Payroll Accounting

A Practical, Real-World Approach

Eric A. Weinstein, CPA

Suffolk County Community College

LABYRINTH

LEARNING™

Payroll Accounting: A Practical, Real-World Approach
by Eric A. Weinstein, CPA

Labyrinth Learning
2560 9th Street, Suite 320
Berkeley, California 94710
800.522.9746
On the web at: lablearning.com

President:
Brian Favro

Product Manager:
Jason Favro

Development Manager:
Laura Popelka

Senior Instructional Designer:
Arl S. Nadel

Senior Editor:
Susan Scharf

Editorial Assistant:
Alexandria Henderson

Production Manager:
Rad Proctor

Production Assistant:
Andrew Kenower

Indexing:
Joanne Sprott

Interior Design:
Mark Ong, Side-by-Side Studio

Cover Design:
Mick Koller, SuperLab Design

eBOOK ITEM: 1-59136-694-1
ISBN-13: 978-1-59136-694-2

PRINT ITEM: 1-59136-691-7
ISBN-13: 978-1-59136-691-1

Manufactured in the United States of America.

10 9 8 7 6 5 4 3 2 1

Contents in Brief

Table of Contents

Preface

This first edition of *Payroll Accounting: A Practical, Real-World Approach* affords an exciting opportunity to address a widespread need among instructors for an applied textbook that is accessible, clear, and resolutely practical for the modern Payroll course.

Grounded in solid pedagogy and the extensive experience of our author, this text focuses on the hands-on tools students and instructors need for building fundamental learning, without overwhelming students with unnecessary theory far removed from practical applications.

The clear, logical, step-by-step approach—highlighting basics such as how to perform calculations and complete forms—guides students through exercises that build understanding and skills.

Supported by an online Student Resource Center and a robust instructor support package, the text is designed to teach the complete payroll accounting cycle to students with little or no prior accounting knowledge.

Key features include:

- Useful chapter organizational items that help guide readers, such as start-of-chapter Learning Objectives, Case Studies, and engaging in-chapter features that break-up content and focus attention.
- Excel templates, PDFs of payroll forms, and myriad resources to provide students with support and direction.
- Progressive exercises that build simply and reinforce key concepts, including:
  - Case in Point case studies
  - Concepts Reviews
  - Knowledge Check A & B reviews
  - Continuing Payroll Practice
  - Critical Thinking Exercises
  - Comprehensive Projects
  - Fresh, engaging, and easily-understood design and graphics

Visual Conventions

In addition to the core features noted above, the text employs a variety of functional, engaging visual graphics to help students incorporate key content and find useful information.

Accounting Terms included in the glossary are set in bold face. If you are using an eBook, note that the terms are linked to the associated glossary definitions.

TIP! Tip! graphics identify helpful shortcuts, advice, or suggestions.

NOTE! Note! graphics call attention to key points, unusual exceptions, or other key information that may not be included the main text.

WARNING! Warning! graphics highlight important points for students to be aware of and on the lookout for.

On the Web On the Web sections provide URLs that lead students to documents or webpages specifically relating to the content.

Acknowledgements

Many individuals contribute to the development and completion of a textbook. We deeply appreciate the careful attention and informed contributions of Carol Rogers, Accounting Program Chair at Central New Mexico Community College, and Rick Street, Accounting and Entrepreneurship Instructor at Spokane Community College.

Labyrinth would also like to express our appreciation for the important contributions of the following advisory group members in the development of this text.

Gwen Bean, *Tennessee College of Applied Technology*
Lyle Hicks, *Danville Area Community College*
Pamela Hillman, *Gateway Technical College*
Carol Rogers, *Central New Mexico Community College*
Rick Street, *Spokane Community College*
Lori Sweat, *Southeastern Technical College*

We are also deeply grateful to the instructors and professionals who reviewed the text and suggested improvements for this first edition. This book has benefited significantly from the feedback and suggestions of the following reviewers.

Mark Aruda, *Hillsborough Community College*

Adam Baker, *Minnesota State Community and Technical College*

Barry Bomboy, *J. Sargeant Reynolds Community College*

Kathy Bowen, *Murray State College*

Marie Campbell, *Idaho State University*

Ilda Casanova, *Palo Alto College*

Christina Chavez, *Elk Grove Adult & Community Education*

Gerald Childs, *Waukesha County Technical College*

Ronda Copple, *North Central Missouri College*

Tiffany DeGraff, *River Valley Community College*

Kerry Dolan, *Great Falls College, Montana State University*

About the Author

Eric A. Weinstein (MBA, CPA) is an Associate Professor of Business Administration at Suffolk County Community College on Long Island, NY. Eric graduated Summa Cum Laude from Georgetown University in 1999, where he earned a BS in Business Administration and majored in Accounting. In 2004, he earned an MBA from the Fuqua School of Business at Duke University. Eric has received many awards in his career, including the State University of New York Chancellor's Award for Excellence in Teaching. Eric has also been a practicing Certified Public Accountant in New York for more than ten years, where he provides accounting services for small businesses and individuals. Eric and his beautiful wife, Cara, are the proud parents of twin sons, Tyler and Lucas. The family lives in Huntington, NY, where they enjoy being bossed around by their two mini-dachshunds, Nathan and Molly.

1

Processing a New Employee

LEARNING OBJECTIVES

After studying this chapter, you will be able to:

- Define the Fair Labor Standards Act

- Utilize the Circular E

- Complete various forms for new employees

- Convey the importance of Workers' Compensation Insurance

- Create an employee earnings record

Accurately determining payroll can be a complex and confusing process. A careful examination of the step-by-step procedures involved is necessary. In this chapter, you'll begin by reviewing the regulations and forms related to hiring a new employee. You'll also examine a number of basic payroll records, including a pay stub and an employee earnings record. Lastly, you'll learn the ways in which many companies employ a payroll service to handle payroll-related matters.

Hiring a New Employee for Lucky Ties Apparel

Lucky Ties Apparel is a clothing store in Rochester, NY. It has been in business for over 15 years, and is a favorite location for local college students. You've worked at the store for three years and have recently taken over all payroll responsibilities. You feel confident that you can complete all the payroll tasks, but intend to review the entire payroll process in preparation for this new role.

The store's sales increase during school months, and Lucky Ties Apparel typically hires new employees for these months. You've just interviewed and hired a new employee, in anticipation of the upcoming fall term, and are eager to review all related payroll tasks.

The Employer's Tax Guide (Circular E) provides excellent guidance for payroll-related matters.

Department of the Treasury
Internal Revenue Service

Publication 15
Cat. No. 10000W

(Circular E), Employer's Tax Guide

For use in **2013**

Get forms and other Information faster and easier by:

Internet IRS.gov

Feb 05, 2013

Contents

Future Developments

For the latest information about developments related to Publication 15 (Circular E), such as legislation enacted after it was published, go to *www.irs.gov/pub15*.

What's New

2013 withholding tables. Employers should implement the 2013 withholding tables as soon as possible, but not later than February 15, 2013. Use the 2012 withholding tables until you implement the 2013 withholding tables.

Social security and Medicare tax for 2013. The employee tax rate for social security is 6.2%. Previously, the employee tax rate for social security was 4.2%. The employer tax rate for social security remains unchanged at 6.2%. The social security wage base limit is $113,700. *(Continued on page 2.)*

Examining the Employee Paystub

If you have ever received a **paycheck**, you know that the attached **paystub** lists a variety of amounts that are not included in your check. Although you've earned these amounts, they are withheld from your check, each for a different reason. In addition to the withholdings, other pertinent payroll information is also found on the paystub.

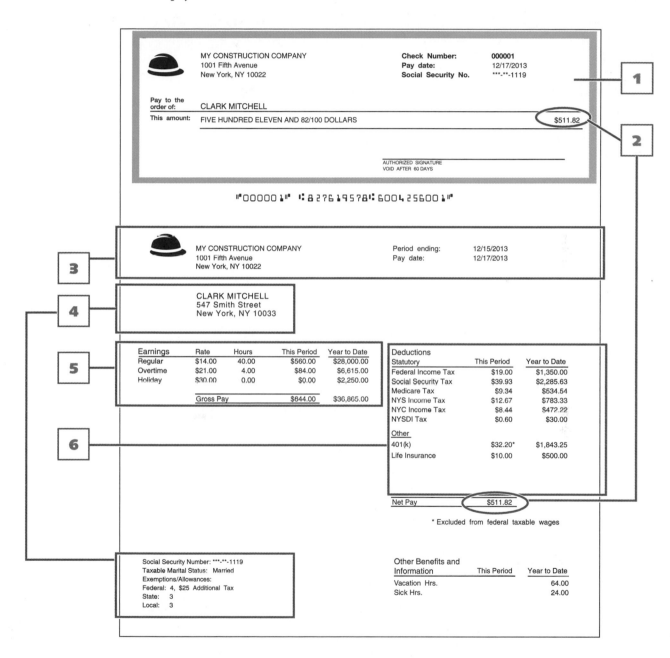

1. Paycheck
2. Net Pay (Paycheck Amount)
3. Company & Pay Period Information
4. Employee Information
5. Current & Year-to-Date Earnings (Chapter 2)
6. Amounts Withheld (Deducted) from Employee Pay (Chapter 3 & Chapter 4)

Aside from standard employee information such as name and address, the pay stub also indicates the employee's marital status and the number of exemptions claimed. This information is used to determine the amount of state and federal income tax withholding that is subtracted from **gross pay** (total amount earned by the employee). Once these and other deductions are subtracted from gross pay, the result is **net pay** (amount actually paid to the employee). Notice in the previous figure that the calculated net pay on the paystub equals the amount of the employee's check.

NOTE!   Don't worry if you are unsure about some of these elements at this stage. You will examine each in further detail in the upcoming chapters.

Previewing a Summary of Tax Rates

Tax Type	Tax Rate
State Income Tax Withholding	5%
Social Security (OASDI) Tax	6.2%
Social Security Wage Base (Threshold)	$113,700
Medicare (HI) Tax	1.45%
FUTA (Federal Unemployment)Tax	0.6%
FUTA Wage Base (Threshold)	$7,000
SUTA (State Unemployment) Tax	3.4%
SUTA Wage Base (Threshold)	$8,500

Before moving forward with our examination of the various elements of the pay stub, it's necessary to identify certain assumptions made within each chapter. Throughout this book you will employ consistent tax rates. While you learn how to utilize each of these rates, you can return to the summary table (at left) whenever necessary.

The State income tax withholding amount varies for each employee based on his or her state, marital status, and number of exemptions. An examination of each of these rates is beyond the scope of this book, so we will employ one consistent rate of 5%.

The Social Security and Medicare tax rates listed, along with the Social Security Wage Base (over which Social Security tax is not levied) of $113,700, are consistent with rates in effect for 2013. The **Federal Unemployment Tax (FUTA)** tax rate for 2013 is 6.0%, however it may be reduced by a maximum of 5.4%, which employers are permitted to deduct for paying state unemployment taxes. Therefore, we will utilize 0.6% (6.0% – 5.4%) as the FUTA tax rate, along with a FUTA wage base of $7,000. The **State Unemployment Tax (SUTA)** tax rate, which varies from state to state, is assumed to be 3.4%, while the SUTA Wage Base is assumed to be $8,500.

Case In Point 1-1	Examine the Paystub

In these examples, we further examine a number of paystub elements.

1. What is the difference between the *Period Ending Date* and the *Pay Date*?

   The Period Ending date represents the final day for which the employee is being paid in the current paycheck. The Pay Date is the date on which the actual check is written.

2. Why are more allowances claimed for federal taxes (3) than for state and local (2)?

This can be due to a number of reasons, but the most likely is that an employee can claim a federal allowance for him/herself, but cannot do so in New York State (where this individual is employed) for state and local taxes. We will examine allowances further in the W-4 Form section later in this chapter.

3. Why are there four different earnings categories on the paystub?

    Employers offer different pay rates for different types of hours worked. For example, employees typically earn 1.5 times more pay for overtime hours than for regular hours. Therefore, hours worked are broken down by type, so that the correct pay rate may be applied to each.

4. Is every displayed deduction withheld from all employee paychecks?

    No, certain deductions, such as Federal Income Tax and Medicare tax, are **Mandatory Deductions** (i.e., they must be withheld from all paychecks), while others such as 401(k) and Life Insurance are **Voluntary Deductions** (the employee can elect to have withheld). We will examine these deductions in detail in Chapter 3.

Complying with the Fair Labor Standards Act

Before the paystub elements are calculated, and the paycheck is distributed, an employer must ensure compliance with the **Fair Labor Standards Act (FLSA)**. The FLSA dictates a variety of regulations that the majority of employers must follow. The act, originally passed into law in 1938, has been amended many times. Among its most influential provisions are the establishment of a **federal minimum wage**, the mandating of 1.5 times pay (time and a half) for overtime hours, and the restriction of child labor.

Complying with the Federal Minimum Wage

Historical Federal Minimum Wage Rates

Effective Date	Minimum Wage Rate
July 24, 2009	$7.25
July 24, 2008	$6.55
July 24, 2007	$5.85
September 1, 1997	$5.15
October 1, 1996	$4.75
April 1, 1991	$4.25
April 1, 1990	$3.80

To comply with the FLSA, employers must be aware of the federal minimum wage. As of July 24, 2009, the United States Congress increased the federal minimum wage rate to $7.25. Individual states have also passed their own minimum-wage laws. When these state-enacted rates disagree with the federal rate of $7.25, the larger wage rate takes precedence. Recent historical federal wage rates are as shown here, at left.

Exceptions to the Federal Minimum Wage

There are a several exceptions to the current federal minimum-wage rate. One is for *workers with disabilities*, who may be paid a lower minimum wage. This wage is a percentage of the current prevailing wage rate for a comparable position, and is based on the productivity level of the employee with the disability.

Full-time students working for specific employers (colleges & universities, agriculture, and retail or service stores) may be paid 85% of the current minimum-wage rate, and are limited to a maximum of 8 hours/day, 20 hours/week while school is in session.

Young workers (under 20 years old) may be paid $4.25/hour for the first 90 days of employment, as long as they do not replace another employee. The pay reverts to the federal minimum after 90 days or after the employee turns 20, whichever comes first.

Tipped employees may be paid $2.13/hour, as long as their tips, when added to this amount, equal or exceed the federal minimum wage. These employees must retain all their tips, and regularly receive at least $30 in tips per month. Any deficit (below the federal minimum wage rate) must be made up by the employer. Certain states provide greater benefits to tipped employees.

Student learners enrolled in a vocational school may be paid 75% of the federal minimum wage, as long as they remain in the educational program while employed. Employers must obtain an authorizing certificate from the US Dept. of Labor to pay these reduced wages.

Who Must Pay the Federal Minimum Wage?

The federal minimum wage applies to employees of all of the following:

- Businesses with gross revenues of at least $500,000
- Federal, state, or local government agencies
- Hospitals
- Schools

Domestic workers, and a wide range of employees working for businesses engaged in interstate commerce, are also covered by the federal minimum wage.

TIP! The federal government allows a wide range of exemptions to the federal minimum wage and other provisions of the FLSA. The most notable exemptions are executive, administrative, and professional employees.

Calculating Overtime Wages

Per the FLSA, employees must be paid 1.5 times regular wages (time and a half) for all hours worked beyond the first 40 in any given workweek. Similar to the federal minimum wage, certain employees are exempted from this overtime-wage provision, including executive, administrative, and professional employees.

To calculate overtime wages, a **workweek** is defined as any 7-day period designated by the employer. It must begin and end consistently each week, but does not need to coincide with the standard calendar, and can vary for different groups of employees.

Adhering to Child Labor Restrictions

The FLSA dictates the type of work that may be performed by children of various ages. Children younger than 14 years of age may only perform specific activities, such as performing arts, newspaper delivery, and working for their parents' sole proprietorships (certain business types are prohibited).

Children aged 14 and 15 may work in a variety of jobs outside of manufacturing and mining, but they are subject to extensive hour limitations. They may work for only three hours on a school day, 18 hours in a school week, 8 hours on a non-school day, and 40 hours in a non-school week. They may work only between 7:00 a.m. and 7:00 p.m. (or 9:00 p.m. between June 1 and Labor Day). Certain children may take advantage of other special programs with more relaxed requirements.

Children aged 16 & 17 may work an unlimited number of hours.

WARNING! Under no circumstances may a child 17 years of age or younger work in a job classified as hazardous, including coal mining, explosives manufacturing, and roofing.

Children employed in agricultural jobs are subject to less stringent requirements, and children employed by their parents on a farm may perform any job duties.

Case In Point 1-2 | ## Interpret the Fair Labor Standards Act

In this example, we'll review four independent employment circumstances and determine whether each employer complies with the Fair Labor Standards Act. Since Lucky Ties Apparel must comply with the FLSA, these examples provide a fuller understanding of FLSA requirements.

1. Robert is a tax advisor for a regional accounting firm in Macon, GA. During one long evening at the office, he uses his annual salary to calculate how much he earns on an hourly basis. He discovers that he is earning $6.85/hour during the current year. Is Robert's employer violating the FLSA?

   No, Robert's employer is not in violation of the FLSA. White-collar workers (executive, administrative, and professional employees) are exempted from the federal minimum wage requirements. Therefore, regardless of the number of hours Robert works, he is entitled only to his agreed-upon annual salary.

2. Maria is 15 years old, and works each weekend during the school year as a roofer. She works seven hours each Saturday and five hours each Sunday. During non-school weeks Maria works an additional eight hours per day, Monday through Wednesday. Is Maria's employer violating the FLSA?

   Yes, although Maria is working fewer than the maximum number of permissible hours, children aged 17 and younger may not work in a variety of hazardous professions, including roofing. Maria's employer is in violation of the FLSA.

3. Kenneth works for a local diner. On a recent Wednesday he worked six hours, was paid $2.13/hour by his employer, and earned $29.46 in tips throughout the day (which he fully retained). In Kenneth's state, the federal and state minimum wages are identical. Is Kenneth's employer violating the FLSA?

   Yes, Kenneth's employer is in violation of the FLSA. When employers use the tip credit provision to pay tipped employees $2.13/hour, they're responsible for demonstrating that the combination of wages and tips exceeds the hourly federal minimum wage of $7.25. Kenneth earned $29.46 in tips, which when divided by the 6 hours he worked, yields $4.91/hour. The sum of hourly wages ($2.13) plus tips ($4.91) is $7.04, which is below the minimum wage of $7.25. It is the employer's responsibility to pay Kenneth the difference of $0.21/hour.

4. Tina is a full-time college student who works in her university's bookstore. She works six hours/day on Tuesday, Friday, and Saturday each week, and is paid $6.20/hour. Is Tina's employer violating the FLSA?

   No, Tina's employer is not in violation of the FLSA. Full-time college students working for certain employers (including universities) may be paid 85% of the federal minimum wage. Tina's $6.20/hour wage is higher than this 85% threshold.

Examining the Circular E & Form SS-4

On the Web

www.irs.gov/pub/
irs-pdf/p15.pdf

The **Circular E** is an Employer's Tax Guide written and distributed free of cost by the US Internal Revenue Service (IRS). Also referred to as *Publication 15*, the Circular E provides employers with an excellent starting point when hiring employees. Becoming familiar with the Circular E helps ensure employers comply with all elements of the FLSA.

Among the benefits provided in the Circular E are a list of due dates for payroll-related forms, tables used to calculate federal income tax withholding, and a summary of new payroll regulations.

TIP! You'll benefit by keeping a copy of the Circular E as a reference guide, so be certain to obtain one as soon as possible.

If an employee has questions not addressed in the publication, the final page of the Circular E provides contact information.

Quick and Easy Access to IRS Tax Help and Tax Products

Internet

You can access the IRS website at IRS.gov 24 hours a day, 7 days a week to:

- *E-file* your return. Find out about commercial tax preparation and *e-file* services available free to eligible taxpayers.
- Download forms, including talking tax forms, instructions, and publications.
- Order IRS products online.
- Research your tax questions online.
- Search publications online by topic or keyword.
- Use the online Internal Revenue Code, Regulations, or other official guidance.
- View Internal Revenue Bulletins (IRBs) published in the last few years.
- Sign up to receive local and national tax news by email.
- Get information on starting and operating a small business.

Phone

Order current year forms, instructions, and publications, and prior year forms and instructions by calling 1-800-TAX-FORM (1-800-829-3676). You should receive your order within 10 days.

Walk-In

You can pick up some of the most requested forms, instructions, and publications at many IRS offices, post offices, and libraries. Some grocery stores, copy centers, city and county government offices, credit unions, and office supply stores have a collection of reproducible tax forms available to photocopy or print from a CD-ROM.

Mail

Send your order for tax products to:
Internal Revenue Service
1201 N. Mitsubishi Motorway
Bloomington, IL 61705-6613

You should receive your products within 10 days after we receive your order.

DVD For Tax Products

You can order Publication 1796, IRS Tax Products, DVD, and obtain:

- Current-year forms, instructions, and publications.
- Prior-year forms, instructions, and publications.
- Tax Map: an electronic research tool and finding aid.
- Tax law frequently asked questions.
- Tax topics from the IRS telephone response system.
- Internal Revenue Code —Title 26 of the U.S. Code.
- Links to other Internet based Tax Research materials.
- Fill-in, print, and save features for most tax forms.
- Internal Revenue Bulletins.
- Toll-free and email technical support.
- Two releases during the year.
  - The first release will ship the beginning of January 2013.
  - The final release will ship the beginning of March 2013.

Purchase the DVD from National Technical Information Service at *www.irs.gov/cdorders* for $30 (no handling fee) or call 1-877-233-6767 toll-free to purchase the DVD for $30 (plus a $6 handling fee).

Obtaining an Employer Identification Number

On the Web

www.irs.gov/pub/
irs-pdf/fss4.pdf

To report employment taxes or provide employees with tax statements, which are both required if a company hires employees, a company must first obtain an **employer identification number (EIN)** by completing Form SS-4 (Application for Employer Identification Number). If a company intends to pay any employees, obtaining an EIN should be one of the first actions taken after it is formed.

TIP! An employer may also apply for an EIN number via the internet or telephone if a faster response is desired.

Examine the Form: SS-4

Completion of Form SS-4 is necessary prior to remitting employee payroll.

Form **SS-4** (Rev. January 2010) Department of the Treasury Internal Revenue Service	**Application for Employer Identification Number** (For use by employers, corporations, partnerships, trusts, estates, churches, government agencies, Indian tribal entities, certain individuals, and others.) ⌧ See separate instructions for each line. ⌧ Keep a copy for your records.	OMB No. 1545-0003 EIN

Type or print clearly.

1 Legal name of entity (or individual) for whom the EIN is being requested

2 Trade name of business (if different from name on line 1)   **3** Executor, administrator, trustee, "care of" name

4a Mailing address (room, apt., suite no. and street, or P.O. box)   **5a** Street address (if different) (Do not enter a P.O. box.)

4b City, state, and ZIP code (if foreign, see instructions)   **5b** City, state, and ZIP code (if foreign, see instructions)

6 County and state where principal business is located

7a Name of responsible party   **7b** SSN, ITIN, or EIN

8a Is this application for a limited liability company (LLC) (or a foreign equivalent)? . . . . ☐ Yes ☐ No   **8b** If 8a is "Yes," enter the number of LLC members . . . . . ⌧

8c If 8a is "Yes," was the LLC organized in the United States? . . . . ☐ Yes ☐ No

9a **Type of entity** (check only one box). **Caution.** If 8a is "Yes," see the instructions for the correct box to check.

☐ Sole proprietor (SSN) _____ : _____
☐ Partnership
☐ Corporation (enter form number to be filed) ⌧ _____
☐ Personal service corporation
☐ Church or church-controlled organization
☐ Other nonprofit organization (specify) ⌧ _____
☐ Other (specify) ⌧

☐ Estate (SSN of decedent) _____
☐ Plan administrator (TIN) _____
☐ Trust (TIN of grantor) _____
☐ National Guard   ☐ State/local government
☐ Farmers' cooperative   ☐ Federal government/military
☐ REMIC   ☐ Indian tribal governments/enterprises
Group Exemption Number (GEN) if any ⌧

9b If a corporation, name the state or foreign country (if applicable) where incorporated   State | Foreign country

10 **Reason for applying** (check only one box)

☐ Started new business (specify type) ⌧ _____
_____
☐ Hired employees (Check the box and see line 13.)
☐ Compliance with IRS withholding regulations
☐ Other (specify) ⌧

☐ Banking purpose (specify purpose) ⌧ _____
☐ Changed type of organization (specify new type) ⌧ _____
☐ Purchased going business
☐ Created a trust (specify type) ⌧ _____
☐ Created a pension plan (specify type) ⌧ _____

11 Date business started or acquired (month, day, year). See instructions.   **12** Closing month of accounting year

13 Highest number of employees expected in the next 12 months (enter -0- if none). If no employees expected, skip line 14.

Agricultural	Household	Other

14 If you expect your employment tax liability to be $1,000 or less in a full calendar year **and** want to file Form 944 annually instead of Forms 941 quarterly, check here. (Your employment tax liability generally will be $1,000 or less if you expect to pay $4,000 or less in total wages.) If you do not check this box, you must file Form 941 for every quarter. ☐

15 First date wages or annuities were paid (month, day, year). **Note.** If applicant is a withholding agent, enter date income will first be paid to nonresident alien (month, day, year) . . . . ⌧

16 Check **one** box that best describes the principal activity of your business.   ☐ Health care & social assistance   ☐ Wholesale-agent/broker
☐ Construction   ☐ Rental & leasing   ☐ Transportation & warehousing   ☐ Accommodation & food service   ☐ Wholesale-other   ☐ Retail
☐ Real estate   ☐ Manufacturing   ☐ Finance & insurance   ☐ Other (specify)

17 Indicate principal line of merchandise sold, specific construction work done, products produced, or services provided.

18 Has the applicant entity shown on line 1 ever applied for and received an EIN? ☐ Yes ☐ No
If "Yes," write previous EIN here ⌧

Third Party Designee   Complete this section **only** if you want to authorize the named individual to receive the entity's EIN and answer questions about the completion of this form.

Designee's name   Designee's telephone number (include area code) ( )
Address and ZIP code   Designee's fax number (include area code) ( )

Under penalties of perjury, I declare that I have examined this application, and to the best of my knowledge and belief, it is true, correct, and complete.   Applicant's telephone number (include area code) ( )

Name and title (type or print clearly) ⌧

Signature ⌧   Date ⌧   Applicant's fax number (include area code) ( )

For Privacy Act and Paperwork Reduction Act Notice, see separate instructions.   Cat. No. 16055N   Form **SS-4** (Rev. 1-2010)

Line 1: Enter the full name of the individual requesting an EIN, or the legal name of the business making the request.

Line 2: Complete this line if the request is being made by a business operating under a different name (a *Doing Business As* or *DBA* name) than is declared on line 1.

Line 3: This line is primarily used by estates and trusts, and may be left blank when the form is being completed for the purposes of remitting payroll.

Line 4a & 4b: Enter the Company's mailing address.

Line 5a & 5b: Enter the Company's physical address if different from line 4.

Line 6: Enter the county and state of the business' physical location.

Line 7a & 7b: Enter the name and social security number (SSN) of the responsible person (individual who exerts control over the business).

Line 8a – 8c: Complete these lines only if the business was formed as a limited liability company (LLC).

Line 9a: Check the box that correlates with the type of business making the request.

Line 9b: Complete this section only if you selected one of the corporation options on line 9a.

Line 10: For payroll purposes, you will typically check either *Started new business* or *Hired employees*, depending on the circumstance.

Line 11: Enter the starting date, or date the business was acquired. If the corporate form was changed, enter the effective date of the new ownership form.

Line 12: Enter the final month of the Company's fiscal year. While this is commonly December, a company may elect to end its fiscal year during any month.

Line 13: Enter an estimate of the number of each type of listed employee.

Line 14: For all businesses except those with the smallest annual payroll, do not check this box. When unchecked, a quarterly Form 941 will be required.

Line 15: Disregard this line if you are starting a new business. For an existing business that has now hired employees, enter the first date on which wages are paid.

Line 16: Check the box that most closely represents the Company's line of business. If checking *Other*, include a brief description.

Line 17: Provide a one- or two-sentence synopsis of the business.

Line 18: Check the appropriate box, and if a previous EIN was issued include it here.

Third Party Designee: Complete this section only if you want an outside party (such as an outside accountant) to answer questions regarding the form on the Company's behalf.

Signature Line: Fully complete all components within this section.

TIP! For a fuller examination of the elements of Form SS-4 (or any other federal form), refer to the instructions provided by the IRS. A simple online search can quickly locate any desired IRS instructions.

Case In Point 1-3	**Complete Form SS-4**

In this example, we'll complete Form SS-4 for a newly-formed company named Wood Furniture Builders, Inc., which creates custom wood furniture. It was started on September 1, 2014 as a sole proprietorship by its President, Samuel Williams (SSN 555-55-5555). His phone number is 516-555-5555, and his fax number is 516-555-5556. The company is located at 748 Negra Arroyo Lane, Massapequa, NY 11758 (in Nassau county), where it receives all mail. The company uses the calendar year as its fiscal year and expects to employ five individuals (earning an average of $36,500/year) in the first 24 months of operations. Payroll is to be paid bi-weekly on Fridays, with the first pay date scheduled for September 12, 2014.

1. Complete lines 1 through 7 with basic information. Leave Line 2 blank, as nothing indicates that the company uses a DBA name. Leave Line 3 blank, as it is not applicable for a new business. Leave Lines 5a & 5b blank, as the mailing address and physical address are identical.

2. Complete Lines 8 through 10 using information provided about the business entity. Select "No" on Line 8a, as this company is a sole proprietorship and not a limited liability company. As a result of this selection, lines 8b & 8c are left blank. Select "Sole Proprietor" on line 9a, and enter the company president's social security number beside this box. Leave Line 9b blank, as this company is not a corporation. Select "Started new business" on line 10, and include the basic business description.

3. Lines 11 through 15 relate to the company's start date, fiscal year, and payroll. Enter the business start date of 9/1/2014 on Line 11 and "December" on Line 12, as the company follows a calendar year (operations are reported annually from January through December). The company's five employees don't qualify as agricultural or household employees; therefore enter "5" in the "Other" category on line 13. Employees are projected to earn an average of $36,500 each per year, and therefore the company must file Form 941 quarterly. As a result, do not check the box on line 14. Enter the first pay date of 9/12/2014 on line 15.

4. Lines 16 through 18 provide information about the company's current and prior operations. Check "Manufacturing" on line 16. Line 17 contains a more extensive description of the business than was written on line 10. As this is a new business, and therefore has not previously applied for an EIN, check "No" on this line.

5. No third-party designee is referenced, so leave this section blank. Finally, Samuel Williams completed all information in the final section, and has signed the form.

Form **SS-4**	**Application for Employer Identification Number**	OMB No. 1545-0003
(Rev. January 2010) Department of the Treasury Internal Revenue Service	(For use by employers, corporations, partnerships, trusts, estates, churches, government agencies, Indian tribal entities, certain individuals, and others.) ► See separate instructions for each line. ► Keep a copy for your records.	EIN

Type or print clearly.

1 Legal name of entity (or individual) for whom the EIN is being requested
Wood Furniture Builders, Inc.

2 Trade name of business (if different from name on line 1)	**3** Executor, administrator, trustee, "care of" name

4a Mailing address (room, apt., suite no. and street, or P.O. box) **748 Negra Arroyo Lane**	**5a** Street address (if different) (Do not enter a P.O. box.)
4b City, state, and ZIP code (if foreign, see instructions) **Massapequa NY 11758**	**5b** City, state, and ZIP code (if foreign, see instructions)

6 County and state where principal business is located
Nassau County, NY

7a Name of responsible party **Samuel Williams**	**7b** SSN, ITIN, or EIN **555-55-5555**

8a Is this application for a limited liability company (LLC) (or a foreign equivalent)? ☐ Yes ☒ No
8b If 8a is "Yes," enter the number of LLC members ►

8c If 8a is "Yes," was the LLC organized in the United States? ☐ Yes ☐ No

9a **Type of entity** (check only one box). **Caution.** If 8a is "Yes," see the instructions for the correct box to check.

☒ Sole proprietor (SSN) **555 55 5555**
☐ Partnership
☐ Corporation (enter form number to be filed) ►
☐ Personal service corporation
☐ Church or church-controlled organization
☐ Other nonprofit organization (specify) ►
☐ Other (specify) ►

☐ Estate (SSN of decedent)
☐ Plan administrator (TIN)
☐ Trust (TIN of grantor)
☐ National Guard   ☐ State/local government
☐ Farmers' cooperative ☐ Federal government/military
☐ REMIC   ☐ Indian tribal governments/enterprises
Group Exemption Number (GEN) if any ►

9b If a corporation, name the state or foreign country (if applicable) where incorporated | State | Foreign country

10 **Reason for applying** (check only one box)
☒ Started new business (specify type) ►
Furniture Builders
☐ Hired employees (Check the box and see line 13.)
☐ Compliance with IRS withholding regulations
☐ Other (specify) ►

☐ Banking purpose (specify purpose) ►
☐ Changed type of organization (specify new type) ►
☐ Purchased going business
☐ Created a trust (specify type) ►
☐ Created a pension plan (specify type) ►

11 Date business started or acquired (month, day, year). See instructions. **09/01/2014**	**12** Closing month of accounting year **DECEMBER**

13 Highest number of employees expected in the next 12 months (enter -0- if none).
If no employees expected, skip line 14.

14 If you expect your employment tax liability to be $1,000 or less in a full calendar year **and** want to file Form 944 annually instead of Forms 941 quarterly, check here. (Your employment tax liability generally will be $1,000 or less if you expect to pay $4,000 or less in total wages.) If you do not check this box, you must file Form 941 for every quarter. ☐

Agricultural	Household	Other
0	**0**	**5**

15 First date wages or annuities were paid (month, day, year). **Note.** If applicant is a withholding agent, enter date income will first be paid to nonresident alien (month, day, year) . . . . ► **09/12/2014**

16 Check **one** box that best describes the principal activity of your business.
☐ Construction ☐ Rental & leasing ☐ Transportation & warehousing ☐ Accommodation & food service ☐ Wholesale-agent/broker
☐ Real estate ☒ Manufacturing ☐ Finance & insurance ☐ Other (specify) ☐ Wholesale-other ☐ Retail
☐ Health care & social assistance

17 Indicate principal line of merchandise sold, specific construction work done, products produced, or services provided.
Sale of custom built furniture based on client-provided specifications

18 Has the applicant entity shown on line 1 ever applied for and received an EIN? ☐ Yes ☒ No
If "Yes," write previous EIN here ►

Third Party Designee

Complete this section **only** if you want to authorize the named individual to receive the entity's EIN and answer questions about the completion of this form.

Designee's name	Designee's telephone number (include area code) ( )
Address and ZIP code	Designee's fax number (include area code) ( )

Under penalties of perjury, I declare that I have examined this application, and to the best of my knowledge and belief, it is true, correct, and complete.

Name and title (type or print clearly) ► **Samuel Williams - President**   Applicant's telephone number (include area code) (**516**) **555-5555**

Signature ► *Samuel Williams*   Date ► **9/1/14**   Applicant's fax number (include area code) (**516**) **555-5556**

For Privacy Act and Paperwork Reduction Act Notice, see separate instructions.   Cat. No. 16055N   Form **SS-4** (Rev. 1-2010)

Hiring an Employee

When a new employee is hired, a number of considerations must be made by both the employee and the employer. These considerations not only provide the employer with information required to properly process payroll, but also enable them to comply with applicable federal and state laws.

Examining the Personal Responsibility and Work Opportunity Reconciliation Act of 1996

The **Personal Responsibility and Work Opportunity Reconciliation Act of 1996 (PRWORA)** significantly strengthened child support throughout the United States. This was achieved in various ways, including through the mandatory reporting of new employees within 20 days of hire, enabling better enforcement of child-support laws. Employers can satisfy the provisions of this act by submitting the newly-hired employee's W-4 Form to the state. We'll examine the W-4 form in more detail further ahead in this chapter.

WARNING!   Some states have more stringent requirements than those required in the federal provisions for PRWORA.

Completing Form SS-5

On the Web

www.socialsecurity.gov/online/ss-5.pdf

The W-4 Form requires the employee's social security number. Employees who don't have a social security card can obtain one by completing and submitting Form SS-5 to their local social security office..

TIP!   Form SS-5 is also used to obtain a replacement social security card or to correct information in the social security record.

Examine the Form: SS-5

Form SS-5 is completed by any employee who does not have a social security number.

SOCIAL SECURITY ADMINISTRATION
Application for a Social Security Card

Form Approved
OMB No. 0960-0066

	NAME TO BE SHOWN ON CARD	First	Full Middle Name	Last
1	FULL NAME AT BIRTH IF OTHER THAN ABOVE	First	Full Middle Name	Last
	OTHER NAMES USED			

2 Social Security number previously assigned to the person listed in item 1 ☐☐☐ – ☐☐ – ☐☐☐☐

3 **PLACE OF BIRTH** _____ (Do Not Abbreviate) City   State or Foreign Country

Office Use Only   FCI

4 **DATE OF BIRTH** _____ MM/DD/YYYY

5 **CITIZENSHIP** (Check One)
☐ U.S. Citizen
☐ Legal Alien Allowed To Work
☐ Legal Alien **Not** Allowed To Work(See Instructions On Page 3)
☐ Other (See Instructions On Page 3)

6 **ETHNICITY** Are You Hispanic or Latino? (Your Response is Voluntary)
☐ Yes ☐ No

7 **RACE** Select One or More (Your Response is Voluntary)
☐ Native Hawaiian ☐ American Indian ☐ Other Pacific Islander
☐ Alaska Native ☐ Black/African American ☐ White
☐ Asian

8 **SEX** ☐ Male ☐ Female

9
A. PARENT/ MOTHER'S NAME AT HER BIRTH | First | Full Middle Name | Last
B. PARENT/ MOTHER'S SOCIAL SECURITY NUMBER (See instructions for 9 B on Page 3) ☐☐☐ – ☐☐ – ☐☐☐☐ ☐ Unknown

10
A. PARENT/ FATHER'S NAME | First | Full Middle Name | Last
B. PARENT/ FATHER'S SOCIAL SECURITY NUMBER (See instructions for 10B on Page 3) ☐☐☐ – ☐☐ – ☐☐☐☐ ☐ Unknown

11 Has the person listed in item 1 or anyone acting on his/her behalf ever filed for or received a Social Security number card before?
☐ Yes (If "yes" answer questions 12-13)   ☐ No   ☐ Don't Know (If "don't know," skip to question 14.)

12 Name shown on the most recent Social Security card issued for the person listed in item 1 | First | Full Middle Name | Last

13 Enter any different date of birth if used on an earlier application for a card _____ MM/DD/YYYY

14 **TODAY'S DATE** _____ MM/DD/YYYY

15 **DAYTIME PHONE NUMBER** _____ Area Code   Number

16 **MAILING ADDRESS** (Do Not Abbreviate)
Street Address, Apt. No., PO Box, Rural Route No.
City   State/Foreign Country   ZIP Code

I declare under penalty of perjury that I have examined all the information on this form, and on any accompanying statements or forms, and it is true and correct to the best to my knowledge.

17 **YOUR SIGNATURE**

18 **YOUR RELATIONSHIP TO THE PERSON IN ITEM 1 IS:**
☐ Self ☐ Natural Or Adoptive Parent ☐ Legal Guardian ☐ Other Specify _____

DO NOT WRITE BELOW THIS LINE (FOR SSA USE ONLY)

NPN			DOC	NTI	CAN		ITV
PBC	EVI	EVA	EVC	PRA	NWR	DNR	UNIT

EVIDENCE SUBMITTED

SIGNATURE AND TITLE OF EMPLOYEE(S) REVIEWING EVIDENCE AND/OR CONDUCTING INTERVIEW

DATE

DCL   DATE

Form **SS-5** (08-2011) ef (08-2011)   Destroy Prior Editions   Page 5

Examine the Form: SS-5 (continued)

Most lines within Form SS-5 are self-explanatory. Those lines that warrant specific mention are as follows:

Line 2: Leave this blank if requesting a social security card for the first time.

Lines 6 & 7: These lines are optional and may be left blank.

Lines 9b & 10b: Complete these lines only when the application is for a child under the age of 18.

Line 17: If the application is for a child under the age of 18, the child's parent or legal guardian may sign on behalf of the child.

When submitting Form SS-5, additional documentation is required to corroborate information about the applicant, such as the applicant's age, identity, and U.S. citizenship (or immigration status). While the combination of a U.S. Birth Certificate and U.S. Driver's License suffice, other documents such as a Final Adoption Decree, U.S. Passport, or a current document from the Department of Homeland Security indicating immigration status can corroborate some details.

Completing Form W-4

On the Web

www.irs.gov/w4

Every employee must complete a W-4 Form (Employee's Withholding Allowance Certificate), which provides the employer with information necessary to calculate both federal income tax withholding and applicable state income tax withholding. Completing the W-4 Form should be one of the first steps taken by a newly-hired employee.

The employer retains the W-4 Form in its files. If his or her circumstances change, the employee may submit a new W-4 Form.

Line 5 of the W-4 Form requires the employee to indicate the number of tax allowances being claimed. The IRS provides a worksheet (attached to the top of the W-4 Form) that helps determine the appropriate number of allowances. This worksheet is retained by the employee.

The Personal Allowances Worksheet provides guidance on the tax allowances an employee may claim.

	Personal Allowances Worksheet (Keep for your records.)	
A	Enter "1" for **yourself** if no one else can claim you as a dependent	**A** _____
B	Enter "1" if: { • You are single and have only one job; or • You are married, have only one job, and your spouse does not work; or • Your wages from a second job or your spouse's wages (or the total of both) are $1,500 or less. } . . .	**B** _____
C	Enter "1" for your **spouse.** But, you may choose to enter "-0-" if you are married and have either a working spouse or more than one job. (Entering "-0-" may help you avoid having too little tax withheld.)	**C** _____
D	Enter number of **dependents** (other than your spouse or yourself) you will claim on your tax return	**D** _____
E	Enter "1" if you will file as **head of household** on your tax return (see conditions under **Head of household** above) . .	**E** _____
F	Enter "1" if you have at least $1,900 of **child or dependent care expenses** for which you plan to claim a credit . . . (**Note.** Do **not** include child support payments. See Pub. 503, Child and Dependent Care Expenses, for details.)	**F** _____
G	**Child Tax Credit** (including additional child tax credit). See Pub. 972, Child Tax Credit, for more information. • If your total income will be less than $65,000 ($95,000 if married), enter "2" for each eligible child; then **less** "1" if you have three to six eligible children or **less** "2" if you have seven or more eligible children. • If your total income will be between $65,000 and $84,000 ($95,000 and $119,000 if married), enter "1" for each eligible child	**G** _____
H	Add lines A through G and enter total here. (**Note.** This may be different from the number of exemptions you claim on your tax return.) ▶ **H** _____	
	For accuracy, complete all worksheets that apply. { • If you plan to **itemize** or **claim adjustments to income** and want to reduce your withholding, see the **Deductions and Adjustments Worksheet** on page 2. • If you are **single and have more than one job** or are **married and you and your spouse both work** and the combined earnings from all jobs exceed $40,000 ($10,000 if married), see the **Two-Earners/Multiple Jobs Worksheet** on page 2 to avoid having too little tax withheld. • If **neither** of the above situations applies, **stop here** and enter the number from line H on line 5 of Form W-4 below. }	

Examine the Form: W-4

Form W-4 is completed by all employees upon their hiring.

-------------------------- **Separate here and give Form W-4 to your employer. Keep the top part for your records.** --------------------------

Form **W-4**	**Employee's Withholding Allowance Certificate**	OMB No. 1545-0074
Department of the Treasury Internal Revenue Service	▶ Whether you are entitled to claim a certain number of allowances or exemption from withholding is subject to review by the IRS. Your employer may be required to send a copy of this form to the IRS.	20**13**

1 Your first name and middle initial	Last name	2 **Your social security number**

Home address (number and street or rural route)	3 ☐ Single ☐ Married ☐ Married, but withhold at higher Single rate. **Note.** If married, but legally separated, or spouse is a nonresident alien, check the "Single" box.
City or town, state, and ZIP code	4 If your last name differs from that shown on your social security card, check here. You must call 1-800-772-1213 for a replacement card. ▶ ☐

5	Total number of allowances you are claiming (from line **H** above **or** from the applicable worksheet on page 2)	5	
6	Additional amount, if any, you want withheld from each paycheck	6	$
7	I claim exemption from withholding for 2013, and I certify that I meet **both** of the following conditions for exemption.		

• Last year I had a right to a refund of **all** federal income tax withheld because I had **no** tax liability, **and**
• This year I expect a refund of **all** federal income tax withheld because I expect to have **no** tax liability.
If you meet both conditions, write "Exempt" here . . . . ▶ | 7 |

Under penalties of perjury, I declare that I have examined this certificate and, to the best of my knowledge and belief, it is true, correct, and complete.

Employee's signature
(This form is not valid unless you sign it.) ▶   **Date** ▶

8 Employer's name and address (Employer: Complete lines 8 and 10 only if sending to the IRS.)	9 Office code (optional)	10 Employer identification number (EIN)

For Privacy Act and Paperwork Reduction Act Notice, see page 2.   Cat. No. 10220Q   Form **W-4** (2013)

The lines an employee enters on the W-4 form are as follows:

Line 1: Enter their name and home address.

Line 2: Enter their social security number.

Line 3: Typically, check either "Single" or "Married." A married employee may obtain some tax advantages by checking "Married, but withhold at higher Single rate." A tax professional can provide advice as to when this is appropriate.

Line 4: This is commonly checked when an employee is recently married or divorced and has not yet changed their social security card to match the name reported on Line 1.

Line 5: Complete the Personal Allowances Worksheet to determine the correct number of allowances. The final instructions indicate that, in some circumstances, employees should complete one of two additional worksheets that provide guidance for employees who intend to itemize deductions on their personal tax return, and for those who work a second job or whose spouse also works. As more allowances are reported, fewer taxes are withheld from the employee's pay.

TIP! The number of allowances claimed does not necessarily equal the number of exemptions reported on the employee's personal tax return.

Line 6: Employees may elect to withhold more from each paycheck by listing an additional amount. Although this is not usually necessary, it further reduces the employee's tax burden (and may lead to a refund) when the personal tax return is submitted.

Examine the Form: W-4 (continued)

Line 7: The employee can enter "Exempt" here only when both listed conditions are met. For those who qualify, this entry prevents taxes from being withheld for federal withholding, therefore simplifying their personal tax return. In this instance, they must only complete lines 1-4 & 7.

Signature Line: The employee must sign and date the completed form before it is submitted to the employer.

Lines 8-10: These lines are only completed by the employer if the W-4 Form is submitted to the IRS. This is necessary when the IRS requests a specific W-4 Form to review an employee's indicated allowances or exempt status.

Case In Point 1-4	Complete Form W-4

In this example, we'll complete Form W-4 for Ryan Jackson (SSN 333-33-3332), a newly hired employee of Apex Textiles. Ryan is single, lives at 37 McDonald Lane, Nashville, TN 37204, does not want any additional withholding amounts, and is not exempt from federal income tax withholding. Ryan has no children and does not hold any other jobs. He claims his elderly father as an exemption on his personal tax return, and he therefore files as Head of Household. He also intends to claim a credit for dependent care expenses of approximately $3,000 on his personal tax return.

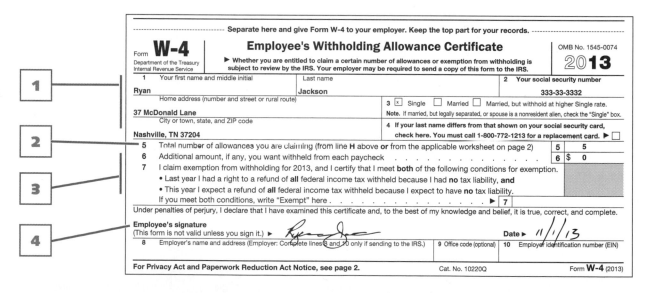

1. Complete lines 1 through 4 with Ryan's name, address, social security number, and single status. No provided information indicates that Ryan's name is different from that on his social security card, so leave line 4 blank.

2. To complete line 5, use the Personal Allowances Worksheet to arrive at the proper number of allowances. Note that in the worksheet below, lines D, E, and F all display "1," since Ryan has one dependent, files as Head of Household, and plans to claim a dependent-care expenses credit of over $1,900. Because the allowances on the worksheet total 5, this figure is entered on line 5 of the Form W-4.

	Personal Allowances Worksheet (Keep for your records.)		
A	Enter "1" for **yourself** if no one else can claim you as a dependent	**A**	1
B	Enter "1" if: { • You are single and have only one job; or / • You are married, have only one job, and your spouse does not work; or / • Your wages from a second job or your spouse's wages (or the total of both) are $1,500 or less. } . . .	**B**	1
C	Enter "1" for your **spouse.** But, you may choose to enter "-0-" if you are married and have either a working spouse or more than one job. (Entering "-0-" may help you avoid having too little tax withheld.)	**C**	0
D	Enter number of **dependents** (other than your spouse or yourself) you will claim on your tax return	**D**	1
E	Enter "1" if you will file as **head of household** on your tax return (see conditions under **Head of household** above)	**E**	1
F	Enter "1" if you have at least $1,900 of **child or dependent care expenses** for which you plan to claim a credit . . . (**Note.** Do **not** include child support payments. See Pub. 503, Child and Dependent Care Expenses, for details.)	**F**	1
G	**Child Tax Credit** (including additional child tax credit). See Pub. 972, Child Tax Credit, for more information. • If your total income will be less than $65,000 ($95,000 if married), enter "2" for each eligible child; then **less** "1" if you have three to six eligible children or **less** "2" if you have seven or more eligible children.		
	• If your total income will be between $65,000 and $84,000 ($95,000 and $119,000 if married), enter "1" for each eligible child . . .	**G**	0
H	Add lines A through G and enter total here. (**Note.** This may be different from the number of exemptions you claim on your tax return.) ▶ **H**	**H**	5
	For accuracy, complete all worksheets that apply. { • If you plan to **itemize** or **claim adjustments to income** and want to reduce your withholding, see the **Deductions and Adjustments Worksheet** on page 2. / • If you are **single and have more than one job** or are **married and you and your spouse both work** and the combined earnings from all jobs exceed $40,000 ($10,000 if married), see the **Two-Earners/Multiple Jobs Worksheet** on page 2 to avoid having too little tax withheld. / • If **neither** of the above situations applies, **stop here** and enter the number from line H on line 5 of Form W-4 below. }		

3. Leave Lines 6 & 7 blank, as Ryan doesn't want additional monies withheld from his paycheck, nor is he exempt from federal income-tax withholding.

4. Sign and date the form below line 7.

Checking Additional Hiring Considerations

Before an individual can become an employee of any company, the employer must confirm that he/she is permitted to work in the United States. The Immigration Reform and Control Act of 1986 (IRCA) outlines these regulations. All employees must complete Form I-9 (Employment Eligibility Verification) as part of the verification process.

Examining the Immigration Reform and Control Act of 1986

The **Immigration Reform and Control Act (IRCA)**, which was passed on November 6, 1986, strengthened immigration law in the United States. As part of this legislation, employers became responsible for maintaining I-9 Forms for all employees. To complete these forms, employers must verify both the employee's identity and employment authorization. Completion of Form I-9 by all employers is intended to reduce the illegal employment of foreign workers in the United States.

Completing Form I-9

On the Web

www.uscis.gov/files/
form/i-9.pdf

Form I-9 (Employment Eligibility Verification) contains three sections. The first section is completed by the employee, and the employer completes either the second or third section, depending on the circumstances. The employee must complete section A of Form I-9 no later than the first day of employment, but the employer has three business days from the first day of employment to complete section B for new hires. Section C, which is completed by the employer, is only utilized when an employee is rehired, or when reverification of an employee's eligibility is required (such as when a previously examined employee document has expired).

Attached to Form I-9 is a list of acceptable documents that an employee may furnish for the purpose of verification. Depending on the document(s) provided, an employer may need to review one or more of these, and record information about them in Section 2. An employer may not specify which of the listed documents the employee must furnish, as all are acceptable. Additionally, an employer may not request that the employee complete Form I-9 prior to the acceptance of a job offer.

Employees may provide either one document from List A, or one from both List B and List C.

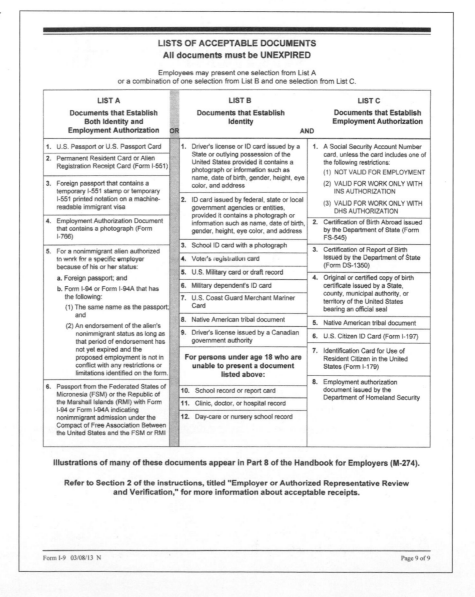

LISTS OF ACCEPTABLE DOCUMENTS
All documents must be UNEXPIRED

Employees may present one selection from List A
or a combination of one selection from List B and one selection from List C.

LIST A	LIST B	LIST C
Documents that Establish Both Identity and Employment Authorization	**Documents that Establish Identity**	**Documents that Establish Employment Authorization**
OR	AND	
1. U.S. Passport or U.S. Passport Card	1. Driver's license or ID card issued by a State or outlying possession of the United States provided it contains a photograph or information such as name, date of birth, gender, height, eye color, and address	1. A Social Security Account Number card, unless the card includes one of the following restrictions: (1) NOT VALID FOR EMPLOYMENT (2) VALID FOR WORK ONLY WITH INS AUTHORIZATION (3) VALID FOR WORK ONLY WITH DHS AUTHORIZATION
2. Permanent Resident Card or Alien Registration Receipt Card (Form I-551)		
3. Foreign passport that contains a temporary I-551 stamp or temporary I-551 printed notation on a machine-readable immigrant visa	2. ID card issued by federal, state or local government agencies or entities, provided it contains a photograph or information such as name, date of birth, gender, height, eye color, and address	
4. Employment Authorization Document that contains a photograph (Form I-766)		2. Certification of Birth Abroad issued by the Department of State (Form FS-545)
	3. School ID card with a photograph	
5. For a nonimmigrant alien authorized to work for a specific employer because of his or her status: a. Foreign passport; and b. Form I-94 or Form I-94A that has the following: (1) The same name as the passport; and (2) An endorsement of the alien's nonimmigrant status as long as that period of endorsement has not yet expired and the proposed employment is not in conflict with any restrictions or limitations identified on the form.	4. Voter's registration card	3. Certification of Report of Birth issued by the Department of State (Form DS-1350)
	5. U.S. Military card or draft record	
	6. Military dependent's ID card	4. Original or certified copy of birth certificate issued by a State, county, municipal authority, or territory of the United States bearing an official seal
	7. U.S. Coast Guard Merchant Mariner Card	
	8. Native American tribal document	5. Native American tribal document
	9. Driver's license issued by a Canadian government authority	6. U.S. Citizen ID Card (Form I-197)
	For persons under age 18 who are unable to present a document listed above:	7. Identification Card for Use of Resident Citizen in the United States (Form I-179)
6. Passport from the Federated States of Micronesia (FSM) or the Republic of the Marshall Islands (RMI) with Form I-94 or Form I-94A indicating nonimmigrant admission under the Compact of Free Association Between the United States and the FSM or RMI	10. School record or report card	8. Employment authorization document issued by the Department of Homeland Security
	11. Clinic, doctor, or hospital record	
	12. Day-care or nursery school record	

Illustrations of many of these documents appear in Part 8 of the Handbook for Employers (M-274).

Refer to Section 2 of the instructions, titled "Employer or Authorized Representative Review and Verification," for more information about acceptable receipts.

Form I-9 03/08/13 N   Page 9 of 9

Examine the Form: I-9

The employee completes Section 1 of Form I-9.

	Employment Eligibility Verification		**USCIS**
	Department of Homeland Security		**Form I-9**
	U.S. Citizenship and Immigration Services		OMB No. 1615-0047
			Expires 03/31/2016

▶**START HERE.** **Read instructions carefully before completing this form. The instructions must be available during completion of this form.**
ANTI-DISCRIMINATION NOTICE: It is illegal to discriminate against work-authorized individuals. Employers **CANNOT** specify which document(s) they will accept from an employee. The refusal to hire an individual because the documentation presented has a future expiration date may also constitute illegal discrimination.

Section 1. Employee Information and Attestation (Employees must complete and sign Section 1 of Form I-9 no later than the **first day of employment**, but not before accepting a job offer.)

Last Name (Family Name)	First Name (Given Name)	Middle Initial	Other Names Used (if any)

Address (Street Number and Name)	Apt. Number	City or Town	State	Zip Code

Date of Birth (mm/dd/yyyy)	U.S. Social Security Number	E-mail Address	Telephone Number
	☐☐☐-☐☐-☐☐☐☐		

I am aware that federal law provides for imprisonment and/or fines for false statements or use of false documents in connection with the completion of this form.

I attest, under penalty of perjury, that I am (check one of the following):

☐ A citizen of the United States

☐ A noncitizen national of the United States (See instructions)

☐ A lawful permanent resident (Alien Registration Number/USCIS Number): _____

☐ An alien authorized to work until (expiration date, if applicable, mm/dd/yyyy) _____ . Some aliens may write "N/A" in this field. (See instructions)

For aliens authorized to work, provide your Alien Registration Number/USCIS Number **OR** Form I-94 Admission Number:

   1. Alien Registration Number/USCIS Number:_____

                 OR

   2. Form I-94 Admission Number: _____

    If you obtained your admission number from CBP in connection with your arrival in the United States, include the following:

      Foreign Passport Number: _____

      Country of Issuance: _____

    Some aliens may write "N/A" on the Foreign Passport Number and Country of Issuance fields. (See instructions)

> 3-D Barcode
> Do Not Write in This Space

Signature of Employee:	Date (mm/dd/yyyy):

Preparer and/or Translator Certification (To be completed and signed if Section 1 is prepared by a person other than the employee.)

I attest, under penalty of perjury, that I have assisted in the completion of this form and that to the best of my knowledge the information is true and correct.

Signature of Preparer or Translator:	Date (mm/dd/yyyy):

Last Name (Family Name)	First Name (Given Name)

Address (Street Number and Name)	City or Town	State	Zip Code

🛑 *Employer Completes Next Page* 🛑

Form I-9 03/08/13 N   Page 7 of 9

Examine the Form: I-9 (continued)

While completing *Section 1*, the employee should be mindful of the following:

- Other Names Used: Include any previously used maiden name.
- Address: Unless the employee commutes to work from a Canadian or Mexican location close to the border, this must be a United States address.
- Social Security Number, E-mail address, and telephone number are optional unless the employer utilizes e-verify (an online federal government system that verifies employee eligibility), in which case a social security number is required. Write "N/A" if omitting the e-mail address and telephone.
- Remaining checkboxes: Check the appropriate box related to citizenship/immigration status. Complete all requested information.
- Signature Line: Sign and date Form I-9.
- Preparer and/or Translator Certification: Completed by the preparer or translator only if the employee required assistance.

Upon receiving verifying documents from the employee, the employer completes Section 2 of Form I-9.

Section 2. Employer or Authorized Representative Review and Verification

(Employers or their authorized representative must complete and sign Section 2 within 3 business days of the employee's first day of employment. You must physically examine one document from List A OR examine a combination of one document from List B and one document from List C as listed on the "Lists of Acceptable Documents" on the next page of this form. For each document you review, record the following information: document title, issuing authority, document number, and expiration date, if any.)

Employee Last Name, First Name and Middle Initial from Section 1:

List A Identity and Employment Authorization	OR	List B Identity	AND	List C Employment Authorization
Document Title:		Document Title:		Document Title:
Issuing Authority:		Issuing Authority:		Issuing Authority:
Document Number:		Document Number:		Document Number:
Expiration Date *(if any)(mm/dd/yyyy)*:		Expiration Date *(if any)(mm/dd/yyyy)*:		Expiration Date *(if any)(mm/dd/yyyy)*:
Document Title:				
Issuing Authority:				
Document Number:				
Expiration Date *(if any)(mm/dd/yyyy)*:				
Document Title:				3-D Barcode Do Not Write in This Space
Issuing Authority:				
Document Number:				
Expiration Date *(if any)(mm/dd/yyyy)*:				

Certification

I attest, under penalty of perjury, that (1) I have examined the document(s) presented by the above-named employee, (2) the above-listed document(s) appear to be genuine and to relate to the employee named, and (3) to the best of my knowledge the employee is authorized to work in the United States.

The employee's first day of employment *(mm/dd/yyyy)*: _____ *(See instructions for exemptions.)*

Signature of Employer or Authorized Representative	Date *(mm/dd/yyyy)*	Title of Employer or Authorized Representative
Last Name *(Family Name)*	First Name *(Given Name)*	Employer's Business or Organization Name

Employer's Business or Organization Address *(Street Number and Name)*	City or Town	State	Zip Code

While completing *Section 2*, the employer should be mindful of the following:

- Complete the List A column or the List B and C columns only, based on employee-submitted documents. Although you may photocopy documents (in which case, you must do so for all employees), you must complete this section.

- Some acceptable documents for List A are combination documents (such as a Foreign Passport & Form I-94), which necessitates recording the information for each document.

- Certification section: The individual reviewing documents on behalf of the employer must complete and sign the certification.

Section 3 of Form I-9 is only completed by the employer in certain circumstances.

Section 3. Reverification and Rehires *(To be completed and signed by employer or authorized representative.)*			
A. New Name *(if applicable)* Last Name *(Family Name)* First Name *(Given Name)*		Middle Initial	B. Date of Rehire *(if applicable) (mm/dd/yyyy)*:
C. If employee's previous grant of employment authorization has expired, provide the information for the document from List A or List C the employee presented that establishes current employment authorization in the space provided below.			
Document Title:	Document Number:		Expiration Date *(if any)(mm/dd/yyyy)*:
I attest, under penalty of perjury, that to the best of my knowledge, this employee is authorized to work in the United States, and if the employee presented document(s), the document(s) I have examined appear to be genuine and to relate to the individual.			
Signature of Employer or Authorized Representative:	Date *(mm/dd/yyyy)*:	Print Name of Employer or Authorized Representative:	

Form I-9 03/08/13 N   Page 8 of 9

If *Section 3* must be completed, the employer should be mindful of the following:

- New Name & Date of Rehire: Leave these sections blank if not applicable.

- Date of Rehire: This section is only applicable if the employee is rehired within three years of completing the original I-9, and if the information in the original form remains valid.

- Document section: List B documents never require reverification. Complete this section based on the employee's List A or List C document if either reverification is necessary (previously submitted document has expired) or employee is rehired within three years of completing the original I-9 and a previously submitted document has expired.

- Signature Line: If section 3 is completed, it must be signed and dated by the individual completing the section on behalf of the employer.

TIP! The Handbook for Employers, which may be found at www.uscis.gov/I-9Central, provides further guidance on the completion of Form I-9.

E-Verify

Most employers are not required to use the online e-verify system, which enables employers to verify employment eligibility quickly, securely, and accurately. However, using this free system provided by the federal government can provide reassurance that employees are eligible to work in the United States.

The system operates by comparing information provided by the employee with information contained in records from both the Social Security Administration and the United States Department of Homeland Security. While matching information typically results in an "Employment Authorized" response, any discrepancies result in a "Tentative Nonconfirmation (TNC)." When a TNC response is received, the employee is given an opportunity to resolve the discrepancy.

WARNING! Receiving a Tentative Nonconfirmation does not necessarily mean that an employee is unauthorized to work. A variety of reasons (such as accidentally incorrect information on Form I-9) can result in a TNC for an eligible employee. The employee has eight workdays to take action to correct the TNC.

Case In Point 1-5	Complete Form I-9

In this example, we will complete Sections 1 & 2 of Form I-9 based on the information provided below.

1. Warren Franklin (SSN 901-23-4444) has requested assistance in completing the employee portion of Form I-9. Warren was born on April 2, 1981, is a United States citizen, and (although you are providing him with assistance) completes the employee section of Form I-9 himself on his first day of employment (7/21/14). He lives at 212 Steeple Place, Madison, WI 53704.

Employment Eligibility Verification

Department of Homeland Security
U.S. Citizenship and Immigration Services

USCIS
Form I-9
OMB No. 1615-0047
Expires 03/31/2016

▶**START HERE.** Read instructions carefully before completing this form. The instructions must be available during completion of this form.
ANTI-DISCRIMINATION NOTICE: It is illegal to discriminate against work-authorized individuals. Employers **CANNOT** specify which document(s) they will accept from an employee. The refusal to hire an individual because the documentation presented has a future expiration date may also constitute illegal discrimination.

Section 1. Employee Information and Attestation *(Employees must complete and sign Section 1 of Form I-9 no later than the first day of employment, but not before accepting a job offer.)*

Last Name *(Family Name)*	First Name *(Given Name)*	Middle Initial	Other Names Used *(if any)*
Franklin	Warren		

Address *(Street Number and Name)*	Apt. Number	City or Town	State	Zip Code
212 Steeple Place		Madison	WI	53704

Date of Birth *(mm/dd/yyyy)*	U.S. Social Security Number	E-mail Address	Telephone Number
04/02/1981	9 0 1 - 2 3 - 4 4 4 4	N/A	N/A

I am aware that federal law provides for imprisonment and/or fines for false statements or use of false documents in connection with the completion of this form.

I attest, under penalty of perjury, that I am (check one of the following):

[X] A citizen of the United States

[ ] A noncitizen national of the United States *(See instructions)*

[ ] A lawful permanent resident (Alien Registration Number/USCIS Number): _____

[ ] An alien authorized to work until (expiration date, if applicable, mm/dd/yyyy) _____ . Some aliens may write "N/A" in this field. *(See instructions)*

*For aliens authorized to work, provide your Alien Registration Number/USCIS Number **OR** Form I-94 Admission Number:*

    1. Alien Registration Number/USCIS Number: _____

                OR

    2. Form I-94 Admission Number: _____

      If you obtained your admission number from CBP in connection with your arrival in the United States, include the following:

        Foreign Passport Number: _____

        Country of Issuance: _____

      Some aliens may write "N/A" on the Foreign Passport Number and Country of Issuance fields. *(See instructions)*

3-D Barcode
Do Not Write in This Space

Signature of Employee: *Warren Franklin*	Date *(mm/dd/yyyy):* 07/21/2014

Preparer and/or Translator Certification *(To be completed and signed if Section 1 is prepared by a person other than the employee.)*

I attest, under penalty of perjury, that I have assisted in the completion of this form and that to the best of my knowledge the information is true and correct.

Signature of Preparer or Translator:	Date *(mm/dd/yyyy):*

Last Name *(Family Name)*	First Name *(Given Name)*

Address *(Street Number and Name)*	City or Town	State	Zip Code

🛑 **Employer Completes Next Page** 🛑

Form I-9 03/08/13 N

Page 7 of 9

2. Warren's employer (Chapman Industries; 91784 Buttress Court, Madison, WI 53704) uses the e-verify system to determine employment eligibility. Warren provides his U.S. Passport (issued by US Dept. of State, #000022222, expires 3/9/16) to his employer (Dexter Hall, President), who completes the form on Warren's first day of employment.

2

Section 2. Employer or Authorized Representative Review and Verification

(Employers or their authorized representative must complete and sign Section 2 within 3 business days of the employee's first day of employment. You must physically examine one document from List A OR examine a combination of one document from List B and one document from List C as listed on the "Lists of Acceptable Documents" on the next page of this form. For each document you review, record the following information: document title, issuing authority, document number, and expiration date, if any.)

Employee Last Name, First Name and Middle Initial from Section 1:

List A	OR	List B	AND	List C
Identity and Employment Authorization		**Identity**		**Employment Authorization**

Document Title: U.S. Passport	Document Title:	Document Title:
Issuing Authority: U.S. Dept. of State	Issuing Authority:	Issuing Authority:
Document Number: #000022222	Document Number:	Document Number:
Expiration Date *(if any)(mm/dd/yyyy)*: 03/09/2016	Expiration Date *(if any)(mm/dd/yyyy)*:	Expiration Date *(if any)(mm/dd/yyyy)*:
Document Title:		
Issuing Authority:		
Document Number:		
Expiration Date *(if any)(mm/dd/yyyy)*:		
Document Title:		**3-D Barcode** **Do Not Write in This Space**
Issuing Authority:		
Document Number:		
Expiration Date *(if any)(mm/dd/yyyy)*:		

Certification

I attest, under penalty of perjury, that (1) I have examined the document(s) presented by the above-named employee, (2) the above-listed document(s) appear to be genuine and to relate to the employee named, and (3) to the best of my knowledge the employee is authorized to work in the United States.

The employee's first day of employment *(mm/dd/yyyy)*: 07/21/2014 *(See instructions for exemptions.)*

Signature of Employer or Authorized Representative *Dexter Hall*	Date *(mm/dd/yyyy)* 07/21/2014	Title of Employer or Authorized Representative President
Last Name *(Family Name)* Hall	First Name *(Given Name)* Dexter	Employer's Business or Organization Name Chapman Industries

Employer's Business or Organization Address *(Street Number and Name)* 91784 Buttress Court	City or Town Madison	State WI	Zip Code 53704

Section 3. Reverification and Rehires *(To be completed and signed by employer or authorized representative.)*

A. New Name *(if applicable)* Last Name *(Family Name)* First Name *(Given Name)*	Middle Initial	B. Date of Rehire *(if applicable)* *(mm/dd/yyyy)*

C. If employee's previous grant of employment authorization has expired, provide the information for the document from List A or List C the employee presented that establishes current employment authorization in the space provided below.

Document Title:	Document Number:	Expiration Date *(if any)(mm/dd/yyyy)*:

I attest, under penalty of perjury, that to the best of my knowledge, this employee is authorized to work in the United States, and if the employee presented document(s), the document(s) I have examined appear to be genuine and to relate to the individual.

Signature of Employer or Authorized Representative:	Date *(mm/dd/yyyy)*:	Print Name of Employer or Authorized Representative:

Form I-9 03/08/13 N

Page 8 of 9

Considering General Payroll Topics

Additional considerations must be made prior to, or concurrent with, the hiring of employees. Among these are the acquisition of Workers' Compensation Insurance and the establishment of an employee earning's record for each employee. Other payroll topics that warrant consideration include the decision to use a payroll services provider, or whether to pursue a specialized payroll certification.

Obtaining Workers' Compensation Insurance

On the Web

www.dol.gov/owcp/
dfec/regs/compliance/
wc.htm

Most businesses are required by their state to obtain **Workers' Compensation** insurance, which provides financial assistance to employees injured during the course of their employment. In most instances, employers may obtain Workers' Compensation Insurance either by purchasing it from a state-operated fund or private insurance carrier, or by becoming authorized by the state to be self-insured.

Insurance premiums paid by employers are based on the relative risk associated with different job types. For example, the premium required for an employee working in an office setting is far less than that required for an employee who chops down trees. Depending on the state, benefits that employees receive are used to pay medical bills, make up for lost wages, compensate for permanent injury, and/or provide an employee's beneficiaries with a death benefit.

Obtaining Payroll Certifications

For those who pursue a career in payroll, obtaining a professional certification can lead to enhanced job opportunities as well as to promotions. The American Payroll Association offers payroll professionals the opportunity to earn two different professional certifications:

- The Fundamental Payroll Certification (FPC) establishes that an individual has a baseline level of payroll competency. This is the lower-level certification offered by the American Payroll Association.
- The Certified Payroll Professional (CPP) designates a higher level of payroll mastery, and the examination can only be taken upon the satisfaction of specific criteria. These criteria involve both the length of time worked in the payroll profession and the payroll courses completed.

Utilizing a Payroll Service

As you'll discover throughout this textbook, payroll can be a complicated topic. While it's possible for a business to handle all of its payroll-related tasks, many instead choose to hire a **payroll service**. These services (some of the most prominent include Paychex, and Intuit) can calculate employee net pay; generate employee paychecks; complete and file all monthly, quarterly, and annual payroll tax forms; and provide many additional services. Given the potential penalties associated with mishandling payroll (which can be levied at both the federal and state levels), and the amount of time spent on payroll tasks, many companies decide that a payroll service is worth the added expense.

Establishing an Employee Earnings Record

An **employee earnings record** should be established upon the hiring of each employee. This record contains both key employee information (name, social security number, marital status, etc.) and payroll information for a given year. By providing a summary of annual payroll figures for a single employee, the employee earnings record facilitates completion of a variety of payroll tax forms.

Most businesses use computerized payroll systems, which automatically generate these records. However, understanding the components of the employee earnings record, and the manner in which they are generated, is vital. Therefore, we'll work with manual versions of the earnings record throughout multiple chapters.

The Employee Earnings Record displays a summary of payroll information for a single employee.

Employee Earnings Record

Name _____   Marital Status _____

Address _____   Fed. Withholding Allow. _____

_____   State Withholding Allow. _____

SS# _____

	Earnings							Deductions									
Pay Period Ending	Regular Hours Worked	Regular Pay Rate	Regular Wages	Overtime Hours Worked	Overtime Pay Rate	Overtime Wages	Gross Pay	Federal Withholding Tax	State Withholding Tax	Social Security Tax	Medicare Tax	Retirement Contribution	Life Insurance	Charitable Contribution	Additional Withholding	Check Number	Net Pay

Case In Point 1-6   Create an Employee Earnings Record

In this example, we will establish an employee earnings record for Stacey Rodriguez, a newly-hired employee of Acme Safes Co. Ms. Rodriguez (SSN 333-44-5555) is single, lives at 1986 Series Drive, Reno, NV 89509, and claims one allowance for both her federal and state taxes. She has agreed to a regular wage rate of $9.25/hour, and an overtime wage rate of $13.88, both of which will initially be applied to her first week of employment, ending on 7/25/14.

1

Employee Earnings Record

Name	Stacey Rodriguez	Marital Status — Single
Address	1986 Series Drive	Fed. Withholding Allow. — 1
	Reno, NV 89509	State Withholding Allow. — 1
SS#	333-44-5555	

	Earnings							Deductions									
Pay Period Ending	Regular Hours Worked	Regular Pay Rate	Regular Wages	Overtime Hours Worked	Overtime Pay Rate	Overtime Wages	Gross Pay	Federal Withholding Tax	State Withholding Tax	Social Security Tax	Medicare Tax	Retirement Contribution	Life Insurance	Charitable Contribution	Additional Withholding	Check Number	Net Pay
7/25/14		$ 9.25			$ 13.88												

2

1. Complete the top portion of the employee earnings record. This section is unlikely to change frequently, and therefore does not need to be listed for every pay period.

2. Fill in those items for the first pay period that have already been determined. The majority of columns, such as Regular Hours Worked and Social Security Tax, are left blank. These items cannot be determined until after the first pay period has ended (i.e. after 7/25/14).

Concepts Review

All of the Concepts Review quizzes for this book are also available in the Student Resource Center. Check with your instructor on how to complete the quizzes (in the book or online).

True/False Questions

1. An employee's paycheck displays the gross pay amount. *True False*

2. Certain employees are not subject to the federal minimum wage of $7.25. *True False*

3. The federal minimum-wage rate takes precedence, regardless of whether it is the same as the applicable state minimum wage rate. *True False*

4. The Internal Revenue Service charges users a nominal fee for the Circular E. *True False*

5. Form SS-4 is used by an employer to apply for an Employer Identification Number. *True False*

6. The provisions of The Personal Responsibility and Work Opportunity Reconciliation Act can be satisfied through the submission of the W-4 Form to the state. *True False*

7. Form SS-5 (Application for a Social Security Card) should be submitted to the employee's local social security office. *True False*

8. Form I-9 (Employment Eligibility Verification) is completed entirely by the employer. *True False*

9. E-verify is an online system that allows employers to verify a prospective employee's employment eligibility status. *True False*

10. Workers' Compensation Insurance costs the same regardless of the type of work performed by the insured employees. *True False*

Multiple Choice Questions

1. Which of the following cannot be found on a standard pay stub?
   a. Employee address
   b. Prior year's gross wages
   c. Overtime hours worked (if any)
   d. Pay date

2. The Fair Labor Standards Act requires that, for non-exempt employees, the overtime hourly pay rate be at least what percentage of the regular hourly pay rate?
   a. 75%
   b. 100%
   c. 150%
   d. 200%

3. Which of the following groups may not be paid less than the federal minimum wage?
   a. Tipped employees
   b. Full-time students
   c. State government workers
   d. Executive employees

4. Which of the following jobs may be held by an individual younger than 18 years of age?
   a. Roofer
   b. Explosives Manufacturer
   c. Coal Miner
   d. Landscaper bagging leaves

5. The Personal Responsibility and Work Opportunity Reconciliation Act (PRWORA) was designed to strengthen what?
   a. Child Support Program
   b. Workers' Compensation Coverage
   c. Federal Minimum Wage Rates
   d. Immigration Law

6. Which of the following is not requested on Form SS-5?
   a. Father's Social Security Number
   b. Ethnicity
   c. Number of Allowances
   d. Place of Birth

7. The Immigration Reform and Control Act (IRCA) was signed into legislation in what year?
   a. 1960
   b. 1974
   c. 1986
   d. 1990

8. Which of the following is insufficient for the purposes of verifying employment eligibility on Form I-9?
   a. Driver's license & Native American tribal document
   b. Voter's registration card & U.S. Coast Guard Merchant Mariner Card.
   c. Military dependent's ID card & an unrestricted Social Security Account Number card
   d. United States passport

9. An Employee Earnings Record typically displays each of the following except?
   a. State Withholding Allowances
   b. Employee Signature
   c. Overtime Pay Rate
   d. Marital Status

10. The Workers' Compensation Insurance requirement may typically be satisfied through all of the following methods except:
    a. Submitting applicable state forms verifying that all full-time employees have approved an uninsured status.
    b. Becoming authorized by the applicable state to be self-insured.
    c. Purchasing Workers' Compensation Insurance from a state-operated fund.
    d. Purchasing Workers' Compensation Insurance from a private insurance carrier.

Knowledge Check A

For all assignments in this section, necessary IRS forms and/or Excel templates are located in the Student Resource Center.

KCa 1-1 Define Paystub Elements

Define a number of items found within a typical paystub.

1. Paycheck

2. Gross Pay

3. Deductions

4. Net Pay

KCa 1-2 Identify Compliance with the Fair Labor Standards Act

Examine the following independent circumstances and identify whether each complies with the Fair Labor Standards Act.

1. A hospital employee is paid $6.95/hour.

2. A full-time student earns $7.20/hour for working 4 hours/day, 4 days/week, during the school year.

3. An administrative (office) employee earns an annual salary which, when divided by total hours worked during the year, is the equivalent of $6.68/hour.

4. An employee at a local bakery begins working on June 1. He turns 20 on October 14, and earns $4.25/hour during his first six months of employment.

5. A student learner in a qualified vocational program earns $5.50/hour. The employer has not yet applied for an authorizing certificate.

6. A federal government employee earns $7.48/hour.

KCa 1-3 Use the Internet to Explore the Circular E

Examine the Circular E to answer a series of questions. (Recall that the Circular E is found at: http://www.irs.gov/pub/irs-pdf/p15.pdf)

1. How long should an employer retain records of employment taxes?

2. What forms should be furnished to employees and filed with the IRS by January 31 each year?

3. Define the term *Payroll Period*.

4. Is income tax withholding handled differently for part-time workers than for full-time workers?

5. If payday falls on a Friday for a semiweekly depositor of social security, Medicare, and withheld income taxes, by what day of the following week must taxes be deposited?

KCa 1-4 Complete Form SS-4

Complete Form SS-4 for a newly-formed company.

1. Adam's Diner is a new eatery that was formed as a sole proprietorship by Adam Spruce (SSN 777-77-7777) on January 28, 2014, and serves only locally-sourced foods. The diner is located at 95 Main Street, Atlanta, GA 30311 (it is in Fulton county and the only address associated with the business), and both its telephone and fax number are 478-555-8129. The company uses the calendar year as its fiscal year, and expects to employ four people (earning an average of $19,900/year) throughout the first 12 months of operations. Payroll is to be paid weekly on Fridays, with the first pay date scheduled for Friday, February 1, 2014.

KCa 1-5 Complete Form W-4

Assist a friend in completing Form W-4. As part of this process, you will also assist him in completing the Personal Allowances Worksheet.

1. David Valentine (SSN 888-88-8888) is single, lives at 752 Amusement Court, St. Louis, MO 63108, does not want any additional withholding amounts, and is not exempt from federal income tax withholding. David has no children or dependents, does not hold any other jobs, and files as single on his tax return.

KCa 1-6 Complete Form I-9

Complete both Section 1 & Section 2 of Form I-9.

1. Thomas Quinn (SSN 999-99-9999) has requested assistance in completing the employee portion of Form I-9. Thomas was born on November 13, 1972, is a United States citizen, and (although you are providing him with assistance) completes the employee section of Form I-9 himself on his first day of employment (7/21/14). He lives at 950 Harvard Place, Newport, RI 02840.

2. Thomas' employer (Carpet Warehouse; 8114 Princeton Avenue, Newport, RI 02840) utilizes the e-verify system to determine employment eligibility. Thomas provides his U.S. Passport (issued by US Dept. of State, #000055555, expires 8/12/19) to his employer (Barry Coleman, HR Manager), who completes the form on Thomas' first day of employment.

KCa 1-7 Create an Employee Earnings Record

Create an employee earnings record for a new employee.

1. Patrick Workman (SSN 123-45-6789) begins working for Fishing Experts Co. on 6/23/14. He lives at 817 Remote Lane, Bentonville, AR 72712, is single, and claims both two federal and state withholding allowances. He earns $9.00/hour in regular wages, and $13.50/hour in overtime wages, and payroll is paid every Friday.

Knowledge Check B

For all assignments in this section, necessary IRS forms and/or Excel templates are located in the Student Resource Center.

KCb 1-1 Identify the Appropriate Paystub Section

Identify the standard paystub section (Company and Pay Period Information, Employee Information, Current and Year-to-Date Earnings, Amounts Withheld (Deducted) from Employee Pay, Paycheck, or Net Pay) that corresponds to each item below.

1. Overtime hours worked

2. Period ending date

3. Marital status

4. Gross Pay

5. Social Security tax amount

6. Social Security number

7. Check number

8. Federal Income tax amount

KCb 1-2 Determine Compliance with Child Labor Restrictions

Determine the youngest age (if any) at which an employee may perform each of the job duties below.

1. Milking cows on a parent's farm.

2. Taking measurements for roof construction.

3. Working as a teller at a grocery store on Monday, Tuesday, and Wednesday from 4:00 p.m. to 7:00 p.m.

4. Performing as lead actor in a local play.

5. Stocking shelves at a convenience store during the school year on Saturday and Sunday from 6:00 a.m. to 3:00 p.m.

KCb 1-3 Use the Internet to Explore the Circular E

Examine the Circular E to answer the following questions. (Recall that the Circular E is found at: http://www.irs. gov/pub/irs-pdf/p15.pdf.)

1. What phone number may an individual with disabilities call in order to ask a federal tax question?

2. If a husband and wife jointly run a business, is it treated as a sole proprietorship, partnership, or corporation for tax purposes?

3. If wages are not paid in money (cash or check), is an employer obligated to remit federal income tax withholding, social security, Medicare, and FUTA taxes based on these wages?

4. Identify three examples of fringe benefits provided to employees that are not taxable.

5. May an employer substitute his own version of Form W-4 for the IRS-Published version? If so, are there any restrictions on this policy?

KCb 1-4 Complete Form SS-4

Complete Form SS-4 for an insurance agency.

1. Local Insurance Corp. is an agency that was formed as a corporation by Jane Detworth (SSN 111-11-1111) on May 4, 2014, and operates under the name JD Insurance. The company specializes in homeowner's insurance, and files Form SS-4 so that it may begin distributing payroll checks as of May 26, 2014. It is located at 2 State Avenue, Tuscaloosa, AL 35405 (it is in Tuscaloosa county and is the only address associated with the business). It was incorporated in the state of Alabama. The company will file form 1120S each year. Its telephone number is 205-555-9991, and fax is 205-555-8000. The fiscal year runs from May through April, and it expects to employ three people (each earning an average of $30,000/year) throughout the first 12 months of operations. Payroll is to be paid semi-monthly on the 15th and final day of the month, with the first pay date scheduled for Monday, June 2, 2014.

KCb 1-5 Complete Form W-4

Assist a friend in completing Form W-4. As part of this process, you will also assist him in completing the Personal Allowances Worksheet.

1. Billy Darling (SSN 343-43-4343) is single, lives at 40 Tabasco Lane, Minneapolis, MN 55423, and is not exempt from federal income tax withholding. Billy files as single on his tax return, has one job, and has no children or dependents.

KCb 1-6 Complete Form I-9

Complete both Section 1 & Section 2 of Form I-9.

1. Alan Strawberry (SSN 111-11-1111) has requested assistance in completing the employee portion of Form I-9. Alan was born on January 4, 1965, is a Lawful Permanent Resident (USCIS #555-555-555), and (although you are providing him with assistance) completes the employee section of Form I-9 himself on his first day of employment (9/1/14). He lives at 214 Indian Lane, Billings, MT 59107.

2. Alan's employer (Uniform Specialists; 12 Pent Drive, Billings, MT 59107) utilizes the e-verify system to determine employment eligibility. Alan provides his Permanent Resident Card (issued by US Citizenship & Immigration Services, expires 11/28/21) to his employer (Joel Weiner, Director of Personnel), who completes the form on Alan's first day of employment. The document number displayed on the Permanent Resident Card is 567-890-123.

KCb 1-7 Complete an Employee Earnings Record

Create an employee earnings record for a new employee.

1. Brian Price (SSN 252-52-5252) begins working for Costume Creativity on 12/15/14. He lives at 8888 Searcher Blvd., Wheeling, WV 26003, is married, claims three federal withholding allowances, and two state withholding allowances. He earns $12.50/hour in regular wages, and $18.75/hour in overtime wages, and payroll is paid twice/month, on the 15th and final days.

Continuing Payroll Problem

For all assignments in this section, necessary IRS forms and/or Excel templates are located in the Student Resource Center.

CPP 1-1 Starting a New Business & Assisting a New Employee

Complete Form SS-4 for TCLH Industries, a manufacturer of cleaning products. You will then work with Zachary Fox, a new employee, to ensure that all necessary payroll forms are completed.

1. Complete Form SS-4 for TCLH Industries. The company was formed on April 15, 2013 as a partnership between Michael Sierra (CEO; SSN 232-32-3232) and David Alexander (President; SSN 454-54-5454). Day-to-day operations, such as the filing of federal and state forms, are handled by the CEO, whose phone number and fax number are 919-555-7485 & 919-555-2000 respectively. The company is located at 202 Whitmore Avenue, Durham, NC 27701 (in Durham county), where it receives all mail. The company uses the calendar year as its fiscal year, and expects to employ four individuals (earning an expected average of $29,300/year) throughout the first 18 months of operations. Payroll is to be paid weekly on Fridays, with the first pay date scheduled for Friday, April 26, 2013 (for the one-week period ending that day).

2. Complete the W-4 Form for Zachary Fox, a new employee who is hired on April 29, 2013. Zachary (SSN 121-21-2121) is married (and files this way), lives at 1483 Independence Road, Durham, NC 27701, does not want any additional withholding amounts, and is not exempt from federal income tax withholding. Zachary (who expects to earn approximately $84,000 this year) has one child, does not hold any other jobs, and his spouse earns $68,200/year (Zachary does not claim an allowance for his spouse). He does not file as Head of Household, and anticipates having $1,720 of child care expenses.

    TIP! To accurately complete Form W-4, you should first fill out the Personal Allowances Worksheet.

3. Complete the I-9 Form for Zachary Fox, a new employee. He requests assistance in completing the employee portion of the form. Zachary was born on February 27, 1977, is a United States citizen, and (although you are providing him with assistance) completes the employee section of Form I-9 himself on his first day of employment. TCLH Industries utilizes the e-verify system to confirm employment eligibility. Zachary provides his driver's license number (NYS, 888 888 888, expires 2/27/18) and social security card (issued by Social Security Administration) to his employer, who completes the form on Zachary's first day of employment (April 29, 2013).

4. Establish an Employee Earnings Record for Zachary Fox, so that payroll may be entered at the end of every pay period. Zachary claims the same number of federal and state withholding allowances, earns regular wages of $7.75/hour, and earns overtime wages of $11.63/hour.

Critical Thinking

CT 1-1 Examine the E-Verify System

The E-verify system, although not mandatory for most employers, is an important tool that should be utilized regularly. For this system to yield beneficial results, the employer must fully understand how it functions. In this exercise, you will study and report on the functionality of the E-verify system.

Open a new Microsoft Word document (or use a comparable document program) and save the file as **PA01-CT1-[Your Last Name]-Everify**. Use the internet to research the E-verify process (Hint: The E-verify system is on the United States Citizenship & Immigration Services website). Write at least three paragraphs in which you discuss the E-verify enrollment process, the E-verify verification process, and the steps an employee should take in the event of a Tentative Nonconfirmation.

Submit your final file(s) based on the guidelines provided by your instructor.

CT 1-2 Research Major Payroll Services

Understanding the differences between available payroll services can allow an organization to select the service that is most suitable for its needs. In this exercise, you will research four major payroll services, and list two benefits of utilizing each.

Open a new Microsoft Word document (or use a comparable document program) and save the file as **PA01-CT2-[Your Last Name]-PayrollService**. Use the internet to identify major payroll services, and select four of the most prominent. Research the services provided by each, and write at least one paragraph for each in which you identify two ways that the payroll service distinguishes itself from its competitors. Lastly, write one paragraph in which, based on these characteristics, you select your preferred payroll service, and discuss why you made this selection.

Submit your final file(s) based on the guidelines provided by your instructor.

2 Calculating Employee Pay

LEARNING OBJECTIVES

After studying this chapter, you will be able to:

■ **Identify various pay period options**

■ **Distinguish between salaries and wages**

■ **Define overtime pay**

■ **Determine employee pay using multiple methods**

■ **Calculate incentives, commissions, and bonuses**

■ **Establish the Payroll Register**

When calculating employee pay, a number of considerations must be taken into account. Primarily, the job duties determine the most appropriate method for calculating employee pay. In this chapter, you will first examine the distinction between salaries and wages. You will also consider a number of additional types of pay, as well as methods for determining each. Lastly, you will practice entering employee pay data within both the employee earnings record and the Payroll Register.

Calculating Employee Pay for Lucky Ties Apparel

Lucky Ties Apparel employs a number of people who occupy different positions, and thus uses a variety of compensation methods. Some employees are paid on an hourly basis, while others have agreed to annual pay. The company is considering allowing employees who work on the sales floor the opportunity to earn commissions in addition to their hourly pay, and a few managers would be eligible for bonuses based on the store's overall performance.

Having recently taken over all payroll responsibilities, you want to be certain that you fully comprehend not only how to calculate the various types of compensation, but also the regulations relating to each. You decide to review the process underlying all of the store's payroll calculations, and to examine the store's payroll-recording process.

A variety of components are used to calculate an employee's gross pay.

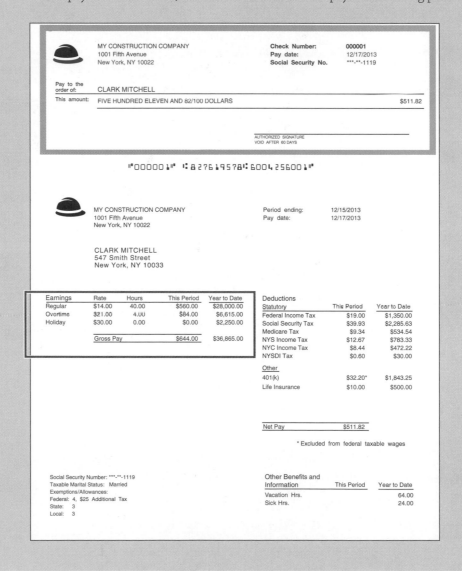

MY CONSTRUCTION COMPANY
1001 Fifth Avenue
New York, NY 10022

Check Number: 000001
Pay date: 12/17/2013
Social Security No. ***-**-1119

Pay to the order of: CLARK MITCHELL

This amount: FIVE HUNDRED ELEVEN AND 82/100 DOLLARS $511.82

AUTHORIZED SIGNATURE
VOID AFTER 60 DAYS

⑈000001⑈ ⑆827619578⑆ 6004256001⑈

MY CONSTRUCTION COMPANY
1001 Fifth Avenue
New York, NY 10022

Period ending: 12/15/2013
Pay date: 12/17/2013

CLARK MITCHELL
547 Smith Street
New York, NY 10033

Earnings	Rate	Hours	This Period	Year to Date
Regular	$14.00	40.00	$560.00	$28,000.00
Overtime	$21.00	4.00	$84.00	$6,615.00
Holiday	$30.00	0.00	$0.00	$2,250.00
		Gross Pay	$644.00	$36,865.00

Deductions		
Statutory	This Period	Year to Date
Federal Income Tax	$19.00	$1,350.00
Social Security Tax	$39.93	$2,285.63
Medicare Tax	$9.34	$534.54
NYS Income Tax	$12.67	$783.33
NYC Income Tax	$8.44	$472.22
NYSDI Tax	$0.60	$30.00
Other		
401(k)	$32.20*	$1,843.25
Life Insurance	$10.00	$500.00

Net Pay	$511.82

* Excluded from federal taxable wages

Social Security Number: ***-**-1119
Taxable Marital Status: Married
Exemptions/Allowances:
Federal: 4, $25 Additional Tax
State: 3
Local: 3

Other Benefits and Information	This Period	Year to Date
Vacation Hrs.		64.00
Sick Hrs.		24.00

Defining Pay Periods and Workweeks

Employees are paid periodically throughout the year. The necessary payroll calculations are based on consistent definitions of the **pay period** and workweek for each employee. Understanding these terms is necessary so that an employee may verify the accuracy of his/her paycheck.

Choosing from Pay Period Options

Employers can choose to pay employees on any of a number of different schedules. The most common options are weekly, bi-weekly, semi-monthly, and monthly.

Pay Period Definitions

Pay Period Type	Frequency of Pay Dates
Weekly	Pay dates occur once per week, on the same day of the week
Bi-weekly	Pay dates occur once every other week, on the same day of the week
Semi-monthly	Pay dates occur twice per month, typically at the midpoint and on the final day each month
Monthly	Pay dates occur once per month, typically on the same date each month

This weekly pay period runs from Monday through Sunday.

July 2014

Sun.	Mon.	Tues.	Wed.	Thurs.	Fri.	Sat
		1	2	3	4	5
6	7	8	9	10	11	12
13	14	15	16	17	18	19
20	21	22	23	24	25	26
27	28	29	30	31		

This bi-weekly pay period covers the equivalent of two consecutive weekly periods.

July 2014

Sun.	Mon.	Tues.	Wed.	Thurs.	Fri.	Sat.
		1	2	3	4	5
6	7	8	9	10	11	12
13	14	15	16	17	18	19
20	21	22	23	24	25	26
27	28	29	30	31		

This semi-monthly pay period covers either the first or second half of a month.

July 2014

Sun.	Mon.	Tues.	Wed.	Thurs.	Fri.	Sat.
		1	2	3	4	5
6	7	8	9	10	11	12
13	14	15	16	17	18	19
20	21	22	23	24	25	26
27	28	29	30	31		

This monthly pay period covers a full month, regardless of the days on which it begins and ends.

July 2014

Sun.	Mon.	Tues.	Wed.	Thurs.	Fri.	Sat.
		1	2	3	4	5
6	7	8	9	10	11	12
13	14	15	16	17	18	19
20	21	22	23	24	25	26
27	28	29	30	31		

Payroll processing can be time-consuming, particularly if employees are paid on an hourly basis. In many instances, when employees are paid on any of the above schedules, they are not being paid for the most recent week(s). Therefore, it is common for a lag to exist between the dates during which employees earn their pay, and the date on which they receive a paycheck.

For example, a weekly schedule could call for employees to be paid every Friday. If employees earn a total of $1,000 from Monday (4/14) through Friday (4/18), they would not receive the $1,000 until the following Friday (4/25). The check they receive on Friday, 4/18 would compensate them for the time that they worked during the prior week (Monday 4/7 through Friday 4/11).

Defining the Workweek

As mentioned in Chapter 1, a workweek, as defined in the Fair Labor Standards Act (FLSA), is any consecutive seven-day period. It can differ from a calendar week (it does not need to run from Sunday through Saturday), and can begin at any hour. For example, an acceptable workweek could begin at 8:00 a.m. on Tuesday and run through the following Tuesday at 7:59 a.m.

It is important that a business clearly define its workweek so that payroll is properly calculated. For example, if an employee receives overtime pay for any hours worked after the first 40 in a given week, there must be a clear beginning and end to the workweek, so that overtime hours are accurately determined.

WARNING! The workweek must be consistent from one week to another. It may only be altered if the change is intended to be permanent, and if it is not made in order to circumvent overtime requirements.

Case In Point 2-1	**Evaluate Pay Periods & Workweeks**

In these examples, we will review a number of pay periods, and determine whether certain specified workweeks are acceptable under the FLSA.

1. Jason Ivory receives two paychecks every month, each of which compensates him for half of the current month. What type of pay period is Jason's employer utilizing?

   This employer is compensating Jason on a semi-monthly basis. This is the only pay period type under which an employee receives two paychecks every month.

2. Lance Quigley receives 52 paychecks every year. What type of pay period is Lance's employer utilizing?

   This employer is compensating Lance on a weekly basis. As a result, Lance receives one paycheck for each of the 52 weeks in a given year.

3. Drew Graham began working for his employer on Monday, 9/15. He receives his first paycheck on Wednesday, 9/24, and his second paycheck on Wednesday, 10/8. The second paycheck was twice as large as the first, and every paycheck after the 10/8 check compensates Drew for the same period of time. What type of pay period is Drew's employer utilizing?

    This employer is compensating Drew on a bi-weekly basis. The 9/24 paycheck compensated Drew for his first week of employment (Monday, 9/15 through Friday, 9/19). The 10/8 paycheck compensated Drew for his second and third weeks of employment (Monday, 9/22 through Friday, 10/3). We know that Drew is not paid on a semi-monthly basis because each paycheck compensates him for the same period of time. Because the number of days within each month differs, semi-monthly paychecks do not all compensate employees for the same number of days.

4. Vincent Meacham's employer has traditionally utilized a workweek running from Monday morning through Sunday evening. During the summer months. the company experiences an increased workload over the weekends. Vincent's employer has decided to alter the workweek so that it begins on Saturday morning each week. The employer expects to return to the Monday through Sunday schedule at the end of the summer. Is Vincent's employer in violation of the Fair Labor Standards Act?

    Yes, the employer is in violation of the FLSA. While it is acceptable for an employer to change a workweek, there must be an expectation that the change is permanent. Temporary changes are not permissible under the FLSA.

5. Gino Lofton's employer pays employees on a bi-weekly basis. As a result, the employer defines a workweek as the two-week period running from Monday through the second Sunday of the period. Is Gino's employer in violation of the Fair Labor Standards Act?

    Yes, the employer is in violation of the FLSA. Regardless of the pay period in use, a workweek must be defined as a consistent seven-day period. Defining a workweek like this means that, regardless of the frequency of paychecks, a number of payroll-related items, such as overtime hours, are determined on a week-by-week basis.

Considering Wage-Determination Issues

When establishing the wage rate for an employee, several considerations should be made. An employer must ensure compliance with the Equal Pay Act. Additionally, in certain states there are mandated minimum wages that exceed the current federal minimum wage. Employers are required to pay employees no less than these higher state minimum-wage rates. Lastly, employers must establish time cards for each employee, which may then be used to track all hours worked.

Complying with the Equal Pay Act

On the Web

www.eeoc.gov/laws/
statutes/epa.cfm

The **Equal Pay Act (EPA)** of 1963 is one of the most prominent amendments to the Fair Labor Standards Act. It dictates that no employer may discriminate against any employee by paying a lower wage than is paid to an employee of the opposite gender for a similar job. While the Equal Pay Act prohibits discrimination against employees of either gender, it was enacted primarily to protect female employees.

WARNING! Employers cannot reduce the wage rate of any employee as a way to comply with the Equal Pay Act. If a wage disparity exists, the lower wage must be increased so that it equals the higher wage.

According to the US Department of Labor, in 1963 women earned, on average, 59 cents for every dollar earned by a man in a similar job. In 2013, fifty years after the enactment of the Equal Pay Act, this figure had risen to 81 cents. This statistic underscores the fact that gender-based wage discrimination is still prevalent today, and employers must be vigilant to ensure that it does not exist in their organizations.

The Equal Pay Act allows for a disparity in pay between employees of different genders under a small number of prescribed circumstances. These include the existence of:

- a seniority system
- a merit system
- a system based on quantity or quality of output produced
- any other non-gender-based system that results in a pay differential.

Paying State Minimum Wages

On the Web

www.dol.gov/whd/
minwage/america.htm

Under the FLSA, if an employee's state mandates a higher minimum wage than the current federal minimum wage of $7.25/hr, the employee is required to be paid at least the higher state rate. Such state minimum wages can be significantly higher than the federal minimum wage, as in Washington, where the state minimum wage is currently $9.19/hour.

NOTE! Some municipalities have enacted minimum-wage rates that are higher than the applicable federal and state rates. For example, San Francisco's 2014 minimum wage rate is $10.74.

Using Time Cards

For employees who are paid on an hourly basis, an employee **time card** offers a method by which hours worked are tracked. Since employee pay is based on hours worked, this is a vital component of the payroll process.

This employee time card allows employees to enter hours worked for a one-week period.

Employee Time Card

Employee Name _____

Employee SS# _____

Day	Date	Morning		Afternoon		Daily Total
		Time In	Time Out	Time In	Time Out	
Monday						
Tuesday						
Wednesday						
Thursday						
Friday						
Saturday						
Sunday						
				Weekly Total:		

Employee Signature _____

Note that the Daily Total column displays the total hours worked by the employee each day. Per the FLSA, employers are permitted to round employee time worked to the nearest 15 minute increment. Employee time cards must be verified by one or more supervisors prior to calculating employee pay.

NOTE! In many work environments, even salaried employees complete time cards, so that the employer has verification of hours worked.

Alternative Timekeeping Methods

While many employers continue to use time cards, an increasing number are turning to electronic timekeeping methods. Examples include Badge Terminals (at which employees swipe badges), and Biometric Terminals (at which employees apply handprints, fingerprints, or other biological data). In both instances, the computer system logs employee hours based on the entries at these terminals.

Case In Point 2-2 # Complete Time Cards for Two Employees

In this example, we'll complete a time card for two different employees. Note that this employer rounds employee time to the nearest fifteen-minute increment.

1. Angelo Dorsett (SSN 444-44-4444) worked five days for Lucky Ties Apparel during the week of 4/21/14 through 4/27/14 (he had Monday and Sunday off). Each working day he arrived at 8:00 a.m. (except Wednesday, when he was 3 minutes early, and Friday, when he arrived at 6:59 a.m.). He left for lunch at 12:00 p.m. each day (except Tuesday, when he left at 12:07 p.m.), and arrived back at 1:00 p.m. (except Friday and Saturday, when he arrived back at 12:57 p.m. and 1:02 p.m. respectively). He left each day at 5:00 p.m. (except Wednesday and Thursday, when he stayed until 5:10 p.m. and 5:59 p.m. respectively). His completed timecard appears as follows:

Employee Time Card

Employee Name **Angelo Dorsett**

Employee SS# **444-44-4444**

Day	Date	Morning		Afternoon		Daily Total
		Time In	Time Out	Time In	Time Out	
Monday	4/21/14	--	--	--	--	--
Tuesday	4/22/14	8:00	12:07	1:00	5:00	8
Wednesday	4/23/14	7:57	12:00	1:00	5:10	8.25
Thursday	4/24/14	8:00	12:00	1:00	5:59	9
Friday	4/25/14	6:59	12:00	12:57	5:00	9
Saturday	4/26/14	8:00	12:00	1:02	5:00	8
Sunday	4/27/14	--	--	--	--	--
					Weekly Total:	42.25

Employee Signature *Angelo Dorsett*

Notice that the **Daily Total** column lists full hours for each day except Wednesday. Since this employer rounds employee time to the nearest 15-minute increment, Angelo is credited with an extra quarter hour (15 minutes) on Wednesday. Rounding resulted in full hours worked for all other workdays. For example, instead of listing 7 hours and 58 minutes for Saturday, the employer rounded to 8 hours.

2. Lucy Marshall (SSN 777-77-7777) worked six days for Lucky Ties Apparel during the week of 12/1/14 through 12/7/14 (she had Wednesday off). Each working day she arrived at 6:00 a.m. (except Monday, when she was 5 minutes early, and Friday, when she arrived at 7:02 a.m.). She left for lunch at 11:00 a.m. each day (except Thursday, when she left at 10:58 a.m., and Sunday, when she left at 11:29 a.m.), and arrived back at 12:00 p.m. (except Saturday, when she arrived back at 12:06 p.m.). She left work each day at 4:00 p.m. (except for Tuesday and Friday, when she stayed until 2:54 p.m. and 4:01 p.m. respectively). Her completed timecard appears as follows:

Employee Time Card

Employee Name **Lucy Marshall**

Employee SS# **777-77-7777**

Day	Date	Morning		Afternoon		Daily Total
		Time In	Time Out	Time In	Time Out	
Monday	12/1/14	5:55	11:00	12:00	4:00	9
Tuesday	12/2/14	6:00	11:00	12:00	2:54	8
Wednesday	12/3/14	--	--	--	--	--
Thursday	12/4/14	6:00	10:58	12:00	4:00	9
Friday	12/5/14	7:02	11:00	12:00	4:01	8
Saturday	12/6/14	6:00	11:00	12:06	4:00	9
Sunday	12/7/14	6:00	11:29	12:00	4:00	9.5
					Weekly Total:	52.5

Employee Signature *Lucy Marshall*

Because this employee worked an extra half hour on Sunday, the **Daily Total** column displays 9.5 hours. Since it's common to credit an employee with an extra quarter hour when he/she works at least an extra 8 minutes, the employer calculated the gross pay based on this additional time. Therefore, Lucy receives credit for two additional 15-minute increments on Sunday as a result of her extra time worked.

Comparing Salaries & Wages

Employees are most commonly paid either wages or salaries by their employers.

- A **wage** is an amount typically paid to employees on an hourly basis.
- A **salary** is typically an annual pay amount (monthly or semi-monthly may also be used) agreed upon by the employer and the employee.

NOTE!   Alternative base wages may also be used, such as daily wage rates, and rates based on employee output (such as for the number of products assembled).

Regular wages are calculated by multiplying an employee's wage rate by the number of hours worked. For example, an employee earning $8.00/hour, who works 38 hours a week, earns $304 ($8 x 38 hours). If the employee didn't earn any other type of pay (such as overtime), the $304 total also represents the employee's **gross wages**. Gross wages are earned wages, as we will see later, that are not equal to the amount actually paid to the employee in their paychecks.

Regular earnings for salaried employees are calculated differently. For these employees, the employer must divide the annual salary by 52 weeks. For example, if an employer earns a salary of $52,000/year, then the employee's regular weekly earnings are $1,000 ($52,000/52 weeks).

Weekly Regular Earnings	
Wage-Earning Employee:	Regular Wage Rate x Regular Hours Worked
Salaried Employee:	Annual Salary / 52 Weeks

Calculating Overtime Pay

As discussed previously, the Fair Labor Standards Act requires that overtime be paid for any hours employees work after the first 40 in a workweek. This pay must equal at least 1.5 times the regular wages (*time and a half*) paid to the employee.

TIP!   While the FLSA mandates that overtime pay cannot be below 1.5 times the regular wages, it is acceptable for an employer to offer overtime pay that is more than 1.5 times regular pay.

One common misconception is that overtime must be paid to employees who work nights and/or weekends. The FLSA does not require that employers pay overtime during these work shifts, as long as the 40 hour/week threshold has not yet been met.

When an employee earns overtime pay, total gross wages (which include both regular and overtime earnings) may be calculated in two different ways.

- First method – the employer adds the regular wages to the overtime wages (overtime wage rate x overtime hours worked).

- Second method – the employer first determines a total for all hours worked based on the regular wage rate (total hours worked x regular rate). To this the employer adds the additional pay earned for working overtime hours ([overtime rate – regular rate] x overtime hours worked).

Total Gross Wages	
Method 1:	Regular Wages + Overtime Wages
Method 2:	Total Regular Wages for all Hours Worked + Additional Pay Earned for Overtime Hours Worked

Total gross wages are the same regardless of which method is used to calculate them.

TIP! In some circumstances, it's possible for an employee to have a workweek in which regular hours diverge from the 40-hour standard. Assume throughout this book, unless otherwise noted, that all employees operate with a regular 40-hour workweek.

Case In Point 2-3   **Calculate Employee Regular and Overtime Earnings**

In these examples, we'll review calculations for both regular and overtime earnings for Lucky Ties Apparel employees. We will also determine gross pay.

NOTE! For simplicity, all calculations throughout the textbook, both intermediate and final, may be rounded to two decimal places at each calculation.

1. Paul Rogers has worked for Lucky Ties Apparel for four years. During the most recent year he was paid regular wages of $11.50/hour. In the most recent week, he worked 35 hours. Calculate his gross pay for the week.

   As Paul did not work any overtime hours, his regular earnings are equal to his gross pay. These regular earnings are calculated as follows:

   $11.50 (Regular Wage Rate) x 35 hours (Regular Hours Worked) = $402.50.

2. Lucky Ties Apparel hired Maryanne Sherman at the beginning of the current year at an annual salary of $40,000. Calculate her gross pay for the most recent week, assuming that she's paid on a weekly basis.

   Maryanne earns the same gross pay every week, since her annual salary is evenly divided over all 52 weeks of each year. Her regular earnings for a single week are calculated as follows:

   $40,000 (Annual Salary) / 52 weeks = $769.23.

3. Bill Novak has worked for Lucky Ties Apparel for ten years. He currently earns regular wages of $14.75/hour, and overtime wages of $22.50. During a recent week, Bill worked 46 hours. Calculate his gross pay using both methods.

Bill's gross pay is the same for both methods. Remember that the FLSA dictates that any hours worked beyond the first 40 in a week must be compensated at the overtime-wage rate. Bill's gross pay is calculated as follows:

Method 1: $14.75 (Regular Wage Rate) x
            40 hours (Regular Hours Worked) = $590

            $22.50 (Overtime Wage Rate) x
            6 hours (Overtime Hours Worked) = $135

            $590 (Regular Wages) +
            $135 (Overtime Wages) = $725 (gross pay)

Method 2: $14.75 (Regular Wage Rate) x
            46 hours (Total Hours Worked) = $678.50

            $22.50 (Overtime Rate) –
            $14.75 (Regular Rate) = $7.75

            $7.75 (calculated above) x
            6 hours (Overtime hours worked) = $46.50

            $678.50 (calculated above) +
            $46.50 (calculated above) = $725 (gross pay)

Converting to Hourly Rates

It's common for employers to comply with the FLSA by compensating employees with an overtime pay rate of 1.5 times the regular rate (the minimum requirement). If an employee is not compensated with an hourly wage, his/her compensation must be converted to an hourly rate in order to calculate the applicable overtime earned.

As discussed previously, certain employees are exempt from the provisions of the FLSA, and employers are not compelled to compensate these employees at the standard overtime rate. While many salaried employees (such as executive, administrative, and professional employees) fit this description, others are non-exempt and must be compensated at the overtime rate for any overtime hours worked. The following conversion process may be used to calculate overtime wages for employees not paid on an hourly basis.

Calculating Weekly Wage Conversions

If an employee earns $820/week, and works 44 hours during one week, the employee is owed overtime pay (for working more than 40 hours in a week). Since the employee is not paid on an hourly basis, how can the employer determine the proper amount of overtime pay? Assuming that the employer offers overtime pay at 1.5 times regular pay, the overtime pay can be calculated by converting the weekly rate to an hourly rate.

Use this four-step process to make the conversion, and then calculate total gross pay.

Process for Determining Weekly Gross Pay based on Weekly Wages	
Step 1:	Determine the hourly regular wage rate.
Step 2:	Convert to an hourly overtime wage rate.
Step 3:	Calculate overtime wages earned.
Step 4:	Determine gross pay by adding regular earnings to overtime earnings.

Based on the above example, gross pay is calculated as follows:

- Step 1: Determine the hourly regular wage rate by dividing the weekly rate by 40 hours (total number of regular hours worked during the week). In this instance, $820 / 40 hours = $20.50.

- Step 2: Multiply the regular hourly rate by 1.5 to convert it to the overtime hourly rate. Here, that is $20.50 x 1.5 = $30.75.

- Step 3: Multiply the overtime hourly rate by the number of overtime hours worked. In this example, $30.75 x 4 hours = $123.

- Step 4: Add the weekly wage rate to the overtime earnings. The total gross pay for this employee is $820 + $123 = $943.

TIP! If an employee receives a biweekly wage, you must begin the conversion process by dividing the biweekly wage by 2 (to convert it to a weekly wage). The above four-step process may then be followed as shown.

Annual Salary Conversions

A similar series of calculations are required when converting an annual salary to an hourly rate. For annual salary conversions, use a five-step process:

Conversion of Annual Salary to Weekly Gross Pay	
Step 1:	Determine the Weekly Salary
Step 2:	Determine the Hourly Regular Wage Rate
Step 3:	Convert to an Hourly Overtime Wage Rate
Step 4:	Calculate Overtime Wages Earned
Step 5:	Determine Gross Pay by adding Regular Earnings to Overtime Earnings

To put these steps in concrete terms, assume that an employee receives $58,000/year, works 48 hours in a recent week, and is paid 1.5 times the regular wage rate for overtime hours. This employee's gross pay is calculated as follows:

- Step 1: Divide the annual salary by 52 weeks to determine the weekly salary. Here, the weekly salary is calculated as $58,000 / 52 weeks = $1,115.38.

- Step 2: Determine the hourly regular wage rate by dividing the weekly rate by 40 hours (total number of regular hours worked during the week). In this instance, $1,115.38 / 40 hours = $27.88.

- Step 3: Multiply the regular hourly rate by 1.5, to convert it to the overtime hourly rate. Here, that is $27.88 x 1.5 = $41.82.

- Step 4: Multiply the overtime hourly rate by the number of overtime hours worked. In this example, $41.82 x 8 hours = $334.56.

- Step 5: Add the weekly wage rate to the overtime earnings. The total gross pay for this employee is $1,115.38 + $334.56 = $1,449.94.

TIP! If an employee receives a monthly or semi-monthly salary, you must begin the conversion process by multiplying either the monthly salary by 12 months, or the semi-monthly salary by 24 (to convert them to an annual salary). The five-step process above may then be followed.

| Case In Point 2-4 | **Convert to Hourly Rates & Calculate Weekly Gross Pay** |

In these examples, we will examine five independent circumstances, and determine both the hourly wage rates and gross pay for each employee.

1. Angelo Dorsett is a salesman for Lucky Ties Apparel. He earns regular wages of $700/week, does not receive commission, and worked 47 hours during the most recent week. Assuming that Lucky Ties Apparel pays Angelo an overtime rate of 1.5 times his regular rate, what should Angelo's gross pay be for the week?

    Step 1: Angelo's hourly regular wage rate is $700 / 40 regular hours = $17.50

    Step 2: Angelo's hourly overtime wage rate is $17.50 x 1.5 = $26.25

    Step 3: Angelo's overtime wages earned are $26.25 x 7 overtime hours = $183.75

    Step 4: Angelo's gross pay for the week is $700 + $183.75 = $883.75

2. Melissa Kubiak has worked in the warehouse of Lucky Ties Apparel for two years. She earns a bi-weekly wage of $1,200, and worked 41 hours during the most recent week. Assuming that Lucky Ties Apparel pays Melissa an overtime rate of 1.5 times her regular rate, what should Melissa's gross pay be for the week?

    Pre-Step: Melissa's weekly salary is $1,200 / 2 weeks = $600

    Step 1: Melissa's hourly regular wage rate is $600 / 40 regular hours = $15

    Step 2: Melissa's hourly overtime wage rate is $15 x 1.5 = $22.50

    Step 3: Melissa's overtime wages earned are $22.50 x 1 overtime hour = $22.50

    Step 4: Melissa's gross pay for the week is $600 + $22.50 = $622.50

3. Stacie Martin works in the warehouse of Lucky Ties Apparel, and is paid an annual salary of $43,992. During the most recent week, Stacie worked 51 hours, and she is paid overtime wages of 1.5 times her regular wage rate. What should Stacie's gross pay be for the week?

    Step 1: Stacie's weekly salary is $43,992 / 52 weeks = $846

    Step 2: Stacie's hourly regular wage rate is $846 / 40 regular hours = $21.15

    Step 3: Stacie's hourly overtime wage rate is $21.15 x 1.5 = $31.73

    Step 4: Stacie's overtime wages earned are $31.73 x 11 overtime hours = $349.03

    Step 5: Stacie's gross pay for the week is $846 + $349.03 = $1,195.03

4. Lucy Marshall has been a member of the janitorial staff at Lucky Ties Apparel for six years, and earns a monthly salary of $2,730. During the most recent week, Lucy worked 49 hours, and she is paid overtime wages of 1.5 times her regular wage rate. What should Lucy's gross pay be for the week?

   Pre-Step: Lucy's annual salary is $2,730 x 12 months = $32,760

   Step 1: Lucy's weekly salary is $32,760 / 52 = $630

   Step 2: Lucy's hourly regular wage rate is $630 / 40 regular hours = $15.75

   Step 3: Lucy's hourly overtime wage rate is $15.75 x 1.5 = $23.63

   Step 4: Lucy's overtime wages earned are $23.63 x 9 overtime hours = $212.67

   Step 5: Lucy's gross pay for the week is $630 + $212.67 = $842.67

5. Donald McHenry has been a member of the janitorial staff at Lucky Ties Apparel for four years, and earns a semi-monthly salary of $1,326. During the most recent week, Donald worked 45 hours, and he is paid overtime wages of 1.5 times his regular wage rate. What should Donald's gross pay be for the week?

   Pre-Step: Donald's annual salary is $1,326 x 24 months = $31,824

   Step 1: Donald's weekly salary is $31,824 / 52 = $612

   Step 2: Donald's hourly regular wage rate is $612 / 40 regular hours = $15.30

   Step 3: Donald's hourly overtime wage rate is $15.30 x 1.5 = $22.95

   Step 4: Donald's overtime wages earned are $22.95 x 5 overtime hours = $114.75

   Step 5: Donald's gross pay for the week is $612 + $114.75 = $726.75

Offering Commissions, Bonuses, and Incentive Plans

Wages and Salaries are not the only types of compensation an employee may receive. Employers can also compensate employees through **commissions** (a percentage of each sale), **bonuses** (either planned or unplanned additional amounts), and **incentive plans** (more pay for increased productivity).

Paying Commissions

Commissions are typically paid to employees as a percentage of sales. For example, if an employee sells a product for $2,000, and earns a 10% commission on every sale, he/she is paid a $200 ($2,000 x 10%) commission. Commissions can be the only form of income earned by an employee, or earned in conjunction with a wage or salary.

Commissions are considered to be a component of an employee's regular pay. To calculate the overtime pay of an employee who earns commissions, the regular hourly wages and the commissions must be combined to determine an overall hourly rate. This combined rate is then multiplied by 1.5 (or the higher applicable rate of compensation offered by the employer) to arrive at the overtime hourly rate.

For example, if an employee works 44 hours, earns a regular hourly wage of $10/hour, and earns commissions of $200, a combined regular hourly wage rate (which takes the commission into account) must be determined. Use the following three-step process to arrive at this figure:

Calculation of Regular Hourly Wage Rate Including Commission	
Step 1:	Determine Total Regular Wages ($10 x 40 hours = $400)
Step 2:	Add the Commission to the above amount ($400 + $200 = $600)
Step 3:	Divide the combined total by the Regular Hours Worked ($600 / 40 hours = $15)

If this employer offers an overtime wage rate of 1.5 times the regular rate, the overtime wage rate is $22.50 ($15 x 1.5). Since this employee worked 4 hours of overtime, total overtime earnings are $90 ($22.50 x 4). Total gross wages are therefore $690 ($400 regular wages + $200 commissions + $90 overtime wages).

NOTE! Employees of retail and service businesses who are paid commissions and who meet certain requirements set by the FLSA are exempt from the mandate that overtime pay exceed regular pay by at least 1.5 times.

Awarding Bonuses

A bonus is an amount awarded to an employee outside of regular and overtime pay. There are two types of bonuses: discretionary and non-discretionary.

- A **discretionary bonus** is one that is unplanned and not contingent on the employee reaching specific goals. An example is a surprise holiday bonus given to employees at the end of the year.
- A **non-discretionary bonus** is one that is planned and an employer pays as a result of a specific metric being met. An example is a longevity bonus paid to an employee on his/her tenth anniversary with the company.

The distinction between these two bonus types is important, because non-discretionary bonuses are considered part of regular pay, while discretionary bonuses are not. Similar to commissions, non-discretionary bonuses must be combined with regular hourly wages prior to determining an employee's overtime pay.

Offering Incentive Plans

An employer may offer a variety of incentive plans to employees, which are designed to reward employees for their performance and/or loyalty to the company. The most common types of incentive plans are:

- Cash paid for reaching specified sales or production goals.
- Profit-sharing plans in which employees receive a share of profits once they exceed a predetermined level.
- Stock Option plans in which employees who meet predetermined goals may purchase shares of stock with pre-tax dollars.
- Additional vacation days for employees whose tenure with the company surpasses preset lengths.
- Sabbaticals, which are common in academic institutions, provide employees with paid leave after working for a predetermined number of years.

When a cash incentive is offered, it may be paid in a lump sum, or as an increase in the hourly (or per unit) rate paid. In the case of an increased pay rate, the increase is typically earned upon employee performance exceeding a preset, quantifiable level.

TIP!   For the purposes of the FLSA, cash paid for reaching specified goals is considered a non-discretionary bonus, and therefore is a component of regular pay. This must be considered when calculating overtime pay.

| Case In Point 2-5 | Calculate Employee Commissions, Bonuses, and Incentive Pay |

In these examples, we'll review four independent circumstances, and will calculate the pay earned by each employee.

1. An employee who sells automobiles is paid $8/hour in regular wages. In addition, he earns another $300 for every car he sells. During the most recent week, he works 46 hours and sells 5 cars. His employer pays overtime of 1.5 times regular hourly wages.

   Step 1: Total regular wages are $8 x 40 hours = $320

   Step 2: Total combined regular earnings are $1,500 (5 cars x $300) + $320 = $1,820

   Step 3: The regular earnings hourly rate is $1,820 / 40 hours = $45.50

   Now that the regular earnings hourly rate is determined, the overtime hourly rate can be calculated as follows: $45.50 x 1.5 = $68.25

   Using this overtime hourly rate, the overtime earnings are $68.25 x 6 hours = $409.50

   This results in total earnings of $1,820 + $409.50 = $2,229.50

2. After his company made a particularly large sale, an employee is awarded a discretionary bonus of $2,000. During this same week, the employee works 42 hours, earning regular wages of $13/hour, with overtime pay calculated as 1.5 times the regular wage rate.

   Since a discretionary bonus is not considered to be part of regular earnings, overtime pay is calculated using the standard 1.5 x regular earnings formula.

   Regular pay therefore is $13 x 40 hours = $520. The overtime hourly rate is $13 x 1.5 = $19.50, which results in overtime pay of $19.50 x 2 hours = $39.

   Total earnings for the week are $520 (regular earnings) + $39 (overtime earnings) + $2,000 (discretionary bonus) = $2,559.

3. An employee who earns regular wages of $9.50/hour, and overtime pay of 1.5 times his regular wage rate, works 53 hours during the most recent week. As a result of total company sales exceeding $1,000,000 for the year, the employee also received a predetermined bonus of $1,500.

    Because this bonus was planned and paid out once company sales reached $1,000,000, it's considered to be a non-discretionary bonus. As a result, it's considered part of regular earnings. The three-step process for combining regular wages and commissions outlined above may be used to combine regular wages and non-discretionary bonuses as well.

    Step 1: Total regular wages are $9.50 x 40 hours = $380

    Step 2: Total combined regular earnings are $1,500 + $380 = $1,880

    Step 3: The regular earnings hourly rate is $1,880 / 40 hours = $47

    The overtime hourly rate, based on the above calculation, is $47 x 1.5 = $70.50

    Using this overtime hourly rate, the overtime earnings are $70.50 x 13 hours = $916.50

    Therefore, total earnings are $1,880 + $916.50 = $2,796.50

4. An employee works in a factory where she earns regular wages of $8/hour, with overtime pay calculated as 1.5 times regular earnings. If, during any week, she is able to assemble more than 1,000 product units, her regular rate increases to $9/hour for the week. Her rate similarly increases to $10/hour if she assembles more than 1,200 units and $11/hour if she assembles more than 1,400 units. During the most recent week she worked 44 hours and assembled 1,352 units.

    This employee has earned incentive pay, since she assembled more than 1,000 product units. For her level of production (1,352 units), she has earned an increased regular wage rate of $10/hour.

    Regular wages are calculated as follows: $10 x 40 hours = $400

    Her overtime hourly wage rate is $10 x 1.5 = $15

    Therefore, her overtime pay is calculated as follows: $15 x 4 hours = $60

    Her total earnings for the week are $400 + $60 = $460

Examining Alternative Pay Considerations

In certain instances, based on an employee's job duties, it's appropriate to use alternative methods of compensation.

- For individuals who are their own boss (such as Certified Public Accountants who earn income outside of a large organization), **self-employment income** must be determined.
- For employees who regularly receive tips from customers (such as waiters and waitresses), special minimum wage and overtime rules apply.
- For employees who produce a measurable output (such as seamstresses creating dresses), compensation may be based on the number of units produced. This is referred to as a **piecework** system.

Earning Self-Employment Income

Individuals who operate a sole proprietorship or partnership must account for and report annual self-employment income. This consists of the revenue an owner may claim based on the company operations, minus expenses incurred. These individuals do not have to be concerned with the minimum wage and overtime provisions of the FLSA, however they still must track total income to ensure that appropriate taxes are paid. We'll examine the tax implications of self-employment income in further detail in Chapter 5.

Considering Tipped Employees

Employees who receive tips are covered by the FLSA, and therefore must be paid the applicable hourly minimum wage. A tipped employee is someone who typically receives more than $30/month in tips. Employers can take advantage of a maximum tip credit of $5.12, which results in employees receiving an hourly wage of $2.13 ($7.25 minimum wage minus $5.12 tip credit). Employers who elect to take advantage of this tip credit must inform employees of their intention to do so, and must use a consistent tip credit for both regular and overtime hours.

Employers cannot use an employee's tips for any purpose other than a tip credit against wages owed, or as part of a **tip pool**. A tip pool, in which all employee tips are added together (pooled) and then divided amongst employees, is permissible under the FLSA. However, these employees each must receive the applicable hourly minimum wage, and the pool must include only employees who regularly receive tips.

WARNING! Regardless of whether an employer elects to utilize a tip credit, under no circumstance may that employer retain an employee's tips.

If the employee's total hourly wage (the sum of the hourly wage received and employee tips) does not exceed the applicable minimum wage, the employer must compensate the employee for the difference. In addition, the employer must calculate the overtime hourly rate for a tipped employee based on the applicable minimum wage. No tip credit may be factored into this calculation.

Tipped Employees Overtime Calculation	
Step 1:	Regular Hourly Rate x Regular Hours Worked = Regular Earnings
Step 2:	Minimum Wage – Regular Hourly Rate = Hourly Tip Credit
Step 3:	(Minimum Wage x Overtime Factor) – Hourly Tip Credit = Overtime Hourly Rate
Step 4:	Overtime Hourly Rate x Overtime Hours Worked = Overtime Earnings
Step 5:	Total Hours Worked x Hourly Tip Credit = Total Tip Credit
Step 6:	Regular Earnings + Overtime Earnings + Total Tips = Total Earnings

NOTE!   The Tip Credit cannot exceed Total Tips Received, so the employer should compare these figures when performing this calculation. In this instance, the employer must reduce the tip credit such that it does not exceed total tips received.

Utilizing Piecework Systems

In certain instances it's logical to compensate employees based on their output, rather than on hours worked. Under this piecework system, an employee receives a fixed amount for each unit of output. These units can take many forms, such as products assembled, telemarketing phone calls made, or packages filled.

One important element that the employer must remember is that the minimum wage requirements of the FLSA apply to employees compensated under a piecework system. To confirm compliance with the FLSA, an employer must determine each piecework employee's hourly rate. This may be done by dividing total weekly compensation by the number of hours worked.

Piecework Overtime Calculation	
Step 1:	Piece Rate x Units of Output = Regular Earnings For All Hours
Step 2:	Regular Earnings for All Hours / Total Hours Worked = Regular Hourly Rate
Step 3:	Regular Hourly Rate * Additional Overtime Factor = Additional Overtime Hourly Rate
Step 4:	Additional Overtime Hourly Rate x Overtime Hours Worked = Additional Overtime Earnings
Step 5:	Regular Earnings For All Hours + Additional Overtime Earnings = Total Earnings

NOTE! Additional Overtime Factor is typically 0.5 (1.5 overtime rate – 1.0 regular rate)

The Additional Overtime Hourly Rate, in Step 3 above, is often also called the Premium Rate, because it represents the premium over the regular hourly rate to which the piecework employee is entitled for overtime hours worked.

NOTE! An alternative to the calculation shown above is to pay an employee at least 1.5 times the regular piece rate for all units of output produced during overtime hours (all hours after the first 40). In this approach, the employer must ensure that the regular hourly rate exceeds the applicable minimum wage rate.

Case In Point 2-6	# Calculate Earnings for Tipped and Piecework Employees

In these examples, we'll examine three independent circumstances, and will determine how total compensation was calculated for each employee.

1. Eric Parker works for a small restaurant chain as a waiter. He is paid $2.13/hour by his employer, and receives $150 in tips during a 35-hour workweek. What is Eric's total compensation for the week?

   Eric's employer pays regular wages of $74.55 ($2.13 regular wage rate x 35 regular hours worked). As a result, if the FLSA were ignored, Eric's total compensation would be $224.55 ($74.55 regular wages + $150 tips).

   Because this is less than the FLSA mandated minimum of $253.75 ($7.25 minimum wage x 35 hours worked), the employer must compensate Eric for the difference. Therefore, Eric receives an additional $29.20 ($253.75 – $224.55) to increase his total compensation to $253.75.

2. Meredith Baer works as an automobile valet at a steak house. She is paid $3.00/hour by her employer, and receives $310 in tips during the most recent 44-hour workweek. Meredith's employer pays overtime hourly wages at a rate of 1.5 times regular hourly wages. What is Meredith's total compensation for the week?

   Using the six-step process detailed previously (in Tipped Employees Overtime Calculation table on page 60), total compensation is calculated as follows:

   Step 1: Meredith's employer pays regular earnings of $120 ($3 regular wage rate x 40 regular hours worked).

   Step 2: This is the result of her employer taking a tip credit of $4.25 ($7.25 minimum wage – $3 regular wage rate).

   Step 3: When calculating overtime compensation, this tip credit must be maintained at the same level. Therefore, total overtime compensation is based on an hourly rate of $6.63 ($7.25 minimum wage x 1.5 overtime factor, minus $4.25 tip credit).

   Step 4: This results in overtime earnings totaling $26.52 ($6.63 overtime hourly rate x 4 overtime hours worked).

Step 5: Before total compensation is finalized, the employer must ensure that the total tip credit does not exceed tips received by the employee. In this instance, the total tip credit of $187 ($4.25 tip credit x 44 hours worked) does not exceed total tips received of $310, and therefore the employer owes no additional compensation.

Step 6: Total compensation is then calculated as $456.52 ($120 regular earnings + $26.52 overtime earnings + $310 tips).

3. Nancy Winchester assembles children's toys and is paid $0.06 for each unit assembled. During the most recent week Nancy worked 48 hours and assembled 8,528 units. Nancy's employer pays overtime hourly wages at a rate of 1.5 times regular hourly wages. What is Nancy's total compensation for the week?

    Using the five-step process detailed previously (in Piecework Overtime Calculation table on page 60), total compensation is calculated as follows:

    Step 1: Regular earnings for all hours are calculated as $0.06 (piece rate) x 8,528 (units of output) = $511.68.

    Step 2: The regular hourly rate is then calculated as $511.68 (regular earnings) / 48 (hours worked) = $10.66.

    Step 3: The additional overtime hourly rate is then $10.66 (regular hourly rate) x 0.5 (additional overtime rate) = $5.33.

    Step 4: Additional overtime earnings are calculated as $5.33 (additional overtime hourly rate) x 8 (overtime hours worked) = $42.64.

    Step 5: Total earnings are then calculated as $511.68 (regular earnings) + $42.64 (additional overtime earnings) = $554.32.

4. Andrew Fitzpatrick is a telemarketer who is paid $0.32 for every telemarketing phone call he places. During the most recent week Andrew worked 43 hours and placed 1,722 calls, 124 of which were placed during the final three hours he worked. Andrew's employer pays an overtime piece rate 1.5 times the regular rate. Using the alternative method outlined earlier, determine Andrew's total week's compensation.

    During regular hours Andrew placed 1,598 (1,722 – 124) calls, and therefore earned $511.36 (1,598 x $0.32) in regular earnings. As the overtime hourly piece rate is $0.48 ($0.32 x 1.5), Andrew earns overtime pay of $59.52 (124 x $0.48). Therefore, total earnings is $570.88 ($511.36 + $59.52).

Payroll Register

Unlike the Employee Earnings Record, which displays the earnings for a single employee over a range of pay periods, the **Payroll Register** shows each employee's pay for a single period.

The Payroll Register displays both Total Earnings (gross pay) and each employee's paycheck amount (net pay).

Payroll Register

Pay Period _____

Pay Date _____

Employee Name	Earnings							Deductions					Check Number	Net Pay
	Regular Hours	Regular Rate	Regular Earnings	Overtime Hours	Overtime Rate	Overtime Earnings	Total Earnings	FWT	SWT	Social Security	Medicare	Vol. With.		
Totals:														

As discussed earlier, the net pay is calculated by subtracting all deductions from the gross pay (Total Earnings) in the Payroll Register. Depending on the business, other columns may appear in the Payroll Register. For example, if a business' employees are unionized, the *Deductions* section may contain a separate column for *Union Dues* that are withheld from each employee's gross pay. Additionally, for some employees not all columns are necessary. For example, a salaried executive is exempt from the minimum wage provision of the FLSA, and therefore no hourly rate information is necessary.

TIP! Just as with the Employee Earnings Record, the Payroll Register is typically completed in a computerized payroll system. However, we'll work with manual versions of the Payroll Register throughout the textbook.

Case In Point 2-7 — Complete a Payroll Register

In this example, we will complete a Payroll Register for Lucky Ties Apparel. Earlier we calculated the weekly pay for eight different employees of Lucky Ties Apparel. Their partially-completed employee earnings records for the most recent week appear below. The employees' address, social security number (SSN), marital status, and withholding allowances have been entered into each employee earnings record as well. Based on these, we'll complete the earnings portion of the Payroll Register.

NOTE! We'll return to this example in the next chapter, where we'll complete the *Deductions* and *Net Pay* sections of both the employee earnings records and the payroll register.

Employee Earnings Record

Name	Paul Rogers		Marital Status	Single
Address	657 Flicker Lane		Fed. Withholding Allow.	1
	Brockport, NY 14420		State Withholding Allow.	1
SS#	111-11-1111			

	Earnings							Deductions									
Pay Period Ending	Regular Hours Worked	Regular Pay Rate	Regular Wages	Overtime Hours Worked	Overtime Pay Rate	Overtime Wages	Gross Pay	Federal Withholding Tax	State Withholding Tax	Social Security Tax	Medicare Tax	Retirement Contribution	Life Insurance	Charitable Contribution	Additional Withholding	Check Number	Net Pay
12/6/13	35	$ 11.50	$ 402.50	0	n/a	$ -	$ 402.50										

Employee Earnings Record

Name	Maryanne Sherman		Marital Status	Single
Address	8171 Winston Court		Fed. Withholding Allow.	2
	Rochester, NY 14604		State Withholding Allow.	1
SS#	222-22-2222			

	Earnings							Deductions									
Pay Period Ending	Regular Hours Worked	Regular Pay Rate	Regular Wages	Overtime Hours Worked	Overtime Pay Rate	Overtime Wages	Gross Pay	Federal Withholding Tax	State Withholding Tax	Social Security Tax	Medicare Tax	Retirement Contribution	Life Insurance	Charitable Contribution	Additional Withholding	Check Number	Net Pay
12/6/13	n/a	n/a	$ 769.23	0	n/a	$ -	$ 769.23										

Employee Earnings Record

Name	Bill Novak		Marital Status	Married
Address	536A North Yellow Lake Avenue		Fed. Withholding Allow.	4
	Hamlin, NY 14464		State Withholding Allow.	3
SS#	333-33-3333			

	Earnings							Deductions									
Pay Period Ending	Regular Hours Worked	Regular Pay Rate	Regular Wages	Overtime Hours Worked	Overtime Pay Rate	Overtime Wages	Gross Pay	Federal Withholding Tax	State Withholding Tax	Social Security Tax	Medicare Tax	Retirement Contribution	Life Insurance	Charitable Contribution	Additional Withholding	Check Number	Net Pay
12/6/13	40	$ 14.75	$ 590.00	6	$ 22.50	$ 135.00	$ 725.00										

Employee Earnings Record

Name	Angelo Dorsett	Marital Status	Single
Address	400 Hillside Court	Fed. Withholding Allow.	2
	Hilton, NY 14468	State Withholding Allow.	2
SS#	444-44-4444		

	Earnings							Deductions									
Pay Period Ending	Regular Hours Worked	Regular Pay Rate	Regular Wages	Overtime Hours Worked	Overtime Pay Rate	Overtime Wages	Gross Pay	Federal Withholding Tax	State Withholding Tax	Social Security Tax	Medicare Tax	Retirement Contribution	Life Insurance	Charitable Contribution	Additional Withholding	Check Number	Net Pay
12/6/13	40	$ 17.50	$ 700.00	7	$ 26.25	$ 183.75	$ 883.75										

Employee Earnings Record

Name	Melissa Kubiak	Marital Status	Married
Address	254 Cheesehead Drive	Fed. Withholding Allow.	5
	Pittsford, NY 14534	State Withholding Allow.	4
SS#	555-55-5555		

	Earnings							Deductions									
Pay Period Ending	Regular Hours Worked	Regular Pay Rate	Regular Wages	Overtime Hours Worked	Overtime Pay Rate	Overtime Wages	Gross Pay	Federal Withholding Tax	State Withholding Tax	Social Security Tax	Medicare Tax	Retirement Contribution	Life Insurance	Charitable Contribution	Additional Withholding	Check Number	Net Pay
12/6/13	40	$ 15.00	$ 600.00	1	$ 22.50	$ 22.50	$ 622.50										

Employee Earnings Record

Name	Stacie Martin	Marital Status	Married
Address	2 Lava Lane	Fed. Withholding Allow.	2
	Brockport, NY 14420	State Withholding Allow.	1
SS#	666-66-6666		

	Earnings							Deductions									
Pay Period Ending	Regular Hours Worked	Regular Pay Rate	Regular Wages	Overtime Hours Worked	Overtime Pay Rate	Overtime Wages	Gross Pay	Federal Withholding Tax	State Withholding Tax	Social Security Tax	Medicare Tax	Retirement Contribution	Life Insurance	Charitable Contribution	Additional Withholding	Check Number	Net Pay
12/6/13	40	$ 21.15	$ 846.00	11	$ 31.73	$ 349.03	$ 1,195.03										

Employee Earnings Record

Name	Lucy Marshall	Marital Status	Single
Address	232 Muscle Road	Fed. Withholding Allow.	3
	Hamlin, NY 14464	State Withholding Allow.	2
SS#	777-77-7777		

	Earnings							Deductions									
Pay Period Ending	Regular Hours Worked	Regular Pay Rate	Regular Wages	Overtime Hours Worked	Overtime Pay Rate	Overtime Wages	Gross Pay	Federal Withholding Tax	State Withholding Tax	Social Security Tax	Medicare Tax	Retirement Contribution	Life Insurance	Charitable Contribution	Additional Withholding	Check Number	Net Pay
12/6/13	40	$ 15.75	$ 630.00	9	$ 23.63	$ 212.67	$ 842.67										

Employee Earnings Record

Name	Donald McHenry	Marital Status	Married
Address	22 Iceberg Lane	Fed. Withholding Allow.	6
	Fairport, NY 14450	State Withholding Allow.	5
SS#	888-88-8888		

	Earnings							Deductions									
Pay Period Ending	Regular Hours Worked	Regular Pay Rate	Regular Wages	Overtime Hours Worked	Overtime Pay Rate	Overtime Wages	Gross Pay	Federal Withholding Tax	State Withholding Tax	Social Security Tax	Medicare Tax	Retirement Contribution	Life Insurance	Charitable Contribution	Additional Withholding	Check Number	Net Pay
12/6/13	40	$ 15.30	$ 612.00	5	$ 22.95	$ 114.75	$ 726.75										

To complete the *Earnings* portion of the Payroll Register, simply transfer the payroll information from each individual employee earnings record. The only calculations that must be performed are those relating to the total figures for the Regular, Overtime, and Total Earnings columns.

Payroll Register

Pay Period 12/6/2013

Pay Date 12/12/2013

Employee Name	Earnings							Deductions					Check Number	Net Pay
	Regular Hours	Regular Rate	Regular Earnings	Overtime Hours	Overtime Rate	Overtime Earnings	Total Earnings	FWT	SWT	Social Security	Medicare	Vol. With.		
Rogers, P	35	$ 11.50	$ 402.50	0	n/a	$ -	$ 402.50							
Sherman, M	n/a	n/a	$ 769.23	0	n/a	$ -	$ 769.23							
Novak, B	40	$ 14.75	$ 590.00	6	$ 22.50	$ 135.00	$ 725.00							
Dorsett, A	40	$ 17.50	$ 700.00	7	$ 26.25	$ 183.75	$ 883.75							
Kubiak, M	40	$ 15.00	$ 600.00	1	$ 22.50	$ 22.50	$ 622.50							
Martin, S	40	$ 21.15	$ 846.00	11	$ 31.73	$ 349.03	$ 1,195.03							
Marshall, L	40	$ 15.75	$ 630.00	9	$ 23.63	$ 212.67	$ 842.67							
McHenry, D	40	$ 15.30	$ 612.00	5	$ 22.95	$ 114.75	$ 726.75							
Totals:			$ 5,149.73				$ 1,017.70	$ 6,167.43							

Concepts Review

All of the Concepts Review quizzes for this book are also available in the Student Resource Center. Check with your instructor on how to complete the quizzes (in the book or online).

True/False Questions

1. Per the FLSA, a Workweek is any non-consecutive 7-day period designated by the employer.   *True   False*

2. An employer may change its workweek, as long as the change is meant to be permanent and is not designed to circumvent overtime requirements.   *True   False*

3. The Equal Pay Act protects only female employees from wage discrimination.   *True   False*

4. An Employee Time Card lists total hours worked for all employees during a single workweek.   *True   False*

5. An employee's overtime wage rate must always be 1.5 times his/her regular wage rate.   *True   False*

6. The FLSA does not mandate that employees be compensated at the overtime wage rate for hours worked during nights and weekends, unless the 40-hour threshold has been reached.   *True   False*

7. Commissions are considered to be a component of an employee's regular pay.   *True   False*

8. A Discretionary Bonus is one that is planned and paid out upon an employee reaching a specific milestone.   *True   False*

9. The maximum tip credit that an employer may take advantage of is $2.13.   *True   False*

10. A Payroll Register displays compensation information for a single pay period.   *True   False*

Multiple Choice Questions

1. Which of the following is not a common pay period used by employers?
   a. Semi-monthly
   b. Monthly
   c. Bi-weekly
   d. Daily

2. Under the provisions of the Equal Pay Act, employers may compensate employees differently for the same job based on each of the following except _____.
   a. gender
   b. seniority
   c. output quantity
   d. a merit system

3. When different minimum wage rates are in effect, which rate takes precedence, and therefore must be met by an employer?
   a. Federal minimum wage
   b. The highest applicable minimum wage
   c. Local (municipality) minimum wage
   d. State minimum wage

4. An employee who works 38 hours during the current workweek, and receives $11.25/hour, has earned gross pay of _____.
   a. $450.00
   b. $427.50
   c. $1,125.00
   d. $380.00

5. An employee who works 44 hours during the current workweek, receives regular wages of $9.50/hour, and is paid overtime wages of 1.5 times his regular wage rate, has earned gross pay of _____.
   a. $418.00
   b. $380.00
   c. $437.00
   d. $627.00

6. What is the hourly wage rate of an employee who typically has a 40-hour workweek, and who earns a monthly salary of $1,768?
   a. $10.20
   b. $20.40
   c. $442.00
   d. $408.00

7. Each of the following is a type of incentive plan except _____.
   a. stock options
   b. sabbaticals
   c. overtime compensation
   d. profit sharing plans

8. Under which of the following circumstances may an employer retain an employee's tips?
   a. The full tip credit is utilized by the employer.
   b. No tip credit is utilized by the employer.
   c. A tip pool is utilized by all employees.
   d. Under no circumstance may an employer retain an employee's tips.

9. A tipped employee is paid $2.13/hour, during a week in which he works 40 hours. During this week he receives $195 in tips from customers. How much additional compensation (beyond the hourly rate and tips) must his employer remit in order to comply with the FLSA??
   a. $0
   b. $92.87
   c. $290.00
   d. $9.80

10. An employee works 44 hours during a week in which he produces 3,057 units at a piece rate of $0.14/unit. What is the employee's regular hourly rate across all hours worked?
    a. $69.48
    b. $9.73
    c. $4.96
    d. $10.70

Knowledge Check A

For all assignments in this section, necessary IRS forms and/or Excel templates are located in the Student Resource Center.

KCa 2-1 Identify Pay Periods & Evaluate Workweeks

Examine each of the following independent circumstances and identify the type of pay period (weekly, bi-weekly, semi-monthly, or monthly) being utilized. Then indicate whether the specified workweek is FLSA *compliant* or *non-compliant*.

1. Touchdown Corporation's most recent pay period ended on Thursday, 7/31/14, with paychecks printed and distributed one week later. The subsequent pay period ended on Friday, 8/15/14. To coincide with the pay periods, the employer's last work week ran from Friday, 8/1/14 through Friday, 8/15/14.

2. Dachshund Inc. recently changed its pay period such that it now runs from Wednesday through Tuesday each week. The workweek also begins on Wednesday, however it starts at 8:00 a.m., and runs through the following Wednesday at 7:59 a.m.

3. Electronics Depot compensates its employees 26 times each year. Its workweek begins on Monday at 12:00 a.m., and runs through Sunday at 11:59 p.m.

KCa 2-2 Complete a Time Card

Complete a time card for each employee below.

1. Audra Moyer (SSN 888-22-4444) worked seven days during the week of 10/13/14 through 10/19/14. She arrived at 8:00 a.m. each day (except Monday when she was 6 minutes early, and Tuesday when she arrived at 6:57 a.m.). She left for lunch at 12:00 p.m. each day (except Tuesday when she left at 11:58 a.m., and Saturday when she left at 12:03 p.m.), and arrived back at 1:00 p.m. (except for Friday, when she arrived back at 1:02 p.m.). She left work at 4:00 p.m. each day (except for Tuesday, Wednesday and Sunday, when she stayed until 5:02 p.m., 3:58 p.m., and 5:31 p.m. respectively).

2. Stephen Fitzpatrick (SSN 333-99-7777) worked four days during the week of 5/26/14 through 6/1/14 (he was off work on Monday, Wednesday, and Friday). He arrived at 7:00 a.m. each day (except Tuesday, when he arrived at 5:58 a.m.). He left for lunch at 11:00 a.m. each day (except Tuesday, when he left at 11:03 a.m., and Saturday, when he did not take a lunch break), and arrived back at 12:00 p.m. (except for Thursday, when he arrived back at 12:32 p.m., and Saturday). He left work at 5:00 p.m. each day (except for Sunday, when he stayed until 6:04 p.m.).

KCa 2-3 Calculate Weekly Regular Earnings

Calculate the weekly regular earnings for each of the following employees.

1. Jason Richards earns $8.45/hour, and worked 37 hours during the most recent week.

2. Drew Johnson earns an annual salary of $72,000.

3. Lucas Short earns $10.20/hour, and worked 40 hours during the most recent week.

4. Anna Graham earns an annual salary of $122,500.

5. Molly Mitchell earns $13/hour, and worked 38 hours during the most recent week.

KCa 2-4 Calculate Weekly Gross Pay

Calculate gross pay (regular earnings + overtime earnings) for each of the following employees. Every employee earns hourly overtime wages 1.5 times greater than their regular wage rate.

1. Luisa Williams earns $7.50/hour, and worked 44 hours during the most recent week.

2. Jonathan Olsen earns $9.10/hour, and worked 47 hours during the most recent week.

3. Nathan Upton earns $11.80/hour, and worked 42 hours during the most recent week.

4. Juan Rodriguez earns $14/hour, and worked 48 hours during the most recent week.

5. Drew Painter earns $16.60/hour, and worked 51 hours during the most recent week.

KCa 2-5 Determine Hourly Regular and Overtime Wage Rates

Determine both the regular and overtime wage rates for each of the following employees. All are paid an overtime wage rate 1.5 times their respective regular wage rates.

1. Nancy Bowie earns a weekly wage of $950. During the most recent week, she worked 46 hours.

2. Ronald McHenry earns a bi-weekly wage of $2,100. During the most recent week, he worked 48 hours.

3. Frank Wayne earns an annual salary of $62,000. During the most recent week, he worked 52 hours.

4. Michelle Connolly earns a monthly salary of $5,000. During the most recent week, she worked 43 hours.

5. Howie Gillette earns a semi-monthly salary of $1,900. During the most recent week, he worked 41 hours.

KCa 2-6 Calculate Gross Pay

Calculate gross pay for each of the five employees listed in the prior exercise.

KCa 2-7 Calculate Gross Pay With Commissions

Calculate gross pay for each of the following employees. All are paid an overtime wage rate that is 1.5 times their respective regular wage rates.

1. Samuel Worthy earns both $7.25/hour, and a 10% commission on all sales. During the most recent week, Samuel worked 42 hours, and made total sales of $11,000.

2. Charlotte Denning earns both $9/hour, and $25 for every sale she completes. During the most recent week, Charlotte worked 48 hours, and made a total of 62 sales.

3. James Finch earns both $11.70/hour, and a 12% commission on all sales. During the most recent week, James worked 45 hours, and made total sales of $7,200.

4. Keri Weinberg earns both $10/hour, $10 for every sale of Product A, and $14 for every sale of Product B. During the most recent week, Keri worked 54 hours, sold 26 units of Product A, and 41 units of Product B.

5. Tom Wilson earns both $16.20/hour, and a 15% commission on all sales. During the most recent week, Tom worked 47 hours, and made total sales of $13,000.

KCa 2-8 Calculate Gross Pay With Bonuses

Calculate gross pay for each of the following employees. All are paid an overtime wage rate that is 1.5 times their respective regular wage rates.

1. Jefferson Dodge earns $8.50/hour. During the most recent week he receives a discretionary bonus of $1,000 and works 47 hours.

2. Julia Jones earns $12/hour. During the most recent week she receives a non-discretionary bonus of $3,100 and works 42 hours.

3. Joseph Marshall earns $7.40/hour. During the most recent week he receives a non-discretionary bonus of $720 and works 50 hours.

4. Philip Lucas earns $10/hour. During the most recent week he receives a non-discretionary bonus of $2,200 and works 49 hours.

KCa 2-9 Calculate Gross Pay Based on an Incentive Plan

Calculate gross pay for each of the following employees of Launchpad Co. The company offers a regular wage rate of $8.20/hour to all employees. Under an incentive plan in place for all employees, this rate increases for any employee who can meet weekly production goals. The increased rates and corresponding thresholds that must be met are as follows:

- $9.40/hour for producing at least 2,000 units
- $10.60/hour for producing at least 2,800 units
- $11.80/hour for producing at least 3,700 units
- $13/hour for producing at least 4,700 units

All employees are paid an overtime wage rate that is 1.5 times their respective regular wage rates.

1. Bronson Chau worked 45 hours and produced 3,251 units.

2. Pauline Myers worked 48 hours and produced 2,054 units.

3. Angela Smith worked 54 hours and produced 5,157 units.

4. Angelo Balducci worked 48 hours and produced 3,986 units.

KCa 2-10 Calculate Gross Pay for a Tipped Employee

Calculate gross pay for each of the following employees. All are paid an overtime wage rate that is 1.5 times their respective regular wage rates.

1. Anita Workman receives tips from customers as a standard component of her weekly pay. She is paid $2.50/hour by her employer, and receives $284 in tips during the most recent 46-hour workweek.

2. Cole Earnhardt receives tips from customers as a standard component of his weekly pay. He is paid $2.13/hour by his employer, and receives $442 in tips during the most recent 42-hour workweek.

3. Calista Flood receives tips from customers as a standard component of her weekly pay. She is paid $4.10/hour by her employer, and receives $350 in tips during the most recent 38-hour workweek.

4. Bethany Pugh receives tips from customers as a standard component of her weekly pay. She is paid $3.60/hour by her employer, and receives $162 in tips during the most recent 51-hour workweek.

KCa 2-11 Calculate Gross Pay for a Piecework Employee

Calculate gross pay for each of the following employees. All are paid an overtime wage rate that is 1.5 times their respective regular wage rates.

1. Walter Pinkman assembles merchandise and is paid $0.11 for each unit assembled. During the most recent week Walter worked 46 hours and assembled 5,628 units.

2. Sidney Darling is a telemarketer, who is paid $0.34 for every telemarketing call he places. During the most recent week Sidney worked 41 hours, and placed 1,642 calls.

3. Pete Brees assembles merchandise and is paid $0.04 for each unit assembled. During the most recent week Pete worked 52 hours and assembled 13,284 units.

4. Roy Carter is a telemarketer who is paid $0.30 for every telemarketing phone call he places. During the most recent week Roy worked 51 hours and placed 1,536 calls.

KCa 2-12 Populate Employee Earnings Records

Complete the top portion and **EARNINGS** section of an employee's earnings record for the five employees in KCa 2-4. The associated pay period ends on 9/15/14. Additional data for each employee is as follows:

- Luisa Williams (SSN 678-90-1111) lives at 345 Mountain View Lane, Juneau, AK, 99801, is single, and claims 1 withholding allowance for both federal and state.
- Jonathan Olsen (SSN 123-45-6789) lives at 25 Harvard Path, Winston-Salem, NC 27101, is single, claims 2 federal withholding allowances, and 1 state withholding allowance.
- Nathan Upton (SSN 232-23-2323) lives at 5672 Hillside Lane, St. Louis, MO 63101, is married, and claims 3 withholding allowances for both federal and state.
- Juan Rodriguez (SSN 343-43-3434) lives at 432B Main Street, Baton Rouge, LA 70801, is single, and claims 1 withholding allowance for both federal and state.
- Drew Painter (SSN 454-45-4545) lives at 12 State Road, Dallas, TX 75201, is married, claims 5 federal withholding allowances, and 4 state withholding allowances.

KCa 2-13 Populate a Payroll Register

Complete the top portion and **EARNINGS** section of a Payroll Register using the employee data from KCa 2-4 and KCa 2-12. The associated pay period ends on 9/15/14, with paychecks being printed and distributed six days later.

Knowledge Check B

For all assignments in this section, necessary IRS forms and/or Excel templates are located in the Student Resource Center.

KCb 2-1 Identify Pay Periods & Evaluate Workweeks

Examine each of the following independent circumstances and identify the type of pay period (weekly, bi-weekly, semi-monthly, or monthly) being utilized. Then indicate whether the specified workweek is FLSA *compliant* or *non-compliant*.

1. Carpets 'r Us pays its employees 24 times each year. Its workweek is based on activity level and varies from week to week, but never exceeds a seven-day period.

2. Flagpole Enterprises distributes paychecks to employees every other week, on Friday afternoon. These pay dates fall exactly seven days after the end of every pay period. The workweek begins Monday at 8:00 a.m. and ends Friday afternoon at 6:00 p.m.

3. Radio World prints and distributes checks for its employees 12 times each year. Its workweek begins Tuesday at 2:43 p.m., and ends a week later on Tuesday at 2:42 p.m.

KCb 2-2 Complete a Time Card

Complete a time card for each employee below.

1. Adam Spruce (SSN 565-56-5656) worked six days during the week of 1/20/14 through 1/26/14 (he was off work on Tuesday). He arrived at 9:00 a.m. each day (except Friday, when he was 4 minutes early, and Sunday, when he was 2 minutes late). He left for lunch at 12:30 p.m. each day (except Wednesday, when he left at 12:28 p.m., and Thursday, when he left at 1:01 p.m.), and arrived back at 1:30 p.m. (except Friday, when he arrived back at 2:02 p.m.). He left work at 5:00 p.m. each day (except Monday, when he stayed until 6:28 p.m.).

2. Tyson Newton (SSN 676-67-6767) worked five days during the week of 4/14/14 through 4/20/14 (he was off work on Saturday and Sunday). He arrived at 8:30 a.m. each day (except Monday, when he was 30 minutes early, and Tuesday, when he was 1 hour late). He left for lunch at 12:00 p.m. each day (except Wednesday, when he left at 12:04 p.m., and Thursday, when he didn't take a lunch break), and arrived back at 1:00 p.m. (except Friday, when he arrived back at 1:04 p.m.). He left work at 6:00 p.m. each day (except Friday, when he left work at 4:31 p.m.).

KCb 2-3 Calculate Weekly Regular Earnings

Calculate the weekly regular earnings for each of the following employees.

1. Phillip Hilton earns $9.05/hour, and worked 34 hours during the most recent week.

2. Suzanne Milliner earns an annual salary of $51,000.

3. Sally Russell earns $11.55/hour, and worked 38 hours during the most recent week.

4. Wendy Parker earns an annual salary of $91,500.

5. Robert Norton earns $18.20/hour, and worked 40 hours during the most recent week.

KCb 2-4 Calculate Weekly Gross Pay

Calculate gross pay (regular earnings + overtime earnings) for each of the following employees. Each of them earns hourly overtime wages 1.5 times greater than their regular wage rate.

1. Jimmy Troffa earns $7.80/hour, and worked 41 hours during the most recent week.

2. Tyler Thomas earns $10.90/hour, and worked 45 hours during the most recent week.

3. Ryan Brown earns $14.60/hour, and worked 48 hours during the most recent week.

4. Michael Kaminski earns $16/hour, and worked 55 hours during the most recent week.

5. Tina Baldwin earns $17.10/hour, and worked 50 hours during the most recent week.

KCb 2-5 Determine Hourly Regular and Overtime Wage Rates

Determine both the regular and overtime wage rates for each of the following employees. All are paid an overtime wage rate that is 1.5 times their respective regular wage rates.

1. Kevin Williams earns a weekly wage of $740. During the most recent week, he worked 42 hours.

2. Charles Joyner earns a bi-weekly wage of $2,720. During the most recent week, he worked 45 hours.

3. Julio Valdez earns an annual salary of $81,000. During the most recent week, he worked 44 hours.

4. Bridget Stein earns a monthly salary of $6,200. During the most recent week, she worked 56 hours.

5. Betsy Cranston earns a semi-monthly salary of $2,200. During the most recent week, she worked 49 hours.

KCb 2-6 Calculate Gross Pay

Calculate gross pay for each of the five employees listed in the prior exercise.

KCb 2-7 Calculate Gross Pay With Commissions

Calculate gross pay for each of the following employees. All are paid an overtime wage rate that is 1.5 times their respective regular wage rates.

1. Billy Fortuna earns both $11.45/hour, and a 10% commission on all sales. During the most recent week, Billy worked 47 hours, and made total sales of $8,800.

2. Emily Robinson earns both $8.10/hour, and $35 for every sale she completes. During the most recent week, Emily worked 55 hours, and made a total of 49 sales.

3. Richard Eisenhower earns both $14.90/hour, and a 14% commission on all sales. During the most recent week, Richard worked 43 hours, and made total sales of $5,700.

4. Zoey Jefferson earns both $19.10/hour, $5 for every sale of Product A, and $18 for every sale of Product B. During the most recent week, Zoey worked 50 hours, sold 37 units of Product A, and 29 units of Product B.

5. Bruce Wright earns both $13.50/hour, and a 20% commission on all sales. During the most recent week, Bruce worked 41 hours, and made total sales of $15,200.

KCb 2-8 Calculate Gross Pay With Bonuses

Calculate gross pay for each of the following employees. All are paid an overtime wage rate that is 1.5 times their respective regular wage rates.

1. Neil Mitchell earns $11/hour. During the most recent week he receives a discretionary bonus of $7,200 and works 43 hours.

2. Francine Palmer earns $7.90/hour. During the most recent week she receives a non-discretionary bonus of $2,450 and works 45 hours.

3. Martin Green earns $11.10/hour. During the most recent week he receives a non-discretionary bonus of $1,360 and works 51 hours.

4. Melvin Waxman earns $17.60/hour. During the most recent week he receives a non-discretionary bonus of $440 and works 56 hours.

KCb 2-9 Calculate Gross Pay Based on an Incentive Plan

Calculate gross pay for each of the following four employees of Person Mover Corp. The company offers a regular wage rate of $7.90/hour to all employees. Under an incentive plan in place for all employees, this rate increases for any employee who can meet weekly production goals. The increased rates and corresponding thresholds that must be met are as follows:

- $8.30/hour for producing at least 550 units
- $10.70/hour for producing at least 720 units
- $13.20/hour for producing at least 1,000 units
- $17.70/hour for producing at least 1,310 units

All employees are paid an overtime wage rate that is 1.5 times their respective regular wage rates.

1. Willy Tripp worked 42 hours and produced 882 units.

2. Louise Franklin worked 49 hours and produced 591 units.

3. Maya James worked 44 hours and produced 1,302 units.

4. Mason Winston worked 53 hours and produced 302 units.

KCb 2-10 Calculate Gross Pay for a Tipped Employee

Calculate gross pay for each of the following employees. All are paid an overtime wage rate that is 1.5 times their respective regular wage rates.

1. Stanley Smothers receives tips from customers as a standard component of his weekly pay. He is paid $5.10/hour by his employer, and receives $305 in tips during the most recent 41-hour workweek.

2. Arnold Weiner receives tips from customers as a standard component of his weekly pay. He is paid $4.40/hour by his employer, and receives $188 in tips during the most recent 47-hour workweek.

3. Katherine Shaw receives tips from customers as a standard component of her weekly pay. She is paid $2.20/hour by her employer, and receives $553 in tips during the most recent 56-hour workweek.

4. Tracey Houseman receives tips from customers as a standard component of her weekly pay. She is paid $3.90/hour by her employer, and receives $472 in tips during the most recent 45-hour workweek.

KCb 2-11 Calculate Gross Pay for a Piecework Employee

Calculate gross pay for each of the following employees. All are paid an overtime wage rate that is 1.5 times their respective regular wage rates.

1. Shane Bryan is a telemarketer who is paid $0.28 for every telemarketing phone call he places. During the most recent week, he worked 47 hours and placed 2,084 calls.

2. Zeke Saunders assembles merchandise and is paid $0.18 for each unit assembled. During the most recent week, he worked 48 hours and assembled 3,436 units.

3. Luke Hernandez is a telemarketer who is paid $0.41 for every telemarketing phone call he places. During the most recent week, he worked 42 hours and placed 1,374 calls.

4. Quincy Finkelstein assembles merchandise and is paid $0.08 for each unit assembled. During the most recent week, he worked 42 hours and assembled 6,209 units.

KCb 2-12 Populate Employee Earnings Records

Complete the top portion and **EARNINGS** section of an employee's earnings record for the five employees in KCb 2-4. The associated pay period ends on 7/25/14. Additional data for each employee is as follows:

- Jimmy Troffa (SSN 787-78-7878) lives at 81 Jackson Road, Berkeley, CA, 94701, is married, and claims 3 withholding allowances for both the federal and state.
- Tyler Thomas (SSN 898-89-8989) lives at 4004 Dartmouth Court, Reno, NV 89501, is single, claims 3 federal withholding allowances, and 2 state withholding allowance.
- Ryan Brown (SSN 100-00-0000) lives at 3 Fireside Avenue, Bentonville, AR 72716, is single, and claims 2 withholding allowances for both federal and state.
- Michael Kaminski (SSN 200-00-0000) lives at 881 Sawmill Street, Nashville, TN 37201, is single, and claims 3 withholding allowance for both federal and state.
- Tina Baldwin (SSN 300-00-0000) lives at 91845 Village Path, Trenton, NJ 08601, is married, claims 4 federal withholding allowances, and 3 state withholding allowances.

KCb 2-13 Populate a Payroll Register

Complete the top portion and **EARNINGS** section of a Payroll Register using the employee data from KCb 2-4 & KCb 2-12. The associated pay period ends on 7/25/14, with paychecks being printed and distributed six days later.

Continuing Payroll Problem

For all assignments in this section, necessary IRS forms and/or Excel templates are located in the Student Resource Center.

CPP 2-1 Calculating & Documenting Gross Pay

Calculate gross pay for a number of employees of TCLH Industries, a manufacturer of cleaning products. Then complete a Payroll Register based on your calculations.

1. Complete Timecards for the following employees:
   - Zachary Fox (SSN 121-21-2121) worked five days for TCLH Industries during the week of 5/6/13 through 5/12/13 (he had both Saturday and Sunday off that week). On each working day he arrived at 7:00 a.m. (except Tuesday, when he was 4 minutes early, and Wednesday, when he arrived at 8:02 a.m.). He left for lunch at 11:00 a.m. each day (except Tuesday & Friday, when he left at 10:59 a.m.), and arrived back at 12:00 p.m. (except Friday, when he arrived back at 11:53 p.m.). He left at 4:00 p.m. each day (except Monday and Thursday, when he stayed until 6:02 p.m. and 4:01 p.m. respectively).

   - Calvin Bell (SSN 500-00-0000) worked six days for TCLH Industries during the week of 5/6/13 through 5/12/13 (he had Wednesday off that week). On each working day he arrived at 8:00 a.m. (except Monday and Saturday, when he was 7 minutes early and 2 minutes late, respectively). He left for lunch each day at noon (except Tuesday, when he left at 11:56 a.m., and Saturday, when he didn't take lunch), and arrived back (except Saturday) at 1:00 p.m. He left at 5:00 p.m. each day (except Monday, when he stayed until 6:02, and Friday, when he stayed until 6:29).

2. Complete an employee earnings record for each of the four employees of TCLH Industries. (Recall that you began this record for Zachary Fox in Chapter 1.)
   - Zachary Fox, whose timecard you completed above, lives at 1483 Independence Road, Durham, NC 27701. He is married, claims 2 withholding allowances for both the federal and state, earns regular wages of $7.75/hour, and overtime wages of $11.63/hour.

   - Calvin Bell, whose timecard you completed above, lives at 2222 Sacker Place, Durham, NC 27701. He is single, claims 2 federal withholding allowances and 1 state withholding allowance, earns regular wages of $7.30/hour, and earns overtime wages of 1.5 times his regular wage rate.

   - Michaela Walton (SSN 654-32-1098) worked 47 hours during the week of 5/6/13 through 5/12/13 (she completed her timecard, which has been verified). She lives at 1 Freedom Blvd., Durham, NC 27701, is single, and claims 1 withholding allowance for both the federal and state. She earns regular wages of $8.70/hour, and overtime wages of $13.20/hour.

   - Suzanne Steinberg (SSN 222-22-2222) worked 51 hours during the week of 5/6/13 through 5/12/13 (she completed her timecard, which has been verified). She lives at 200 Mississippi Road, Durham, NC 27701, is married, claims 4 federal withholding allowances and 3 state withholding allowances. She earns regular wages of $9.00/hour, and overtime wages of 1.5 times her regular wage rate.

3. Lastly, complete the earnings section of the Payroll Register for the week of 5/6/13 through 5/12/13. TCLH Industries prints and distributes paychecks each week on the Thursday following the completion of the pay period.

Critical Thinking

CT 2-1 Review Various Incentive Plans

You were introduced earlier to some of the most common incentive plans used by employers. In all cases, these plans are designed to encourage specific employee behaviors that align with the goals of the organization. In this exercise, you'll use the internet to research alternate incentive plans beyond those listed earlier.

Incentive plans can be divided into monetary (providing employees with the opportunity to earn additional money) and non-monetary (incentivizing employees with a benefit other than money). Use the internet to identify four employee incentives (two monetary and two non-monetary) not listed in this chapter. For each incentive, write at least three sentences in which you describe the incentive, and discuss the circumstance in which it is most appropriate. Lastly, write at least two sentences in which you select the one of these incentives that you deem to be most effective, and discuss your reasoning.

Submit your final file(s) based on the guidelines provided by your instructor.

CT 2-2 Research State Minimum Wages

In states in which the State Minimum Wage exceeds the Federal Minimum Wage, employers must comply with the higher state wage. In this exercise, you'll research current state minimum wages, identifying those states that currently require a minimum wage higher than the federal requirement.

Begin by researching state minimum wages on the internet, and identify those states that require higher minimum wages than the current federal rate. Write a paragraph of at least five sentences in which you list these states, identify the state(s) with the highest current state minimum wage, identify the current state minimum wage in your state, and discuss reasons why you believe that certain states have mandated higher minimum wage rates.

Submit your final file(s) based on the guidelines provided by your instructor.

Federal & State Income Tax Withholding

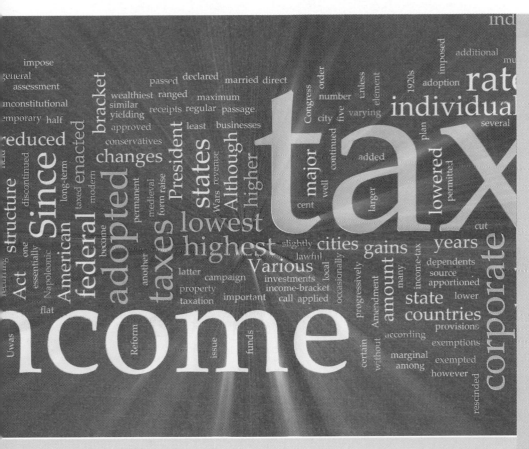

LEARNING OBJECTIVES

After studying this chapter, you will be able to:

- Identify and distingulsh between mandatory & voluntary deductions

- Determine taxable earnings

- Calculate federal income tax withholding using the Wage-Bracket Method

- Calculate federal income tax withholding using the Percentage Method

- Understand state & local income tax withholding

Once an employee's earnings are determined, the next step is to calculate the amounts withheld from the earnings. While some of these deductions are mandatory (such as Medicare tax), others are voluntary and may be elected by the employee. In this chapter, you will identify a wide range of both mandatory and voluntary deductions. Next you will examine federal income tax withholding more closely, and learn two methods for calculating the tax. You will then review state and local income tax withholding, and will conclude by entering both federal & state income tax withholding figures in the payroll register.

CASE STUDY

Determining Federal & State Income Tax Withholding for Lucky Ties Apparel

Lucky Ties Apparel is required to withhold a variety of taxes from each employee's pay. Among these are federal & state income tax withholdings. As not all employees of Lucky Ties Apparel earn the same amount and all have a different number of federal and state withholding allowances, the applicable calculations differ from one employee to the next.

Because these deductions from gross pay are among your payroll-related responsibilities, you decide that a thorough examination of each is warranted. You begin by examining both the federal & state income tax withholding, so that you understand the different methods that may be used to calculate each. You then fill out the payroll register with these newly-calculated deductions.

Federal, state, and local income tax withholding (where applicable) are some of the mandatory deductions withheld from employee pay.

MY CONSTRUCTION COMPANY
1001 Fifth Avenue
New York, NY 10022

Period ending: 12/15/2013
Pay date: 12/17/2013

CLARK MITCHELL
547 Smith Street
New York, NY 10033

Earnings	Rate	Hours	This Period	Year to Date		Deductions		
Regular	$14.00	40.00	$560.00	$28,000.00		Statutory	This Period	Year to Date
Overtime	$21.00	4.00	$84.00	$6,615.00		Federal Income Tax	$19.00	$1,350.00
Holiday	$30.00	0.00	$0.00	$2,250.00		Social Security Tax	$39.93	$2,285.63
						Medicare Tax	$9.34	$534.54
		Gross Pay	$644.00	$36,865.00		NYS Income Tax	$12.67	$783.33
						NYC Income Tax	$8.44	$472.22
						NYSDI Tax	$0.60	$30.00
						Other		
						401(k)	$32.20*	$1,843.25
						Life Insurance	$10.00	$500.00

Federal Income Tax Withholding ———

State Income Tax Withholding ———

Local Income Tax Withholding ———

Net Pay	$511.82

* Excluded from federal taxable wages

Social Security Number: ***-**-1119
Taxable Marital Status: Married
Exemptions/Allowances:
Federal: 4, $25 Additional Tax
State: 3
Local: 3

Other Benefits and Information	This Period	Year to Date
Vacation Hrs.		64.00
Sick Hrs.		24.00

Examining Deductions From Employee Earnings

Once an employee's gross pay is calculated, certain amounts are withheld by the employer and therefore not included in the employee's paycheck. These amounts are referred to as **deductions**. Some of these amounts must be withheld, and are referred to as **mandatory deductions**. Others may be requested by the employee, and are referred to as **voluntary deductions**.

Reviewing Mandatory Deductions

Employees are subject to a number of mandatory deductions that their employers are required to withhold from each paycheck. Among these deductions are the following:

- **Federal Income Tax Withholding** – This tax (also called *Federal Income Tax*) is collected by the federal government to fund a wide range of governmental agencies. A small percentage of employees are exempt from this tax, as you will see later in this chapter.

- **State Income Tax Withholding** – The majority of states collect this tax (also called *State Income Tax*) to fund state operations. As of 2013, nine states (Alaska, Florida, Nevada, New Hampshire, South Dakota, Texas, Tennessee, Washington, Wyoming) did not collect state taxes on individual incomes.

NOTE! In 2013, New Hampshire and Tennessee did collect taxes on dividend and interest income.

- **Local Income Tax Withholding** – Some municipalities, such as Manhattan in New York State, require that local income tax withholding (also called *Local Income Tax*) be deducted from employee earnings to fund governmental operations in their respective municipalities.

- **Social Security Tax (OASDI)** – This tax is withheld from employee earnings to fund the social security system, which pays benefits to retired or disabled workers, as well as their dependents and survivors. This tax is subject to an income threshold, and therefore (in 2013) was only calculated as 6.2% of the first $113,700 earned during the year. To be discussed in detail in Chapter 4.

- **Medicare Tax (HI)** – This tax (in 2013) was calculated as 1.45% of all employee earnings. These funds operate the Medicare federal health insurance program that covers individuals 65 years of age or older, and certain disabled individuals. To be discussed in detail in Chapter 4.

TIP! Social Security tax and Medicare tax, in conjunction, are referred to as FICA (Federal Insurance Contributions Act) Taxes.

- **State Disability Insurance Tax** – Five states (California, Hawaii, New Jersey, New York, Rhode Island) and the territory of Puerto Rico require that disability insurance be withheld from employee pay. With these funds, the states provide benefits to temporarily disabled employees who are unable to work for a period of time. To be discussed in detail in Chapter 4.

Reviewing Voluntary Deductions

In addition to the items that must be withheld from an employee's pay, there are a number of amounts that an employee may elect to have withheld. Common examples of these voluntary deductions, which will be examined further in Chapter 4, are as follows:

- **Union Dues** – For those employees who are unionized, the associated dues may be withheld from their earnings and remitted directly to the union.

- **Retirement Plans** – Employees may elect to have monies withheld for retirement plans, certain of which can be tax-deferred (no federal income tax is paid on these funds when they are withheld). These are called *Defined Contribution Plans*, as the employee's contribution percentage (portion of gross pay deducted) is fixed.

- **Medical Plans** – Depending on various criteria, employees may realize a tax benefit from having funds withheld and directed to a medical savings plan. These plans differ from Flexible Spending Accounts (discussed next) in that the funds roll over and can be used in subsequent years.

NOTE!   Medical Plans differ from Health Insurance Premiums, which employees can elect to have withheld from gross earnings, and which pay for (either in part or entirely) the employee's health insurance coverage.

- **Cafeteria Plans** – Offered by some employers, these plans can provide a variety of benefits, and designated funds are not subject to federal income tax withholding. One common type of cafeteria plan is a **Flexible Spending Account**, through which employees may be reimbursed for qualified benefits such as dependent care and medical expenses.

Not technically a voluntary deduction for the employee to whom it is applied, a *wage garnishment* represents monies withheld from pay as a result of a court order. These amounts may fund a wide range of monetary obligations, including child support. Individual states have varying requirements regarding the reporting of newly-hired employees, primarily to identify those employees for whom garnishments should be made.

Distinguishing Between Gross Pay and Taxable Pay

As you saw in the previous chapter, gross pay encompasses all earnings of an employee for a given period. However, each of the above-listed taxes is not necessarily calculated based on this gross pay. For example, since certain retirement plans, dependent care expenses, and cafeteria plans are tax-deferred, the amount contributed to these must be subtracted from Gross Pay before determining federal income tax withholding. Additionally, 401(k) and 403 (b) plans are both tax-deferred retirement plans that are exempt from federal income tax. Taxable pay (also called Taxable Income) represents the portion of gross pay used to calculate each of the Mandatory Deductions.

WARNING! Taxable pay used to calculate federal income tax withholding can be different from taxable pay used to calculate Social Security or Medicare tax. For example, deductions for a 401(k) or 403(b) retirement plan are not taxable for federal income tax withholding, but are taxable for Social Security and Medicare taxes.

Depending on the regulations in place, taxable income for both state and local income tax withholdings can also differ from that for federal income tax withholding. For simplicity, we will assume throughout the text that, for every employee, taxable income is the same for federal, state, and local income tax withholding.

Case In Point 3-1 Determine Gross and Taxable Pay

Based on the information provided below, determine the gross pay for each employee. Then calculate taxable pay for federal income tax withholding, Social Security tax, and Medicare tax.

1. An employee works 37 regular hours during the first workweek of 2013, and earns $8.25/hour. He has requested that his employer withhold 8% of gross pay, which is to be contributed to a 401(k) plan.

    Gross pay for this employee, who did not work any overtime hours, was $305.25 (37 hours x $8.25).

    As 401(k) contributions are tax-deferred for the purposes of federal income tax withholding, this employee's contribution must be subtracted from gross pay in order to determine taxable pay for federal income tax withholding. The 401(k) contribution is $24.42 ($305.25 x 8%), therefore taxable pay for federal income tax withholding is $280.83 ($305.25 – $24.42).

    For this employee, there are no amounts which must be subtracted from gross pay in order to arrive at taxable pay for Social Security tax or Medicare tax (401(k) contributions are taxable for these two taxes). Therefore, taxable pay for both Social Security tax and Medicare tax is $305.25.

2. An employee works 43 hours (3 of which were overtime hours) during a workweek in November of 2013. The employee earns $37.50/hour, with his employer paying 1.5 times the regular rate of pay for overtime hours. To date, he has earned $112,900 during the year (these earnings include hourly wages, as well as bonus payments, which are also subject to FICA tax). He has requested that his employer withhold 10% of gross pay, which is to be contributed to a 403(b) plan.

    Regular Earnings for this employee were $1,500 (40 hours x $37.50/hour). The overtime rate of pay is $56.25/hour ($37.50/hour x 1.5), and the Overtime Earnings were $168.75 (3 hours x $56.25/hour). Therefore, gross pay for the week was $1,668.75 ($1,500 regular earnings + $168.75 overtime earnings).

    Taxable Earnings for federal income tax withholding must exclude the 403(b) contribution. This contribution was $166.88 ($1,668.75 gross pay ÷10%), therefore the taxable earnings for federal income tax withholding were $1,501.87 ($1,668.75 gross pay minus $166.88 403(b) contribution).

The previous annual earnings of $112,900, when added to the gross pay of $1,668.75, totals $114,568.75. As this exceeds the 2013 Social Security tax threshold of $113,700, only a portion of the gross pay is taxable for Social Security tax. The portion of gross pay that falls below the threshold totals $800 ($113,700 threshold – $112,900 previous annual earnings), and therefore this $800 represents the taxable pay for Social Security tax.

Medicare tax is not subject to an earnings threshold. In addition, 403(b) contributions are not exempt from Medicare tax. Therefore, taxable pay for Medicare tax is the same as the gross pay of $1,668.75

Collecting Federal Income Tax Withholding

The manner in which federal income tax withholding is remitted to the United Sates government is referred to as a **pay-as-you-go** system. Under this system, income tax must be paid as the income is earned.

The pay-as-you-go system was established as a result of the **Current Tax Payment Act of 1943**. This act modified the federal income tax system such that payments could no longer be made in the subsequent year, but instead must be paid in the year that the income is earned. To facilitate the collection of these taxes, the act stipulated that employers must withhold these taxes from employee pay, and remit the withholdings to the federal government.

Under limited circumstances, employees may be exempted from paying federal income tax withholding. Typically, an employee who qualifies for exemption did not owe federal income tax during the prior year, and does not expect to owe it in the current year. In this instance, the employee must file a W-4 Form with the employer indicating the exempt status. These qualifying employees are often low-income earners who, in many instances, qualify for the *Earned Income Credit*, which reduces the tax burden on their year-end personal tax returns.

For the employer to withhold the correct amount of federal income tax for each non-exempt employee, a number of calculation methods may be utilized. The two primary methods are the Wage-Bracket method, and the Percentage Method.

Using the Wage-Bracket Method

Under the **Wage-Bracket Method**, an employee's marital status, withholding allowances, and taxable pay are used to locate the correct amount of withholding on a Federal Income Tax Withholding Table. This is one of the primary instances in which key information from the employee's W-4 Form (marital status & federal withholding allowances) is utilized to determine applicable taxes.

Updated Federal Income Tax Withholding Tables are published each year in the Circular E.

	**SINGLE** Persons—**WEEKLY** Payroll Period
	**(For Wages Paid through December 2013)**
	And the wages are—	colspan="11"	And the number of withholding allowances claimed is—
At least	But less than	0	1	2	3	4	5	6	7	8	9	10
			The amount of income tax to be withheld is—
$ 0	$55	$0	$0	$0	$0	$0	$0	$0	$0	$0	$0	$0
55	60	2	0	0	0	0	0	0	0	0	0	0
60	65	2	0	0	0	0	0	0	0	0	0	0
65	70	3	0	0	0	0	0	0	0	0	0	0
70	75	3	0	0	0	0	0	0	0	0	0	0
75	80	4	0	0	0	0	0	0	0	0	0	0
80	85	4	0	0	0	0	0	0	0	0	0	0
85	90	5	0	0	0	0	0	0	0	0	0	0
90	95	5	0	0	0	0	0	0	0	0	0	0
95	100	6	0	0	0	0	0	0	0	0	0	0
100	105	6	0	0	0	0	0	0	0	0	0	0
105	110	7	0	0	0	0	0	0	0	0	0	0
110	115	7	0	0	0	0	0	0	0	0	0	0
115	120	8	0	0	0	0	0	0	0	0	0	0
120	125	8	1	0	0	0	0	0	0	0	0	0
125	130	9	1	0	0	0	0	0	0	0	0	0
130	135	9	2	0	0	0	0	0	0	0	0	0
135	140	10	2	0	0	0	0	0	0	0	0	0
140	145	10	3	0	0	0	0	0	0	0	0	0
145	150	11	3	0	0	0	0	0	0	0	0	0
150	155	11	4	0	0	0	0	0	0	0	0	0
155	160	12	4	0	0	0	0	0	0	0	0	0
160	165	12	5	0	0	0	0	0	0	0	0	0
165	170	13	5	0	0	0	0	0	0	0	0	0
170	175	13	6	0	0	0	0	0	0	0	0	0
175	180	14	6	0	0	0	0	0	0	0	0	0
180	185	14	7	0	0	0	0	0	0	0	0	0
185	190	15	7	0	0	0	0	0	0	0	0	0
190	195	15	8	0	0	0	0	0	0	0	0	0
195	200	16	8	1	0	0	0	0	0	0	0	0
200	210	16	9	1	0	0	0	0	0	0	0	0
210	220	17	10	2	0	0	0	0	0	0	0	0
220	230	19	11	3	0	0	0	0	0	0	0	0
230	240	20	12	4	0	0	0	0	0	0	0	0
240	250	22	13	5	0	0	0	0	0	0	0	0
250	260	23	14	6	0	0	0	0	0	0	0	0
260	270	25	15	7	0	0	0	0	0	0	0	0
270	280	26	16	8	1	0	0	0	0	0	0	0
280	290	28	17	9	2	0	0	0	0	0	0	0
290	300	29	18	10	3	0	0	0	0	0	0	0
300	310	31	20	11	4	0	0	0	0	0	0	0
310	320	32	21	12	5	0	0	0	0	0	0	0
320	330	34	23	13	6	0	0	0	0	0	0	0
330	340	35	24	14	7	0	0	0	0	0	0	0
340	350	37	26	15	8	0	0	0	0	0	0	0
350	360	38	27	16	9	1	0	0	0	0	0	0
360	370	40	29	17	10	2	0	0	0	0	0	0
370	380	41	30	19	11	3	0	0	0	0	0	0
380	390	43	32	20	12	4	0	0	0	0	0	0
390	400	44	33	22	13	5	0	0	0	0	0	0

The withholding table shown above is for an employee whose marital status is single and who is paid on a weekly basis. Weekly wage ranges are provided on the left of the table and federal withholding allowances are at the top. To determine an employee's federal income tax withholding, an employer locates the intersection of the applicable wage range of the employee's taxable pay, and number of withholding allowances (found on the employee's W-4 Form).

For example, if a single employee is paid on a weekly basis and claims one federal withholding allowance and earns wages of $312, he/she is subject to $21 of federal income tax withholding. This employee would look at the intersection of the $310 to $320 wages row and the 1 withholding allowance column to determine this tax amount.

If this same employee earned wages of $330, the $330 to $340 row is applicable, resulting in federal income tax withholding of $24. The wage increments represent *at least... but less than*; therefore, wages of $330 correspond with the $330 to $340 row. Using the $320 to $330 row, in this instance, is incorrect.

TIP!   Notice that, as the number of withholding allowances increases, the federal income tax withholding decreases. To ensure that sufficient tax is withheld during the year, employees may elect to claim fewer withholding allowances than they are permitted, thus increasing total withholding.

On the Web

www.irs.gov/pub/
irs-pdf/p15.pdf

Many different withholding tables are published by the Internal Revenue Service (IRS) in Circular E. Aside from the *Single: Weekly* table, a portion of which is shown above, the following tables are also available:

- Married: Weekly
- Single: Biweekly
- Married: Biweekly
- Single: Semimonthly
- Married: Semimonthly
- Single: Monthly
- Married: Monthly
- Single: Daily
- Married: Daily

These tables can all be viewed in Appendix A. Each table is two pages long, and displays the appropriate federal income tax withholding for an employee with up to ten withholding allowances. The Circular E provides instruction regarding the federal income tax withholding calculation (under the wage-bracket method) for employees claiming more than ten withholding allowances. However, in the event that an employee earns more than the largest wage range on the appropriate table, the percentage method must be used.

Using the Percentage Method

An alternative method for determining federal income tax withholding is the **Percentage Method**. To use this method the employer completes a three-step process:

- Step 1: Multiply the employee's number of federal withholding allowances by the applicable figure shown in the table below.

This *One Withholding Allowance* table is published each year in the Circular E.

Payroll Period	One Withholding Allowance
Weekly	$ 75.00
Biweekly	150.00
Semimonthly	162.50
Monthly	325.00
Quarterly	975.00
Semiannually	1,950.00
Annually	3,900.00
Daily or miscellaneous (each day of the payroll period)	15.00

- Step 2: Subtract the Step 1 result from the employee's taxable pay.
- Step 3: Use the percentage method tables (provided annually in the Circular E) to calculate the federal income tax withholding, based on the result from Step 2.

This percentage method table provides calculation instruction for both single and married employees earning weekly pay.

(For Wages Paid in 2013)							
TABLE 1—WEEKLY Payroll Period							
(a) SINGLE person (including head of household)—				**(b) MARRIED person—**			
If the amount of wages (after subtracting withholding allowances) is:		The amount of income tax to withhold is:		If the amount of wages (after subtracting withholding allowances) is:		The amount of income tax to withhold is:	
Not over $42		$0		Not over $160		$0	
Over—	But not over—		of excess over—	Over—	But not over—		of excess over—
$42	—$214 . .	$0.00 plus 10%	—$42	$160	—$503 . .	$0.00 plus 10%	—$160
$214	—$739 . .	$17.20 plus 15%	—$214	$503	—$1,554 . .	$34.30 plus 15%	—$503
$739	—$1,732 . .	$95.95 plus 25%	—$739	$1,554	—$2,975 . .	$191.95 plus 25%	—$1,554
$1,732	—$3,566 . .	$344.20 plus 28%	—$1,732	$2,975	—$4,449 . .	$547.20 plus 28%	—$2,975
$3,566	—$7,703 . .	$857.72 plus 33%	—$3,566	$4,449	—$7,820 . .	$959.92 plus 33%	—$4,449
$7,703	—$7,735 . .	$2,222.93 plus 35%	—$7,703	$7,820	—$8,813 . .	$2,072.35 plus 35%	—$7,820
$7,735		$2,234.13 plus 39.6%	—$7,735	$8,813		$2,419.90 plus 39.6%	—$8,813

Percentage Method Example:

$95.95 + (25% * ($1,000 - $739)) = $161.20

For example, if a single employee has $1,075 of taxable pay, is paid weekly, and claims one federal withholding allowance, Step 1 results in $75 (1 allowance x $75 weekly figure in table). Step 2 results in $1,000 ($1,075 taxable pay minus $75 step 1 result). Step 3 results in the employee having federal income tax withholding of $95.95 + (25% ÷ ($1,000 minus $739)) = $161.20. Based on the third row of the *single* portion of the table, the excess of the $1,000 wages over $739 must be multiplied by 25%. This is how we determine the amount that is added to the $95.95 starting point to arrive at federal income tax withholding.

NOTE!   The percentage method often yields a different withholding amount than the wage-bracket method for the same circumstance. In spite of this difference, both methods are acceptable.

Seven other versions of the percentage method table are also provided in the Circular E. These allow for the calculation of federal income tax withholding for employees paid on the following bases: biweekly, semimonthly, monthly, quarterly, semiannually, annually, and daily.

TIP!   More types of tables are provided under the percentage method than the wage-bracket method. For this reason, the wage-bracket method cannot be used for employees with quarterly, semiannual, or annual pay periods.

Case In Point 3-2   # Calculate Federal Income Tax Withholding

For each of the following employees of Lucky Ties Apparel, let's calculate the federal income tax withholding for the current weekly pay period. We'll use the wage-bracket method for the first three employees, and the percentage method for the final two employees.

Before You Begin: Federal withholding tax tables for both the wage-bracket method and the percentage method are in Appendix A.

1. Paul Rogers (single; 1 federal withholding allowance) earned gross pay of $402.50. For each period, he makes a 401(k) contribution of 8% of gross pay.

   Wage-Bracket Method:

   Taxable pay for federal income tax withholding excludes the 401(k) contribution. This retirement plan contribution totals $32.20 ($402.50 x 8%), and therefore taxable pay is $370.30 ($402.50 minus $32.20).

   Using the Single: Weekly withholding table, this taxable pay falls in the $370 to $380 range. The intersection of this row and the 1 withholding allowance column yields federal income tax withholding of $30.

2. Maryanne Sherman (single; 2 federal withholding allowances) earned gross pay of $769.23. She does not make any retirement-plan contributions.

   Wage-Bracket Method:

   All of the gross pay is taxable for federal income tax withholding purposes, therefore taxable pay is $769.23.

   Using the Single: Weekly withholding table, this taxable pay falls in the $760 to $770 range. The intersection of this row and the 2 withholding allowance column yields federal income tax withholding of $77.

3. Bill Novak (married; 4 federal withholding allowances) earned gross pay of $725. For each period, he makes a flexible spending account contribution of 6% of gross pay.

   Wage-Bracket Method:

   Taxable pay for federal income tax withholding excludes the flexible spending account contribution. This contribution totals $43.50 ($725 x 6%), and therefore taxable pay is $681.50 ($725 minus $43.50).

   Using the Married: Weekly withholding table, this taxable pay falls in the $680 to $690 range. The intersection of this row and the 4 withholding allowance column yields federal income tax withholding of $23.

4. Angelo Dorsett (single; 2 federal withholding allowances) earned gross pay of $883.75. For each period, he makes a dependent-care flexible spending account contribution of 10% of gross pay.

   Percentage Method:

   Before undertaking the 3-step process for the percentage method, taxable pay must first be determined. Taxable pay for federal income tax withholding excludes the dependent-care flexible spending account contribution. This dependent-care flexible spending account contribution totals $88.38 ($883.75 ÷ 10%), and therefore taxable pay is $795.37 ($883.75 minus $88.38).

   Step 1: 2 withholding allowances x $75 (weekly One Withholding Allowance amount) = $150.

   Step 2: $795.37 (taxable pay) minus $150 = $645.37

   Step 3: Using the *single* side of the *weekly* table, taxable pay falls in the $214 to $739 range. Therefore, federal income tax withholding is calculated as $17.20 ı (15% ÷ ($645.37 minus $214)), which equals $81.91.

5. Melissa Kubiak (married; 5 federal withholding allowances) earned gross pay of $622.50. She does not make any retirement plan contributions.

   Percentage Method:

   Before undertaking the 3-step process for the percentage method, taxable pay must first be determined. All of the gross pay is taxable for federal income tax withholding purposes, therefore taxable pay is $622.50.

   Step 1: 5 withholding allowances x $75 (weekly One Withholding Allowance amount) = $375.

   Step 2: $622.50 (taxable pay) minus $375 = $247.50

   Step 3: Using the *married* side of the *weekly* table, taxable pay falls in the $160-$503 range. Therefore, federal income tax withholding is calculated as $0 + (10% ÷ [$247.50 minus $160]), which equals $8.75.

Examining Other Federal Income Tax Withholding Considerations

An employee's federal income tax withholding can be impacted by a number of other circumstances. Among the most common are the passing away or termination of an employee, and changes in the number of dependents (or other similar changes) that require the submission of an updated W-4 Form.

Accounting for Deceased & Terminated Employees

In the event that an employee dies, it is likely that a portion of the employee's earnings will be paid by the employer after death. Any such payments are not subject to federal income tax withholding, and should be excluded from the calculation of taxable pay.

When an individual's employment ends, either voluntarily or involuntarily, he/she is entitled to all compensation earned prior to termination. The required timing of this payment differs from state to state, and ranges from immediately upon involuntary termination to the time of the subsequent pay date. These earnings are subject to federal income tax withholding in the same manner as were the employee's prior earnings.

Changing the W-4 Form

Employees may need to change their W-4 Forms for a variety of reasons, including marriage, divorce, the birth of children, or change of job status for the employee or his/her spouse.

WARNING! For changes that either reduce the number of withholding allowances, or alter the status from *married* to *single*, the employee is required to complete a new W-4 Form within ten days. No time limit exists for other changes; the employee may submit a new W-4 Form for other changes at his/her discretion.

When an updated W-4 Form is submitted by the employee, the employer must process the change (and therefore adjust the federal income tax withholding) no later than the start of the first payroll period that ends at least 30 days after submission of the new form. Although there is no limit to the number of W-4 Form changes that may be submitted by an employee, this timeframe over which an employer is permitted to implement the change effectively limits the total number of changes that can be processed in a given year.

TIP! Accepting an updated W-4 Form is not optional for an employer. New W-4 Forms resulting from circumstances described earlier must be processed by the employer.

| Case In Point 3-3 | ## Determine Timing of Employer Responsibilities |

For each of the following circumstances, let's determine the date on which the referenced action must take place.

1. Samuel Wildhorn's divorce was finalized on Sunday, June 15. When must he submit a revised W-4 Form to his employer?

   When an employee's divorce is finalized, he/she has 10 days to provide the employer with a revised W-4 Form. Therefore, Samuel must furnish a new W-4 Form no later than Wednesday, June 25.

2. Maggie Yang decides on Monday, March 3 that she would like to increase her number of federal withholding allowances from 3 to 5. When must she submit a revised W-4 Form to her employer?

   In this instance, there is no time limit for submitting a new W-4 Form, as this is not one of the circumstances under which notification must be made within 10 days. Maggie is free to submit the new form whenever she would like.

3. Brandon Rosenberg decides on Tuesday, October 21 that he would like to reduce his number of federal withholding allowances from 3 to 2. He submits a revised W-4 Form, on which he makes this change, on Friday, October 24. Brandon is compensated on a semimonthly basis (at the middle and end of each month), and receives his paycheck five days after the end of each pay period. By which pay date must this change be in effect?

   The next two pay periods that end after submission of the new form have end dates of October 31 & November 15, neither of which is 30 days after submission. The pay period ending on November 30 is the first pay period that ends at least 30 days after submission; therefore the W-4 Form must be processed prior to the beginning of this pay period (November 16). The associated pay date, which is five days after the end of the period, is December 5. The W-4 Form change must be in effect for this pay date.

Calculating State Income Tax Withholding

On the Web

www.sba.gov/content/
learn-about-your-state-
and-local-tax-obligations

In addition to federal income tax withholdings, the majority of employees are also subject to state income tax withholding. These taxes are calculated based on state taxable income, which in many states is the same as federal taxable income.

As was noted previously, nine states do not collect state income tax on employee taxable income. The tax rates imposed in the other 41 states vary widely from one to the next. Furthermore, while some states levy a flat tax on all employee earnings, others levy a graduated tax, which increases as the employee's earnings increase. Refer to your eLab course for links to state taxing authorities in each of the 50 states. Further details regarding each state's specific withholding tax provisions can be found there.

Due to the variability in state income tax withholding rates and methods, we will utilize a flat 5% state tax rate throughout the textbook.

Determining Local Income Tax Withholding

In addition to both federal and state income tax withholding, employees living and/or working in certain jurisdictions are subject to local income tax withholding. These taxes vary widely in terms of the tax rates applied, and the form in which the taxes are levied. For example, some local jurisdictions (such as cities or towns) impose local income tax withholding as a percentage of gross pay, others do so as a percentage of federal or state income tax withholding, while still others impose a simple flat tax (specific, identical dollar amount for each employee) on a weekly basis.

Local jurisdictions may also elect to impose different local income tax withholding on residents and non-residents. The justification for this practice is that residents utilize the services of the jurisdiction to a greater extent than non-residents, and therefore should bear a greater tax burden.

Case In Point 3-4	# Calculate State & Local Income Tax Withholding

For each of the following employees, let's calculate the applicable state and local income tax withholding.

Before You Begin: Assume a state income tax withholding rate of 5% of taxable earnings.

1. Julio Ordonez earned gross pay of $847, all of which is taxable for state and local income tax withholding. The city in which he both lives and works levies a tax of 2% of an employee's gross pay.

   State income tax withholding for this employee is $42.35 ($847 gross pay x 5% state tax rate). Local income tax withholding is $16.94 ($847 gross pay x 2% local tax rate).

2. Alyona Gaponovitch earned gross pay of $1,620. Of this amount, $1,598 is taxable for state and local income tax withholding. The city in which she works (she lives elsewhere) levies a tax of 1.5% of an employee's gross pay on residents, and 0.8% of an employee's gross pay on non-residents.

   State income tax withholding for this employee is $79.90 ($1,598 taxable pay x 5% state tax rate). Local income tax withholding is based on a rate of 0.8%, as Alyona is a non-resident. Therefore, her local income tax withholding is $12.78 ($1,598 taxable pay x 0.8% local tax rate).

3. Lucy Farmington earned gross pay of $1,100. Of this amount, $1,065 is taxable for state and local income tax withholding. The city in which she lives and works levies a tax of 2.1% of an employee's gross pay on residents, and 0.5% of an employee's gross pay on non-residents.

   State income tax withholding for this employee is $53.25 ($1,065 taxable pay x 5% state tax rate). Local income tax withholding is based on a rate of 2.1%, as Lucy is a resident. Therefore, her local income tax withholding is $22.37 ($1,065 taxable pay x 2.1% local tax rate).

4. Gabrielle Fernandez earned weekly gross pay of $740, all of which is taxable for state and local income tax withholding. The city in which she lives and works levies a tax of $10/week on employees who work within city limits.

   State income tax withholding for this employee is $37 ($740 taxable pay x 5% state tax rate). Local income tax withholding is unrelated to Gabrielle's gross pay, and is $10.

Using the Payroll Register

As you saw in the last chapter, the payroll register is completed based on the earnings and deductions calculated in the employee earnings records. Note that the city of Rochester, NY, in which Lucky Ties Apparel is located, does not levy local income tax withholding. As a result, there is no column in either the employee earnings record or the payroll register in which local income tax withholding can be entered. Both of these forms may be modified by the employer in this manner to suit a company's circumstance.

As with the employee earnings record, the payroll register columns can be modified to suit a specific company's circumstances.

Payroll Register

Pay Period _____

Pay Date _____

Employee Name	Regular Hours	Regular Rate	Regular Earnings	Overtime Hours	Overtime Rate	Overtime Earnings	Total Earnings	FWT	SWT	Social Security	Medicare	Health Ins.	Union Dues	Check Number	Net Pay
Totals:															

Case In Point 3-5   Complete a Payroll Register

In this example, we'll complete a payroll register for Lucky Ties Apparel. Earlier we calculated the federal income tax withholding for five different employees of Lucky Ties Apparel. Their partially-completed employee earnings records for the most recent week appear below (federal income tax withholding for Angelo Dorsett & Melissa Kubiak differ slightly from earlier calculations, as Lucky Ties Apparel has elected to use the wage-bracket method for all employees).

Additionally, the partially-completed employee earnings records of three other employees (whose earnings were determined in the last chapter) also appear below. The state income tax withholding has been completed for all employees based on the previously-assumed 5% tax rate. Based on these employee earnings records, we will complete a portion of the deductions section of the payroll register.

Assume that any deductions which are exempt from federal income tax withholding are also exempt from state income tax withholding. Further note that Lucy Marshall has requested that a voluntary deduction of 8% of gross earnings be contributed to a 401(k) retirement plan.

Employee Earnings Record

Name	Paul Rogers	Marital Status	Single
Address	657 Flicker Lane	Fed. Withholding Allow.	1
	Brockport, NY 14420	State Withholding Allow.	1
SS#	111-11-1111		

	Earnings							Deductions									
Pay Period Ending	Regular Hours Worked	Regular Pay Rate	Regular Wages	Overtime Hours Worked	Overtime Pay Rate	Overtime Wages	Gross Pay	Federal Withholding Tax	State Withholding Tax	Social Security Tax	Medicare Tax	Retirement Contribution	Life Insurance	Charitable Contribution	Additional Withholding	Check Number	Net Pay
12/6/13	35	$ 11.50	$ 402.50	0	n/a	$ -	$ 402.50	$ 30.00	$ 18.52								

Employee Earnings Record

Name	Maryanne Sherman	Marital Status	Single
Address	8171 Winston Court	Fed. Withholding Allow.	2
	Rochester, NY 14604	State Withholding Allow.	1
SS#	222-22-2222		

	Earnings							Deductions									
Pay Period Ending	Regular Hours Worked	Regular Pay Rate	Regular Wages	Overtime Hours Worked	Overtime Pay Rate	Overtime Wages	Gross Pay	Federal Withholding Tax	State Withholding Tax	Social Security Tax	Medicare Tax	Retirement Contribution	Life Insurance	Charitable Contribution	Additional Withholding	Check Number	Net Pay
12/6/13	n/a	n/a	$ 769.23	0	n/a	$ -	$ 769.23	$ 77.00	$ 38.46								

Employee Earnings Record

Name	Bill Novak	Marital Status	Married
Address	536A North Yellow Lake Avenue	Fed. Withholding Allow.	4
	Hamlin, NY 14464	State Withholding Allow.	3
SS#	333-33-3333		

	Earnings							Deductions									
Pay Period Ending	Regular Hours Worked	Regular Pay Rate	Regular Wages	Overtime Hours Worked	Overtime Pay Rate	Overtime Wages	Gross Pay	Federal Withholding Tax	State Withholding Tax	Social Security Tax	Medicare Tax	Retirement Contribution	Life Insurance	Charitable Contribution	Additional Withholding	Check Number	Net Pay
12/6/13	40	$ 14.75	$ 590.00	6	$ 22.50	$ 135.00	$ 725.00	$ 23.00	$ 34.08								

Employee Earnings Record

Name	Angelo Dorsett	Marital Status	Single
Address	400 Hillside Court	Fed. Withholding Allow.	2
	Hilton, NY 14468	State Withholding Allow.	2
SS#	444-44-4444		

	Earnings							Deductions									
Pay Period Ending	Regular Hours Worked	Regular Pay Rate	Regular Wages	Overtime Hours Worked	Overtime Pay Rate	Overtime Wages	Gross Pay	Federal Withholding Tax	State Withholding Tax	Social Security Tax	Medicare Tax	Retirement Contribution	Life Insurance	Charitable Contribution	Additional Withholding	Check Number	Net Pay
12/6/13	40	$ 17.50	$ 700.00	7	$ 26.25	$ 183.75	$ 883.75	$ 82.00	$ 39.77								

Employee Earnings Record

Name	Melissa Kubiak	Marital Status	Married
Address	254 Cheesehead Drive	Fed. Withholding Allow.	5
	Pittsford, NY 14534	State Withholding Allow.	4
SS#	555-55-5555		

	Earnings							Deductions									
Pay Period Ending	Regular Hours Worked	Regular Pay Rate	Regular Wages	Overtime Hours Worked	Overtime Pay Rate	Overtime Wages	Gross Pay	Federal Withholding Tax	State Withholding Tax	Social Security Tax	Medicare Tax	Retirement Contribution	Life Insurance	Charitable Contribution	Additional Withholding	Check Number	Net Pay
12/6/13	40	$ 15.00	$ 600.00	1	$ 22.50	$ 22.50	$ 622.50	$ 9.00	$ 31.13								

Employee Earnings Record

Name	Stacie Martin	Marital Status	Married
Address	2 Lava Lane	Fed. Withholding Allow.	2
	Brockport, NY 14420	State Withholding Allow.	1
SS#	666-66-6666		

	Earnings							Deductions									
Pay Period Ending	Regular Hours Worked	Regular Pay Rate	Regular Wages	Overtime Hours Worked	Overtime Pay Rate	Overtime Wages	Gross Pay	Federal Withholding Tax	State Withholding Tax	Social Security Tax	Medicare Tax	Retirement Contribution	Life Insurance	Charitable Contribution	Additional Withholding	Check Number	Net Pay
12/6/13	40	$ 21.15	$ 846.00	11	$ 31.73	$ 349.03	$ 1,195.03	$ 116.00	$ 59.75								

Employee Earnings Record

Name	Lucy Marshall	Marital Status	Single
Address	232 Muscle Road	Fed. Withholding Allow.	3
	Hamlin, NY 14464	State Withholding Allow.	2
SS#	777-77-7777		

	Earnings							Deductions									
Pay Period Ending	Regular Hours Worked	Regular Pay Rate	Regular Wages	Overtime Hours Worked	Overtime Pay Rate	Overtime Wages	Gross Pay	Federal Withholding Tax	State Withholding Tax	Social Security Tax	Medicare Tax	Retirement Contribution	Life Insurance	Charitable Contribution	Additional Withholding	Check Number	Net Pay
12/6/13	40	$ 15.75	$ 630.00	9	$ 23.63	$ 212.67	$ 842.67	$ 68.00	$ 38.76								

Employee Earnings Record

Name	Donald McHenry	Marital Status	Married
Address	22 Iceberg Lane	Fed. Withholding Allow.	6
	Fairport, NY 14450	State Withholding Allow.	5
SS#	888-88-8888		

	Earnings							Deductions									
Pay Period Ending	Regular Hours Worked	Regular Pay Rate	Regular Wages	Overtime Hours Worked	Overtime Pay Rate	Overtime Wages	Gross Pay	Federal Withholding Tax	State Withholding Tax	Social Security Tax	Medicare Tax	Retirement Contribution	Life Insurance	Charitable Contribution	Additional Withholding	Check Number	Net Pay
12/6/13	40	$ 15.30	$ 612.00	5	$ 22.95	$ 114.75	$ 726.75	$ 12.00	$ 36.34								

As in the previous chapter, when transferring earnings amounts, all federal income tax withholding & state income tax withholding figures from the employee earnings records are now transferred to the payroll register. Totals for the two applicable columns are then calculated.

Payroll Register

Pay Period	12/6/2013
Pay Date	12/12/2013

Employee Name	Earnings							Deductions					Check Number	Net Pay
	Regular Hours	Regular Rate	Regular Earnings	Overtime Hours	Overtime Rate	Overtime Earnings	Total Earnings	FWT	SWT	Social Security	Medicare	Vol. With.		
Rogers, P	35	$ 11.50	$ 402.50	0	n/a	$ -	$ 402.50	$ 30.00	$ 18.52					
Sherman, M	n/a	n/a	$ 769.23	0	n/a	$ -	$ 769.23	$ 77.00	$ 38.46					
Novak, B	40	$ 14.75	$ 590.00	6	$ 22.50	$ 135.00	$ 725.00	$ 23.00	$ 34.08					
Dorsett, A	40	$ 17.50	$ 700.00	7	$ 26.25	$ 183.75	$ 883.75	$ 82.00	$ 39.77					
Kubiak, M	40	$ 15.00	$ 600.00	1	$ 22.50	$ 22.50	$ 622.50	$ 9.00	$ 31.13					
Martin, S	40	$ 21.15	$ 846.00	11	$ 31.73	$ 349.03	$ 1,195.03	$ 116.00	$ 59.75					
Marshall, L	40	$ 15.75	$ 630.00	9	$ 23.63	$ 212.67	$ 842.67	$ 68.00	$ 38.76					
McHenry, D	40	$ 15.30	$ 612.00	5	$ 22.95	$ 114.75	$ 726.75	$ 12.00	$ 36.34					
Totals:			$ 5,149.73			$ 1,017.70	$ 6,167.43	$ 417.00	$ 296.81					

Concepts Review

All of the Concepts Review quizzes for this book are also available in the Student Resource Center. Check with your instructor on how to complete the quizzes (in the book or online).

True/False Questions

1. State income tax withholding must be deducted from gross pay for employees of every state.   *True*   *False*

2. Social Security tax is subject to an income threshold, and therefore is only levied on an employee's wages until he/she has earned more than the threshold level in a single year.   *True*   *False*

3. Taxable pay used to calculate federal income tax withholding can differ from taxable pay used to calculate Social Security tax.   *True*   *False*

4. The current pay-as-you-go system of remitting federal income tax withholding was established by The Current Tax Payment Act of 1943.   *True*   *False*

5. Employees who are exempt from federal income tax withholding are only required to verbally inform their employer of this status.   *True*   *False*

6. The number of federal withholding allowances impacts the withholding amount calculated under the wage-bracket method, but not under the percentage method.   *True*   *False*

7. Employers who utilize quarterly pay periods must use the percentage method to determine federal income tax withholdings.   *True*   *False*

8. Employees are either subject to both federal and state income tax withholding, or to neither of these.   *True*   *False*

9. State income tax withholding calculations differ from one state to another.   *True*   *False*

10. Because not all employees are subject to local income tax withholding, this amount never appears in the payroll register.   *True*   *False*

Multiple Choice Questions

1. Which of the following is not a mandatory deduction from gross pay?
   a. Federal income tax withholding
   b. Union dues
   c. Social Security tax
   d. Medicare tax

2. Which of the following was not a result of The Current Tax Payment Act of 1943?
   a. Use of a pay-as-you-go system
   b. Requirement that taxes no longer be paid in the year after the associated taxable pay is earned
   c. Employer withholding of federal income tax
   d. One increased federal income tax withholding rate that was consistent for all employees.

3. Which of the following is not a withholding table available for use with the wage-bracket method of calculating federal income tax withholding?
   a. Married; Biweekly
   b. Single; Semimonthly
   c. Single; Daily
   d. Married; Semiannually

4. Under the wage-bracket method, what would the federal income tax withholding be for a married employee with three federal withholding allowances, who has weekly taxable earnings of $786?
   a. $2
   b. $26
   c. $43
   d. $69

5. For which of the following employees may the wage-bracket method not be used?
   a. A single employee claims 6 withholding allowances, and earns weekly pay of $1,047.
   b. A married employee claims 11 withholding allowances, and earns monthly pay of $4,275.
   c. A single employee claims 4 withholding allowances, and earns biweekly pay of $1,320.
   d. A married employee claims 9 withholding allowances, and earns semimonthly pay of $2,950.

6. Which of the following employees is subject to federal income tax withholding of $0 for the specified period?
   a. A married employee claims 2 withholding allowances, and earns weekly pay of $324.
   b. A single employee claims 1 withholding allowance, and earns weekly pay of $40.
   c. A married employee claims 3 withholding allowances, and earns weekly pay of $421.
   d. A single employee claims 2 withholding allowances, and earns weekly pay of $232.

7. Under the percentage method, what is the federal income tax withholding for a single employee with two federal withholding allowances, who has biweekly taxable pay of $862?
   a. $24.30
   b. $54.40
   c. $69.40
   d. $76.90

8. When an employee gets a divorce, how many days does he/she have to file a new W-4 Form with his/her employer?
   a. 10
   b. 30
   c. 45
   d. Unlimited

9. Which of the following statements about state income tax withholding is inaccurate?
   a. State income tax withholding is not levied in all 50 states.
   b. Some states charge higher state income tax withholding to employees with high earnings, as compared with employees whose earnings are smaller.
   c. State income tax withholding cannot be levied on an employee who is subject to local income tax withholding.
   d. For those states that levy a flat state income tax withholding, the applicable rate varies from state to state.

10. Which of the following is not considered a municipality from which local income tax withholding could be levied?
    a. West Virginia
    b. Manhattan
    c. San Francisco
    d. Yonkers

Knowledge Check A

For all assignments in this section, necessary IRS forms and/or Excel templates are located in the Student Resource Center.

KCa 3-1 Identify Deductions

For each of the deductions listed, indicate whether it is a mandatory deduction or a voluntary deduction.

1. Medicare tax

2. State Income Tax Withholding

3. Union dues

4. Federal income tax withholding

5. Medical plans

KCa 3-2 Calculate Gross Pay & Taxable Pay

For each employee, first calculate gross pay. Then determine taxable income used to calculate federal income tax withholding, Social Security tax, and Medicare tax.

1. An employee works 47 hours (7 were overtime hours) during a workweek in December of 2013. The employee earns $39/hour, with his employer paying 1.5 times the regular rate of pay for overtime hours. To date, he has earned $111,850 during the year. He has requested that his employer withhold 6% of gross pay, which is to be contributed to a 401(k) plan.

2. An employee works 39 regular hours during a workweek in August of 2013. The employee earns a salary of $115,000/year, and is exempt from the overtime provisions of the FLSA. To date, he has received no compensation beyond his annual salary. He has requested that his employer withhold 12% of gross pay, which is to be contributed to a 403(b) plan.

3. An employee works 51 hours (11 were overtime hours) during a workweek in December of 2013. The employee earns $10,000/month, with his employer paying 1.5 times the regular rate of pay for overtime hours. To date, he has earned $117,200 during the year. He has requested that his employer withhold 9% of gross pay, which is to be contributed to a 401(k) plan.

KCa 3-3 Calculate Federal Income Tax Withholding Using the Wage-Bracket Method

Refer to Appendix A, 2013 Federal Tax Tables

For each employee listed, use the wage-bracket method to calculate federal income tax withholding.

1. Sam Coleridge (married; 4 federal withholding allowances) earned weekly gross pay of $565. For each period, he makes a 403(b) retirement plan contribution of 5% of gross pay.

2. Michael Kolk (single; 2 federal withholding allowances) earned biweekly gross pay of $975. He participates in a flexible spending account, to which he contributes $100 during the period.

3. Anita McLachlan (single; 0 federal withholding allowances) earned monthly gross pay of $2,440. For each period, she makes a 401(k) contribution of 9% of gross pay.

4. Stacey Williamson (married; 3 federal withholding allowances) earned semimonthly gross pay of $1,250. She participates in a cafeteria plan, to which she contributes $150 during the period.

KCa 3-4 Calculate Federal Income Tax Withholding Using the Percentage Method

Refer to Appendix A, 2013 Federal Tax Tables

For each employee listed, use the percentage method to calculate federal income tax withholding.

1. Billy Rainer (married; 5 federal withholding allowances) earned weekly gross pay of $602. For each period, he makes a 403(b) retirement plan contribution of 7% of gross pay.

2. Angel Rodriguez (married; 4 federal withholding allowances) earned biweekly gross pay of $1,020. He participates in a flexible spending account, to which he contributes $50 during the period.

3. Julie Smithers (single; 2 federal withholding allowances) earned monthly gross pay of $2,170. For each period, she makes a 401(k) contribution of 10% of gross pay.

4. Anna Marquez (single; 0 federal withholding allowances) earned semimonthly gross pay of $1,700. She participates in a cafeteria plan, to which she contributes $110 during the period.

KCa 3-5 Calculate Federal Income Tax Withholding Using Two Methods

Refer to Appendix A, 2013 Federal Tax Tables

For each employee listed, use both the wage-bracket method, and the percentage method to calculate federal income tax withholding. Show all work for each method.

1. Thomas Fortuna (married; 6 federal withholding allowances) earned weekly gross pay of $745. For each period, he makes a 401(k) retirement plan contribution of 10% of gross pay.

2. Barbara Houlihan (single; 1 federal withholding allowance) earned daily gross pay of $320. For each period, she makes a 401(k) contribution of 12% of gross pay.

3. Marcus Xavier (married; 5 federal withholding allowances) earned monthly gross pay of $3,650. He participates in a flexible spending account, to which he contributes $200 during the period.

KCa 3-6 Calculate Federal (Wage-Bracket Method), State, and Local Income Tax Withholding

Refer to Appendix A, 2013 Federal Tax Tables

For each employee listed, use the wage-bracket method to calculate federal income tax withholding. Then calculate both the state income tax withholding (assuming a state tax rate of 5% of taxable pay, with taxable pay being the same for federal & state income tax withholding), and the local income tax withholding.

1. Paul Bronson (single; 1 federal withholding allowance) earned weekly gross pay of $1,247. For each period, he makes a 401(k) retirement plan contribution of 10% of gross pay. The city in which he works (he lives elsewhere) levies a tax of 1.5% of an employee's taxable pay (which is the same for federal & local income tax withholding) on residents, and 0.8% of an employee's taxable pay on non-residents.

2. Stephen McPherson (married; 5 federal withholding allowances) earned weekly gross pay of $980. He participates in a flexible spending account, to which he contributes $75 during the period. The city in which he lives and works levies a tax of 2.3% of an employee's taxable pay (which is the same for federal & local income tax withholding) on residents, and 1.6% of an employee's taxable pay on non-residents.

3. Tyler Howard (married; 4 federal withholding allowances) earned weekly gross pay of $1,310. For each period, he makes a 403(b) retirement plan contribution of 7% of gross pay. The city in which he lives and works levies a tax of 1.4% of an employee's taxable pay (which is the same for federal & local income tax withholding) on both residents and non-residents.

4. Alejandro Garcia (single; 3 federal withholding allowances) earned weekly gross pay of $1,110. He participates in a cafeteria plan, to which he pays $50 during the period. The city in which he works levies a tax of $12/week on employees who work within city limits.

KCa 3-7 Calculate Federal (Percentage Method), State, and Local Income Tax Withholding

Refer to Appendix A, 2013 Federal Tax Tables

For each employee listed, use the percentage method to calculate federal income tax withholding. Then calculate both the state income tax withholding (assuming a state tax rate of 5% of taxable pay, with taxable pay being the same for federal & state income tax withholding), and the local income tax withholding.

1. Walter Ferrell (married; 4 federal withholding allowances) earned weekly gross pay of $1,030. For each period, he makes a 401(k) retirement plan contribution of 14% of gross pay. The city in which he works (he lives elsewhere) levies a tax of 1.3% of an employee's taxable pay (which is the same for federal & local income tax withholding) on residents, and 1.1% of an employee's taxable pay on non-residents.

2. Lucas Sedaris (married; 3 federal withholding allowances) earned weekly gross pay of $2,800. He participates in a flexible spending account, to which he contributes $150 during the period. The city in which he lives and works levies a tax of 3.1% of an employee's taxable pay (which is the same for federal & local income tax withholding) on residents, and 2.4% of an employee's taxable pay on non-residents.

3. Darrell Roper (married; 6 federal withholding allowances) earned weekly gross pay of $1,540. He does not request that any voluntary deductions be made from his gross pay. The city in which he lives and works levies a tax of 2.5% of an employee's taxable pay (which is the same for federal & local income tax withholding) on both residents and non-residents.

4. Giuseppe Fortuna (single; 2 federal withholding allowances) earned weekly gross pay of $3,820. He participates in a cafeteria plan, to which he pays $175 during the period. The city in which he works levies a tax of $13/week on employees who work within city limits.

KCa 3-8 Populate Employee Earnings Record

This problem is a continuation of exercise KCa 2-12 from Chapter 2.

Complete the federal withholding tax (wage-bracket method) and state withholding tax columns of the employee earnings record for the five employees whose information was provided in KCa 2-4 & KCa 2-12. The state income tax withholding rate is 5% of taxable pay, with taxable pay being the same for federal & state income tax withholding. Additional information for each employee is provided below.

*   Luisa Williams makes a 401(k) retirement plan contribution of 14% of gross pay each period.
*   Jonathan Olsen participates in a cafeteria plan, to which he pays $100 each period.
*   Nathan Upton does not make any voluntary deductions each period.
*   Juan Rodriguez makes a 403(b) retirement plan contribution of 13% of gross pay.
*   Drew Painter participates in a flexible spending account, to which he contributes $50 each period.

KCa 3-9 Populate a Payroll Register

This problem is a continuation of exercise KCa 2-13 from Chapter 2.

Complete the federal income tax withholding (FWT) and state income tax withholding (SWT) columns of the payroll register for the five employees from KCa 3-8. The Earnings section of the payroll register was previously completed in KCa 2-13.

Knowledge Check B

For all assignments in this section, necessary IRS forms and/or Excel templates are located in the Student Resource Center.

KCb 3-1 Identify Deductions

For each of the deductions listed, indicate whether it is a mandatory deduction or a voluntary deduction.

1. Cafeteria plans

2. Social Security tax

3. State Disability Insurance

4. Local income tax withholding

5. Retirement plans

KCb 3-2 Calculate Gross Pay & Taxable Pay

For each employee, first calculate gross pay. Then determine taxable income used to calculate federal income tax withholding, Social Security tax, and Medicare tax.

1. An employee works 42 hours (2 were overtime hours) during a workweek in December of 2013. He earns $40.50/hour, with his employer paying 1.5 times the regular rate of pay for overtime hours. To date, he has earned $113,100 during the year. He has requested that his employer withhold 7% of gross pay to contribute to a 403(b) plan.

2. An employee works 37 regular hours during a workweek in August of 2013. He earns a salary of $125,000/year, and is exempt from the overtime provisions of the FLSA. To date, he has received no compensation beyond his annual salary. He has requested that his employer withhold 8% of gross pay to contribute to a 401(k) plan.

3. An employee works 50 hours (10 of which were overtime hours) during a workweek in December of 2013. He earns $9,500/month, with his employer paying 1.5 times the regular rate of pay for overtime hours. To date, he has earned $108,200 during the year. He has requested that his employer withhold 13% of gross pay to contribute to a 403(b) plan.

KCb 3-3 Calculate Federal Income Tax Withholding Using the Wage-Bracket Method

Refer to Appendix A, 2013 Federal Tax Tables

For each employee listed, use the wage-bracket method to calculate federal income tax withholding.

1. Paul Yount (married; 7 federal withholding allowances) earned weekly gross pay of $605. For each period, he contributes 7% of gross pay to a 403(b) retirement plan.

2. Paulina Robinson (single; 3 federal withholding allowances) earned biweekly gross pay of $1,245. She contributes $75 to a flexible spending account during the period.

3. Lacey Kunis (single; 2 federal withholding allowances) earned monthly gross pay of $3,090. For each period, she makes a 401(k) contribution of 11% of gross pay.

4. Francine Stewart (married; 4 federal withholding allowances) earned semimonthly gross pay of $1,420. She contributes $125 to a cafeteria plan during the period.

KCb 3-4 Calculate Federal Income Tax Withholding Using the Percentage Method

Refer to Appendix A, 2013 Federal Tax Tables

For each employee listed, use the percentage method to calculate federal income tax withholding.

1. Juan Hoffman (single; 2 federal withholding allowances) earned weekly gross pay of $445. For each period, he makes a 403(b) retirement plan contribution of 5% of gross pay.

2. William Harrison (single; 1 federal withholding allowance) earned biweekly gross pay of $990. He contributes $75 to a flexible spending account during the period.

3. Loretta Goulet (married; 3 federal withholding allowances) earned monthly gross pay of $2,800. For each period, she makes a 401(k) contribution of 14% of gross pay.

4. Louise Simpson (married; 10 federal withholding allowances) earned semimonthly gross pay of $2,300. She contributes $100 to a cafeteria plan during the period.

KCb 3-5 Calculate Federal Income Tax Withholding Using Two Methods

Refer to Appendix A, 2013 Federal Tax Tables

For each employee listed, use both the wage-bracket method, and the percentage method to calculate federal income tax withholding. Show all work for each method.

1. Warren Cavanagh (single; 0 federal withholding allowances) earned weekly gross pay of $620. For each period, he makes a 401(k) retirement plan contribution of 5% of gross pay.

2. Stacey Vaughn (married; 4 federal withholding allowances) earned daily gross pay of $275. For each period, she makes a 401(k) contribution of 8% of gross pay.

3. Jordan Peters (single; 3 federal withholding allowances) earned monthly gross pay of $3,300. He contributes $150 to a flexible spending account, during the period.

KCb 3-6 Calculate Federal (Wage-Bracket Method), State, and Local Income Tax Withholding

Refer to Appendix A, 2013 Federal Tax Tables

For each employee listed, use the wage-bracket method to calculate federal withholding tax. Then calculate both the state withholding tax (assuming a state tax rate of 5% of taxable pay, with taxable pay being the same for federal & state income tax withholding), and the local withholding tax.

1. Jay Monroe (single; 2 federal withholding allowances) earned weekly gross pay of $1,145. For each period, he makes a 401(k) retirement plan contribution of 12% of gross pay. The city in which he works (he lives elsewhere) levies a tax of 2% of an employee's taxable pay (which is the same for federal & local income tax withholding) on residents, and 1.7% of an employee's taxable pay on non-residents.

2. Gus Damon (married; 9 federal withholding allowances) earned weekly gross pay of $1,200. He contributes $125 to a flexible spending account during the period. The city in which he lives and works levies a tax of 3% of an employee's taxable pay (which is the same for federal & local income tax withholding) on residents, and 0.4% of an employee's taxable pay on non-residents.

3. Kenneth Riley (single; 0 federal withholding allowances) earned weekly gross pay of $1,000. For each period, he makes a 403(b) retirement plan contribution of 5% of gross pay. The city in which he lives and works levies a tax of 1.7% of an employee's taxable pay (which is the same for federal & local income tax withholding) on both residents and non-residents.

4. Ross McMichael (married; 2 federal withholding allowances) earned weekly gross pay of $970. He pays $60 to a cafeteria plan during the period. The city in which he works levies a tax of $8/week on employees who work within city limits.

KCb 3-7 Calculate Federal (Percentage Method), State, and Local Income Tax Withholding

Refer to Appendix A, 2013 Federal Tax Tables

For each employee listed, use the percentage method to calculate federal income tax withholding. Then calculate both the state income tax withholding (assuming a state tax rate of 5% of taxable pay, with taxable pay being the same for federal & state income tax withholding), and the local income tax withholding.

1. Armand Giroux (single; 0 federal withholding allowances) earned weekly gross pay of $1,500. For each period, he makes a 401(k) retirement plan contribution of 8% of gross pay. The city in which he works (he lives elsewhere) levies a tax of 1% of an employee's taxable pay (which is the same for federal & local income tax withholding) on residents, and 0.6% of an employee's taxable pay on non-residents.

2. Peter Quigley (married; 8 federal withholding allowances) earned weekly gross pay of $2,350. He contributes $100 to a flexible spending account during the period. The city in which he lives and works levies a tax of 2.7% of an employee's taxable pay (which is the same for federal & local income tax withholding) on residents, and 1.9% of an employee's taxable pay on non-residents.

3. Eric Belanger (married; 4 federal withholding allowances) earned weekly gross pay of $1,275. He does not request that any voluntary deductions be made from his gross pay. The city in which he lives and works levies a tax of 1.5% of an employee's taxable pay (which is the same for federal & local income tax withholding) on both residents and non-residents.

4. Christopher Martin (single; 4 federal withholding allowances) earned weekly gross pay of $2,780. He pays $85 to a cafeteria plan during the period. The city in which he works levies a tax of $7/week on employees who work within city limits.

KCb 3-8 Populate Employee Earnings Record

This problem is a continuation of exercise KCb 2-12 from Chapter 2.

Complete the federal withholding tax (wage-bracket method) and state withholding tax columns of the employee earnings record for the five employees whose information was provided in KCb 2-4 & KCb 2-12. Note that the state income tax withholding rate is 5% of taxable pay, with taxable pay being the same for federal & state income tax withholding. Additional information for each employee is provided below.

- Jimmy Troffa makes a 401(k) retirement plan contribution of 9% of gross pay each period.
- Tyler Thomas pays $75 to a cafeteria plan during each period.
- Ryan Brown does not make any voluntary deductions each period.
- Michael Kaminski makes a 403(b) retirement plan contribution of 10% of gross pay.
- Tina Baldwin contributes $110 to a flexible spending account each period.

KCb 3-9 Populate a Payroll Register

This problem is a continuation of exercise KCb 2-13 from Chapter 2.

Complete the federal income tax withholding (FWT) and state income tax withholding (SWT) columns of the payroll register for the five employees from KCb 3-8. Note that the Earnings section of the payroll register was previously completed in KCb 2-13.

Continuing Payroll Problem

For all assignments in this section, necessary IRS forms and/or Excel templates are located in the Student Resource Center.

CPP 3-1 Calculating & Documenting Federal & State Income Tax Withholding

Calculate federal (wage-bracket method) and state income tax withholding for a number of employees of TCLH Industries, a manufacturer of cleaning products. We assume the state income tax withholding rate to be 5% of taxable pay (which is the same for federal & state income tax withholding). Then, continue to fill out the employee earnings records and the payroll register based on your calculations.

1. Calculate the federal and state income tax withholdings for each employee, based on information from the prior chapters' Continuing Payroll Problem, as well as the following:

   • Zachary Fox does not make any voluntary deductions that impact earnings subject to federal income tax withholding.

   • Calvin Bell makes a 401(k) retirement plan contribution of 6% of gross pay,

   • Michaela Walton makes a 401(k) retirement plan contribution of 12% of gross pay.

   • Suzanne Steinberg contributes $50 to a flexible spending account each period.

2. Complete the federal and state withholding tax columns of the employee earnings record (which you established during an earlier Continuing Payroll Problem) for each of the four employees of TCLH Industries.

3. Lastly, complete the federal (FWT) and state (SWT) income tax withholding columns of the payroll register of TCLH Industries.

Critical Thinking

CT 3-1 Investigate Federal Withholding Allowances

As you have seen, the number of federal withholding allowances claimed by an employee has a significant impact on the amount of federal income tax withheld from each paycheck. In Chapter 1 you examined the W-4 Form, and learned that an employee claims his/her desired number of federal withholding allowances on this form. But how does an employee determine the optimal number of allowances? While the Personal Allowances Worksheet, which you reviewed in Chapter 1, provides guidance on this topic, an employee may still choose to alter the suggested number of allowances from this worksheet. In this exercise, we will use the internet to research common reasons why employees may choose to either increase or decrease the number of allowances claimed.

Begin by researching different reasons why an employee may choose to alter his/her number of federal withholding allowances. Next, write a paragraph of at least five sentences, in which you identify and discuss the two most compelling reasons you identified for reducing the number of allowances. Then, write a second paragraph of at least five sentences, in which you identify and discuss the two most compelling reasons you identified for increasing the number of allowances.

Submit your final file based on the guidelines provided by your instructor.

CT 3-2 Examine State Income Tax Withholding

Earlier you learned that, as of 2013, nine states do not levy state income tax withholdings on their residents. Two of these (New Hampshire & Tennessee) collect tax on dividend and interest income, but how do the other seven states (Alaska, Florida, Nevada, South Dakota, Texas, Washington, and Wyoming) raise funds to run governmental operations? In this exercise, we will use the internet to research the manner in which some of these states generate revenues.

Select three of the seven states listed above to research. If you either live or work in one of these states, include it in your selection. Use the internet to research the alternative methods utilized by these states to generate funds. These may include different tax types, state-specific revenue-generating activities, or other methods. For each state, write a paragraph of at least four sentences in which you discuss the manner in which these funds are raised.

Submit your final file based on the guidelines provided by your instructor.

FICA Taxes and Voluntary Deductions

LEARNING OBJECTIVES

After studying this chapter, you will be able to:

- Calculate Social Security tax

- Calculate Medicare tax

- Identify states in which State Disability Insurance is withheld

- Apply various voluntary deductions

- Record employee payroll journal entries

Having calculated federal and state tax withholdings in the last chapter, you're now ready to examine the remaining mandatory deductions from gross earnings. These include Social Security tax and Medicare tax, which are collectively referred to as FICA taxes. In this chapter, you'll review the purpose and application of FICA taxes. You'll also examine state disability insurance and voluntary deductions in detail. After completing the employee earnings record and payroll register, you'll conclude by examining the journal entries related to the deductions examined in Chapter 3 and Chapter 4.

CASE STUDY

Determining FICA Taxes & Voluntary Deductions for Lucky Ties Apparel

After having deducted federal & state income tax withholding from employee earnings, Lucky Ties Apparel must then calculate further deductions. FICA taxes include Social Security & Medicare tax, both of which must be withheld from employee pay. While the applicable rates for these taxes are the same for each employee, there is an annual per-employee ceiling on Social Security taxes that must be taken into consideration.

To complete your understanding of employee deductions, you review both Social Security and Medicare tax. You then examine State Disability Insurance (which is only applicable in some states), and further review a number of voluntary deductions. After including these tax calculations in both the employee earnings record and the payroll register, you finish by reviewing the required journal entry to account for both deductions and net pay.

Social Security & Medicare taxes are mandatory for all employees, while State Disability Insurance & voluntary deductions are also withheld for some employees.

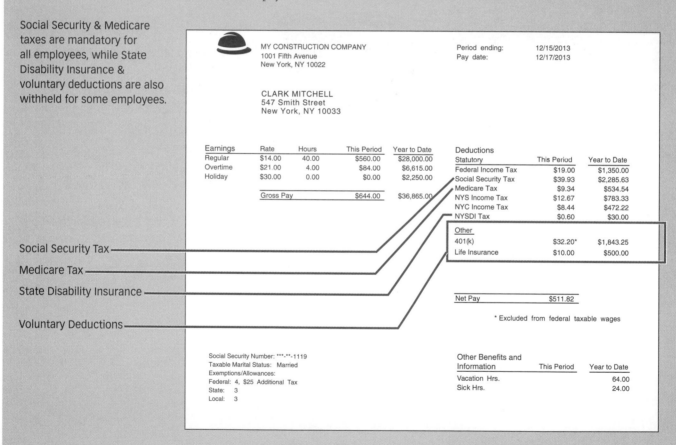

MY CONSTRUCTION COMPANY
1001 Fifth Avenue
New York, NY 10022

Period ending: 12/15/2013
Pay date: 12/17/2013

CLARK MITCHELL
547 Smith Street
New York, NY 10033

Earnings	Rate	Hours	This Period	Year to Date
Regular	$14.00	40.00	$560.00	$28,000.00
Overtime	$21.00	4.00	$84.00	$6,615.00
Holiday	$30.00	0.00	$0.00	$2,250.00
Gross Pay			$644.00	$36,865.00

Deductions		
Statutory	This Period	Year to Date
Federal Income Tax	$19.00	$1,350.00
Social Security Tax	$39.93	$2,285.63
Medicare Tax	$9.34	$534.54
NYS Income Tax	$12.67	$783.33
NYC Income Tax	$8.44	$472.22
NYSDI Tax	$0.60	$30.00
Other		
401(k)	$32.20*	$1,843.25
Life Insurance	$10.00	$500.00

Social Security Tax

Medicare Tax

State Disability Insurance

Voluntary Deductions

Net Pay	$511.82

* Excluded from federal taxable wages

Social Security Number: ***-**-1119
Taxable Marital Status: Married
Exemptions/Allowances:
Federal: 4, $25 Additional Tax
State: 3
Local: 3

Other Benefits and Information	This Period	Year to Date
Vacation Hrs.		64.00
Sick Hrs.		24.00

Computing the Social Security Tax

Also referred to as OASDI (old age, survivors, and disability insurance), Social Security tax was initially established to provide employees with retirement benefits. Over time the program was expanded to provide financial support to the employee's survivors, and to disabled employees.

Initially, the Social Security tax rate was 1% of taxable earnings. This rate was in place from 1937-1949, after which it has steadily increased over the years. A number of credits have, for certain years, been passed into law, and have reduced the effective Social Security tax rate remitted on the employee's behalf. The most recent tax rates (before taking these credits into account) are shown here.

Year(s)	Social Security Tax Rate	Year(s)	Social Security Tax Rate
1974 – 1977	4.95%	1982 – 1983	5.40%
1978	5.05%	1984 – 1987	5.70%
1979 – 1980	5.08%	1988 – 1989	6.06%
1981	5.35%	1990 – 2013	6.20%

NOTE!   Whereas employees are permitted to increase federal & state income tax withholdings by a set amount each pay period, this is neither necessary nor permissible for Social Security tax.

Applying the Social Security Taxable Wage Base

Aside from the applicable Social Security tax rate, which is presently 6.2%, you must also consider the earnings threshold over which Social Security tax is not levied. Once an employee's year-to-date taxable earnings reaches this threshold (referred to as the Social Security Taxable Wage Base), no further Social Security tax is withheld until the beginning of the following year. The result is that no Social Security tax is paid by the employee after he/she earns a specified amount during the year. From 1937-1950, the first taxable wage base was $3,000. Therefore, Social Security tax was levied on the first $3,000 earned by each employee during these years. Annual earnings above $3,000 for each employee were not subject to the tax. Similar to the

Social Security tax rate, the taxable wage base has increased steadily since that time. As of 2013, the applicable taxable wage base is $113,700.

Year(s)	Social Security Taxable Wage Base	Year(s)	Social Security Taxable Wage Base
2002	$84,900	2007	$97,500
2003	$87,000	2008	$102,000
2004	$87,900	2009 – 2011	$106,800
2005	$90,000	2012	$110,100
2006	$94,200	2013	$113,700

Determining Taxable Earnings for Social Security Tax

Similar to the taxable earnings for federal & state income tax withholding, taxable earnings for Social Security tax also exclude certain portions of gross pay. Among those amounts that must be subtracted from gross pay to arrive at taxable earnings for Social Security tax are those deducted for Cafeteria Plans (including flexible spending accounts, such as those for dependent-care expenses).

WARNING!   Retirement plan contributions (such as those for 401(k) and 403(b) Plans) are taxable for Social Security tax and should not be subtracted from gross pay when calculating taxable earnings for Social Security tax.

Calculating Social Security Tax

To calculate an employee's Social Security tax, the employer must undertake a four-step process, outlined below.

Step #1   Determine current period taxable earnings for Social Security tax

Step #2   Add the step #1 result to the year-to-date taxable earnings for Social Security tax

Step #3   • If the step #2 result exceeds the taxable wage base, determine the amount by which it is higher and subtract this amount from the step #1 result. Your new amount (if it is positive) is used to determine Social Security tax in step #4 (a negative result indicates that $0 should be used in step #4).

• If the step #2 result does not exceed the taxable wage base, use the step #1 result when determining Social Security tax in step #4.

Step #4   Multiply the current 6.2% tax rate by the step #3 result.

| Case In Point 4-1 | # Calculate Social Security Tax |

For each of the following employees of Lucky Ties Apparel, we'll calculate the Social Security tax for the current weekly pay period.

1. Paul Rogers earned gross pay of $402.50. Each period he makes a 401(k) contribution of 8% of gross pay. His current year taxable earnings for Social Security tax, to date, are $82,400.

   Step 1: Here, taxable earnings for Social Security tax are the same as gross pay. The only voluntary deduction is the retirement plan, which is taxable for the purposes of Social Security. Therefore, the current period taxable earnings are $402.50.

   Step 2: When the current period taxable earnings of $402.50 are added to the year-to-date earnings of $82,400, the result is $82,802.50.

   Step 3: The step 2 result does not exceed the taxable wage base of $113,700, and therefore all of the current week's taxable earnings of $402.50 (the step 1 result) are subject to Social Security tax.

   Step 4: The Social Security tax for this employee is $24.96 ($402.50 current period taxable earnings x 6.2% Social Security tax rate).

2. Maryanne Sherman earned gross pay of $769.23. She does not make any retirement plan contributions. Her current year taxable earnings for Social Security tax, to date, are $119,850.

   Step 1: Here, taxable earnings for Social Security tax are the same as gross pay. There are no voluntary deductions that would reduce taxable earnings for Social Security tax. Therefore, the current period taxable earnings are $769.23.

   Step 2: When the current period taxable earnings of $769.23 are added to the year-to-date earnings of $119,850, the result is $120,619.23.

   Step 3: The step 2 result exceeds the taxable wage base by $6,919.23 (step 2 result of $120,619.23 – taxable wage base of $113,700). When subtracted from the current period taxable earnings of $769.23, the result is –$6,150. Because the wage base was exceeded before adding any of the current week's earnings, we arrive here at a negative result. We therefore utilize $0 in step 4, as none of the current period earnings are subject to Social Security tax.

   Step 4: The Social Security tax for this employee is $0 ($0 current period taxable earnings x 6.2% Social Security tax rate).

3. Bill Novak earned gross pay of $725. Each period he contributes 6% of gross pay to a flexible spending account. His current year taxable earnings for Social Security tax, to date, are $113,000.

   Step 1: Here, taxable earnings for Social Security tax are less than gross pay. The employee contributes $43.50 ($725 gross pay x 6% rate) to a flexible spending account. This amount is not taxable for Social Security tax, and therefore taxable earnings are $681.50 ($725 gross pay minus $43.50 non-taxable portion).

   Step 2: When the current period taxable earnings of $681.50 are added to the year-to-date earnings of $113,000, the result is $113,681.50.

   Step 3: The step 2 result does not exceed the taxable wage base of $113,700, and therefore all of the current week's taxable earnings of $681.50 (the step 1 result) are subject to Social Security tax.

   Step 4: The Social Security tax for this employee is $42.25 ($681.50 current period taxable earnings x 6.2% Social Security tax rate).

4. Angelo Dorsett earned gross pay of $883.75. Each period he designates 10% of gross pay for a dependent-care flexible spending account. His current year taxable earnings for Social Security tax, to date, are $113,600.

   Step 1: Here, taxable earnings for Social Security tax are less than gross pay. The employee designates $88.38 ($883.75 gross pay x 10% rate) for a dependent-care flexible spending account. This amount is not taxable for Social Security tax, and therefore taxable earnings are $795.37 ($883.75 gross pay minus $88.38 non-taxable portion).

   Step 2: When the current period taxable earnings of $795.37 are added to the year-to-date earnings of $113,600, the result is $114,395.37.

   Step 3: The step 2 result exceeds the taxable wage base by $695.37 (step 2 result of $114,395.37 minus taxable wage base of $113,700). When subtracted from the current period taxable earnings of $795.37, the result is $100. We therefore utilize $100 in step 4, as this is the only portion of current period earnings that are subject to Social Security tax.

   Step 4: The Social Security tax for this employee is $6.20 ($100 current period taxable earnings x 6.2% Social Security tax rate).

Computing the Medicare Tax

Also referred to as HI (hospital insurance), Medicare tax funds health care coverage for individuals 65 or older. Taxable earnings for Medicare tax are the same as Social Security tax.

TIP! Because they are both mandated under the Federal Insurance Contributions Act, Social Security tax and Medicare tax are collectively referred to as FICA taxes.

Initially, the Medicare tax rate was 0.35% of taxable earnings. This rate was in place in 1966, after which it increased repeatedly before reaching the current rate of 1.45%. A complete history of Medicare tax rates is shown here.

Year(s)	Medicare Tax Rate	Year(s)	Medicare Tax Rate
1966	0.35%	1978	1.00%
1967	0.50%	1979 – 1980	1.05%
1968 – 1972	0.60%	1981 – 1984	1.30%
1973	1.00%	1985	1.35%
1974 – 1977	0.90%	1986 – 2013	1.45%

Determining the Additional Medicare Tax

Beginning in 2013, an additional Medicare tax of 0.9% is imposed on individuals whose earnings exceed specified levels. This tax was implemented as a result of the Patient Protection and Affordable Care Act, which was signed into law in 2010. The extra revenue generated by the additional Medicare tax is designed to fund the expanded health care coverage that is provided through this legislation.

The income threshold over which additional Medicare tax is levied is based on an individual's filing status. The filing status that an individual elects on his/her year-end tax return, while primarily impacted by their marital status, can be influenced by other factors (such as a desire to file separately from one's spouse, or the payment of at least half of the cost of keeping up a home for an unmarried individual). The applicable thresholds for additional Medicare tax are shown here.

Filing Status	Earnings Threshold
Single/Head of Household/Qualifying Widower	$200,000
Married filing jointly	$250,000
Married filing separately	$125,000

WARNING!   Unlike for Social Security tax, there is no upper earnings limit above which Medicare tax is not levied. All employee earnings are subject to standard Medicare tax, while additional Medicare tax is also levied on high-income individuals.

During the pay period in which an employee reaches the additional Medicare tax threshold, only the portion of taxable earnings that exceeds the threshold is subject to the additional Medicare tax rate.

Case In Point 4-2	**Calculating Medicare Tax**

For each of the following employees, we will calculate the Medicare tax for the current weekly pay period.

1. Beverly Itzin's filing status is married filing jointly, and she has earned gross pay of $3,525. Each period she makes a 401(k) contribution of 8% of gross pay, and contributes $100 to a flexible spending account. Her current year taxable earnings for Medicare tax, to date, are $122,400.

   Beverly's taxable earnings for Medicare tax do not include her contribution to the flexible spending account, and therefore are $3,425 ($3,525 gross pay minus $100 flexible spending account contribution). The 401(k) payment is fully taxable for Medicare tax. She has not yet reached the earnings threshold over which the additional Medicare tax is assessed, so her Medicare tax is $49.66 ($3,425 taxable earnings x 1.45% Medicare tax rate).

2. Willard Poe's filing status is single, and he has earned gross pay of $4,100. Each period he makes a 403(b) contribution of 10% of gross pay, and contributes $200 to a cafeteria plan. His current year taxable earnings for Medicare tax, to date, are $207,400.

   Willard's taxable earnings for Medicare tax do not include his contribution to the cafeteria plan, and therefore are $3,900 ($4,100 gross pay – $200 cafeteria plan contribution). Note that the 403(b) payment is fully taxable for Medicare tax. He has reached the earnings threshold of $200,000 for a single taxpayer, and therefore additional Medicare tax is assessed on these earnings. The total Medicare tax rate on these earnings is 2.35% (1.45% standard tax rate + 0.90% additional tax rate). Therefore, his resulting Medicare tax is $91.65 ($3,900 taxable earnings x 2.35% total Medicare tax rate).

3. Yelena Phillips' filing status is single, and she has earned gross pay of $2,000. Her current year taxable earnings for Medicare tax, to date, are $199,600

   Yelena reached the $200,000 earnings threshold during the current period. The portion of her earnings that does not exceed the threshold is $400 ($200,000 threshold minus $199,600 earnings to date), while the portion of her earnings that does exceed the threshold is $1,600 ($2,000 gross pay minus $400 portion not exceeding threshold). While $400 is only subject to Medicare tax of 1.45%, $1,600 is subject to additional Medicare tax (2.35% rate). Therefore, total Medicare tax owed is $43.40 ($400 x 1.45% + $1,600 x 2.35%).

Exploring Additional Withholding Tax Considerations

Aside from the mandatory deductions that you have examined thus far, there are a wide variety of other amounts that may be withheld from gross pay. Among these are state disability insurance, wage garnishment, retirement plans, cafeteria plans, union dues, and charitable contributions.

Withholding State Disability Insurance

Disability insurance programs provide short-term benefits to employees who are unable to work as a result of an off-the-job circumstance. Presently there are five states (California, Hawaii, New Jersey, New York, and Rhode Island), as well as the commonwealth of Puerto Rico, that require employers to carry disability insurance for their employees. Depending on each state's regulations, employees may be required to contribute toward the insurance coverage through payroll withholding. For example, in New York State an employer may require that 0.5% of an employee's earnings (not to exceed $0.60/week) be withheld for this purpose.

Applying Wage Garnishments

A **wage garnishment** is the withholding of a portion of an employee's earnings, in compliance with a court order or other legal proceeding. Wage garnishments are limited to the lesser of 25% of disposable earnings (gross pay – mandatory deductions) or the amount of disposable earnings that exceed 30 times the federal minimum wage (disposable earnings minus [30 x federal minimum wage]). This limit may be increased in certain instances, such as garnishments for child support, bankruptcy, and federal or state tax payments.

NOTE! If the state regulations applicable to an employee limit wage garnishments to a smaller amount than is permissible under federal regulations (as described earlier), the smaller, state regulations take precedence.

Contributing to Retirement Plans

Depending on the circumstance, an employee may choose from a wide variety of retirement plans. Contributions to these plans constitute voluntary deductions from gross earnings. Some of the most common retirement plans, as well as the federal law regulating these plans, are discussed here.

401(k) Plan

A **401(k) Plan** (named after the associated subsection of the Internal Revenue Code) is a defined-contribution retirement plan under which a set amount may be withheld from gross earnings each pay period. These funds are tax-deferred, meaning that they are not subject to federal income tax withholding when earned, but are taxed when the employee withdraws the funds subsequent to retirement.

Some employers choose to match employee contributions to a 401(k) plan. Additionally, an employee is only permitted to contribute up to a specified amount ($17,500 in 2013) to the plan each year.

403(b) Plan

A **403(b) Plan** (named after the associated subsection of the Internal Revenue Code) is also referred to as a Tax-Sheltered Annuity (TSA) Plan. It is very similar to a 401(k) Plan, however 403(b) Plans are only available to certain employees of the following institution types:

*   public education institutions
*   certain tax-exempt organizations

Ministers can also be eligible for a 403(b) plan. For all of these eligible individuals, the annual contribution limit in 2013 is the same $17,500 as for a 401(k) Plan.

TIP!   Both 401(k) and 403(b) Plans allow for *catch-up* withholdings, which are additional annual withholdings (above the initial $17,500) based on employee age and/or years of service.

SIMPLE IRA Plan

A **SIMPLE IRA** Plan is a retirement plan designed for employees of small businesses (fewer than 100 employees). (SIMPLE stands for *Savings Incentive Match Plan for Employees*.) Although these retirement plans are relatively easy for an employer to establish, a significant drawback is that the contribution limit ($12,000 in 2013) is lower than that for a 401(k) or 403(b) Plan. Another difference is that the employer is required to contribute to a SIMPLE IRA Plan, while employer contributions are optional for a 401(k) or 403(b) Plan. The employee may choose to have amounts withheld from gross earnings for a SIMPLE IRA Plan, but is not required to do so. If the employee does choose to contribute, the deduction from gross earnings is exempt from federal income tax withholding.

Payroll Deduction IRA

A **Payroll Deduction IRA** (Individual Retirement Arrangement) is perhaps the simplest retirement plan option. For this reason, it is often utilized by individuals who are self-employed. Only the employee may contribute to a Payroll Deduction IRA, and the 2013 annual contribution is limited to the lesser of $5,500 ($6,500 for employees age 50 or older) or taxable earnings. Although contributions to Payroll Deduction IRA's are subject to federal income tax withholding, the employee does receive a tax deduction on their year-end tax return for contributions made during the year.

NOTE! A number of other retirement plans are often utilized, including a Traditional IRA and a Roth IRA, however as these do not involve deductions from employee earnings, they are not discussed here.

The Employee Retirement Income Security Act of 1974

Commonly referred to as ERISA, the **Employee Retirement Income Security Act** of 1974 regulates retirement plans offered by employers. While it does not require that employers offer such plans, for those that do ERISA sets forth a number of requirements.

Employees must be provided with pertinent retirement plan information, such as the manner in which it is funded. Secondly, fiduciaries of the retirement plan (individuals who can make investment decisions) may be held accountable for breaches of responsibility. This results in more conscientious investing of the funds. Additionally, ERISA sets forth requirements for retirement plan participation, the accumulation of benefits, and the timeframe over which plan benefits become non-forfeitable.

Offering Cafeteria Plans

A cafeteria plan is a group of benefits offered by employers. To offer a cafeteria plan, the employer must give each employee a choice of at least one taxable option (compensation on which tax is levied; this is typically cash) and one non-taxable option. The voluntary non-taxable deductions afforded to employees through a cafeteria plan can include:

- Medical Care Reimbursements
- Adoption Assistance
- Group-Term Life Insurance
- Health Savings Account
- Flexible Spending Account

A flexible spending account is a type of cafeteria plan that sets aside funds to be used for health care expenses during the year. Some of these plans are designated for a specific purpose, such as a Dependent Care Flexible Spending Account. These plans contain a *use it or lose it* feature that traditionally prevented employees from carrying over the contributed funds for use in the subsequent year, although this provision has been relaxed in recent years.

If desired, an employee may choose from any of the available options. With a few notable exceptions (such as for adoption assistance & group-term life insurance coverage exceeding $50,000), cafeteria plans are exempt from both federal income tax withholding and FICA tax.

Withholding Charitable Contributions, Union Dues, & Insurance Premiums

Employees may choose to have charitable contributions voluntarily deducted from gross earnings and remitted directly to the charity by the employer. Some employers choose to match employee charitable contributions, thereby magnifying the impact of the employee's donation. Although these amounts are subject to federal income tax withholding, the employee typically may claim a deduction on his/her year-end tax return for the contribution amount.

Many different types of employees, such as college faculty members and auto workers, may be eligible to join a union. These organizations negotiate a variety of employment terms on behalf of their members. Union dues are typically withheld from gross earnings as a voluntary deduction, but are subject to federal income tax withholding. Similar to charitable contributions, union dues may be claimed as a deduction on the employee's year-end tax return.

Insurance premiums, such as those for health insurance and life insurance, may also be withheld and remitted to the insurance company on behalf of the employee as a voluntary deduction. Except when it is associated with a cafeteria plan, health insurance is subject to federal income tax withholding when it is paid by the employee through a deduction. In this instance, the amount spent may be claimed as a deduction on the employee's year-end tax return.

Case In Point 4-3	**Identify Miscellaneous Deductions**

See if you can match each of the voluntary deduction types listed in the left column to the corresponding withholding description in the right column. Answers are below.

1.	Wage garnishment	A.	An employee elects to withhold amounts to fund multiple benefits on a pre-tax basis.
2.	401(k)		
3.	Charitable contribution	B.	An amount withheld as a result of a court order.
		C.	An employee working for a public university withholds funds for a retirement plan.
4.	Cafeteria plan		
5.	Union dues	D.	A steelworker elects to withhold funds that are remitted to an organization that advocates on his behalf for work-related issues.
6.	403(b)		
		E.	An employee chooses to withhold funds that are remitted directly to a local soup kitchen.

The items match up as follows:

1 → B   2 → F   3 → E
4 → A   5 → D   6 → C

F.	An employee withholds the maximum permissible amount ($17,500) for a retirement plan.

Remember the following:

- Wage garnishments are required as a result of a legal proceeding

- The maximum 401(k) contribution is $17,500

- Charitable contributions can be made to both large and small organizations

- A cafeteria plan allows for the selection of multiple options

- Union dues are paid to a union that advocates on the employee's behalf

- 403(b) plans are only available to certain employees (such as those who are employed by a public university).

Completing the Payroll Register

Once the withholding amounts identified throughout this chapter have been properly calculated, both the employee earnings record and the payroll register can be completed. The final figure in the employee earnings record is the net pay. As you have seen, this is the amount for which each employee's paycheck is written. To facilitate the tracking of employee paychecks, the check number is included beside net pay for each pay period.

Case In Point 4-4	**Complete a Payroll Register**

In this example, we will complete a payroll register for Lucky Ties Apparel. Earlier we calculated the Social Security tax for four different employees of Lucky Ties Apparel. Their completed employee earnings records for the most recent week appear below. Additionally, the completed employee earnings records of four other employees (whose earnings were determined in Chapter 2) also appear below.

Note that none of these remaining four employees exceed the Social Security tax annual wage base as of the end of the current pay period. Additionally, Medicare, life insurance, and charitable contribution deductions have been entered for each employee. Lastly, the additional withholding column contains appropriate withholdings for cafeteria plans and State Disability Insurance (Lucky Ties Apparel conducts business in New York State, which requires the withholding of disability insurance). Based on these employee earnings records, we will complete the payroll register for the pay period.

Employee Earnings Record

Name	Paul Rogers		Marital Status	Single
Address	657 Flicker Lane		Fed. Withholding Allow.	1
	Brockport, NY 14420		State Withholding Allow.	1
SS#	111-11-1111			

	Earnings							Deductions									
Pay Period Ending	Regular Hours Worked	Regular Pay Rate	Regular Wages	Overtime Hours Worked	Overtime Pay Rate	Overtime Wages	Gross Pay	Federal Withholding Tax	State Withholding Tax	Social Security Tax	Medicare Tax	Retirement Contribution	Life Insurance	Charitable Contribution	Additional Withholding	Check Number	Net Pay
12/5/14	35	$ 11.50	$ 402.50	0	n/a	$ -	$ 402.50	$ 30.00	$ 18.52	$ 24.96	$ 5.84	$ 32.20	$ -	$ 10.00	$ 0.60	1462	$ 280.38

Employee Earnings Record

Name	Maryanne Sherman		Marital Status	Single
Address	8171 Winston Court		Fed. Withholding Allow.	2
	Rochester, NY 14604		State Withholding Allow.	1
SS#	222-22-2222			

	Earnings							Deductions									
Pay Period Ending	Regular Hours Worked	Regular Pay Rate	Regular Wages	Overtime Hours Worked	Overtime Pay Rate	Overtime Wages	Gross Pay	Federal Withholding Tax	State Withholding Tax	Social Security Tax	Medicare Tax	Retirement Contribution	Life Insurance	Charitable Contribution	Additional Withholding	Check Number	Net Pay
12/5/14	n/a	n/a	$ 769.23	0	n/a	$ -	$ 769.23	$ 77.00	$ 38.46	$ -	$ 11.15	$ -	$ -	$ 10.00	$ 0.60	1463	$ 632.02

Employee Earnings Record

Name	Bill Novak		Marital Status	Married
Address	536A North Yellow Lake Avenue		Fed. Withholding Allow.	4
	Hamlin, NY 14464		State Withholding Allow.	3
SS#	333-33-3333			

	Earnings							Deductions									
Pay Period Ending	Regular Hours Worked	Regular Pay Rate	Regular Wages	Overtime Hours Worked	Overtime Pay Rate	Overtime Wages	Gross Pay	Federal Withholding Tax	State Withholding Tax	Social Security Tax	Medicare Tax	Retirement Contribution	Life Insurance	Charitable Contribution	Additional Withholding	Check Number	Net Pay
12/5/14	40	$ 14.75	$ 590.00	6	$ 22.50	$ 135.00	$ 725.00	$ 23.00	$ 34.08	$ 42.25	$ 9.88	$ -	$ 25.00	$ -	$ 44.10	1464	$ 546.69

Employee Earnings Record

Name	Angelo Dorsett	Marital Status	Single
Address	400 Hillside Court	Fed. Withholding Allow.	2
	Hilton, NY 14468	State Withholding Allow.	2
SS#	444-44-4444		

	Earnings							Deductions										
Pay Period Ending	Regular Hours Worked	Regular Pay Rate	Regular Wages	Overtime Hours Worked	Overtime Pay Rate	Overtime Wages	Gross Pay	Federal Withholding Tax	State Withholding Tax	Social Security Tax	Medicare Tax	Retirement Contribution	Life Insurance	Charitable Contribution	Additional Withholding	Check Number	Net Pay
12/5/14	40	$17.50	$700.00	7	$26.25	$183.75	$883.75	$82.00	$39.77	$6.20	$11.53	$ -	$20.00	$5.00	$88.98	1465	$630.27

Employee Earnings Record

Name	Melissa Kubiak	Marital Status	Married
Address	254 Cheesehead Drive	Fed. Withholding Allow.	5
	Pittsford, NY 14534	State Withholding Allow.	4
SS#	555-55-5555		

	Earnings							Deductions										
Pay Period Ending	Regular Hours Worked	Regular Pay Rate	Regular Wages	Overtime Hours Worked	Overtime Pay Rate	Overtime Wages	Gross Pay	Federal Withholding Tax	State Withholding Tax	Social Security Tax	Medicare Tax	Retirement Contribution	Life Insurance	Charitable Contribution	Additional Withholding	Check Number	Net Pay
12/5/14	40	$15.00	$600.00	1	$22.50	$22.50	$622.50	$9.00	$31.13	$38.60	$9.03	$ -	$ -	$15.00	$20.60	1466	$499.14

Employee Earnings Record

Name	Stacie Martin	Marital Status	Married
Address	2 Lava Lane	Fed. Withholding Allow.	2
	Brockport, NY 14420	State Withholding Allow.	1
SS#	666-66-6666		

	Earnings							Deductions										
Pay Period Ending	Regular Hours Worked	Regular Pay Rate	Regular Wages	Overtime Hours Worked	Overtime Pay Rate	Overtime Wages	Gross Pay	Federal Withholding Tax	State Withholding Tax	Social Security Tax	Medicare Tax	Retirement Contribution	Life Insurance	Charitable Contribution	Additional Withholding	Check Number	Net Pay
12/5/14	40	$21.15	$846.00	11	$31.73	$349.03	$1,195.03	$116.00	$59.75	$74.09	$17.33	$ -	$35.00	$25.00	$0.60	1467	$867.26

Employee Earnings Record

Name	Lucy Marshall	Marital Status	Single
Address	232 Muscle Road	Fed. Withholding Allow.	3
	Hamlin, NY 14464	State Withholding Allow.	2
SS#	777-77-7777		

	Earnings							Deductions									
Pay Period Ending	Regular Hours Worked	Regular Pay Rate	Regular Wages	Overtime Hours Worked	Overtime Pay Rate	Overtime Wages	Gross Pay	Federal Withholding Tax	State Withholding Tax	Social Security Tax	Medicare Tax	Retirement Contribution	Life Insurance	Charitable Contribution	Additional Withholding	Check Number	Net Pay
12/5/14	40	$ 15.75	$ 630.00	9	$ 23.63	$ 212.67	$ 842.67	$ 68.00	$ 38.76	$ 52.25	$ 12.22	$ 67.41	$ -	$ 10.00	$ 0.60	1468	$ 593.43

Employee Earnings Record

Name	Donald McHenry	Marital Status	Married
Address	22 Iceberg Lane	Fed. Withholding Allow.	6
	Fairport, NY 14450	State Withholding Allow.	5
SS#	888-88-8888		

	Earnings							Deductions									
Pay Period Ending	Regular Hours Worked	Regular Pay Rate	Regular Wages	Overtime Hours Worked	Overtime Pay Rate	Overtime Wages	Gross Pay	Federal Withholding Tax	State Withholding Tax	Social Security Tax	Medicare Tax	Retirement Contribution	Life Insurance	Charitable Contribution	Additional Withholding	Check Number	Net Pay
12/5/14	40	$ 15.30	$ 612.00	5	$ 22.95	$ 114.75	$ 726.75	$ 12.00	$ 36.34	$ 45.06	$ 10.54	$ -	$ -	$ -	$ 0.60	1469	$ 622.21

The payroll register can now be completed in full. Although not explicitly discussed earlier, a number of deductions (life insurance, charitable contributions, state disability insurance) were entered for each employee. When these, as well as the previously-discussed withholding amounts, are subtracted from gross pay, each employee's net pay is determined.

Payroll Register

Pay Period: **12/6/2013**

Pay Date: **12/12/2013**

	Earnings							Deductions						
Employee Name	Regular Hours	Regular Rate	Regular Earnings	Overtime Hours	Overtime Rate	Overtime Earnings	Total Earnings	FWT	SWT	Social Security	Medicare	Vol. With.	Check Number	Net Pay
Rogers, P	35	$ 11.50	$ 402.50	0	n/a	$ -	$ 402.50	$ 30.00	$ 18.52	$ 24.96	$ 5.84	$ 42.80	1462	$ 280.38
Sherman, M	n/a	n/a	$ 769.23	0	n/a	$ -	$ 769.23	$ 77.00	$ 38.46	$ -	$ 11.15	$ 10.60	1463	$ 632.02
Novak, B	40	$ 14.75	$ 590.00	6	$ 22.50	$ 135.00	$ 725.00	$ 23.00	$ 34.08	$ 42.25	$ 9.88	$ 69.10	1464	$ 546.69
Dorsett, A	40	$ 17.50	$ 700.00	7	$ 26.25	$ 183.75	$ 883.75	$ 82.00	$ 39.77	$ 6.20	$ 11.53	$ 113.98	1465	$ 630.27
Kubiak, M	40	$ 15.00	$ 600.00	1	$ 22.50	$ 22.50	$ 622.50	$ 9.00	$ 31.13	$ 38.60	$ 9.03	$ 35.60	1466	$ 499.14
Martin, S	40	$ 21.15	$ 846.00	11	$ 31.73	$ 349.03	$ 1,195.03	$ 116.00	$ 59.75	$ 74.09	$ 17.33	$ 60.60	1467	$ 867.26
Marshall, L	40	$ 15.75	$ 630.00	9	$ 23.63	$ 212.67	$ 842.67	$ 68.00	$ 38.76	$ 52.25	$ 12.22	$ 78.01	1468	$ 593.43
McHenry, D	40	$ 15.30	$ 612.00	5	$ 22.95	$ 114.75	$ 726.75	$ 12.00	$ 36.34	$ 45.06	$ 10.54	$ 0.60	1469	$ 622.21
Totals:			$ 5,149.73			$ 1,017.70	$ 6,167.43	$ 417.00	$ 296.81	$ 283.41	$ 87.52	$ 411.29		$ 4,671.40

Accounting for Payroll (Employee Portion)

Before You Begin: This section assumes prior knowledge of the transaction recording process. Consult with your instructor to determine if you are required to review this material.

Once each employee's earnings, deductions, and net pay are determined, the employer must record a journal entry to account for each element in the payroll register. For the purposes of this journal entry, all gross pay is considered to be either salaries or wages expense. This amount is not in any way impacted by the breakdown of deductions.

A journal entry to account for employee payroll and its associated withholding amounts, would appear as follows:

8/21	Salaries Expense	XXXXX	
	Wages Expense	XXXXX	
	Federal Income Tax Payable		XXXXX
	State Income Tax Payable		XXXXX
	Social Security Tax Payable		XXXXX
	Medicare Tax Payable		XXXXX
	Retirement Plan Payable		XXXXX
	Life Insurance Payable		XXXXX
	Union Dues Payable		XXXXX
	Charitable Contribution Payable		XXXXX
	Cash		XXXXX
	Payment of Salaries & Wages to Employees		

Because the total of salaries and wages expense increases as a result of the employee's earnings (employee earnings are seen as a payroll expense by the employer), these accounts are debited for a total amount equal to gross pay.

The corresponding credits in this journal entry account for each of the amounts owed by the employer, as well as the cash paid to the employees in their paychecks. When the employer withholds amounts from employee paychecks, these amounts are immediately owed to the corresponding entities. For example, once federal income tax withholding is withheld from employee gross pay, it is immediately owed to the U.S. Government.

The same holds true for voluntary deduction; so an amount withheld for a charitable contribution is immediately owed to the intended charity. For this reason, every withheld amount is shown as a credit to a liability account within the necessary journal entry. The credits to payable accounts in this journal entry can change, depending on the types of payroll withholding that a business has during any given pay period. The credit to the Cash account represents the net pay earned by the employee. This is the only amount that is actually paid by the employer on the payroll date, and therefore the only amount displayed as a reduction (credit) to cash.

WARNING!   As with every journal entry, total debits must always equal total credits in the employee payroll journal entry.

Case In Point 4-5	**Record a Payroll Journal Entry**

In this example, we will record a journal entry for Lucky Ties Apparel, in which we account for employee gross pay, payroll withholdings, and net pay. Each employee was subject to $0.60 of State Disability Insurance, and the only other additional withholding amount on the employee earnings records are contributions to cafeteria plans. Refer to the employee earnings records and payroll register at the end of the previous Case in Point to either calculate or locate the figures included in this journal entry.

12/11	Salaries Expense	3,533.68	
	Wages Expense	2,633.75	
	Federal Income Tax Payable		417.00
	State Income Tax Payable		296.81
	Social Security Tax Payable		283.41
	Medicare Tax Payable		87.52
	Retirement Plan Payable		99.61
	Life Insurance Payable		80.00
	Charitable Contribution Payable		75.00
	Disability Insurance Payable		4.80
	Cafeteria Plan Payable		151.88
	Cash		4,671.40
	Payment of Salaries & Wages to Employees		

Many of the amounts listed in the journal entry were taken directly from the payroll register. This is one of the primary reasons why it is beneficial to summarize payroll activity for a single pay period in the payroll register.

Also, the debits for gross pay are divided between two accounts. These amounts are the sum of the gross pay for employees who earn a salary (Sherman, Martin, Marshall, and McHenry) and the gross pay for employees who earn wages (Rogers, Novak, Dorsett, and Kubiak).

Concepts Review

All of the Concepts Review quizzes for this book are also available in the Student Resource Center. Check with your instructor on how to complete the quizzes (in the book or online).

True/False Questions

1. The sole purpose of Social Security taxes is to provide retirement benefits to employees. *True   False*

2. The Social Security taxable wage base for 2013 is $113,700. *True   False*

3. Taxable earnings for Social Security tax are always the same as taxable earnings for federal income tax withholding. *True   False*

4. The income threshold for Medicare tax indicates the income level above which no Medicare taxes are levied. *True   False*

5. Collectively, Social Security tax and Medicare tax are referred to as FICA tax. *True   False*

6. Employees are required to contribute toward the purchase of disability insurance in all fifty states. *True   False*

7. The contribution limit for a SIMPLE IRA is lower than that for a 401(k) or 403(b). *True   False*

8. ERISA is a set of regulations that dictate the manner in which a cafeteria plan may be administered. *True   False*

9. Flexible Spending Accounts contain a use it or lose it feature which, although relaxed in recent years, limits the time over which the account's funds may be utilized. *True   False*

10. Certain withholding amounts are excluded from the calculation of net pay. *True   False*

Multiple Choice Questions

1. Which of the following statements regarding Social Security tax is false?
   a. Social Security tax is also referred to as OASDI tax because it was initially established to benefit retired employees, survivors of employees, and disabled employees.
   b. Social Security tax was first levied on employees in 1937.
   c. All earnings of an employee that exceed the taxable wage base in a single year are not subject to Social Security tax.
   d. Contributions to cafeteria plans are not taxable for Social Security tax.

2. How much Social Security tax would be owed by an employee who has taxable earnings for Social Security tax of $2,000, and who, prior to the current pay period, has earned $113,400 of taxable earnings for Social Security tax?
   a. $0.00
   b. $18.60
   c. $105.40
   d. $124.00

3. Which of the following is taxable for Social Security tax?
   a. Contributions to a 403(b) plan
   b. Contributions to a flexible spending account
   c. Contributions to a dependent-care flexible spending account
   d. Contributions to a cafeteria plan

4. The additional Medicare tax is paid on a portion of employee earnings by which of the following individuals?
   a. Joe Stinson's filing status is married filing jointly. He earns $174,000 during the year.
   b. Jeanette Yancy's filing status is head of household. She earns $194,000 during the year.
   c. Keanu Levine's filing status is married filing separately. He earns $132,000 during the year.
   d. Carolyn Hughes' filing status is qualifying widow. She earns $187,000 during the year.

5. If an individual whose filing status is single earns $256,000 during the year, what portion of the earnings are subject to additional Medicare tax, and what is the total (standard & additional) Medicare tax rate that will be applied to these earnings?
   a. $6,000 & 0.90%
   b. $6,000 & 2.35%
   c. $56,000 & 0.90%
   d. $56,000 & 2.35%

6. Contributions to which of the following retirement plans are subject to federal income tax withholding?
   a. 401(k)
   b. 403(b)
   c. SIMPLE IRA
   d. Payroll Deduction IRA

7. Which of the following is not a retirement plan?
   a. 401(k)
   b. Flexible spending account
   c. 403(b)
   d. SIMPLE IRA

8. Which of the following is not a voluntary deduction from gross earnings?
   a. Union dues
   b. State Disability Insurance
   c. Payroll Deduction IRA
   d. Cafeteria plan

9. Assuming that taxable earnings are $51,200, which of the following is the lowest contribution limit applicable to a Payroll Deduction IRA?
   a. $5,500
   b. $6,500
   c. $12,000
   d. $17,500

10. Which of the following payroll register columns can contain a combination of multiple withholding amounts?
    a. State income tax withholding
    b. Social Security
    c. Medicare
    d. Voluntary withholdings

Knowledge Check A

For all assignments in this section, necessary IRS forms and/or Excel templates are located in the Student Resource Center.

KCa 4-1 Calculate Taxable Earnings for Social Security Tax

For each employee listed below, calculate the taxable earnings for Social Security tax for the described pay period.

1. Devin Moody earned gross pay of $1,450 during a recent pay period. He contributes 11% of gross pay to a 403(b) retirement plan, and $100 each pay period to a cafeteria plan.

2. Jaclyn Connor earned gross pay of $1,820 during a recent pay period. She contributes 7% of gross pay to a 401(k) retirement plan, and 3% of gross pay to a dependent-care flexible spending account.

3. Amy Williams earned gross pay of $990 during a recent pay period. She contributes $75 to a flexible spending account, and 5% of gross pay to a separate dependent-care flexible spending account.

4. Edward Sorkin earned gross pay of $850 during a recent pay period. He contributes 10% of gross pay to a 401(k) retirement plan.

KCa 4-2 Calculate Social Security Tax

For each of the following employees, calculate the Social Security tax for the weekly pay period described.

1. Alfred Morneau earned gross pay of $820. Each period he makes a 401(k) contribution of 5% of gross pay. His current year taxable earnings for Social Security tax, to date, are $37,200.

2. Rachel Schillo earned gross pay of $1,900. She does not make any retirement plan contributions. Her current year taxable earnings for Social Security tax, to date, are $105,000.

3. Rudolph Fabrizio earned gross pay of $3,200. Each period he contributes 3% of gross pay to a flexible spending account. His current year taxable earnings for Social Security tax, to date, are $112,200.

4. Michael Frank earned gross pay of $2,650. Each period he designates 6% of gross pay for a dependent-care flexible spending account. His current year taxable earnings for Social Security tax, to date, are $224,300.

KCa 4-3 Calculate Medicare Tax

For each of the following employees, calculate the Medicare tax for the weekly pay period described.

1. Paul Robinson's filing status is married filing jointly, and he has earned gross pay of $2,650. Each period he makes a 403(b) contribution of 8% of gross pay, and contributes $100 to a cafeteria plan. His current year taxable earnings for Medicare tax, to date, are $274,000.

2. Stephen Belcher's filing status is single, and he has earned gross pay of $1,840. Each period he makes a 401(k) contribution of 6% of gross pay, and contributes 3% of gross pay to a dependent-care flexible spending plan. His current year taxable earnings for Medicare tax, to date, are $198,950.

3. Sidney Black's filing status is head of household, and he has earned gross pay of $970. Each period he contributes $50 to a flexible spending plan. His current year taxable earnings for Medicare tax, to date, are $86,400.

4. Bill Clay's filing status is married filing separately, and he has earned gross pay of $1,900. Each period he makes a 403(b) contribution of 10% of gross pay, and contributes $75 to a cafeteria plan. His current year taxable earnings for Medicare tax, to date, are $124,600.

KCa 4-4 Calculate FICA Taxes

For each of the following employees, calculate both the Social Security tax and the Medicare tax for the weekly pay period described.

1. Bradley Banks' filing status is qualifying widower, and he had earned gross pay of $1,570. Each period he makes a 401(k) contribution of 6% of gross pay, and makes a contribution of 2% of gross pay to a flexible spending account. His current year taxable earnings for Social Security tax & Medicare tax, to date, are $212,900.

2. Kyle Struck's filing status is single, and he had earned gross pay of $2,400. Each period he makes a 403(b) contribution of 9% of gross pay, and makes a contribution of 1.5% of gross pay to a cafeteria plan. His current year taxable earnings for Social Security tax & Medicare tax, to date, are $199,500.

3. Sebastian Wayne's filing status is married filing jointly, and he had earned gross pay of $3,820. Each period he makes a 401(k) contribution of 10% of gross pay, and contributes $150 to a dependent-care flexible spending account. His current year taxable earnings for Social Security tax & Medicare tax, to date, are $92,500.

4. Lukas Douglas' filing status is married filing separately, and he had earned gross pay of $2,000. Each period he makes a 403(b) contribution of 12% of gross pay, and contributes $75 to a cafeteria plan. His current year taxable earnings for Social Security tax & Medicare tax, to date, are $113,400.

KCa 4-5 Define Miscellaneous Deductions

For each of the voluntary deductions listed, write a definition of at least two sentences.

1. 403(b)

2. SIMPLE IRA

3. Flexible Spending Account

4. Union dues

5. Insurance premiums

KCa 4-6 Populate Employee Earnings Record

This problem is a continuation of exercise KCa 3-8 from Chapter 3.

Complete the remaining columns of the employee earnings record for the five employees whose information was provided in KCa 2-4, KCa 2-12, and KCa 3-8. All employees work in a state that does not require the withholding of disability insurance, and none of the employees files their tax return under married filing separately status. Additional information for each employee is provided below.

- Luisa Williams voluntarily deducts life insurance of $15, and a charitable contribution of $5 each pay period. Her year-to-date Social Security tax earnings, prior to the current pay period, are $82,600.

- Jonathan Olsen voluntarily deducts a charitable contribution of $10 each pay period. His year-to-date Social Security tax earnings, prior to the current pay period, are $31,550.

- Nathan Upton does not make any voluntary deductions each period. His year-to-date Social Security tax earnings, prior to the current pay period, are $113,220.

- Juan Rodriguez voluntarily deducts life insurance of $25 each pay period. His year-to-date Social Security tax earnings, prior to the current pay period, are $124,500.

- Drew Painter voluntarily deducts life insurance of $20 and a charitable contribution of $30 each pay period. His year-to-date Social Security tax earnings, prior to the current pay period, are $51,750.

KCa 4-7 Populate a Payroll Register

This problem is a continuation of exercise KCa 3-9 from Chapter 3.

Complete the remainder of the payroll register for the five employees from KCa 4-6. The Earnings section of the payroll register was previously completed in KCa 2-13 & KCa 3-9.

KCa 4-8 Record Employee Payroll Journal Entry

Based on the employee earnings records and the Payroll register that you completed in the prior two exercises, record the necessary journal entry to account for employee payroll. All employees are paid on an hourly basis.

KCa 4-9 Record Employee Payroll Journal Entry

Based on the following figures for all employees during the most recent pay period, record the necessary journal entry to account for employee payroll. A template to be used with this problem is among the Student Exercise Files.

Account Name	Amount
Retirement Plan Payable	$127.10
Social Security Tax Payable	$356.30
Medicare Tax Payable	$110.43
Cafeteria Plan Payable	$193.80
Wages Expense	$4,605.67

Account Name	Amount
Charitable Contribution Payable	$101.82
State Income Tax Payable	$345.23
Salaries Expense	$3,263.98
Life Insurance Payable	$102.08
Federal Income Tax Payable	$516.78

Knowledge Check B

For all assignments in this section, necessary IRS forms and/or Excel templates are located in the Student Resource Center.

KCb 4-1 Calculate Taxable Earnings for Social Security Tax

For each employee listed below, calculate the taxable earnings for Social Security tax for the described pay period.

1. Dustin Woodward earned gross pay of $2,200 during a recent pay period. He contributes 8% of gross pay to a 403(b) retirement plan, and $50 each pay period to a cafeteria plan.

2. Olivia Sutter earned gross pay of $950 during a recent pay period. She contributes 5% of gross pay to a 401(k) retirement plan, and 1% of gross pay to a dependent-care flexible spending account.

3. Ana Grantham earned gross pay of $1,420 during a recent pay period. She contributes $40 to a flexible spending account, and 2.5% of gross pay to a separate dependent-care flexible spending account.

4. Paul Bernstein earned gross pay of $1,100 during a recent pay period. He contributes 14% of gross pay to a 401(k) retirement plan.

KCb 4-2 Calculate Social Security Tax

For each of the following employees, calculate the Social Security tax for the weekly pay period described.

1. Mortimer Klein earned gross pay of $1,340. Each period he makes a 401(k) contribution of 3% of gross pay. His current year taxable earnings for Social Security tax, to date, are $184,600.

2. Helena Smith earned gross pay of $2,000. She does not make any retirement plan contributions. Her current year taxable earnings for Social Security tax, to date, are $113,500.

3. Kasey Wolfe earned gross pay of $1,140. Each period he contributes 1.5% of gross pay to a flexible spending account. His current year taxable earnings for Social Security tax, to date, are $71,900.

4. Matthew Pugh earned gross pay of $880. Each period he designates 2% of gross pay for a dependent-care flexible spending account. His current year taxable earnings for Social Security tax, to date, are $113,700.

KCb 4-3 Calculate Medicare Tax

For each of the following employees, calculate the Medicare tax for the weekly pay period described.

1. Caleb Griffin's filing status is married filing jointly, and he has earned gross pay of $3,100. Each period he makes a 401(k) contribution of 7% of gross pay, and contributes $125 to a cafeteria plan. His current year taxable earnings for Medicare tax, to date, are $248,400.

2. Anderson Fowler's filing status is single, and he has earned gross pay of $2,220. Each period he makes a 403(b) contribution of 11% of gross pay, and contributes 2.5% of gross pay to a dependent-care flexible spending plan. His current year taxable earnings for Medicare tax, to date, are $124,375.

3. Rick Portnoy's filing status is head of household, and he has earned gross pay of $1,300. Each period he contributes $40 to a flexible spending plan. His current year taxable earnings for Medicare tax, to date, are $206,100.

4. Shawn Buffett's filing status is married filing separately, and he has earned gross pay of $2,680. Each period he makes a 401(k) contribution of 14% of gross pay, and contributes $60 to a cafeteria plan. His current year taxable earnings for Medicare tax, to date, are $198,300.

KCb 4-4 Calculate FICA Taxes

For each of the following employees, calculate both the Social Security tax and the Medicare tax for the weekly pay period described.

1. Tyler Samuels' filing status is qualifying widower, and he had earned gross pay of $830. Each period he makes a 401(k) contribution of 9% of gross pay, and makes a contribution of 1% of gross pay to a flexible spending account. His current year taxable earnings for Social Security tax & Medicare tax, to date, are $199,720.

2. Jacob Finney's filing status is single, and he had earned gross pay of $1,240. Each period he makes a 403(b) contribution of 8% of gross pay, and makes a contribution of 0.8% of gross pay to a cafeteria plan. His current year taxable earnings for Social Security tax & Medicare tax, to date, are $112,900.

3. Charlie Lilly's filing status is married filing jointly, and he had earned gross pay of $1,850. Each period he makes a 401(k) contribution of 15% of gross pay, and contributes $60 to a dependent-care flexible spending account. His current year taxable earnings for Social Security tax & Medicare tax, to date, are $84,200.

4. Desmond Carroll's filing status is married filing separately, and he had earned gross pay of $4,120. Each period he makes a 403(b) contribution of 5% of gross pay, and contributes $90 to a cafeteria plan. His current year taxable earnings for Social Security tax & Medicare tax, to date, are $97,200.

KCb 4-5 Define Miscellaneous Deductions

For each of the voluntary deductions listed, write a definition of at least two sentences.

1. State Disability Insurance

2. 401(k)

3. Payroll Deduction IRA

4. Cafeteria plan

5. Charitable contribution

KCb 4-6 Populate Employee Earnings Record

This problem is a continuation of exercise KCb 3-8 from Chapter 3.

Complete the remaining columns of the employee earnings record for the five employees whose information was provided in KCb 2-4, KCb 2-12, and KCb 3-8. All employees work in a state that does not require the withholding of disability insurance, and none of the employees files their tax return under married filing separately status. Additional information for each employee is provided below.

- Jimmy Troffa voluntarily deducts life insurance of $10, and a charitable contribution of $15 each pay period. His year-to-date Social Security tax earnings, prior to the current pay period, are $71,300.
- Tyler Thomas voluntarily deducts a charitable contribution of $35 each pay period. His year-to-date Social Security tax earnings, prior to the current pay period, are $112,950.
- Ryan Brown does not make any voluntary deductions each period. His year-to-date Social Security tax earnings, prior to the current pay period, are $22,400.
- Michael Kaminski voluntarily deducts life insurance of $30 each pay period. His year-to-date Social Security tax earnings, prior to the current pay period, are $79,560.
- Tina Baldwin voluntarily deducts life insurance of $5, and a charitable contribution of $3 each pay period. Her year-to-date Social Security tax earnings, prior to the current pay period, are $119,000.

KCb 4-7 Populate a Payroll Register

This problem is a continuation of exercise KCb 3-9 from Chapter 3.

Complete the remainder of the payroll register for the five employees from KCb 4-6. The Earnings section of the payroll register was previously completed in KCb 2-13 & KCb 3-9.

KCb 4-8 Record Employee Payroll Journal Entry

Based on the employee earnings records and the Payroll register that you completed in the prior two exercises, record the necessary journal entry to account for employee payroll. All employees are paid on an hourly basis.

KCb 4-9 Record Employee Payroll Journal Entry

Based on the following figures for all employees during the most recent pay period, record the necessary journal entry to account for employee payroll.

Account Name	Amount
State Income Tax Payable	$175.32
Salaries Expense	$3,589.82
Cafeteria Plan Payable	$98.42
Medicare Tax Payable	$56.08
Federal Income Tax Payable	$262.44

Account Name	Amount
Charitable Contributions Payable	$51.71
Life Insurance Payable	$51.84
Retirement Plan Payable	$64.55
Social Security Tax Payable	$180.94
Wages Expense	$406.67

Continuing Payroll Problem

For all assignments in this section, necessary IRS forms and/or Excel templates are located in the Student Resource Center.

CPP 4-1 Complete the Payroll Register & Record the Employee Payroll Journal Entry

Calculate Social Security and Medicare tax for a number of employees of TCLH Industries, a manufacturer of cleaning products. None of the employees files as married filing separately for their year-end tax return.

Complete the employee earnings record using these calculations and the additional information provided below. Complete the payroll register, and record the necessary journal entry for employee payroll.

1. Calculate the Social Security tax and Medicare tax for each employee, based on information from the prior chapters' Continuing Payroll Problems, as well as the following:
   - Zachary Fox's current year taxable earnings for Social Security tax, prior to the current pay period, are $2,100.
   - Calvin Bell's current year taxable earnings for Social Security tax, prior to the current pay period, are $109,400.
   - Michaela Walton's current year taxable earnings for Social Security tax, prior to the current pay period, are $141,000.
   - Suzanne Steinberg's current year taxable earnings for Social Security tax, prior to the current pay period, are $113,100.

   Note that Bell, Walton, and Steinberg all received large discretionary signing bonuses when hired, resulting in large year-to-date taxable earnings.

2. Next, complete the remainder of the employee earnings record (which you began in Chapter 2) for each employee. Use the following information to complete the employee earnings record.
   - Zachary Fox has authorized voluntary deductions each pay period of $10 for charitable contributions, $15 for life insurance, and $7 for union dues. He receives check #092.
   - Calvin Bell has authorized voluntary deductions each pay period of $15 for charitable contributions, and $7 for union dues. He receives check #093.
   - Michaela Walton has authorized voluntary deductions each pay period of $7 for union dues. She receives check #094.
   - Suzanne Steinberg has authorized voluntary deductions each pay period of $5 for charitable contributions, $20 for life insurance, and $7 for union dues. She receives check #095.

3. Complete the payroll register based on the completed employee earnings records.

4. Record the journal entry to account for employee payroll based on the employee earnings records, and the totals in the payroll register.

Critical Thinking

CT 4-1 Evaluate the Patient Protection & Affordable Care Act

President Obama signed the Patient Protection & Affordable Care Act into law on March 23, 2010. Commonly referred to as Obamacare, this legislation was designed to ensure that all Americans receive adequate healthcare. As there is an increased cost associated with providing this medical coverage, the federal government needed a method by which it could raise additional funds. The additional Medicare tax, which is levied only after an employee has earned a specified amount of income in a single year, is one such method. In this exercise, we will use the internet to evaluate this legislation, and will decide whether we are in favor of its enactment.

First, research the legislation to learn about its most important elements. While you should focus on all aspects of the act, pay particular attention to the implications of the additional Medicare tax. Write a paragraph of at least four sentences in which you highlight these vital components. Continue your research by examining both the arguments in favor of the act, and against it. Write two more paragraphs (of at least three sentences each) in which you outline these arguments. Lastly, write a concluding paragraph of at least four sentences in which you explain your opinion regarding the effectiveness of this law. Be certain to provide adequate support for your opinion.

Submit your final file based on the guidelines provided by your instructor.

CT 4-2 Review Cafeteria Plan Benefits

A cafeteria plan can provide a wide variety of benefits to an employee. These plans are desirable to both the employer and the employee, as both parties can reduce their tax burden by participating. For this reason, these plans are relatively common. For an employee to derive maximum benefit from a cafeteria plan, he/she must understand the different benefits provided. In this exercise, we will use the internet to research the most common cafeteria plan features, and will describe a number of them.

Begin by researching the possible elements of a cafeteria plan. Identify three components that you believe would be most beneficial for you, either now or in the future. Write a paragraph of at least six sentences in which you discuss your three selected elements. Ensure that you both define the benefit, and discuss why you believe it would be helpful to you.

Submit your final file based on the guidelines provided by your instructor.

Federal & State Unemployment Taxes

The payroll process is not complete once the employee checks have been written. In addition to remitting employee withholdings to the appropriate governmental entity, the employer must pay additional taxes (based on this payroll) that are not withheld from gross earnings. While some of these employer taxes mirror those that were withheld from the employees, others are specific to the employer. These employer taxes represent an additional expense that the employer must bear as a result of compensating employees. In this chapter, you will first examine the manner in which federal unemployment and state unemployment taxes are calculated. You will then examine the matching Social Security & Medicare taxes that are paid by the employer. After reviewing the journal entry to account for these employer taxes you'll finish by examining non-employee compensation and self-employment tax..

CASE STUDY

Determining Employer Taxes for Lucky Ties Apparel

Lucky Ties has now successfully withheld all necessary amounts from the employees' earnings. The next step is for the company to determine the proper amount of employer taxes to remit. These taxes are not withheld from employee pay, and therefore are entirely satisfied by the employer. Although these taxes are all based on employees' taxable earnings, some are matched by the employer, while others are paid solely by the employer.

As part of your examination of these employer taxes, you first look at federal unemployment tax, and the extent to which it is reduced as a result of paying state unemployment tax. You then review state unemployment tax, and the different effective rates in different states. You next examine the manner in which Social Security tax and Medicare tax are matched by the employer, and conclude by reviewing the manner in which the employer payroll taxes are recorded on the company's books.

FUTA & SUTA taxes are not withheld from employee pay (in most states), and therefore do not appear on the check stub.

MY CONSTRUCTION COMPANY		
1001 Fifth Avenue	Check Number:	000001
New York, NY 10022	Pay date:	12/17/2013
	Social Security No.	***-**-1119

Pay to the order of: CLARK MITCHELL

This amount: FIVE HUNDRED ELEVEN AND 82/100 DOLLARS $511.82

AUTHORIZED SIGNATURE
VOID AFTER 60 DAYS

⑈"00000 ⅈ" ⑆8 2 76 ⅈ9 5 78⑆ 6004 25600 ⅈ"

MY CONSTRUCTION COMPANY
1001 Fifth Avenue
New York, NY 10022

Period ending: 12/15/2013
Pay date: 12/17/2013

CLARK MITCHELL
547 Smith Street
New York, NY 10033

Earnings	Rate	Hours	This Period	Year to Date
Regular	$14.00	40.00	$560.00	$28,000.00
Overtime	$21.00	4.00	$84.00	$6,615.00
Holiday	$30.00	0.00	$0.00	$2,250.00
Gross Pay			$644.00	$36,865.00

Deductions		
Statutory	This Period	Year to Date
Federal Income Tax	$19.00	$1,350.00
Social Security Tax	$39.93	$2,285.63
Medicare Tax	$9.34	$534.54
NYS Income Tax	$12.67	$783.33
NYC Income Tax	$8.44	$472.22
NYSDI Tax	$0.60	$30.00
Other		
401(k)	$32.20*	$1,843.25
Life Insurance	$10.00	$500.00
Net Pay	$511.82	

* Excluded from federal taxable wages

Social Security Number: ***-**-1119
Taxable Marital Status: Married
Exemptions/Allowances:
Federal: 4, $25 Additional Tax
State: 3
Local: 3

Other Benefits and Information	This Period	Year to Date
Vacation Hrs.		64.00
Sick Hrs.		24.00

Computing the Federal Unemployment (FUTA) Tax

Federal unemployment tax (also referred to as FUTA, from the Federal Unemployment Tax Act) is levied on the employer, based on the taxable earnings of the employees. The federal government uses these taxes to provide unemployment compensation to individuals who are out of work.

TIP! Certain compensation, such as that paid to agricultural workers, governmental employees, and employees of religious organizations, are exempt from FUTA tax.

As of 2013, the tax is levied on only the first $7,000 of taxable wages for federal income tax withholding. Once an employee has earned $7,000 in a single year, no further FUTA tax is levied on the employer for this employee. As of 2013, the FUTA tax rate is 6.0%. However, employers may take advantage of a credit against this 6.0% rate for having paid state unemployment tax (which we will examine in detail later in this chapter). This credit is 5.4%, resulting in an actual FUTA tax rate of 0.6% (6.0% to 5.4%).

WARNING! The credit of 5.4% is not based on the state unemployment tax rate in an employer's state (this specific rate is dictated by the federal government). The full credit may be used even when the state unemployment tax rate is below 5.4%.

Identifying Credit Reduction States

In some instances, states must take out loans from the federal government in order to provide unemployment benefits to all eligible individuals in the state. If a state maintains an outstanding loan balance as of January 1st for two consecutive years, and has not fully repaid the loan as of November 1st of the second year, it is subject to a credit reduction. Instead of a 5.4% credit, these states receive a lower credit, and therefore their employers must pay a higher FUTA tax rate than the 0.6% that would otherwise be in place.

2013 Credit Reduction States

Credit Reduction; State Credit	State/Territory
0.6%; 4.8%	Delaware
0.9%; 4.5%	Arkansas, California, Connecticut, Georgia, Kentucky, Missouri, New York, North Carolina, Ohio, Rhode Island, Wisconsin
1.2%; 4.2%	Indiana, U.S. Virgin Islands

Regardless of whether or not an employer operates in a credit-reduction state, the same five-step process may be used to determine FUTA tax owed:

Step #1   Determine the applicable FUTA tax rate, based on whether the employee works in a credit-reduction state.

Step #2   Determine current period taxable earnings for FUTA tax.

Step #3   Add the step #2 result to the year-to-date taxable earnings for FUTA tax.

Step #4   • If the step #3 result exceeds the taxable wage base, determine the amount by which it is higher, and subtract this amount from the step #2 result. Your new amount (if it is positive) is used to determine FUTA tax in step #5 (a negative result here indicates that $0 should be used in step #5).

   • If the step #3 result does not exceed the taxable wage base, use the step #2 result when determining FUTA tax in step #5.

Step #5   Multiply the tax rate from step #1 by the step #4 result.

Making FUTA Tax Payments

FUTA tax must be remitted by the employer on a quarterly basis. One exception to this occurs when total FUTA tax owed by the employer is less than $500. In this instance, the employer may postpone payment of applicable FUTA tax either until the total tax owed exceeds $500, or until the end of the year. When FUTA taxes exceed $500 at the end of a quarter, they must be paid by the final day of the first month after the end of the quarter. As a result, the four payment dates for FUTA tax during the year are as follows:

Quarter	FUTA Tax Due Date
1st Quarter	April 30th
2nd Quarter	July 31st
3rd Quarter	October 31st
4th Quarter	January 31st

If the total FUTA tax owed for the fourth quarter exceeds $500, it must be deposited by the due date of January 31st. However, if fourth-quarter FUTA tax does not exceed $500, the employer may mail payment with the year-end Form 940 (which will be examined in detail in Chapter 6).

Case In Point 5-1   Calculate FUTA Tax

For each of the following businesses, we will calculate the FUTA tax that is owed for the pay period described.

1. Caramia Company employs 3 workers in Colorado Springs, Colorado. As of the beginning of the current pay period, these employees have earned $42,500, $6,800, and $2,000 respectively. Let's calculate FUTA tax for the current pay period if these employees earn taxable pay of $3,140, $1,470, and $1,500 respectively.

    Step 1: Colorado is not a credit-reduction state. Therefore, Caramia Company is entitled to claim the entire 5.4% credit, resulting in a FUTA tax rate of 0.6% (6.0% minus 5.4%).

    Step 2: Taxable earnings for the three employees are provided above as $3,140, $1,470, and $1,500.

    Step 3: The first employee earned $3,140 during the current period, with year-to-date earnings of $42,500, for a total of $45,640.

    The second employee earned $1,470 during the current period, with year-to-date earnings of $6,800, for a total of $8,270.

    The third employee earned $1,500 during the current period, with year-to-date earnings of $2,000, for a total of $3,500.

    Step 4: The step 3 result for the first employee exceeds the wage base of $7,000 by $38,640. When subtracted from the step 2 result of $3,140, we arrive at –$35,500. As this is a negative amount, none of the current year taxable earnings are subject to FUTA tax.

    The step 3 result for the second employee exceeds the wage base of $7,000 by $1,270. When subtracted from the step 2 result of $1,470, we arrive at $200. This positive amount is subject to FUTA tax.

    The step 3 result for the third employee does not exceed the wage base of $7,000, therefore all $1,500 of current period taxable earnings are subject to FUTA tax.

    Step 5: With total earnings subject to FUTA tax of $1,700 ($0 + $200 + $1,500), the FUTA tax owed by the employer is $10.20 ($1,700 x 0.6%).

2. Perfect Painting employs 17 workers in Des Moines, Iowa. For the current pay period, the employees earn total taxable pay of $24,500. Of this amount, only $3,250 is subject to FUTA tax, as this is the portion of individual employees' earnings that does not exceed the $7,000 threshold. Calculate FUTA tax based on these earnings.

   Step 1: Iowa is not a credit-reduction state, and therefore Perfect Painting is entitled to the full credit of 5.4%, resulting in a FUTA tax rate of 0.6% (6.0% minus 5.4%).

   Step 2: Taxable earnings are given above as $24,500.

   Step 3 & 4: Although year-to-date earnings are not provided here, the goal of steps 3 & 4 is to determine the portion of current period taxable earnings on which FUTA tax should be calculated. This amount is given as $3,250.

   Step 5: With total earnings subject to FUTA tax of $3,250, the FUTA tax owed by the employer is $19.50 ($3,250 x 0.6%).

3. CJ Industries employs 2 workers in Smithtown, New York. As of the beginning of the current pay period, these employees have earned, to date, $16,300, and $4,100, respectively. Calculate FUTA tax for the current pay period if these employees earn taxable pay of $1,275, and $840 respectively.

   Step 1: As New York is a credit-reduction state, in which the credit is reduced by 0.9%, the FUTA tax rate for CJ Industries is 1.5% (6.0% minus 4.5%).

   Step 2: Taxable earnings are given above as $1,275 and $840.

   Step 3: The first employee earned $1,275 during the current period, with year-to-date earnings of $16,300, for a total of $17,575.

   The second employee earned $840 during the current period, with year-to-date earnings of $4,100, for a total of $4,940.

   Step 4: The step 3 result for the first employee exceeds the wage base of $7,000 by $10,575. When subtracted from the step 2 result of $1,275, we arrive at –$9,300. As this is a negative amount, none of the current year taxable earnings are subject to FUTA tax.

   The step 3 result for the second employee does not exceed the wage base of $7,000, therefore all $840 of current period taxable earnings are subject to FUTA tax.

   Step 5: When the taxable earnings of $840 are multiplied by the applicable tax rate from step 1 of 1.5% (recall that the FUTA tax rate is higher in this credit-reduction state), total FUTA tax owed by the employer is $12.60.

Computing the State Unemployment (SUTA) Tax

Similar to FUTA, state unemployment tax (also referred to as SUTA, from the State Unemployment Tax Act) is levied on the employer, based on the taxable earnings of the employees. Unemployment programs are run through the efforts of both the federal & individual state governments. The majority of unemployment taxes are paid not to the federal government, but to the states through the collection of SUTA tax.

NOTE! As of 2013, there are three states (Alaska, New Jersey, and Pennsylvania) that levy SUTA tax on the employee as well as the employer.

As with FUTA tax, there is a threshold in most states over which SUTA tax is not levied on taxable earnings. The SUTA tax rate applicable to an employer varies from state to state, and in most cases is dependent on the number of employees that have been laid off by the employer. As an employer lays off more employees, and therefore creates more workers who are eligible for unemployment benefits, the employer must contribute more to the unemployment program through higher SUTA taxes.

TIP! Employers are assigned an appropriate SUTA tax rate, based on employee turnover, by their state at the beginning of each year. For employers without an employee track record, states assign a *New Employer* SUTA tax rate.

The SUTA tax rates prescribed by individual states for 2013 range from a low of 0% to a high of 13.5%. The wage threshold over which SUTA tax is not assessed ranges from a low of $7,000 in California to a high of $39,800 in the state of Washington. As discussed in Chapter 1, unless noted otherwise we assume a state unemployment tax rate of 3.4% and a threshold of $8,500 throughout this book.

The *new employer* SUTA tax rate in each state is lower than the maximum SUTA tax rate that may be assigned. As a result, years ago some employers that experienced significant employee turnover, and therefore were subject to high SUTA tax rates, circumvented the application of this high rate by forming new companies and transferring all employees to these new businesses. The result was that the new employer SUTA tax rate was applied to the employees in these newly formed businesses, in spite of the fact that employee turnover for this group of employees was high. To prevent employers from artificially avoiding high SUTA tax rates in this manner, the SUTA Dumping Prevention Act of 2004 was enacted by President George W. Bush. The act requires states to ensure that prior employee turnover impacts the SUTA tax rate, even when a new business is formed by an employer.

The majority of states allow employers to claim a credit for SUTA tax paid for an employee who has already worked (and been subject to SUTA tax) in a different state during the same year. The intent is to ensure that employers do not pay more than a reasonable amount of SUTA tax in a given year, as a result of an employee working in multiple states.

To calculate applicable SUTA tax, the following four-step process may be utilized:

Step #1   Determine current period taxable earnings for SUTA tax.

Step #2   Add the step #1 result to the year-to-date taxable earnings for SUTA tax.

Step #3   • If the step #2 result exceeds the taxable wage base, determine the amount by which it is higher, and subtract this amount from the step #1 result. Your new amount (if it is positive) will be used to determine SUTA tax in step #4 (a negative result here indicates that $0 should be used in step #4).

                  • If the step #2 result does not exceed the taxable wage base, use the step #1 result when determining SUTA tax in step #4.

Step #4   Multiply the SUTA tax rate by the step #3 result.

Case In Point 5-2   Calculate SUTA Tax

For each of the following businesses, let's calculate the SUTA tax for the pay period described. Assume a SUTA tax rate of 3.4%, and a taxable earnings threshold of $8,500.

1. Blast Inc. employs 2 workers who, as of the beginning of the current pay period, have earned $2,450, and $8,100. Calculate SUTA tax for the current pay period if these employees earn taxable pay of $725, and $640 respectively.

   Step 1: Current period taxable earnings for the two employees are given above as $725 and $640.

   Step 2: When current period taxable earnings are added to year-to-date taxable earnings, the first employee totals $3,175 ($725 + $2,450), and the second employee totals $8,740 ($640 + $8,100).

   Step 3: The first employee's step 2 total does not exceed the taxable wage base. Therefore, the entire current period taxable earnings of $725 are subject to SUTA tax.

   The second employee's step 2 total exceeds the taxable wage base of $8,500 by $240. When subtracted from the step 1 result of $640, we arrive at $400, which is subject to FUTA tax.

   Step 4: When total taxable earnings of $1,125 ($725 + $400) are multiplied by the SUTA tax rate of 3.4%, total SUTA tax owed by the employer is $38.25.

2. Football Enterprises employs 43 workers who, for the current pay period, earn total taxable pay of $57,220. Of this amount, only $10,400 are subject to SUTA tax, as this is the portion of individual employee's earnings that does not exceed the $8,500 threshold. Calculate SUTA tax based on these earnings.

Step 1: Current period taxable earnings are given above as $57,220.

Step 2 & 3: Although year-to-date earnings are not provided here, the goal of steps 2 & 3 is to determine the portion of current period taxable earnings on which SUTA tax should be calculated. This amount is given as $10,400.

Step 4: When total taxable earnings of $10,400 are multiplied by the SUTA tax rate of 3.4%, total SUTA tax owed by the employer is $353.60.

Matching Social Security & Medicare Tax

In the last chapter you learned how Social Security and Medicare tax is withheld from employee gross pay. In this way, employees indirectly pay both of these taxes to the federal government. In addition to these withholdings, as of 2013 the employer must then pay an equal amount of Social Security and Medicare tax. For example, if an employer withholds $450 in Social Security and Medicare tax from an employee's earnings, the employer must then pay an additional $450 for the employer portion of these taxes. The resulting total tax remitted by the employer is $900 ($450 employee portion + $450 employer portion). In this instance, the employer is said to be *matching* the employee's taxes.

Similar to FUTA & SUTA tax, these employer Social Security & Medicare taxes are an expense of the employer. As they are matched to the amounts owed by the employee, these taxes are based on the level of employee earnings.

Case In Point 5-3	Calculate Employer Social Security & Medicare Tax

For the following circumstance, determine the employer's matching Social Security and Medicare taxes.

1. For the most recent pay period, total Social Security & Medicare taxes withheld from all employee earnings totaled $601.40 and $140.65, respectively.

Since the employer is required to match all Social Security & Medicare taxes withheld from employee gross pay, the employer's Social Security & Medicare taxes are $601.40 and $140.65, respectively.

Accounting for Payroll (Employer Portion)

Before You Begin: This section assumes prior knowledge of the transaction-recording process. Consult with your instructor to determine if you are required to review this material.

As you saw in the prior chapter, all payroll activity must be recorded in journal entries. Employee gross pay, and its associated withholding amounts, are recorded first. The second journal entry that must be recorded is designed to record the employer taxes we have examined in this chapter.

The first journal entry recorded both salaries expense and wages expense, because all of the amounts discussed in that journal entry (both the withholding amount, and the net pay) had been earned by the employees. This second journal entry instead records payroll tax expense, which is incurred by the employer as a result of maintaining employees. This entry does not include those amounts earned by the employees. Instead, the amounts in this journal entry are paid by the employer himself.

8/21	Payroll Tax Expense	XXXXX	
	Federal Unemployment Tax Payable		XXXXX
	State Unemployment Tax Payable		XXXXX
	Social Security Tax Payable		XXXXX
	Medicare Tax Payable		XXXXX
	Recording of Employer Payroll Tax Expenses		

The credits to Social Security Tax Payable and Medicare Tax Payable are identical in this journal entry to those that we recorded in the prior journal entry. It is important to record these items separately from the first journal entry, so that the different types of expenses are properly recorded.

| Case In Point 5-4 | **Record an Employer Payroll Journal Entry** |

12/11	Payroll Tax Expense	401.38	
	Federal Unemployment Tax Payable		10.90
	State Unemployment Tax Payable		24.71
	Social Security Tax Payable		279.23
	Medicare Tax Payable		86.54
	Recording of Employer Payroll Tax Expenses		

The debit to Payroll Tax Expense of $401.38 is the sum of the credited amounts below. We have already determined the Social Security Tax Payable and Medicare Tax Payable amounts from the prior journal entry.

When Donald's taxable earnings of $726.75 are added to year-to-date earnings of $5,200, neither the $7,000 FUTA taxable wage base, nor the $8,500 SUTA taxable wage base are exceeded, and therefore all of the current period's taxable earnings are subject to FUTA & SUTA tax. The FUTA tax amount of $10.90 is calculated as 1.5% x $726.75, while the SUTA tax amount of $24.71 is calculated as 3.4% x $726.75.

TIP! As in the previous journal entry, all taxes are credited to liability accounts because they are immediately owed to the respective governmental entities.

Paying Nonemployee Compensation

Throughout the textbook thus far, you have only examined the manner in which payroll-related topics impact employees. However, a wide variety of individuals perform services for employers without qualifying as employees. The general rule that employers use to define these individuals as **independent contractors**, instead of employees, is that these workers determine how the employer's work is completed, and what is to be done. For example, a lawyer can provide legal services through whatever method he/she chooses, as long as the legal representation is sufficient. Because the employer can't exert control over the method used by the lawyer, the *employee* classification does not apply. This lawyer would be considered an independent contractor.

When an employer utilizes the services of an independent contractor, a number of forms that are specific to this circumstance must be completed. These include Form W-9 (Request for Taxpayer Identification Number and Certification), Form 1099-MISC (Miscellaneous Income), and Form 1096 (Annual Summary and Transmittal of U.S. Information Returns).

Hiring Independent Contractors

On the Web

www.irs.gov/pub/
irs-pdf/fss8.pdf

Independent contractors, who perform services for employers without qualifying as employees, can do so both with or without having formed a business of their own. Among those professionals who most frequently work as independent contractors are accountants, lawyers, doctors, and subcontractors. The determination of whether an individual is an employee or an independent contractor can be unclear at times, and essentially comes down to whether the employer can control how the work is performed. If the employer is unable to make this determination, Form SS-8 (Determination of Worker Status for Purposes of Federal Employment Taxes and Income Tax Withholding) may be filed. The IRS, upon receipt and review of this form, will render a decision as to the worker's employment classification.

Using Form W-9

On the Web

www.irs.gov/pub/
irs-pdf/fw9.pdf

Although employers (in many instances) are not responsible for withholding taxes from the compensation of independent contractors, they are obligated to report the individual's annual compensation to the federal government. They must also inform the independent contractor of his/her annual compensation at year-end. To accurately complete these forms, the employer must obtain either the independent contractor's social security number, or the applicable employer identification number (for the business under which the independent contractor operates, or for a resident alien, for example). This may be done through the use of Form W-9 (Request for Taxpayer Identification Number and Certification). Upon receipt of Form W-9, the employer retains the form and does not submit it to the IRS.

Examine the Form: W-9

Form W-9 primarily contains the independent contractor's demographic information.

1 | **3** | **5** | **6**

Form **W-9**
(Rev. August 2013)
Department of the Treasury
Internal Revenue Service

Request for Taxpayer
Identification Number and Certification

Give Form to the
requester. Do not
send to the IRS.

2 | **4**

Name (as shown on your income tax return)

Business name/disregarded entity name, if different from above

Check appropriate box for federal tax classification:
☐ Individual/sole proprietor ☐ C Corporation ☐ S Corporation ☐ Partnership ☐ Trust/estate

☐ Limited liability company. Enter the tax classification (C=C corporation, S=S corporation, P=partnership) ▶

☐ Other (see instructions) ▶

Exemptions (see instructions):

Exempt payee code (if any) _____

Exemption from FATCA reporting
code (if any) _____

Address (number, street, and apt. or suite no.)

Requester's name and address (optional)

City, state, and ZIP code

List account number(s) here (optional)

Print or type   See Specific Instructions on page 2.

Part I **Taxpayer Identification Number (TIN)**

Enter your TIN in the appropriate box. The TIN provided must match the name given on the "Name" line
to avoid backup withholding. For individuals, this is your social security number (SSN). However, for a
resident alien, sole proprietor, or disregarded entity, see the Part I instructions on page 3. For other
entities, it is your employer identification number (EIN). If you do not have a number, see *How to get a
TIN* on page 3.

Note. If the account is in more than one name, see the chart on page 4 for guidelines on whose
number to enter.

Social security number

Employer identification number

Part II **Certification**

Under penalties of perjury, I certify that:

1. The number shown on this form is my correct taxpayer identification number (or I am waiting for a number to be issued to me), and

2. I am not subject to backup withholding because: (a) I am exempt from backup withholding, or (b) I have not been notified by the Internal Revenue
Service (IRS) that I am subject to backup withholding as a result of a failure to report all interest or dividends, or (c) the IRS has notified me that I am
no longer subject to backup withholding, and

3. I am a U.S. citizen or other U.S. person (defined below), and

4. The FATCA code(s) entered on this form (if any) indicating that I am exempt from FATCA reporting is correct.

Certification instructions. You must cross out item 2 above if you have been notified by the IRS that you are currently subject to backup withholding
because you have failed to report all interest and dividends on your tax return. For real estate transactions, item 2 does not apply. For mortgage
interest paid, acquisition or abandonment of secured property, cancellation of debt, contributions to an individual retirement arrangement (IRA), and
generally, payments other than interest and dividends, you are not required to sign the certification, but you must provide your correct TIN. See the
instructions on page 3.

Sign
Here

Signature of
U.S. person ▶

Date ▶

1. **Top portion of form:** *Name* (either of the individual or business), *Business Name* (if applicable; typically the Doing Business As name), *Federal Tax Classification* (Individual/Sole Proprietor is typically checked by an independent contractor), and *Address* should be completed.

2. **Exemptions:** Not typically completed by U.S.-based independent contractors. Enter the applicable code from the Form W-9 instructions if you are exempt from backup withholding or Foreign Account Tax Compliance Act (FATCA) reporting.

3. **List account number(s) here:** Typically left blank (accounts already established with the IRS to pay back taxes can be entered here).

4. **Requester's name and address:** This item does not need to be completed for the form to be valid. If utilized, it should include information for the entity requesting that the independent contractor complete the form.

5. **Taxpayer Identification Number:** Either the social security number or employer identification number of the independent contractor should be entered here.

6. **Certification:** Form must be signed and dated to be valid.

Using Form 1099-MISC

At the end of the year, the employer must both furnish the independent contractor with a copy of Form 1099-MISC, and remit a copy of the form to the IRS. Form 1099-MISC displays total annual earnings for the independent contractor. The form must be provided to the independent contractor no later than January 31st of the following year. This is necessary so that the independent contractor has sufficient time to complete his/her individual tax return (due on April 15th) after receiving the form.

TIP! For many items in Form 1099-MISC (such as rents, other income, medical & healthcare benefits, nonemployee compensation, crop insurance proceeds, and gross proceeds paid to an attorney), only annual compensation exceeding $600 must be reported.

Examine the Form: 1099-MISC

Form 1099-MISC reports many different types of income and withholding amounts.

☐ VOID ☐ CORRECTED		
PAYER'S name, street address, city or town, province or state, country, ZIP or foreign postal code, and telephone no.	**1** Rents $	OMB No. 1545-0115
	2 Royalties $	20**13** **Miscellaneous Income**
		Form **1099-MISC**
	3 Other income $	**4** Federal income tax withheld $
PAYER'S federal identification number RECIPIENT'S identification number	**5** Fishing boat proceeds $	**6** Medical and health care payments $	Copy 1 For State Tax Department
RECIPIENT'S name	**7** Nonemployee compensation $	**8** Substitute payments in lieu of dividends or interest $
Street address (including apt. no.)	**9** Payer made direct sales of $5,000 or more of consumer products to a buyer (recipient) for resale ▶ ☐	**10** Crop insurance proceeds $
City or town, province or state, country, and ZIP or foreign postal code	**11** Foreign tax paid $	**12** Foreign country or U.S. possession
Account number (see instructions)	**13** Excess golden parachute payments $	**14** Gross proceeds paid to an attorney $
15a Section 409A deferrals $ **15b** Section 409A income $	**16** State tax withheld $ $	**17** State/Payer's state no.	**18** State income $ $
Form **1099-MISC**	www.irs.gov/form1099misc	Department of the Treasury - Internal Revenue Service

Void/Corrected: The Void box is checked when an employer determines that a partially-completed electronic form contains an inaccuracy. Checking the box ensures that, when submitted, the form is disregarded. The Corrected box is checked when newly-submitted forms are completed to correct a previous error.

Left side of form: Payer and recipient information should be fully completed. The account number box is optional, and may be used by the payer to assign unique numbers to different 1099-MISC forms.

Boxes 1-15: Income and withholding amounts are entered in these boxes. The majority of independent contractors' earnings are considered to be nonemployee compensation, and therefore are reported in box 7.

Boxes 16-18: These boxes are not completed for federal tax purposes. In some instances, these boxes are completed in order to report state earnings and withholding amounts for up to two states.

Using Form 1096

So that the federal government possesses a record of the compensation paid to independent contractors, the employer must complete and submit both Form 1096 (Annual Summary and Transmittal of U.S. Information Returns), and copies of all 1099-MISC forms at the end of each year. When Form 1099-MISC is completed, these two forms must then be submitted to the IRS by March 1st of the following year. Form 1096 provides a total of all compensation paid to every independent contractor during the year.

WARNING! Form 1096 is used to report compensation that has been entered on a wide variety of forms. If an employer has completed multiple types of these forms (such as at least one Form 1099-MISC & one Form 1099-Int, which is used to report interest earned), then the company must submit a separate 1096 form for each type.

Examine the Form: 1096

Form 1096 provides an annual summary of compensation for one of the form types listed at the bottom of the form.

Do Not Staple 6969		OMB No. 1545-0108
Form **1096**	**Annual Summary and Transmittal of U.S. Information Returns**	20**13**
Department of the Treasury Internal Revenue Service		

FILER'S name

Street address (including room or suite number)

City or town, province or state, country, and ZIP or foreign postal code

Name of person to contact	Telephone number	**For Official Use Only**
Email address	Fax number	

1 Employer identification number	**2** Social security number	**3** Total number of forms	**4** Federal income tax withheld $	**5** Total amount reported with this Form 1096 $

6 Enter an "X" in only one box below to indicate the type of form being filed.

7 If this is your **final return**, enter an "X" here . . . . . ▶ ☐

W-2G 32	1097-BTC 50	1098 81	1098-C 78	1098-E 84	1098-T 83	1099-A 80	1099-B 79	1099-C 85	1099-CAP 73	1099-DIV 91	1099-G 86	1099-H 71	1099-INT 92	1099-K 10	1099-LTC 93	1099-MISC 95	1099-OID 96
☐	☐	☐	☐	☐	☐	☐	☐	☐	☐	☐	☐	☐	☐	☐	☐	☐	☐

1099-PATR 97	1099-Q 31	1099-R 98	1099-S 75	1099-SA 94	3921 25	3922 26	5498 28	5498-ESA 72	5498-SA 27
☐	☐	☐	☐	☐	☐	☐	☐	☐	☐

Return this entire page to the Internal Revenue Service. Photocopies are not acceptable.

Under penalties of perjury, I declare that I have examined this return and accompanying documents, and, to the best of my knowledge and belief, they are true, correct, and complete.

Signature ▶   Title ▶   Date ▶

Top of the form: Company name, address, contact person, telephone number, e-mail address, and fax number should be completed.

Boxes 1-2: Either the employer identification number, or the social security number of the company's owner should be entered. Only one of these boxes should be completed.

Box 3: The total number of completed forms (not pages) that are being submitted with Form 1096 should be entered here.

Examine the Form: 1096 (continued)

Box 4: Total federal income tax withheld from form 1099-MISC (or other form type being reported) forms is entered here.

Box 5: Total compensation for all independent contractors is entered here.

Box 6: Only one box should contain an "X," as Form 1096 can only report on one form type. For independent contractors, the Form 1099-MISC box is checked.

Box 7: Unless this is the company's final return (due to the ceasing of operations), this box is left blank.

Signature line: The contact person's signature and title, as well as the date, must be entered for the form to be valid.

| Case In Point 5-5 | Complete Form 1099-MISC & Form 1096 |

In this example, we will complete Form 1099-MISC for Blaine Freemont (SS# 444-44-4444), an independent contractor of Fallen Bear Company (745 Alpine Way, Rapid City, SD 57703). Blaine (who lives at 84 Mountain Ave., Rapid City, SD 57702) earns nonemployee compensation of $21,000 during the year. Fallen Bear Company (federal identification #33-3333333) does not use account numbers, and does not report state data.

We will then complete Form 1096 for Fallen Bear Company which, in addition to Blaine Freemont's Form 1099-MISC, issues three other 1099-MISC forms. Total compensation across these four forms is $62,500, on which no federal income tax was withheld. The CFO of Fallen Bear Company, Jaime Vargas, (telephone number 605-555-8271, fax number 605-555-8270, e-mail address; jvargas@fbc.com) signs and submits the form on the due date.

☐ VOID	☐ CORRECTED			

PAYER'S name, street address, city or town, province or state, country, ZIP or foreign postal code, and telephone no.	**1** Rents $	OMB No. 1545-0115	Miscellaneous Income
Fallen Bear Company 745 Alpine Way Rapid City SD 57702	**2** Royalties $	20**13** Form **1099-MISC**	
	3 Other income $	**4** Federal income tax withheld $	**Copy 1** **For State Tax** **Department**

PAYER'S federal identification number	RECIPIENT'S identification number	**5** Fishing boat proceeds	**6** Medical and health care payments	
33-3333333	444-44-4444	$	$	

RECIPIENT'S name Blaine Freemont	**7** Nonemployee compensation	**8** Substitute payments in lieu of dividends or interest
Street address (including apt. no.) 84 Mountain Ave.	$ 21000.00	$
	9 Payer made direct sales of $5,000 or more of consumer products to a buyer (recipient) for resale ▶ ☐	**10** Crop insurance proceeds $
City or town, province or state, country, and ZIP or foreign postal code Rapid City SD 57702	**11** Foreign tax paid $	**12** Foreign country or U.S. possession
Account number (see instructions)	**13** Excess golden parachute payments $	**14** Gross proceeds paid to an attorney $

15a Section 409A deferrals	**15b** Section 409A income	**16** State tax withheld	**17** State/Payer's state no.	**18** State income
$	$	$		$
		$		$

Form **1099-MISC**	www.irs.gov/form1099misc	Department of the Treasury - Internal Revenue Service

All company information and independent contractor information is entered on the left of the form. As the company does not enter state information, box 7 is the only other box that is populated. No signature (either from the employer or the independent contractor) is included on Form 1099-MISC.

Form **1096** Department of the Treasury Internal Revenue Service	**Annual Summary and Transmittal of U.S. Information Returns**	OMB No. 1545-0108 20**13**

FILER'S name

Fallen Bear Company

Street address (including room or suite number)

745 Alpine Way

City or town, province or state, country, and ZIP or foreign postal code
Rapid City SD 57702

Name of person to contact Jaime Vargas	Telephone number 605 555-8271	**For Official Use Only**
Email address jvargas@fbc.com	Fax number 605 555-8270	

1 Employer identification number 33-3333333	**2** Social security number	**3** Total number of forms 4	**4** Federal income tax withheld $ 0.00	**5** Total amount reported with this Form 1096 $ 62500.00

6 Enter an "X" in only one box below to indicate the type of form being filed.

7 If this is your **final return**, enter an "X" here . . . . ▶ ☐

W-2G 32	1097-BTC 50	1098 81	1098-C 78	1098-E 84	1098-T 83	1099-A 80	1099-B 79	1099-C 85	1099-CAP 73	1099-DIV 91	1099-G 86	1099-H 71	1099-INT 92	1099-K 10	1099-LTC 93	1099-MISC 95	1099-OID 96
☐	☐	☐	☐	☐	☐	☐	☐	☐	☐	☐	☐	☐	☐	☐	☐	☒	☐

1099-PATR 97	1099-Q 31	1099-R 98	1099-S 75	1099-SA 94	3921 25	3922 26	5498 28	5498-ESA 72	5498-SA 27
☐	☐	☐	☐	☐	☐	☐	☐	☐	☐

Return this entire page to the Internal Revenue Service. Photocopies are not acceptable.

Under penalties of perjury, I declare that I have examined this return and accompanying documents, and, to the best of my knowledge and belief, they are true, correct, and complete.

Signature ▶ *Jaime Vargas*   Title ▶ CFO   Date ▶ 3/1/14

In this instance, Form 1096 is issued by a company that possesses an employer identification number (EIN). Therefore, box 1 is populated, while box 2 (which would contain the social security number if the form was completed by an individual employer with an EIN) is left blank. The 1099-MISC box is checked, while all other boxes remain unchecked.

Exploring the Self-Employment Contributions Act (SECA)

On the Web

http://www.irs.
gov/Businesses/
Small-Businesses-
%26-Self-Employed/
Self-Employed-
Individuals-Tax-Center

The **Self-Employment Contributions Act of 1954** established that self-employed individuals must pay self-employment taxes (SE taxes). These taxes are very similar to Social Security and Medicare taxes, which aren't paid by self-employed individuals. SE taxes serve to ensure that self-employed individuals are taxed in a manner similar to standard employees.

As you have seen, an employee pays Social Security tax of 6.2% of taxable earnings, while the employer matches the same 6.2%. This results in total Social Security tax of 12.4% being remitted to the federal government. Similarly, for Medicare, 1.45% of taxable earnings are paid by both the employee and the employer, resulting in a total of 2.9% being remitted. Since a self-employed individual takes on the role of both employer and employee, self-employment taxes total 15.3% (12.4% + 2.9%) of **Net Self-Employment Income**.

Similar to Social Security tax, there is a taxable earnings threshold applied to the 12.4% portion of self-employment taxes. While the full 15.3% self-employment tax is levied on the first $113,700 of net self-employment income (the same 2013 taxable earnings wage base as for Social Security tax), only the 2.9% Medicare portion of the self-employment tax rate is levied on net self-employment income above that level.

Additionally, there is an income floor, below which self-employment taxes need not be paid. self-employment taxes must be remitted by any individual whose net self-employment income totals $400 or more for the year.

NOTE!   Net self-employment income represents income after certain business expenses are subtracted.

Payroll Accounting   Chapter 5: Federal & State Unemployment Taxes

| Case In Point 5-6 | **Calculate Self-Employment Taxes** |

For each of the following individuals, let's calculate the applicable Self-Employment tax.

1. Samuel Henner earns net self-employment income of $97,200. He does not work a second job.

   As Samuel's net self-employment income has not yet exceeded the $113,700 threshold, the entire amount is subject to Self-Employment Tax.

   When the earnings of $97,200 are multiplied by the 15.3% Self-Employment Tax Rate, the self-employment taxes are $14,871.60.

2. Lisa Coleman earns net self-employment income of $119,200. Aside from this self-employment, she works a second job from which she receives FICA taxable earnings of $12,200.

   Lisa's net self-employment income must first be reduced by the earnings received from the second job. This results in a new net self-employment income amount of $107,000 ($119,200 minus $12,200).

   When the earnings of $107,000 (which do not exceed the $113,700 threshold) are multiplied by the 15.3% Self-Employment Tax Rate, the self-employment taxes are $16,371.

3. Penelope Woods earns net self-employment income of $136,400. Aside from this self-employment, she works a second job from which she receives FICA taxable earnings of $20,000.

   Penelope's net self-employment income must first be reduced by the earnings received from the second job. This results in a new net self-employment income amount of $116,400 ($136,400 minus $20,000).

   As this new net self-employment income exceeds the $113,700 threshold by $2,700 ($116,400 minus $113,700), this excess above the threshold is only subject to Self-Employment Tax of 2.9%.

   When self-employment tax on the first $113,700 of $17,396.10 ($113,700 x 15.3%) is added to Self-Employment Tax on the remaining net self-employment income of $78.30 ($2,700 x 2.9%), the total Self-Employment Tax is $17,474.40.

Concepts Review

All of the Concepts Review quizzes for this book are also available in the Student Resource Center. Check with your instructor on how to complete the quizzes (in the book or online).

True/False Questions

1. FUTA tax is paid solely by the employer. *True* *False*

2. The credit for FUTA tax must equal the applicable SUTA tax rate for the employer. *True* *False*

3. FUTA credit reductions are assessed as a result of individual states neglecting to repay federal loans in a timely manner. *True* *False*

4. There are a few states in which SUTA tax is levied on both the employer and the employee. *True* *False*

5. Employers who have experienced significant employee turnover can be levied SUTA tax as high as 25% of taxable earnings. *True* *False*

6. For employers who do not have a track record with employees, a New Employer SUTA tax rate is assigned. *True* *False*

7. It is possible for an employer to pay FUTA tax on a specific employee's pay, while not paying SUTA tax on the same employee's pay. *True* *False*

8. The employer's matching Social Security and Medicare tax may equal those taxes withheld from employee earnings, but will not always do so. *True* *False*

9. An independent contractor is considered to be an employee of the business for which he/she performs work. *True* *False*

10. The self-employment tax rate is the same as the combined employee and employer FICA tax rates. *True* *False*

Multiple Choice Questions

1. The taxable earnings threshold over which FUTA tax is not levied is:
   a. $7,000
   b. $113,700
   c. $200,000
   d. $250,000

2. The FUTA credit applicable to a non-credit-reduction state is:
   a. 4.5%
   b. 4.8%
   c. 5.4%
   d. 6.0%

3. How much FUTA tax would an employer in a non-credit-reduction state owe if an employee has earned $6,400 to date, and has current period taxable pay of $1,500.
   a. $3.60
   b. $9.00
   c. $36.00
   d. $90.00

4. Which of the following is an accurate statement about SUTA tax?
   a. Every state designates a taxable earnings threshold over which SUTA tax is not levied.
   b. SUTA tax paid by an employer is typically less than FUTA tax paid for the same period.
   c. SUTA tax rates differ from one employer to another, but do not change from year to year.
   d. The SUTA tax rate is based on the number of layoffs that an employer has experienced.

5. Based on the range of possible SUTA tax rates and thresholds, which of the following circumstances could occur?
   a. An employee who has year-to-date earnings of $42,000 pays 5.2% SUTA tax on the current period taxable pay.
   b. An employee who has year-to-date earnings of $21,400 pays 17.2% SUTA tax on the current period taxable pay.
   c. An employee who has year-to-date earnings of $26,300 pays 0% SUTA tax on the current period taxable pay.
   d. An employee who has year-to-date earnings of $4,300 pays 14.1% SUTA tax on the current period taxable pay.

6. Which of the following states does not levy SUTA tax on employees?
   a. South Dakota
   b. Alaska
   c. New Jersey
   d. Pennsylvania

7. Which of the following employee taxes is matched by the employer?
   a. State unemployment tax
   b. Federal income tax
   c. Medicare tax
   d. Federal unemployment tax

8. The employer's Social Security tax...
   a. is greater than the employee's Social Security tax
   b. is the same as the employee's Social Security tax
   c. is less than the employee's Social Security tax
   d. can be any of the above

9. Which of the following is accurate regarding self-employment tax?
   a. The taxable wage base (threshold) is the same as that for Social Security tax.
   b. If an individual receives compensation from a business, he/she is not required to pay self-employment tax on a net self-employment income.
   c. Self-employment tax is designed such that the self-employed individual pays the equivalent of only the employee portion of FICA taxes.
   d. Self-employment tax must be paid by all self-employed individuals, regardless of income level.

10. What is the self-employment tax rate levied on the first $113,700 of 2013 net self-employment income?
   a. 2.9%
   b. 12.4%
   c. 15.3%
   d. 18.2%

Knowledge Check A

For all assignments in this section, necessary IRS forms and/or Excel templates are located in the Student Resource Center.

KCa 5-1 Determine the Applicable FUTA Tax Rate

For each of the following businesses, determine the applicable FUTA tax rate for 2013 based on the locations listed below.

1. A business operating in Seattle, Washington.

2. A business operating in Atlanta, Georgia.

3. A business operating in Dover, Delaware.

4. A business operating in Bangor, Maine.

5. A business operating in the U.S. Virgin Islands.

KCa 5-2 Determine the Taxable Earnings Subject to FUTA Tax

For each of the described pay periods, determine the taxable earnings subject to FUTA Tax.

1. A business employs three employees, whose taxable earnings to date (prior to the current pay period) are $5,700, $8,000, and $1,000. During the current pay period, these employees earn $1,800, $3,140, and $2,500, respectively.

2. A business employs two employees, whose taxable earnings to date (prior to the current pay period) are $2,400, and $7,200. During the current pay period, these employees earn $1,250, and $750, respectively.

3. A business employs three employees, whose taxable earnings to date (prior to the current pay period) are $26,700, $4,400, and $6,850. During the current pay period, these employees earn $2,320, $2,550, and $3,100, respectively.

KCa 5-3 Calculate FUTA Tax

For each of the following independent circumstances calculate the FUTA tax owed by the employer.

1. An employer in Macon, Georgia employs two employees, whose taxable earnings to date (prior to the current pay period) are $8,100, and $6,200. During the current pay period, these employees earn $750, and $1,620 respectively.

2. An employer in Bloomington, Illinois employs three employees, whose taxable earnings to date (prior to the current pay period) are $51,500, $32,420 and $7,550. During the current pay period, these employees earn $1,800, $2,250 and $740 respectively.

3. An employer in Los Angeles, California employs two employees, whose taxable earnings to date (prior to the current pay period) are $920, and $5,150. During the current pay period, these employees earn $2,200, and $3,000 respectively.

4. An employer in Honolulu, Hawaii employs three employees, whose taxable earnings to date (prior to the current pay period) are $7,000, $6,100, and $9,400. During the current pay period, these employees earn $650, $980, and $1,100 respectively.

KCa 5-4 Calculate SUTA Tax

For each of the following independent circumstances calculate the SUTA tax owed by the employer. Assume a SUTA tax rate of 3.4%, and a taxable earnings threshold of $8,500.

1. Hometown Bakery employs 3 workers who, as of the beginning of the current pay period, have earned $16,200, $7,150 and $4,000. Calculate SUTA tax for the current pay period if these employees earn taxable pay of $1,450, $2,100, and $960 respectively.

2. Electronics Outlet employs 2 workers who, as of the beginning of the current pay period, have earned $8,400, and $7,200. Calculate SUTA tax for the current pay period if these employees earn taxable pay of $3,450, and $2,250 respectively.

3. Delivery Inc. employs 127 workers who, for the current pay period, earn total taxable pay of $347,540. Of this amount, only $31,400 are subject to SUTA tax, as this is the portion of individual employee's earnings that does not exceed the $8,500 threshold. Calculate SUTA tax based on these earnings.

KCa 5-5 Calculate FUTA & SUTA Tax

For each of the following independent circumstances calculate both the FUTA & SUTA tax owed by the employer.

1. An employer in Louisville, Kentucky employs two individuals, whose taxable earnings to date (prior to the current pay period) are $5,100, and $6,900. During the current pay period, these employees earn $1,700, and $2,650 respectively. The applicable SUTA tax rate is 2.7%, and the 2013 Kentucky SUTA threshold is $9,300.

2. An employer in Newark, New Jersey employs three individuals, whose taxable earnings to date (prior to the current pay period) are $26,200, $30,100 and $6,850. During the current pay period, these employees earn $3,200, $2,750 and $1,620 respectively. The applicable SUTA tax rate is 3.1%, and the 2013 New Jersey SUTA threshold is $30,900.

3. An employer in Indianapolis, Indiana employs two individuals, whose taxable earnings to date (prior to the current pay period) are $4,900, and $8,200. During the current pay period, these employees earn $2,800, and $1,900 respectively. The applicable SUTA tax rate is 2.5%, and the 2013 Indiana SUTA threshold is $9,500.

4. An employer in Juneau, Alaska employs three individuals, whose taxable earnings to date (prior to the current pay period) are $34,500, $41,300, and $5,200. During the current pay period, these employees earn $3,600, $4,200, and $1,200, respectively. The applicable SUTA tax rate is 2.38%, and the 2013 Alaska SUTA threshold is $36,900.

KCa 5-6 Record Employer Payroll Tax Journal Entry

Based on the following figures for the most recent pay period, record the necessary journal entry to account for employer payroll taxes.

Account Name	Amount
Medicare Tax Payable	$31.90
State Unemployment Tax Payable	$74.80
Social Security Tax Payable	$136.40
Payroll Tax Expense	$256.30
Federal Unemployment Tax Payable	$13.20

KCa 5-7 Complete Form 1099-MISC

Complete Form 1099-MISC (available from the SRC) for William Porter (SS# 222-22-2222), an independent contractor of Pronespeed Inc. (6 Snowcap Lane, Jefferson City, MO 65101). William (who lives at 55 Rounding Place, Jefferson City, MO 65101) earns nonemployee compensation of $13,400 during the year. Pronespeed Inc. (federal identification #99-9999999) does not use account numbers, and does not report state data.

KCa 5-8 Complete Form 1096

Complete Form 1096 for Pronespeed Inc., based on the information from KCa 5-7 and the following. In addition to Williams Porter's Form 1099-MISC, the company issued seven other 1099-MISC forms. Total compensation across these eight forms is $101,400, on which no federal income tax was withheld. The Controller of Pronespeed, Inc., William Mancuso, (telephone number 573-555-2320, fax number 573-555-2321, e-mail address; wporter@PSI.com) signs and submits the form on the due date.

KCa 5-9 Calculate Self-Employment Tax

For each of the following individuals, calculate the applicable self-employment tax.

1. Annabelle Jefferson earns net self-employment income of $43,500. She does not work a second job.

2. Alexander Ryan earns net self-employment income of $115,000. He works a second job from which he receives FICA taxable earnings of $41,300.

3. Morgan Cruise earns net self-employment income of $221,000. She works a second job from which she receives FICA taxable earnings of $101,000.

Knowledge Check B

For all assignments in this section, necessary IRS forms and/or Excel templates are located in the Student Resource Center.

KCb 5-1 Determine the Applicable FUTA Tax Rate

For each of the following businesses, determine the applicable FUTA tax rate for 2013 based on the locations listed below.

1. A business operating in Indianapolis, Indiana.

2. A business operating in Columbus, Ohio.

3. A business operating in Austin, Texas.

4. A business operating in Madison, Wisconsin.

5. A business operating in Birmingham, Alabama.

KCb 5-2 Determine the Taxable Earnings Subject to FUTA Tax

For each of the described pay periods, determine the taxable earnings subject to FUTA Tax.

1. A business employs three individuals, whose taxable earnings to date (prior to the current pay period) are $12,200, $5,250, and $3,000. During the current pay period, these employees earn $2,400, $2,000 and $1,350, respectively.

2. A business employs two individuals, whose taxable earnings to date (prior to the current pay period) are $3,000, and $31,400. During the current pay period, these employees earn $3,300 and $1,450, respectively.

3. A business employs three individuals, whose taxable earnings to date (prior to the current pay period) are $5,200, $46,700, and $500. During the current pay period, these employees earn $2,100, $1,140, and $920, respectively.

KCb 5-3 Calculate FUTA Tax

For each of the following independent circumstances, calculate the FUTA tax owed by the employer.

1. An employer in Anchorage, Alaska employs two individuals, whose taxable earnings to date (prior to the current pay period) are $5,000, and $12,000. During the current pay period, these employees earn $1,800, and $2,000, respectively.

2. An employer in St. Louis, Missouri employs three individuals, whose taxable earnings to date (prior to the current pay period) are $6,900, $1,000 and $24,200. During the current pay period, these employees earn $2,400, $1,750, and $3,000, respectively.

3. An employer in Reno, Nevada employs two individuals, whose taxable earnings to date (prior to the current pay period) are $8,500 and $3,400. During the current pay period, these employees earn $880 and $675, respectively.

4. An employer in Providence, Rhode Island employs three individuals, whose taxable earnings to date (prior to the current pay period) are $5,900, $8,900, and $6,600. During the current pay period, these employees earn $940, $1,020, and $850, respectively.

KCb 5-4 Calculate SUTA Tax

For each of the following independent circumstances, calculate the SUTA tax owed by the employer. Assume a SUTA tax rate of 3.4%, and a taxable earnings threshold of $8,500.

1. A-1 Framing employs 3 workers who, as of the beginning of the current pay period, have earned $8,550, $8,200, and $7,400. Calculate SUTA tax for the current pay period if these employees earn taxable pay of $1,000, $1,350, and $1,800, respectively.

2. Mrs. Fix-It Corp. employs 2 workers who, as of the beginning of the current pay period, have earned $4,200 and $6,500. Calculate SUTA tax for the current pay period if these employees earn taxable pay of $2,700 and $2,400, respectively.

3. Burger Bites Restaurant employs 51 workers who, for the current pay period, earn total taxable pay of $87,450. Of this amount, only $11,000 are subject to SUTA tax, as this is the portion of individual employee's earnings that does not exceed the $8,500 threshold. Calculate SUTA tax based on these earnings.

KCb 5-5 Calculate FUTA & SUTA Tax

For each of the following independent circumstances, calculate both the FUTA & SUTA tax owed by the employer.

1. An employer in Delaware City, Delaware employs two individuals, whose taxable earnings to date (prior to the current pay period) are $6,100 and $8,800. During the current pay period, these employees earn $1,450 and $2,000 respectively. The applicable SUTA tax rate is 3.1%, and the 2013 Delaware SUTA threshold is $10,500.

2. An employer in Bridgeport, Connecticut employs three individuals, whose taxable earnings to date (prior to the current pay period) are $5,500, $12,900, and $14,200. During the current pay period, these employees earn $2,200, $1,950, and $2,400 respectively. The applicable SUTA tax rate is 4.2%, and the 2013 Connecticut SUTA threshold is $15,000.

3. An employer in Albuquerque, New Mexico employs two individuals, whose taxable earnings to date (prior to the current pay period) are $8,350 and $21,400. During the current pay period, these employees earn $3,350 and $1,700 respectively. The applicable SUTA tax rate is 2.0%, and the 2013 New Mexico SUTA threshold is $22,900.

4. An employer in Durham, North Carolina employs three individuals, whose taxable earnings to date (prior to the current pay period) are $6,000, $19,500, and $34,500. During the current pay period, these employees earn $980, $1,600, and $1,150 respectively. The applicable SUTA tax rate is 1.2%, and the 2013 North Carolina SUTA threshold is $20,900.

KCb 5-6 Record Employer Payroll Tax Journal Entry

Based on the following figures for the most recent pay period, record the necessary journal entry to account for employer payroll taxes.

Account Name	Amount
Social Security Tax Payable	$217.00
Federal Unemployment Tax Payable	$21.00
Payroll Tax Expense	$407.75
Medicare Tax Payable	$50.75
State Unemployment Tax Payable	$119.00

KCb 5-7 Complete Form 1099-MISC

Complete Form 1099-MISC (included in the Student Exercise Files) for Emma Jamison (SS# 777-77-7777), an independent contractor of SingleStep Industries (993 Valley Court, Detroit, MI 48126). Emma (who lives at 12 Handsome Place, Detroit, MI 48126) earns nonemployee compensation of $32,900 during the year. SingleStep Industries (federal identification #88-8888888) does not use account numbers, and does not report state data.

KCb 5-8 Complete Form 1096

Complete Form 1096 (included in the Student Exercise Files) for Goldbar Company, based on the information from KCb 5-7 and the following. In addition to Emma Jamison's Form 1099-MISC, the company issued one other 1099-MISC form. Total compensation across these two forms is $44,000, on which no federal income tax was withheld. The President of Goldbar Company, George Borstein, (telephone number 313-555-8880, fax number 313-555-8881, e-mail address; gborstein@gcompany.com) signs and submits the form on the due date.

KCb 5-9 Calculate Self-Employment Tax

For each of the following individuals, calculate the applicable self-employment tax.

1. Allison Wilson earns net self-employment income of $74,200. She does not work a second job.

2. Martin Hughes earns net self-employment income of $152,000. He works a second job from which he receives FICA taxable earnings of $93,100.

3. Elisa Grant earns net self-employment income of $198,000. She works a second job from which she receives FICA taxable earnings of $71,000.

Continuing Payroll Problem

For all assignments in this section, necessary IRS forms and/or Excel templates are located in the Student Resource Center.

CPP 5-1 Calculating & Recording Employer Payroll Taxes

Calculate Federal Unemployment Tax Payable & State Unemployment Tax Payable for a number of employees of TCLH Industries, a manufacturer of cleaning products. Conclude by recording the necessary journal entry for employer payroll taxes. As TCLH Industries operates in North Carolina, assume a SUTA tax rate of 1.2%, and a taxable earnings threshold of $20,900.

1. Calculate total employer's FUTA & SUTA tax. Current period taxable earnings for FUTA & SUTA taxes are the same as those for FICA taxes. Year-to-date taxable earnings for FUTA & SUTA taxes are as follows:
   - Zachary Fox: $2,100
   - Calvin Bell: $109,400
   - Michaela Walton: $141,000
   - Suzanne Steinberg: $113,100

2. Record the journal entry to account for employer payroll taxes based on the totals in the payroll register, and the above calculations.

Critical Thinking

CT 5-1 Compare the Federal & State Unemployment Programs

The federal and state unemployment programs are designed to work in conjunction to ensure that all eligible workers receive appropriate unemployment benefits. Naturally, as part of this process, certain elements are handled by the federal government, while others are controlled by the individual states. In this exercise, you will use the internet to research the manner in which the federal government and individual states divide responsibility for distributing unemployment benefits.

Begin by researching the manner in which unemployment benefits are distributed to workers. Continue by examining the elements of the program that are handled by the federal government, and those responsibilities that typically fall to the individual states. Write a paragraph of at least five sentences in which you discuss that which you have learned about the division of responsibilities in the unemployment program.

Submit your final file based on the guidelines provided by your instructor.

CT 5-2 Research Self-Employment Taxes

Self-employment taxes are levied to ensure that the equivalent of Social Security and Medicare taxes are paid by individuals who are self-employed. As you have seen, these taxes were established by the Self Employment Contributions Act of 1954 (SECA). In this exercise, you will use the internet to research both the historical evolution of SECA, and the current impact of the act.

First research the components of SECA, and the historical SECA tax rates. Then examine the primary objections to the act. Write a paragraph of at least five sentences in which you discuss the tax rate trend since the act was established, and the arguments against this taxation. Then write whether you agree with the levying of SECA tax, and provide your reasoning.

Submit your final file(s) based on the guidelines provided by your instructor.

Periodic & Year-End Payroll Reporting

LEARNING OBJECTIVES

After studying this chapter, you will be able to:

- Record the necessary payroll journal entries

- Complete quarterly Form 941

- Complete year-end Form 940

- Complete year-end Form W-2

- Complete year-end Form W-3

At this stage, you've completed all steps for a single payroll cycle. However, you're not done yet, as there are a number of remaining payroll reporting requirements. While some of the necessary forms are completed on a quarterly basis, others are submitted annually. Similarly, there are a number of payroll accounting journal entries that must be recorded as a given year progresses. In this chapter, you'll begin by examining the remaining payroll accounting that must be performed. You'll then review a number of required forms, including Forms 941, 940, W-2, and W-3. As you work through this chapter, note that a calendar of IRS filing due dates may be found in Appendix B in the back of the book.

CASE STUDY

Completing Payroll Recording for Lucky Ties Apparel

Although Lucky Ties Apparel has now accounted for the different payroll taxes that must be remitted, it has not yet completed all payroll-related requirements. The company has a number of federal and state payroll reporting requirements that must be met in order to avoid financial penalties. Lucky Ties Apparel also must record journal entries when payroll-related payments are made.

To meet these requirements, you first examine the remaining journal entries that are necessary when both deducted amounts and employer payroll taxes are paid to the associated organization (federal government, insurance provider, etc.). You then review a number of federal payroll-related forms such as Form 941, 940, W-2, and W-3.

Employers must report payroll-related activity by filing Form 941 on a quarterly basis.

Form **941 for 2013:** **Employer's QUARTERLY Federal Tax Return**
(Rev. January 2013)
Department of the Treasury — Internal Revenue Service
950113
OMB No. 1545-0029

Employer identification number (EIN) ☐☐ – ☐☐☐☐☐☐☐

Name (not your trade name)

Trade name (if any)

Address
Number   Street   Suite or room number
City   State   ZIP code

Report for this Quarter of 2013
(Check one.)

☐ 1: January, February, March
☐ 2: April, May, June
☐ 3: July, August, September
☐ 4: October, November, December

Instructions and prior year forms are available at www.irs.gov/form941.

Read the separate instructions before you complete Form 941. Type or print within the boxes.

Part 1:   Answer these questions for this quarter.

1   Number of employees who received wages, tips, or other compensation for the pay period including: Mar. 12 (Quarter 1), June 12 (Quarter 2), Sept. 12 (Quarter 3), or Dec. 12 (Quarter 4)   1

2   Wages, tips, and other compensation   2

3   Income tax withheld from wages, tips, and other compensation   3

4   If no wages, tips, and other compensation are subject to social security or Medicare tax   ☐ Check and go to line 6.

		Column 1	Column 2
5a	Taxable social security wages		× .124 =
5b	Taxable social security tips		× .124 =
5c	Taxable Medicare wages & tips		× .029 =
5d	Taxable wages & tips subject to Additional Medicare Tax withholding		× .009 =

5e   Add Column 2 from lines 5a, 5b, 5c, and 5d   5e

5f   Section 3121(q) Notice and Demand—Tax due on unreported tips (see instructions)   5f

6   Total taxes before adjustments (add lines 3, 5e, and 5f)   6

7   Current quarter's adjustment for fractions of cents   7

8   Current quarter's adjustment for sick pay   8

9   Current quarter's adjustments for tips and group-term life insurance   9

10   Total taxes after adjustments. Combine lines 6 through 9   10

11   Total deposits for this quarter, including overpayment applied from a prior quarter and overpayment applied from Form 941-X or Form 944-X filed in the current quarter   11

12a   COBRA premium assistance payments (see instructions)   12a

12b   Number of individuals provided COBRA premium assistance

13   Add lines 11 and 12a   13

14   Balance due. If line 10 is more than line 13, enter the difference and see instructions   14

15   Overpayment. If line 13 is more than line 10, enter the difference   Check one: ☐ Apply to next return. ☐ Send a refund.

▶ You MUST complete both pages of Form 941 and SIGN it.   Next ▶

For Privacy Act and Paperwork Reduction Act Notice, see the back of the Payment Voucher.   Cat. No. 17001Z   Form **941** (Rev. 1-2013)

Accounting for Payroll (Periodic Entries)

Before You Begin: This section assumes prior knowledge of the transaction-recording process. Consult with your instructor to determine if you are required to review this material.

You have learned how to record journal entries for employee payroll and employer payroll taxes. In each of these journal entries, multiple liability accounts were credited, because, as of the payroll date, none of the deductions from employee pay or employer taxes were actually remitted to the organization to which they are owed. When these liabilities are actually paid, a different journal entry is booked to account for the payment.

Federal income tax withholding, Social Security tax (employee & employer portions), and Medicare tax (employee & employer portions) must be paid by the employer on either a monthly or semiweekly basis. The applicable payment increment is determined by reviewing the employer's **lookback period**.

The lookback period for a given year is the previous July 1 through June 30. For example, the lookback period for 2013 runs from July 1, 2011 through June 30, 2012. If an employer reports less than $50,000 in combined taxes (the three taxes listed above) during the lookback period, the company is a **monthly depositor**. Alternatively, if the reported taxes exceed $50,000, the employer is a **semiweekly depositor**.

Monthly depositors must submit each month's payment by the 15th of the following month. Semiweekly depositors whose pay date falls from Wednesday to Friday must submit payment by the following Wednesday, while those whose pay date falls from Saturday to Tuesday must submit payment by the following Friday.

Type of Depositor	Payment Dates
Monthly	15th of the following month
Semiweekly (pay date Wed-Fri)	Following Wednesday
Semiweekly (pay date Sat-Tues)	Following Friday

When payment is made, the journal entry appears as follows:

9/15	Federal Income Tax Payable	XXXXX	
	Social Security Tax Payable	XXXXX	
	Medicare Tax Payable	XXXXX	
	Cash		XXXXX
	Monthly Payment of Federal Taxes		

The liability (payable) accounts are debited to reduce their balances. This is appropriate, as the amounts are no longer owed. The corresponding credit is to the Cash account, to illustrate that the employer now has less cash than it did before. Since Social Security tax and Medicare tax are both matched by the employer, the amounts of these taxes in the journal entry will combine the employee and employer portions.

NOTE! State income tax payments are usually made on schedules similar to those for federal payments. In those cases the state payment is included as part of the earlier journal entry. Check your individual state's regulations to determine the exact payment requirements.

Submitting Unemployment Tax Payments

FUTA Tax Payment Schedule

Quarter	Payment Date
1st Quarter (Jan. – Mar.)	April 30
2nd Quarter (Apr. – Jun.)	July 31
3rd Quarter (Jul. – Sept.)	October 31
4th Quarter (Oct. – Dec.)	January 31

While federal unemployment tax is paid on a quarterly basis, many small businesses are permitted to remit payment once at the end of each year. Employers whose FUTA tax owed does not exceed $500 at the end of a quarter, are permitted to delay payment. In these instances, the employer must remit payment either when total FUTA tax owed exceeds $500 at the end of a quarter, or after the 4th quarter of the year, whichever comes first. Stated differently, an employer only must remit payment by the due dates listed here (at left) if the total FUTA tax owed exceeds $500 at the end of a quarter. State unemployment taxes are also typically remitted on a quarterly basis, with specific regulations differing from state to state.

For those quarters in which FUTA tax must be paid, the payment is due at a different time than the other federal taxes, and therefore is typically paid separately. As such, the associated journal entry is as follows:

9/15	FUTA Tax Payable	XXXXX	
	Cash		XXXXX
	Quarterly Payment of Unemployment Taxes		

SUTA tax typically follows a similar payment schedule (depending on the individual state's regulations), and when paid at the same time as FUTA tax, would be included in the above journal entry.

TIP! When a payment date for any of the previously listed taxes falls on either a weekend or holiday, the employer is permitted to submit payment on the next business day.

Making Voluntary Withholding Payments

The payments for voluntary deductions are typically made at set intervals during the year. These intervals differ, based on the deduction in question and the employer. When, for example, withheld charitable contributions are remitted to the designated organization, the associated journal entry appears as follows:

10/1	Charitable Contribution Payable	XXXXX	
	Cash		XXXXX
	Payment of Withheld Charitable Contributions		

Case In Point 6-1 — ## Record a Quarterly Federal Tax Payment Journal Entry

In this example, we'll record the following:

- One journal entry to account for the month-end payment of the federal taxes

- One journal entry to account for the payment of federal unemployment taxes

- One journal entry to account for the payment of the voluntary deductions of Lucky Ties Apparel

The company is a monthly depositor whose December federal taxes, 4th quarter FUTA taxes, and 4th quarter voluntary deductions are displayed below. Assume that each voluntary deduction is remitted to the respective organization on a quarterly basis, on the last day of the first month after the end of the quarter. All tax payments are made in a timely manner on the payment due date (which, for this quarter, is not impacted by a weekend or holiday).

December Tax Totals	
Federal Income Tax	$1,942
Employee's Social Security Tax	$1,215
Employee's Medicare Tax	$395
Employer's Social Security Tax	$1,215
Employer's Medicare Tax	$395

4th Quarter Totals	
FUTA Tax	$66
Retirement Plan	$598
Health Insurance	$480
Charitable Contribution	$450
Cafeteria Plan	$912

1.

1/15	Federal Income Tax Payable	1,942	
	Social Security Tax Payable	2,430	
	Medicare Tax Payable	790	
	Cash		5,162
	Monthly Payment of Federal Taxes		

Social Security and Medicare payments include both the employee and employer portions. The journal entry is recorded on January 15, as the 4th quarter payment (covering October through December, which is the 4th quarter of the year) is due on the 15th day of the month after quarter end (January).

2.

1/31	FUTA Tax Payable	66	
	Cash		66
	Quarterly Payment of Unemployment Taxes		

Based on the FUTA tax payment schedule, the 4th quarter unemployment tax payment is made on January 31.

3.

1/31	Retirement Plan Payable	598	
	Health Insurance Payable	480	
	Charitable Contribution Payable	450	
	Cafeteria Plan Payable	912	
	Cash		2,440
	Quarterly Payment of Voluntary Deductions		

In spite of the fact that these voluntary withholding amounts were paid on the same day as the FUTA tax, it is not advisable to include FUTA tax with these items in one journal entry. By writing two journal entries, each one has a more specific purpose. In fact, many companies would not combine these voluntary deductions into one journal entry, opting instead to write a separate entry for each one. Both the approach illustrated above and this alternative method are acceptable.

Completing Form 941 (Employer's Quarterly Federal Tax Return)

On the Web

www.irs.gov/pub/
irs-pdf/f941.pdf

Employers are required to complete and submit Form 941 on a quarterly basis. This form summarizes the payroll activity (including wages, employee taxes, and employer taxes) of a business for the most recent quarter. The Federal Income Tax Payable, Social Security Tax Payable, and Medicare Tax Payable accounts are (for monthly depositors) debited each month in order to reduce their balances when the taxes are remitted. To enter the correct tax figures in Form 941, the employer may sum the amounts in these journal entries to arrive at the quarterly totals. Similar calculations, based on the payroll register totals, may be made to arrive at the quarterly wage figures.

The due dates for the quarterly Form 941's are the same as the due dates for FUTA payments. Therefore, Form 941 is due by the last day of the first month after each quarter has ended.

NOTE!   If an employer's total annual tax liability for federal income tax withholding, Social Security tax, and Medicare tax is less than $1,000, the employer is not required to file quarterly Form 941, and in their place may instead file Form 944 at the end of the year.

As you saw previously, employers typically make payments on either a monthly or semiweekly basis. However, if an employer owes total taxes of less than $2,500 for either the current or preceding quarter, the company is permitted to disregard the monthly or semiweekly schedule, and instead submit payment either with Form 941 or using another method prior to the Form 941 due date.

WARNING! If total accumulated tax owed exceeds $100,000 at the end of any day, then the **next-day deposit rule** is triggered, and the employer must pay all taxes owed on the following business day.

The quarterly Form 941 payments, and the amounts owed during the quarter, will not necessarily be equal. One common cause of this discrepancy is the rounding of tax payments, resulting in differences of a few cents. Form 941 is designed to reconcile the federal tax payments that have been made with the federal taxes that are owed during a quarter. Any differences between these amounts are accounted for in the form, or result in either a *Balance Due*, or *Overpayment* amount that is reported at the bottom of page 1 of the form.

Using the Electronic Federal Tax Payment System

On the Web

www.eftps.gov

The **Electronic Federal Tax Payment System (EFTPS)** provides the simplest method for employers to submit federal tax payments. To use the system, an employer must enroll by acquiring a pin number which, when combined with the employer identification number, identifies the employer in the system. The pin may be requested either by phone or internet, and is mailed to the employer.

Once the pin is established and the employer has linked the desired bank account, the employer may remit payment either by phone (1-800-555-3453) or internet (a separate internet password must be established to use this method).

TIP! The EFTPS is a free service, and is therefore the most efficient method for remitting federal tax payments.

When using the EFTPS, payments must be submitted by 8:00 p.m. the day before the tax due date. Alternative payment methods (such as wire transfer) must be used when making a same-day payment. If the employer chooses not to use the EFTPS, other available payment methods include credit or debit card and mailing a check (which must be postmarked by the tax due date). When a check is mailed with Form 941, the employer must also mail Form 941-V, which is a payment voucher summarizing basic information related to the payment. The employer is subject to penalties and interest if federal tax payments are not remitted in a timely manner.

NOTE! State tax payments may typically be remitted in a manner similar to that described here for federal tax payments.

Examine the Form: 941

Part 1 of Form 941 summarizes quarterly federal tax liabilities and payments.

Form **941 for 2013:** **Employer's QUARTERLY Federal Tax Return**

950113

(Rev. January 2013)   Department of the Treasury — Internal Revenue Service

OMB No. 1545-0029

Employer identification number (EIN) ☐☐ – ☐☐☐☐☐☐☐

Name (not your trade name)

Trade name (if any)

Address
Number   Street   Suite or room number
City   State   ZIP code

Report for this Quarter of 2013
(Check one.)

☐ **1:** January, February, March

☐ **2:** April, May, June

☐ **3:** July, August, September

☐ **4:** October, November, December

Instructions and prior year forms are available at *www.irs.gov/form941*.

Read the separate instructions before you complete Form 941. Type or print within the boxes.

Part 1:   **Answer these questions for this quarter.**

1   Number of employees who received wages, tips, or other compensation for the pay period
including: *Mar. 12* (Quarter 1), *June 12* (Quarter 2), *Sept. 12* (Quarter 3), or *Dec. 12* (Quarter 4)   **1**

2   Wages, tips, and other compensation **2**

3   Income tax withheld from wages, tips, and other compensation **3**

4   If no wages, tips, and other compensation are subject to social security or Medicare tax   ☐ Check and go to line 6.

		Column 1		Column 2
5a	Taxable social security wages . .		× .124 =	
5b	Taxable social security tips . . .		× .124 =	
5c	Taxable Medicare wages & tips. .		× .029 =	
5d	Taxable wages & tips subject to Additional Medicare Tax withholding		× .009 =	

5e   Add Column 2 from lines 5a, 5b, 5c, and 5d **5e**

5f   Section 3121(q) Notice and Demand—Tax due on unreported tips (see instructions)   . . .   **5f**

6   Total taxes before adjustments (add lines 3, 5e, and 5f) **6**

7   Current quarter's adjustment for fractions of cents **7**

8   Current quarter's adjustment for sick pay **8**

9   Current quarter's adjustments for tips and group-term life insurance **9**

10   Total taxes after adjustments. Combine lines 6 through 9   . . . .   **10**

11   Total deposits for this quarter, including overpayment applied from a prior quarter and
overpayment applied from Form 941-X or Form 944-X filed in the current quarter   . . .   **11**

12a   COBRA premium assistance payments (see instructions) **12a**

12b   Number of individuals provided COBRA premium assistance   . .

13   Add lines 11 and 12a **13**

14   Balance due. If line 10 is more than line 13, enter the difference and see instructions   . . .   **14**

15   Overpayment. If line 13 is more than line 10, enter the difference   ☐ .   Check one: ☐ Apply to next return.   ☐ Send a refund.

▶ **You MUST complete both pages of Form 941 and SIGN it.**   Next ▶

For Privacy Act and Paperwork Reduction Act Notice, see the back of the Payment Voucher.   Cat. No. 17001Z   Form **941** (Rev. 1-2013)

The top portion of the form (including employer identification number, name, and address) must be completed in its entirety. The *Trade name* line is left blank, unless a business has a *doing business as* (DBA) name (a name under which the company conducts its business, and that differs from its legal name). The checkbox for the corresponding quarter should also be selected.

Part 1 of Form 941 should be completed as follows:

Line 1: Only employees who actually received compensation during the current quarter are counted when determining the number of employees to enter here.

Line 2: This box includes all compensation that would appear in box 1 of Form W-2. This includes all compensation that is subject to federal income tax withholding.

Line 3: Federal income tax withholding for the quarter is entered on this line.

Line 4: Compensation is typically subject to FICA taxes, and therefore this box is rarely checked.

Line 5a: Wages subject to Social Security tax, and their associated taxes, are entered here. If, prior to the beginning of the quarter, all employees have exceeded the Social Security wage base ($113,700 for 2013), then both columns are left blank. Social Security wages in Column 1 are multiplied by .124 (12.4%) to arrive at Social Security tax in Column 2. This is double the Social Security tax rate of 6.2%, to account for both the employee withholding and the employer match.

Line 5b: All employee tips that are subject to Social Security tax (namely, those earned prior to each employee reaching the Social Security wage base) are reported in Column 1, while the associated taxes are entered in Column 2.

Line 5c: All wages and tips subject to Medicare tax, and their associated taxes, are entered in Column 1. The employer then calculates Medicare tax and enters it in Column 2. Similar to the Social Security lines above, the Medicare tax rate of 1.45% is doubled (.029, or 2.9%) to account for both the employee and employer portions.

Line 5d: All wages and tips subject to additional Medicare tax (those that exceed $200,000 for the year for an individual employee), and their associated taxes, are entered on this line. Notice that the additional Medicare tax rate of .009 (0.9%) is displayed to assist in calculating the applicable Medicare tax. This figure is not doubled, as the employer does not match this tax.

Line 5e: This line totals all tax figures from lines 5a through 5d, and therefore represents the total Social Security and Medicare tax for the quarter.

Line 5f: When an employer is informed by the IRS that taxes are owed on unreported employee tips, the associated taxes are displayed here.

Line 6: Total federal income tax withholding, Social Security tax, and Medicare tax combined are entered here.

Line 7: Cents may be added or subtracted here in order to eliminate any rounding-related differences between tax owed and tax withheld. There is no penalty for entering these types of differences; however the amount displayed should only be a few cents (either positive or negative). Although the IRS is unlikely to question slightly higher amounts (such as $0.25 or $0.50), there should be no need for adjustments of this magnitude, as rounding issues are highly unlikely to result in such discrepancies. An amount that rounds up to a whole dollar (greater than $0.50) would constitute an additional amount owed to the IRS.

Line 8: If Social Security and Medicare taxes for sick pay were withheld by a third party, these taxes are entered here.

Examine the Form: 941 (continued)

Line 9: Uncollected Social Security and Medicare taxes related to tips and/or group-term life insurance are entered here.

Line 10: The sum of the prior four lines is entered here. The $2,500 threshold, below which total tax may be remitted with Form 941, is compared to this line.

Line 11: Actual federal tax deposits made by the employer are entered here.

Line 12a & 12b: 65% of the insurance premium assistance provided to COBRA-eligible individuals, and the number of individuals for whom assistance is provided, are entered on these lines. COBRA (Consolidated Omnibus Budget Reconciliation Act) health coverage is available to certain employees (and their spouses & dependents) at an increased rate, for a period of time after employment ends.

Line 13: The sum of lines 11 and 12a.

Line 14: This line is only populated if total taxes on line 10 exceed total deposits and credits on line 13. In this case, the difference between these two amounts is placed here, and payment is remitted for this amount.

Line 15: This line is only populated if total deposits and credits on line 13 exceed total taxes on line 10. In this case, the difference between these two amounts is entered, and the employer must elect to either receive a check for the overpayment or apply it to the next return.

Parts 2 through 5 of Form 941 should be completed as follows:

Part 2; Line 16: The employer selects only one of these three options. If the employer qualifies for the first category, then the company does not check either the monthly or semiweekly box, regardless of the deposit schedule utilized. Monthly depositors also must enter monthly tax liability amounts in this section.

Part 3; Lines 17 & 18: Line 17 must be checked if wages will no longer be paid. Line 18 is checked by seasonal employers (those who do not pay wages year-round, and therefore do not file Form 941 for all four quarters) on every Form 941 that is filed.

Part 4: To allow a third-party (such as the employer's accountant) to discuss Form 941 with the IRS, this section must be completed. Note that the third-party may not bind the employer to additional taxes, but instead may only discuss the details with the IRS. The third-party designation lasts for one year, unless terminated early via written request. Additionally, if no pin is selected by the employer, then the third-party designation will not be valid.

Part 5: The employer must sign and complete the top portion of this section for the form to be valid. If a paid preparer (such as the employer's accountant) completed the form, this individual is required to complete the *Paid Preparer Use Only* section.

Parts 2–5 of Form 941 require additional information regarding quarterly deposits and the company itself.

950213

Name *(not your trade name)*	**Employer identification number (EIN)**

Part 2: Tell us about your deposit schedule and tax liability for this quarter.

If you are unsure about whether you are a monthly schedule depositor or a semiweekly schedule depositor, see Pub. 15 (Circular E), section 11.

16   Check one: ☐   Line 10 on this return is less than $2,500 or line 10 on the return for the prior quarter was less than $2,500, and you did not incur a $100,000 next-day deposit obligation during the current quarter. If line 10 for the prior quarter was less than $2,500 but line 10 on this return is $100,000 or more, you must provide a record of your federal tax liability. If you are a monthly schedule depositor, complete the deposit schedule below; if you are a semiweekly schedule depositor, attach Schedule B (Form 941). Go to Part 3.

☐   **You were a monthly schedule depositor for the entire quarter.** Enter your tax liability for each month and total liability for the quarter, then go to Part 3.

Tax liability: Month 1   [_____ . __]

Month 2   [_____ . __]

Month 3   [_____ . __]

Total liability for quarter   [_____ . __]   Total must equal line 10.

☐   **You were a semiweekly schedule depositor for any part of this quarter.** Complete Schedule B (Form 941), Report of Tax Liability for Semiweekly Schedule Depositors, and attach it to Form 941.

Part 3: Tell us about your business. If a question does NOT apply to your business, leave it blank.

17   If your business has closed or you stopped paying wages . . . . ☐ Check here, and

enter the final date you paid wages   [__ / __ / ____] .

18   If you are a seasonal employer and you do not have to file a return for every quarter of the year   . .   ☐ Check here.

Part 4: May we speak with your third-party designee?

Do you want to allow an employee, a paid tax preparer, or another person to discuss this return with the IRS? See the instructions for details.

☐ Yes.   Designee's name and phone number   [_____]   [_____]

Select a 5-digit Personal Identification Number (PIN) to use when talking to the IRS.   ☐ ☐ ☐ ☐ ☐

☐ No.

Part 5: Sign here. You MUST complete both pages of Form 941 and SIGN it.

Under penalties of perjury, I declare that I have examined this return, including accompanying schedules and statements, and to the best of my knowledge and belief, it is true, correct, and complete. Declaration of preparer (other than taxpayer) is based on all information of which preparer has any knowledge.

✗   **Sign your name here**   [_____]

Print your name here   [_____]

Print your title here   [_____]

Date   [__ / __ / ____]

Best daytime phone   [_____]

Paid Preparer Use Only   Check if you are self-employed   . . .   ☐

Preparer's name	[_____]	PTIN	[_____]
Preparer's signature	[_____]	Date	[__ / __ / ____]
Firm's name (or yours if self-employed)	[_____]	EIN	[_____]
Address	[_____]	Phone	[_____]
City	[_____]	State [____]	ZIP code	[_____]

Page **2**

Form **941** (Rev. 1-2013)

Examine the Form: 941 (continued)

Form 941-V is only submitted with Form 941 when payment is included with the form.

✂ ┄┄┄┄ ▼ **Detach Here and Mail With Your Payment and Form 941.** ▼ ┄┄┄┄ ✂

Form 941-V

Department of the Treasury
Internal Revenue Service

Payment Voucher

► Do not staple this voucher or your payment to Form 941.

OMB No. 1545-0029

20**13**

1 Enter your employer identification number (EIN).	2 **Enter the amount of your payment.** ► Make your check or money order payable to **"United States Treasury"**	Dollars	Cents

3 Tax Period	4 Enter your business name (individual name if sole proprietor).
○ 1st Quarter ○ 3rd Quarter	Enter your address.
○ 2nd Quarter ○ 4th Quarter	Enter your city, state, and ZIP code.

Form 941-V: The payment amount entered on Line 2 must match the Balance Due displayed on Line 14 of Form 941. All other information (employer identification number, quarter, business name, and address) must also match Form 941.

Schedule B should be completed as follows:

The top portion of the form must be completed with the employer's identification number, company name, quarter, and year.

The body of the form contains boxes that correspond with each day of the prior quarter. Tax liabilities (not deposits) are entered in these boxes on those days when wages are paid. Monthly and quarterly totals are then entered in the boxes to the right. The total liability for the quarter, which is entered at the bottom-right of the form, should equal Line 10 of Form 941. Therefore, the purpose of Schedule B is to provide a breakdown of the total taxes owed for the quarter.

Schedule B must be submitted with Form 941 for all semiweekly depositors.

Schedule B (Form 941):
Report of Tax Liability for Semiweekly Schedule Depositors

960311

(Rev. January 2014)
Department of the Treasury — Internal Revenue Service

OMB No. 1545-0029

Employer identification number (EIN)

Name *(not your trade name)*

Calendar year

(Also check quarter)

Report for this Quarter...
(Check one.)

- [ ] **1:** January, February, March
- [ ] **2:** April, May, June
- [ ] **3:** July, August, September
- [ ] **4:** October, November, December

Use this schedule to show your TAX LIABILITY for the quarter; DO NOT use it to show your deposits. When you file this form with Form 941 or Form 941-SS, DO NOT change your tax liability by adjustments reported on any Forms 941-X or 944-X. You must fill out this form and attach it to Form 941 or Form 941-SS if you are a semiweekly schedule depositor or became one because your accumulated tax liability on any day was $100,000 or more. Write your daily tax liability on the numbered space that corresponds to the date wages were paid. See Section 11 in Pub. 15 (Circular E), Employer's Tax Guide, for details.

Month 1

				Tax liability for Month 1
1	9	17	25	
2	10	18	26	
3	11	19	27	
4	12	20	28	
5	13	21	29	
6	14	22	30	
7	15	23	31	
8	16	24		

Month 2

				Tax liability for Month 2
1	9	17	25	
2	10	18	26	
3	11	19	27	
4	12	20	28	
5	13	21	29	
6	14	22	30	
7	15	23	31	
8	16	24		

Month 3

				Tax liability for Month 3
1	9	17	25	
2	10	18	26	
3	11	19	27	
4	12	20	28	
5	13	21	29	
6	14	22	30	
7	15	23	31	
8	16	24		

Fill in your total liability for the quarter (Month 1 + Month 2 + Month 3) ▶

Total must equal line 10 on Form 941 or Form 941-SS.

Total liability for the quarter

For Paperwork Reduction Act Notice, see separate instructions.   IRS.gov/form941   Cat. No. 11967Q   Schedule B (Form 941) (Rev. 1-2014)

WARNING!   Be certain to enter tax liabilities in these boxes, not the actual deposits that are made. Schedule B is designed to summarize the actual liabilities incurred for a quarter, not the payments that are remitted.

Completing Quarterly State Payroll Forms

For those states that levy a state income tax, forms must be submitted to summarize the employer's payroll activity. Similar to Form 941, these forms typically are submitted on a quarterly basis, and the taxes summarized in these forms typically must be deposited periodically during the quarter.

Case In Point 6-2	Complete Form 941

In this example, we will complete Form 941 for the 4th quarter of the year for Lucky Ties Apparel (employer identification #11-1111111). Assume that Lucky Ties Apparel (located at 77 Main Street, Rochester, NY 14602) chooses to complete and mail Form 941 on the due date. The form is signed by the President of the company, Harold Cameron (telephone #: 585-555-6281). Based on the lookback period, Lucky Ties Apparel is a monthly depositor, and has deposited all tax amounts in a timely manner. No adjustments are required to align the total deposits with taxes owed, all eight employees worked during each of the three months, and Lucky Ties Apparel does not choose to allow a third-party to discuss the form with the IRS. Fourthquarter earnings, and associated taxes withheld from employee earnings, are as follows:

	October	November	December	4th Quarter	Associated Earnings
FWT	$1,845	$2,120	$1,942	$5,907	$85,472
Social Security	$1,260	$1,305	$1,215	$3,780	$60,968
Medicare	$420	$445	$395	$1,260	$86,897

Form **941 for 2013:** **Employer's QUARTERLY Federal Tax Return**   950113
(Rev. January 2013)   Department of the Treasury — Internal Revenue Service   OMB No. 1545-0029

Employer identification number (EIN)   1 1 — 1 1 1 1 1 1 1 1

Name (not your trade name)   Lucky Ties Apparel

Trade name (if any)

Address   77 Main Street
  Number   Street   Suite or room number

  Rochester   NY   14602
  City   State   ZIP code

Report for this Quarter of 2013
(Check one.)

☐ **1:** January, February, March
☐ **2:** April, May, June
☐ **3:** July, August, September
☒ **4:** October, November, December

Instructions and prior year forms are available at *www.irs.gov/form941*.

Read the separate instructions before you complete Form 941. Type or print within the boxes.

Part 1:   Answer these questions for this quarter.

#	Description			Value
1	Number of employees who received wages, tips, or other compensation for the pay period including: *Mar. 12* (Quarter 1), *June 12* (Quarter 2), *Sept. 12* (Quarter 3), or *Dec. 12* (Quarter 4) **1**			8
2	Wages, tips, and other compensation **2**			85472 .
3	Income tax withheld from wages, tips, and other compensation **3**			5907 .

4   If no wages, tips, and other compensation are subject to social security or Medicare tax   ☐ Check and go to line 6.

		Column 1		Column 2
5a	Taxable social security wages . .	60968 .	× .124 =	7560 .
5b	Taxable social security tips . . .	.	× .124 =	.
5c	Taxable Medicare wages & tips . .	86897 .	× .029 =	2520 .
5d	Taxable wages & tips subject to Additional Medicare Tax withholding	.	× .009 =	.

#	Description	Value
5e	Add Column 2 from lines 5a, 5b, 5c, and 5d **5e**	10080 .
5f	Section 3121(q) Notice and Demand—Tax due on unreported tips (see instructions) **5f**	.
6	Total taxes before adjustments (add lines 3, 5e, and 5f) **6**	15987 .
7	Current quarter's adjustment for fractions of cents **7**	.
8	Current quarter's adjustment for sick pay **8**	.
9	Current quarter's adjustments for tips and group-term life insurance **9**	.
10	Total taxes after adjustments. Combine lines 6 through 9 **10**	15987 .
11	Total deposits for this quarter, including overpayment applied from a prior quarter and overpayment applied from Form 941-X or Form 944-X filed in the current quarter **11**	15987 .
12a	COBRA premium assistance payments (see instructions) **12a**	.
12b	Number of individuals provided COBRA premium assistance . .	
13	Add lines 11 and 12a **13**	15987 .
14	Balance due. If line 10 is more than line 13, enter the difference and see instructions **14**	.
15	Overpayment. If line 13 is more than line 10, enter the difference . Check one: ☐ Apply to next return. ☐ Send a refund.	

▶ You MUST complete both pages of Form 941 and SIGN it.   Next ▶

For Privacy Act and Paperwork Reduction Act Notice, see the back of the Payment Voucher.   Cat. No. 17001Z   Form **941** (Rev. 1-2013)

Earnings for federal income tax withholding, Social Security tax, and Medicare tax are all reported in the first five lines of the form. In addition, the Social Security tax on line 5a, and the Medicare tax on line 5c are displayed with the combined employee and employer portions.

950213

Name *(not your trade name)*	Employer identification number (EIN)

Part 2:   **Tell us about your deposit schedule and tax liability for this quarter.**

If you are unsure about whether you are a monthly schedule depositor or a semiweekly schedule depositor, see Pub. 15 (Circular E), section 11.

16   Check one: ☐   Line 10 on this return is less than $2,500 or line 10 on the return for the prior quarter was less than $2,500, and you did not incur a $100,000 next-day deposit obligation during the current quarter. If line 10 for the prior quarter was less than $2,500 but line 10 on this return is $100,000 or more, you must provide a record of your federal tax liability. If you are a monthly schedule depositor, complete the deposit schedule below; if you are a semiweekly schedule depositor, attach Schedule B (Form 941). Go to Part 3.

☒   **You were a monthly schedule depositor for the entire quarter.** Enter your tax liability for each month and total liability for the quarter, then go to Part 3.

	Tax liability:	Month 1	5205 ∎
		Month 2	5620 ∎
		Month 3	5162 ∎
	Total liability for quarter	15987 ∎	Total must equal line 10.

☐   **You were a semiweekly schedule depositor for any part of this quarter.** Complete Schedule B (Form 941), Report of Tax Liability for Semiweekly Schedule Depositors, and attach it to Form 941.

Part 3:   **Tell us about your business. If a question does NOT apply to your business, leave it blank.**

17   If your business has closed or you stopped paying wages . . . . ☐ Check here, and

enter the final date you paid wages   [/   /   ] .

18   If you are a seasonal employer and you do not have to file a return for every quarter of the year   . .   ☐ Check here.

Part 4:   **May we speak with your third-party designee?**

Do you want to allow an employee, a paid tax preparer, or another person to discuss this return with the IRS? See the instructions for details.

☐   Yes.   Designee's name and phone number   [   ]   [   ]

Select a 5-digit Personal Identification Number (PIN) to use when talking to the IRS.   ☐ ☐ ☐ ☐ ☐

☐   No.

Part 5:   **Sign here. You MUST complete both pages of Form 941 and SIGN it.**

Under penalties of perjury, I declare that I have examined this return, including accompanying schedules and statements, and to the best of my knowledge and belief, it is true, correct, and complete. Declaration of preparer (other than taxpayer) is based on all information of which preparer has any knowledge.

✗	**Sign your name here** *Harold Cameron*	Print your name here	Harold Cameron
		Print your title here	President
	Date *1/31/14*	Best daytime phone	585-555-6281

Paid Preparer Use Only   Check if you are self-employed . . . ☐

Preparer's name		PTIN	
Preparer's signature		Date	/ /
Firm's name (or yours if self-employed)		EIN	
Address		Phone	
City		State		ZIP code	

Page **2**   Form **941** (Rev. 1-2013)

As Lucky Ties Apparel is a monthly depositor, and line 10 exceeds $2,500, line 16 in Part 2 must display the monthly deposits, which in this case are the same as the monthly tax liabilities. Lastly, the form is dated 1/31/14 in Part 5, as this was the due date for the form.

Now let's expand on this example to illustrate how rounding can require the use of line 7 (current quarter's adjustment for fractions of cents). Review the following page 1 of Form 941, in which the figures include the associated cents. Note that, in this example, total deposits for the quarter equal $15,987.33.

Form **941 for 2013:** **Employer's QUARTERLY Federal Tax Return**   950113
(Rev. January 2013) Department of the Treasury — Internal Revenue Service   OMB No. 1545-0029

Employer identification number (EIN) 1 1 – 1 1 1 1 1 1 1

Name (not your trade name) Lucky Ties Apparel

Trade name (if any)

Address 77 Main Street
Number   Street   Suite or room number

Rochester   NY   14602
City   State   ZIP code

Report for this Quarter of 2013
(Check one.)

☐ **1:** January, February, March

☐ **2:** April, May, June

☐ **3:** July, August, September

☒ **4:** October, November, December

Instructions and prior year forms are available at *www.irs.gov/form941*.

Read the separate instructions before you complete Form 941. Type or print within the boxes.

Part 1:   Answer these questions for this quarter.

1   Number of employees who received wages, tips, or other compensation for the pay period including: *Mar. 12* (Quarter 1), *June 12* (Quarter 2), *Sept. 12* (Quarter 3), or *Dec. 12* (Quarter 4)   **1**   8

2   Wages, tips, and other compensation   **2**   85472 . 45

3   Income tax withheld from wages, tips, and other compensation   **3**   5907 . 20

4   If no wages, tips, and other compensation are subject to social security or Medicare tax   ☐ Check and go to line 6.

	Column 1		Column 2
5a Taxable social security wages	60968 . 47	× .124 =	7560 . 09
5b Taxable social security tips	.	× .124 =	.
5c Taxable Medicare wages & tips	86897 . 06	× .029 =	2520 . 01
5d Taxable wages & tips subject to Additional Medicare Tax withholding	.	× .009 =	.

5e   Add Column 2 from lines 5a, 5b, 5c, and 5d   **5e**   10080 . 10

5f   Section 3121(q) Notice and Demand—Tax due on unreported tips (see instructions)   **5f**   .

6   Total taxes before adjustments (add lines 3, 5e, and 5f)   **6**   15987 . 30

7   Current quarter's adjustment for fractions of cents   **7**   . 03

8   Current quarter's adjustment for sick pay   **8**   .

9   Current quarter's adjustments for tips and group-term life insurance   **9**   .

10   Total taxes after adjustments. Combine lines 6 through 9   **10**   15987 . 33

11   Total deposits for this quarter, including overpayment applied from a prior quarter and overpayment applied from Form 941-X or Form 944-X filed in the current quarter   **11**   15987 . 33

12a   COBRA premium assistance payments (see instructions)   **12a**   .

12b   Number of individuals provided COBRA premium assistance

13   Add lines 11 and 12a   **13**   15987 . 33

14   Balance due. If line 10 is more than line 13, enter the difference and see instructions   **14**   .

15   Overpayment. If line 13 is more than line 10, enter the difference   .   Check one: ☐ Apply to next return. ☐ Send a refund.

▶ You MUST complete both pages of Form 941 and SIGN it.   Next ▶

For Privacy Act and Paperwork Reduction Act Notice, see the back of the Payment Voucher.   Cat. No. 17001Z   Form **941** (Rev. 1-2013)

Line 7 displays $0.03, as rounding of the monthly tax payments resulted in a difference between the quarter's deposits and tax owed. Entering this negligible amount on line 7 leads to the figures equaling on page 1 of Form 941.

Completing Form 940 (Employer's Annual Federal Unemployment Tax Return)

On the Web

www.irs.gov/pub/
irs-pdf/f940.pdf

Assuming that an employer has made timely federal tax deposits for each of the four quarters of the year, no payments for federal income tax withholding, Social Security tax, or Medicare tax are owed at year-end. Federal unemployment tax (FUTA tax) operates in the same manner; however, as you have seen, quarterly payments are only made when FUTA tax owed exceeds $500 at the end of a quarter. These quarterly payments may be made using the EFTPS.

Small businesses that employ only a few individuals often do not exceed $500 in FUTA tax for the year, and therefore are not required to remit payment until Form 940 is submitted. When payment is included with Form 940, the form must be submitted by January 31 of the following year. When no payment is remitted with the form, the employer may wait until February 10 of the following year.

TIP! Just as with quarterly federal tax deposits on Form 941, annual FUTA tax payments remitted with Form 940 must be accompanied by a payment voucher (Form 940-V).

In those instances when at least some of an employer's FUTA earnings are not subject to SUTA tax, or when an employer operates in a credit-reduction state, the resulting increase in FUTA tax must be calculated on Schedule A. The total for this form is then transferred to page 1 of Form 940.

WARNING! The four quarterly Form 941's submitted during the year must agree, in total, with the annual figures reported on the year-end Form 940.

Examine the Form: 940

Form 940 requires both payroll and state information that allows for FUTA tax to be determined.

Form **940 for 2013:** **Employer's Annual Federal Unemployment (FUTA) Tax Return**

Department of the Treasury — Internal Revenue Service

850113

OMB No. 1545-0028

Employer identification number (EIN)

□□ – □□□□□□□

Name (not your trade name)

Trade name (if any)

Address

Number   Street   Suite or room number

City   State   ZIP code

Foreign country name   Foreign province/county   Foreign postal code

Type of Return
(Check all that apply.)

□ **a.** Amended

□ **b.** Successor employer

□ **c.** No payments to employees in 2013

□ **d.** Final: Business closed or stopped paying wages

Instructions and prior-year forms are available at *www.irs.gov/form940*.

Read the separate instructions before you complete this form. Please type or print within the boxes.

Part 1:   Tell us about your return. If any line does NOT apply, leave it blank.

1a If you had to pay state unemployment tax in one state only, enter the state abbreviation .   **1a** □ □

1b If you had to pay state unemployment tax in more than one state, you are a multi-state employer . . . .   **1b** □   Check here. Complete Schedule A (Form 940).

2   If you paid wages in a state that is subject to **CREDIT REDUCTION** . . . .   **2** □   Check here. Complete Schedule A (Form 940).

Part 2:   Determine your FUTA tax before adjustments for 2013. If any line does NOT apply, leave it blank.

3   Total payments to all employees . . . .   **3** _____ ▪

4   Payments exempt from FUTA tax . . . .   **4** _____ ▪

    Check all that apply: **4a** □ Fringe benefits   **4c** □ Retirement/Pension   **4e** □ Other
                          4b □ Group-term life insurance **4d** □ Dependent care

5   Total of payments made to each employee in excess of $7,000 . . . .   **5** _____ ▪

6   Subtotal (line 4 + line 5 = line 6) . . . . . .   **6** _____ ▪

7   Total taxable FUTA wages (line 3 – line 6 = line 7) (see instructions) . . . .   **7** _____ ▪

8   FUTA tax before adjustments (line 7 × .006 = line 8) . . . .   **8** _____ ▪

Part 3:   Determine your adjustments. If any line does NOT apply, leave it blank.

9   If ALL of the taxable FUTA wages you paid were excluded from state unemployment tax, multiply line 7 by .054 (line 7 × .054 = line 9). Go to line 12 . . . .   **9** _____ ▪

10 If SOME of the taxable FUTA wages you paid were excluded from state unemployment tax, OR you paid ANY state unemployment tax late (after the due date for filing Form 940), complete the worksheet in the instructions. Enter the amount from line 7 of the worksheet . .   **10** _____ ▪

11 If credit reduction applies, enter the total from Schedule A (Form 940) . . . . . .   **11** _____ ▪

Part 4:   Determine your FUTA tax and balance due or overpayment for 2013. If any line does NOT apply, leave it blank.

12 Total FUTA tax after adjustments (lines 8 + 9 + 10 + 11 = line 12) . . . .   **12** _____ ▪

13 FUTA tax deposited for the year, including any overpayment applied from a prior year .   **13** _____ ▪

14 Balance due (If line 12 is more than line 13, enter the excess on line 14.)
    • If line 14 is more than $500, you must deposit your tax.
    • If line 14 is $500 or less, you may pay with this return. (see instructions) . . . .   **14** _____ ▪

15 Overpayment (If line 13 is more than line 12, enter the excess on line 15 and check a box below.) . . . .   **15** _____ ▪

    ▶ You **MUST** complete both pages of this form and **SIGN** it.   Check one: □ Apply to next return.   □ Send a refund.

    Next ▶

For Privacy Act and Paperwork Reduction Act Notice, see the back of Form 940-V, Payment Voucher.   Cat. No. 11234O   Form **940** (2013)

Examine the Form: 940 (continued)

The top portion of the form (including employer identification number, name, and address) must be completed in its entirety. Boxes in the *Type of Return* section should only be checked if they apply, and may all be left blank when appropriate. Note that a *Successor Employer* is one who purchases the business during the year, and who therefore may be able to apply the FUTA taxes paid by the previous employer toward the $7,000 threshold.

Part 1 of Form 940 should be completed as follows:

Line 1: The two-letter abbreviation for the employer's state is entered on line 1a for employers who operate in only one state, while the checkbox on line 1b is checked when the employer operates in more than one state.

Line 2: The checkbox is checked when the employer operates in a credit-reduction state.

Part 2 of Form 940 should be completed as follows:

Line 3: Total employee compensation, including that which is not subject to FUTA tax, is entered here. Compensation in the payroll register may be summarized to arrive at this amount.

Line 4: Enter compensation exempt from FUTA tax here, and check all boxes that apply to the exempt compensation.

Line 5: Enter total compensation that exceeds $7,000 for each individual employee. This compensation should not include that which was reported on line 4 above.

Line 6: This total represents all compensation on which FUTA tax will not be calculated.

Line 7: This total represents all compensation on which FUTA tax will be calculated.

Line 8: This total represents FUTA tax owed for the year.

Part 3 of Form 940 should be completed as follows:

Line 9: If all compensation is exempt from SUTA tax, this line accounts for the additional FUTA tax that results (as the FUTA rate cannot be reduced by 5.4% if SUTA is not applicable).

Line 10: The same as line 9, in an instance in which a portion of compensation is exempt from SUTA tax.

Line 11: The additional tax attributable to the credit reduction for certain states is entered here.

Part 4 of Form 940 should be completed as follows:

Line 12: Total FUTA tax owed for the year, including adjustments from the prior three lines.

Line 13: Total actual FUTA tax payments made during the year are entered here.

Line 14: The amount due may be remitted with Form 940 if it is less than $500.

Line 15: If deposits exceed tax owed, the difference is entered here. If this line is completed, the employer must choose to either receive a check for the overpayment, or apply it to the next quarter.

Page 2 of Form 940 must be completed for the form to be valid.

850212

Name *(not your trade name)*	**Employer identification number (EIN)**

Part 5:   Report your FUTA tax liability by quarter only if line 12 is more than $500. If not, go to Part 6.

16   Report the amount of your FUTA tax liability for each quarter; do NOT enter the amount you deposited. If you had no liability for a quarter, leave the line blank.

16a   **1st quarter** (January 1 – March 31) . . . .   16a   [.]

16b   **2nd quarter** (April 1 – June 30) . . . .   16b   [.]

16c   **3rd quarter** (July 1 – September 30) . . . .   16c   [.]

16d   **4th quarter** (October 1 – December 31) . . . .   16d   [.]

17   **Total tax liability for the year** (lines 16a + 16b + 16c + 16d = line 17) **17**   [.]   **Total must equal line 12.**

Part 6:   May we speak with your third-party designee?

Do you want to allow an employee, a paid tax preparer, or another person to discuss this return with the IRS? See the instructions for details.

☐ **Yes.**   Designee's name and phone number   [   ]   [   ]

Select a 5-digit Personal Identification Number (PIN) to use when talking to IRS   [ ] [ ] [ ] [ ] [ ]

☐ **No.**

Part 7:   Sign here. You MUST complete both pages of this form and SIGN it.

Under penalties of perjury, I declare that I have examined this return, including accompanying schedules and statements, and to the best of my knowledge and belief, it is true, correct, and complete, and that no part of any payment made to a state unemployment fund claimed as a credit was, or is to be, deducted from the payments made to employees. Declaration of preparer (other than taxpayer) is based on all information of which preparer has any knowledge.

✗ Sign your name here   [   ]

Print your name here   [   ]

Print your title here   [   ]

Date   [/ /]

Best daytime phone   [   ]

Paid Preparer Use Only   Check if you are self-employed   . ☐

Preparer's name	[ ]	PTIN	[ ]
Preparer's signature	[ ]	Date	[/ /]
Firm's name (or yours if self-employed)	[ ]	EIN	[ ]
Address	[ ]	Phone	[ ]
City	[ ] State [ ]	ZIP code	[ ]

Form **940** (2013)

Examine the Form: 940 (continued)

Parts 5-7 of Form 940 should be completed as follows:

Lines 16-17: The quarterly FUTA tax liabilities are reported here. These amounts should include any adjustments from lines 9 through 11, and therefore the total of the four amounts should equal line 12.

Part 6: Similar to Form 941, the third-party designee section is optional.

Part 7: The form must be signed by the employer in order to be valid.

The payment voucher (Form 940-V) must be submitted when payment is included with Form 940.

Form 940-V: This form is completed in the same manner as Form 941-V, with the exception that the quarter is not selected, as this is an annual form.

Schedule A (Form 940): After entering the employer identification number and company name at the top of the form, the employer then must check all states in which the company paid SUTA tax. Then, in those credit-reduction states in which the employer operates, the employer must enter applicable FUTA taxable wages and use the adjacent percentage to calculate the total credit reduction.

Schedule A is only completed when a portion of an employer's FUTA earnings are exempt from SUTA tax, or the employer operates in a credit-reduction state.

Schedule A (Form 940) for 2013:

860312

Multi-State Employer and Credit Reduction Information
Department of the Treasury — Internal Revenue Service

OMB No. 1545-0028

Employer identification number (EIN) ☐☐ – ☐☐☐☐☐☐☐

Name *(not your trade name)*

See the instructions on page 2. File this schedule with Form 940.

Place an "X" in the box of EVERY state in which you had to pay state unemployment tax this year. For each state with a credit reduction rate greater than zero, enter the FUTA taxable wages, multiply by the reduction rate, and enter the credit reduction amount. Do not include in the *FUTA Taxable Wages* box wages that were excluded from state unemployment tax (see the instructions for Step 2). If any states do not apply to you, leave them blank.

Postal Abbreviation	FUTA Taxable Wages	Reduction Rate	Credit Reduction	Postal Abbreviation	FUTA Taxable Wages	Reduction Rate	Credit Reduction
☐ AK	.	× .000	.	☐ NC	.	× .009	.
☐ AL	.	× .000	.	☐ ND	.	× .000	.
☐ AR	.	× .009	.	☐ NE	.	× .000	.
☐ AZ	.	× .000	.	☐ NH	.	× .000	.
☐ CA	.	× .009	.	☐ NJ	.	× .000	.
☐ CO	.	× .000	.	☐ NM	.	× .000	.
☐ CT	.	× .009	.	☐ NV	.	× .000	.
☐ DC	.	× .000	.	☐ NY	.	× .009	.
☐ DE	.	× .006	.	☐ OH	.	× .009	.
☐ FL	.	× .000	.	☐ OK	.	× .000	.
☐ GA	.	× .009	.	☐ OR	.	× .000	.
☐ HI	.	× .000	.	☐ PA	.	× .000	.
☐ IA	.	× .000	.	☐ RI	.	× .009	.
☐ ID	.	× .000	.	☐ SC	.	× .000	.
☐ IL	.	× .000	.	☐ SD	.	× .000	.
☐ IN	.	× .012	.	☐ TN	.	× .000	.
☐ KS	.	× .000	.	☐ TX	.	× .000	.
☐ KY	.	× .009	.	☐ UT	.	× .000	.
☐ LA	.	× .000	.	☐ VA	.	× .000	.
☐ MA	.	× .000	.	☐ VT	.	× .000	.
☐ MD	.	× .000	.	☐ WA	.	× .000	.
☐ ME	.	× .000	.	☐ WI	.	× .009	.
☐ MI	.	× .000	.	☐ WV	.	× .000	.
☐ MN	.	× .000	.	☐ WY	.	× .000	.
☐ MO	.	× .009	.	☐ PR	.	× .000	.
☐ MS	.	× .000	.	☐ VI	.	× .012	.
☐ MT	.	× .000	.				

Total Credit Reduction. Add all amounts shown in the *Credit Reduction* boxes. Enter the total here and on Form 940, line 11   . . . . ☐ .

For Privacy Act and Paperwork Reduction Act Notice, see the Instructions for Form 940.   Cat. No. 16997C   **Schedule A (Form 940) 2013**

Case In Point 6-3   Complete Form 940

In this example, we will complete the 2013 Form 940 for Lucky Ties Apparel (employer identification #11-1111111). Assume that Lucky Ties Apparel (located at 77 Main Street, Rochester, NY 14602) chooses to complete and mail Form 940 on the due date. The form is signed by the President of the company, Harold Cameron (telephone #: 585-555-6281). Lucky Ties Apparel elects to delay remitting FUTA tax until the company is required to do so. Total employee compensation for the year was $1,045,070, annual retirement plan contributions totaled $7,825, and flexible spending account contributions (some of which were for dependent care) totaled $8,300. All earnings subject to FUTA tax are also subject to SUTA tax. Lucky Ties Apparel does not choose to allow a third-party to discuss the form with the IRS. Note that all eight employees of Lucky Ties Apparel earned more than $7,000 in 2013 that was subject to FUTA tax.

Form **940 for 2013:** Employer's Annual Federal Unemployment (FUTA) Tax Return

Department of the Treasury — Internal Revenue Service

850113

OMB No. 1545-0028

Employer identification number (EIN): 1 1 – 1 1 1 1 1 1 1

Name (not your trade name): Lucky Ties Apparel

Trade name (if any):

Address: 77 Main Street
Number — Street — Suite or room number

Rochester — NY — 14602
City — State — ZIP code

Foreign country name — Foreign province/county — Foreign postal code

Type of Return (Check all that apply.)
- ☐ a. Amended
- ☐ b. Successor employer
- ☐ c. No payments to employees in 2013
- ☐ d. Final: Business closed or stopped paying wages

Instructions and prior-year forms are available at *www.irs.gov/form940*.

Read the separate instructions before you complete this form. Please type or print within the boxes.

Part 1: Tell us about your return. If any line does NOT apply, leave it blank.

1a If you had to pay state unemployment tax in one state only, enter the state abbreviation . **1a** N Y

1b If you had to pay state unemployment tax in more than one state, you are a multi-state employer . . . . **1b** ☐ Check here. Complete Schedule A (Form 940).

2 If you paid wages in a state that is subject to CREDIT REDUCTION . . . . **2** ☒ Check here. Complete Schedule A (Form 940).

Part 2: Determine your FUTA tax before adjustments for 2013. If any line does NOT apply, leave it blank.

3	Total payments to all employees	**3**	1045070 .
4	Payments exempt from FUTA tax . . . . . . **4** 16125 .		

Check all that apply: 4a ☒ Fringe benefits   4c ☒ Retirement/Pension   4e ☐ Other
4b ☐ Group-term life insurance   4d ☒ Dependent care

5	Total of payments made to each employee in excess of $7,000 . . . . **5** 972945 .		
6	Subtotal (line 4 + line 5 = line 6)	**6**	989070 .
7	Total taxable FUTA wages (line 3 – line 6 = line 7) (see instructions)	**7**	56000 .
8	FUTA tax before adjustments (line 7 x .006 = line 8)	**8**	336 .

Part 3: Determine your adjustments. If any line does NOT apply, leave it blank.

9 If ALL of the taxable FUTA wages you paid were excluded from state unemployment tax, multiply line 7 by .054 (line 7 × .054 = line 9). Go to line 12 . . . . **9** .

10 If SOME of the taxable FUTA wages you paid were excluded from state unemployment tax, OR you paid ANY state unemployment tax late (after the due date for filing Form 940), complete the worksheet in the instructions. Enter the amount from line 7 of the worksheet . . **10** .

11 If credit reduction applies, enter the total from Schedule A (Form 940) . . . . **11** 504 .

Part 4: Determine your FUTA tax and balance due or overpayment for 2013. If any line does NOT apply, leave it blank.

12 Total FUTA tax after adjustments (lines 8 + 9 + 10 + 11 = line 12) . . . . **12** 840 .

13 FUTA tax deposited for the year, including any overpayment applied from a prior year . **13** 0 .

14 Balance due (If line 12 is more than line 13, enter the excess on line 14.)
- If line 14 is more than $500, you must deposit your tax.
- If line 14 is $500 or less, you may pay with this return. (see instructions) . . . . **14** 840 .

15 Overpayment (If line 13 is more than line 12, enter the excess on line 15 and check a box below.) . . . . **15** .

▶ You **MUST** complete both pages of this form and **SIGN** it.   Check one: ☐ Apply to next return.   ☐ Send a refund.

Next ▶

For Privacy Act and Paperwork Reduction Act Notice, see the back of Form 940-V, Payment Voucher.   Cat. No. 11234O   Form **940** (2013)

Line 2 is checked because Lucky Ties Apparel operates in New York, which is a credit-reduction state. As all employees earned more than the $7,000 FUTA tax threshold for the year, total FUTA tax attributable to each employee is the $7,000 maximum. Therefore, total taxable FUTA wages on line 7 are calculated as $7,000 * 8 employees. Line 5 may then be calculated as total earnings ($1,045,070), minus total annual retirement-plan contributions ($7,825), minus flexible spending account contributions ($8,300), minus taxable FUTA wages ($56,000).

850212

Name *(not your trade name)*	Employer identification number (EIN)

Part 5: Report your FUTA tax liability by quarter only if line 12 is more than $500. If not, go to Part 6.

16 Report the amount of your FUTA tax liability for each quarter; do NOT enter the amount you deposited. If you had no liability for a quarter, leave the line blank.

16a	1st quarter (January 1 – March 31)	16a	336.
16b	2nd quarter (April 1 – June 30)	16b	0.
16c	3rd quarter (July 1 – September 30)	16c	0.
16d	4th quarter (October 1 – December 31)	16d	504.

17 Total tax liability for the year (lines 16a + 16b + 16c + 16d = line 17) 17   840.   Total must equal line 12.

Part 6: May we speak with your third-party designee?

Do you want to allow an employee, a paid tax preparer, or another person to discuss this return with the IRS? See the instructions for details.

☐ Yes. Designee's name and phone number

Select a 5-digit Personal Identification Number (PIN) to use when talking to IRS

☐ No.

Part 7: Sign here. You MUST complete both pages of this form and SIGN it.

Under penalties of perjury, I declare that I have examined this return, including accompanying schedules and statements, and to the best of my knowledge and belief, it is true, correct, and complete, and that no part of any payment made to a state unemployment fund claimed as a credit was, or is to be, deducted from the payments made to employees. Declaration of preparer (other than taxpayer) is based on all information of which preparer has any knowledge.

✗ Sign your name here	*Harold Cameron*	Print your name here	Harold Cameron
		Print your title here	President
Date	1/31/14	Best daytime phone	585-555-6281

Paid Preparer Use Only   Check if you are self-employed . ☐

Preparer's name		PTIN	
Preparer's signature		Date	/ /
Firm's name (or yours if self-employed)		EIN	
Address		Phone	
City		State	ZIP code

Page **2**   Form **940** (2013)

Quarterly FUTA tax payments of $0 are displayed in Part 5 for the second and third quarters. This is because Lucky Ties Apparel chooses not to make FUTA tax payments until required. FUTA tax owed, prior to the credit reduction, was $336 (as all employees' earnings subject to FUTA tax exceeded $7,000 during the first quarter, no FUTA taxes were owed for the second or third quarters). As this amount did not exceed $500, Lucky Ties Apparel was not required to pay the tax after each of the first three quarters. The credit reduction is applied at the end of the fourth quarter, after which the entire FUTA tax payment must be made. When Form 940 is submitted with a payment, it is due by January 31. As Lucky Ties Apparel pays the FUTA tax on the due date, the form is submitted on this same day.

Schedule A (Form 940) for 2013:

860312

Multi-State Employer and Credit Reduction Information

Department of the Treasury — Internal Revenue Service

OMB No. 1545-0028

Employer identification number (EIN) 1 1 – 1 1 1 1 1 1 1

Name (not your trade name) Lucky Ties Apparel

See the instructions on page 2. File this schedule with Form 940.

Place an "X" in the box of EVERY state in which you had to pay state unemployment tax this year. For each state with a credit reduction rate greater than zero, enter the FUTA taxable wages, multiply by the reduction rate, and enter the credit reduction amount. Do not include in the *FUTA Taxable Wages* box wages that were excluded from state unemployment tax (see the instructions for Step 2). If any states do not apply to you, leave them blank.

Postal Abbreviation	FUTA Taxable Wages	Reduction Rate	Credit Reduction	Postal Abbreviation	FUTA Taxable Wages	Reduction Rate	Credit Reduction
AK	.	× .000	.	NC	.	× .009	.
AL	.	× .000	.	ND	.	× .000	.
AR	.	× .009	.	NE	.	× .000	.
AZ	.	× .000	.	NH	.	× .000	.
CA	.	× .009	.	NJ	.	× .000	.
CO	.	× .000	.	NM	.	× .000	.
CT	.	× .009	.	NV	.	× .000	.
DC	.	× .000	.	☒ NY	56000 .	× .009	504 .
DE	.	× .006	.	OH	.	× .009	.
FL	.	× .000	.	OK	.	× .000	.
GA	.	× .009	.	OR	.	× .000	.
HI	.	× .000	.	PA	.	× .000	.
IA	.	× .000	.	RI	.	× .009	.
ID	.	× .000	.	SC	.	× .000	.
IL	.	× .000	.	SD	.	× .000	.
IN	.	× .012	.	TN	.	× .000	.
KS	.	× .000	.	TX	.	× .000	.
KY	.	× .009	.	UT	.	× .000	.
LA	.	× .000	.	VA	.	× .000	.
MA	.	× .000	.	VT	.	× .000	.
MD	.	× .000	.	WA	.	× .000	.
ME	.	× .000	.	WI	.	× .009	.
MI	.	× .000	.	WV	.	× .000	.
MN	.	× .000	.	WY	.	× .000	.
MO	.	× .009	.	PR	.	× .000	.
MS	.	× .000	.	VI	.	× .012	.
MT	.	× .000	.				

Total Credit Reduction. Add all amounts shown in the *Credit Reduction* boxes. Enter the total here and on Form 940, line 11 . . . .

504 ▪

For Privacy Act and Paperwork Reduction Act Notice, see the Instructions for Form 940. Cat. No. 16997C Schedule A (Form 940) 2013

Completing Form W-2 (Wage and Tax Statement)

On the Web

www.irs.gov/pub/
irs-pdf/fw2.pdf

For all employers whose compensation to employees exceeds $600 for the year (from which taxes are withheld), both Forms W-2 and W-3 must be completed. The employer is required to provide three copies of Form W-2, which provides annual earnings information, to each employee by January 31 of the following year. The copies provided to employees are as follows:

- Copy B: To be filed with the employee's federal tax return
- Copy C: To be maintained for the employee's records
- Copy 2: To be filed with the employee's state, city, or local tax return (typically employees receive two copies of this version)

The employer is also required to submit Copy A of Form W-2 to the Social Security Administration. This copy of the form must be submitted by March 1 (for paper copies) or March 31 (for e-filed copies). Form W-3 is a summary of all Form W-2's submitted by the employer, and will be discussed shortly.

TIP! E-filing is an electronic method of submitting both federal and state tax forms. Whenever available, the federal and state government encourages taxpayers to utilize this method (instead of submitting paper versions), due to its increased efficiency.

To arrive at the correct figures in Form W-2, the employer may use the employee earnings records, which when completed as of the end of the year, will each summarize total compensation for a single employee. Although calculations may need to be performed based on the final totals in the employee earnings record, such as to determine the wages subject to federal income tax in Box 1, all necessary figures are available therein.

Examine the Form: W-2

While the IRS-approved W-2 Form appears here, employers may use alternative versions that convey the same information.

a Employee's social security number		
b Employer identification number (EIN)	**1** Wages, tips, other compensation	**2** Federal income tax withheld
c Employer's name, address, and ZIP code	**3** Social security wages	**4** Social security tax withheld
	5 Medicare wages and tips	**6** Medicare tax withheld
	7 Social security tips	**8** Allocated tips
d Control number	**9**	**10** Dependent care benefits
e Employee's first name and initial Last name Suff.	**11** Nonqualified plans	**12a** See instructions for box 12
	13 Statutory employee / Retirement plan / Third-party sick pay	**12b**
	14 Other	**12c**
		12d
f Employee's address and ZIP code		

OMB No. 1545-0008   Safe, accurate, FAST! Use IRS *e-file*   Visit the IRS website at www.irs.gov/efile

15 State Employer's state ID number	16 State wages, tips, etc.	17 State income tax	18 Local wages, tips, etc.	19 Local income tax	20 Locality name

Form **W-2** Wage and Tax Statement   **2013**   Department of the Treasury—Internal Revenue Service

Copy B—To Be Filed With Employee's FEDERAL Tax Return.
This information is being furnished to the Internal Revenue Service.

Parts A-F must be completed with employee and employer information. The control number in Box D is an optional box that may be used by employers to track W-2 Forms.

Boxes 1-2: Earnings subject to federal income tax withholding and the associated tax are entered here.

Boxes 3-4: Earnings subject to Social Security tax (not to exceed the wage base) and the associated tax are entered here.

Boxes 5-6: Earnings subject to Medicare tax and the associated tax are entered here.

Box 7: Tips subject to Social Security tax are entered here. The sum of boxes 3 and 7 cannot exceed the Social Security tax wage base.

Box 8: Food and/or beverage companies enter tips allocated to employees here.

Box 9: Left blank.

Box 10: All dependent-care expenses paid or incurred (which includes the value of healthcare provided to dependents) are entered here. This includes expenses related to dependent-care flexible spending accounts.

Box 11: Contributions made to non-qualified retirement plans (for which taxes are not deferred and which are typically provided to highly compensated employees) are entered here.

Boxes 12a-12d: A wide variety of compensation types (identified by codes that are defined on the back of the form) are listed on the left side of these boxes when applicable. The corresponding compensation amount for each is listed to the right.

The following chart displaying the codes that may be entered can be used for reference when reviewing completed copies of Form W-2:

Code	Compensation Type
A	Uncollected Social Security or RRTA tax on tips
B	Uncollected Medicare tax on tips
C	Taxable cost of group-term life insurance over $50,000
D	Elective deferrals under section 401(k) cash or deferred arrangement (plan)
E	Elective deferrals under a section 403(b) salary-reduction agreement
F	Elective deferrals under a section 408(k)(6) salary-reduction SEP
G	Elective deferrals and employer contributions (including nonelective deferrals) to any governmental or nongovernmental section 457(b) deferred-compensation plan
H	Elective deferrals under section 501(c)(18)(D) tax-exempt organization plan
J	Nontaxable sick pay
K	20% excise tax on excess golden parachute payments (not applicable to Forms W-2AS, W-2CM, W-2GU, or W-2VI)
L	Substantiated employee business-expense reimbursements
M	Uncollected Social Security or RRTA tax on taxable cost of group-term life insurance over $50,000 (for former employees)
N	Uncollected Medicare tax on taxable cost of group-term life insurance over $50,000 (for former employees)
P	Excludable moving expense reimbursements paid directly to employee
Q	Nontaxable combat pay
R	Employer contributions to an Archer MSA
S	Employee salary-reduction contributions under a section 408(p) SIMPLE plan
T	Adoption benefits
V	Income from the exercise of nonstatutory stock option(s)
W	Employer contributions to a health savings account (HSA)
Y	Deferrals under a section 409A nonqualified deferred-compensation plan
Z	Income under a nonqualified deferred compensation plan that fails to satisfy section 409A.
AA	Designated Roth contributions under a section 401(k) plan
BB	Designated Roth contributions under a section 403(b) plan
DD	Cost of employer-sponsored health coverage
EE	Designated Roth contributions under a section 457(b) plan

Examine the Form: W-2 (continued)

Box 13: Employers should check all boxes that apply here. *Statutory employees* are those for whom federal income tax is not withheld, but Social Security & Medicare taxes are withheld (these include certain drivers of food and beverages and certain full-time life insurance sales agents). The *retirement plan* box is checked if the employee is an active participant in a wide variety of plans including a 401(k), 403(b), SEP Plan, or SIMPLE account. The *third-party sick pay* box is checked if an employer is reporting third-party sick pay, or a third party is reporting having remitted sick pay to an insured employee.

Box 14: Any additional information the employer wants to convey to the employee, such as state disability insurance withheld, union dues, and health insurance premiums deducted, are entered here.

Boxes 15-20: State & local taxes withheld, as well as the state names (and corresponding employer state I.D. numbers) are entered here.

Case In Point 6-4	Complete Form W-2

In this example, we will complete two different W-2 Forms. We begin by completing the W-2 Form for Maryanne Sherman (8171 Winston Court, Rochester, NY 14604; Social Security #222-22-2222), an employee of Lucky Ties Apparel (employer identification #11-1111111), which completes Form 941 on a quarterly basis. Lucky Ties Apparel (located at 77 Main Street, Rochester, NY 14602) does not use control or establishment numbers, and compensated 8 employees during 2013. Maryanne's gross earnings for federal income tax withholding, Social Security tax, and Medicare tax was $131,584.61 for the year, while these taxes were $6,250, $7,049.40, and $1,907.98, respectively. State disability insurance for the year was $31.20, while the annual charitable contribution was $520. New York State income tax withholding was $1,999.92 (based on the same gross earnings amount as above), with no local taxes withheld. The employer's New York State ID number is the same as the federal identification number.

Many of the above-provided figures can be found on the total row of Maryanne Sherman's employee earnings record. Note that this employee earnings record has been truncated to display only one week's payroll data, along with the associated totals.

Employee Earnings Record

Name	Maryanne Sherman	Marital Status	Single
Address	8171 Winston Court	Fed. Withholding Allow.	2
	Rochester, NY 14604	State Withholding Allow.	1
SS#	222-22-2222		

Pay Period Ending	Regular Hours Worked	Regular Pay Rate	Regular Wages	Overtime Hours Worked	Overtime Pay Rate	Overtime Wages	Gross Pay	Federal Withholding Tax	State Withholding Tax	Social Security Tax	Medicare Tax	Retirement Contribution	Life Insurance	Charitable Contribution	Additional Withholding	Check Number	Net Pay
12/5/14	n/a	n/a	$ 769.23	0	n/a	$ -	$ 769.23	$ 77.00	$ 38.46	$ -	$ 11.15	$ -	$ -	$ 10.00	$ 0.60	1463	$ 632.02
Totals	n/a	n/a	$ 131,584.61	0	n/a	$ -	$ 131,584.61	$ 6,250.00	$ 1,999.92	$ 7,049.40	$ 1,907.98	$ -	$ -	$ 520.00	$ 31.20	n/a	$ 113,826.11

Upon reviewing the figures in the total row of the employee earnings record, the employer may then complete the Form W-2, as shown here.

22222	Void ☐	**a** Employee's social security number 222-22-2222	For Official Use Only ▶ OMB No. 1545-0008		
b Employer identification number (EIN) 11-1111111			**1** Wages, tips, other compensation 131584.61		**2** Federal income tax withheld 6250.00
c Employer's name, address, and ZIP code Lucky Ties Apparel			**3** Social security wages 113700.00		**4** Social security tax withheld 7049.40
77 Main Street Rochester NY 14602			**5** Medicare wages and tips 131584.61		**6** Medicare tax withheld 1907.98
			7 Social security tips		**8** Allocated tips
d Control number			**9**		**10** Dependent care benefits
e Employee's first name and initial Maryanne	**Last name** Sherman	Suff.	**11** Nonqualified plans		**12a** See instructions for box 12
8171 Winston Court Rochester NY 14604			**13** Statutory employee ☐ Retirement plan ☐ Third-party sick pay ☐		**12b**
			14 Other SDI 31.20 Charity 520.00		**12c**
					12d
f Employee's address and ZIP code					

15 State	Employer's state ID number	**16** State wages, tips, etc.	**17** State income tax	**18** Local wages, tips, etc.	**19** Local income tax	**20** Locality name
NY	11-1111111	131584.61	1999.92			

Form W-2 Wage and Tax Statement **2013**

Copy A For Social Security Administration — Send this entire page with Form W-3 to the Social Security Administration; photocopies are **not** acceptable.

Department of the Treasury—Internal Revenue Service For Privacy Act and Paperwork Reduction Act Notice, see the separate instructions.

Cat. No. 10134D

Do Not Cut, Fold, or Staple Forms on This Page

Notice that Box 3 contains only $113,700, as Social Security tax is not levied on the full gross earnings of Maryanne Sherman, but instead is only levied up to this 2013 Social Security tax wage base. Additionally, both state disability tax and charitable contributions are displayed in box 14, as these were withheld from gross earnings, and not listed elsewhere on the W-2 Form.

We will then complete the W-2 Form for Paul Rogers (657 Flicker Lane, Brockport, NY 14420; Social Security #111-11-1111), an employee of Lucky Ties Apparel (employer identification #11-1111111), which completes Form 941 on a quarterly basis. Lucky Ties Apparel (located at 77 Main Street, Rochester, NY 14602) does not use control or establishment numbers, and compensated 8 employees during 2013. Paul's gross earnings for federal income tax withholding are $114,735, with an associated tax of $8551.68. As a result of his total retirement contributions of $4,140, which were withheld from his gross pay starting in June and are not subject to federal income tax withholding, gross earnings subject to Social Security tax and Medicare tax were $118,875 ($114,735 + $4,140). The associated taxes were $7,049.40 and $1,723.69 respectively. State disability insurance for the year was $31.20, while the annual charitable contribution was $520. New York State income tax withholding was $3,420.67 (based on the gross earnings amount subject to federal income tax withholding provided above), with no local taxes withheld. The employer's New York State ID number is the same as the federal identification number.

22222	Void ☐	a Employee's social security number 111-11-1111	For Official Use Only ▶ OMB No. 1545-0008		
b Employer identification number (FIN) 11-1111111			1 Wages, tips, other compensation 114735.00	2 Federal income tax withheld 8551.68	
c Employer's name, address, and ZIP code Lucky Ties Apparel 77 Main Street Rochester NY 14602			3 Social security wages 113700.00	4 Social security tax withheld 7049.40	
			5 Medicare wages and tips 118875.00	6 Medicare tax withheld 1723.69	
			7 Social security tips	8 Allocated tips	
d Control number			9	10 Dependent care benefits	
e Employee's first name and initial Paul	Last name Rogers	Suff.	11 Nonqualified plans	12a See instructions for box 12 D 4140.00	
657 Flicker Lane Brockport NY 14420			13 Statutory employee ☐ Retirement plan ☒ Third-party sick pay ☐	12b	
			14 Other SDI 31.20 Charity 520.00	12c	
				12d	
f Employee's address and ZIP code					

15 State	Employer's state ID number	16 State wages, tips, etc.	17 State income tax	18 Local wages, tips, etc.	19 Local income tax	20 Locality name
NY	11-1111111	114735.00	3420.67			

Form **W-2** Wage and Tax Statement   **2013**   Department of the Treasury—Internal Revenue Service

Copy A For Social Security Administration — Send this entire page with Form W-3 to the Social Security Administration; photocopies are **not** acceptable.

For Privacy Act and Paperwork Reduction Act Notice, see the separate instructions.

Cat. No. 10134D

Do Not Cut, Fold, or Staple Forms on This Page

In this example, Paul Rogers' Form W-2 displays three different wage amounts for federal income tax, Social Security tax, and Medicare tax. The federal income tax amount represents total gross earnings less the 401(k) retirement contribution that is not subject to federal income tax.

The Social Security tax amount is the 2013 wage-base threshold, over which Social Security tax is not levied. As Paul earned more than this amount, he is subject to Social Security tax on only the first $113,700 of earnings during the year.

The Medicare tax amount is equal to the total gross earnings for the year, as they are all subject to this tax.

Also note that the retirement plan contribution amount is entered in Box 12a (code D indicates a 401(k) contribution).

Completing Form W-3 (Transmittal of Wage and Tax Statements)

On the Web

www.irs.gov/pub/
irs-pdf/fw3.pdf

Form W-3 is an informational form that is submitted to the Social Security Administration by the employer at the same time as the W-2 Forms. The W-3 Form summarizes all of the information contained in the W-2 Forms, and must agree to the totals of these. As the W-3 Form is submitted in conjunction with W-2 Forms, it is subject to the same due dates as those that apply to W-2 Forms (March 1 for paper filing; March 31 for e-filing).

TIP! Form W-3 is only furnished to the Social Security Administration and is not provided to the individual employees.

When completing Form W-3, the employer should not have a need to refer back to the payroll register or the employee earnings records, as all required compensation and tax information may be summarized from the individual Form W-2's that have already been completed.

Examine the Form: W-3

DO NOT STAPLE

33333	**a** Control number	**For Official Use Only ▶** OMB No. 1545-0008		

b Kind of Payer (Check one): 941 ☐ Military ☐ 943 ☐ 944 ☐ CT-1 ☐ Hshld. emp. ☐ Medicare govt. emp. ☐

Kind of Employer (Check one): None apply ☐ 501c non-govt. ☐ State/local non-501c ☐ State/local 501c ☐ Federal govt. ☐

Third-party sick pay (Check if applicable) ☐

c Total number of Forms W-2	**d** Establishment number	**1** Wages, tips, other compensation	**2** Federal income tax withheld
e Employer identification number (EIN)		**3** Social security wages	**4** Social security tax withheld
f Employer's name		**5** Medicare wages and tips	**6** Medicare tax withheld
		7 Social security tips	**8** Allocated tips
		9	**10** Dependent care benefits
		11 Nonqualified plans	**12a** Deferred compensation
g Employer's address and ZIP code			
h Other EIN used this year		**13** For third-party sick pay use only	**12b**
15 State Employer's state ID number		**14** Income tax withheld by payer of third-party sick pay	
16 State wages, tips, etc.	**17** State income tax	**18** Local wages, tips, etc.	**19** Local income tax
Contact person		Telephone number	For Official Use Only
Email address		Fax number	

Under penalties of perjury, I declare that I have examined this return and accompanying documents and, to the best of my knowledge and belief, they are true, correct, and complete.

Signature ▶   Title ▶   Date ▶

Form **W-3** **Transmittal of Wage and Tax Statements**   **2013**   Department of the Treasury Internal Revenue Service

Send this entire page with the entire Copy A page of Form(s) W-2 to the Social Security Administration (SSA).
Photocopies are not acceptable. Do not send Form W-3 if you filed electronically with the SSA.
Do not send any payment (cash, checks, money orders, etc.) with Forms W-2 and W-3.

Examine the Form: W-3 (continued)

Box A: Similar to Box D on the W-2 Form, this control number box may be left blank, or an employer may assign a number.

Box B: One *Kind of Payer* box must be selected (941 applies to all companies examined in this text), and one *Kind of Employer* box must be selected (*None apply* would be applicable for all companies examined in this text). The *Third-party sick pay* box should also be selected where applicable.

Box C: This box displays the number of non-voided W-2 Forms completed.

Box D: This optional box may be used by an employer to distinguish between different W-3 Forms that have been submitted for different establishments in the business.

Boxes E:-G: These boxes all must be completed with the requested company information.

Box H: If another employer identification number (such as that of a previous owner of the business) was used on a federally submitted form during the year, this number is entered here.

Boxes 1-11: These boxes require the same information as the W-2 Form, but display the totals for all W-2s across the establishment (or business as a whole).

Box 12a: This displays one total for all deferred compensation codes entered on the individual W-2 Forms. No code is to be entered on the W-3 Form, as this is a combined amount across multiple codes.

Box 12b: This box is left blank.

Box 13: The phrase "Third-party sick pay recap" is entered here if a third-party payer of sick pay is completing the W-3 Form.

Box 14: Employers enter total income tax withheld from employee earnings for third-party sick pay here. Note that this amount is also included in the Box 2 total.

Box 15: The two-letter state abbreviation and associated state ID number are entered here. This box is left blank if the employer completes W-2 Forms for more than one state.

Boxes 16-19: Totals from the corresponding boxes on the W-2 Forms are entered for each of these boxes, regardless of whether more than one state is represented in these W-2s.

The bottom portion of the form, including contact person, telephone, e-mail, fax, signature, title, and date should all be completed.

| Case In Point 6-5 | **Complete Form W-3** |

In this example, we will complete the W-3 Form for Lucky Ties Apparel (employer identification #11-1111111). Lucky Ties Apparel (located at 77 Main Street, Rochester, NY 14602) does not use control numbers. Total employee compensation for the year was $1,045,070, annual retirement-plan contributions totaled $7,825, and flexible spending account contributions ($4,200 of which were for dependent care) totaled $8,300. Federal income tax withholding totaled $116,400 for the year. Only two employees, Bill Novak & Melissa Kubiak earned less than the $113,700 subject to Social Security tax (these employees earnings were $82,400 & $75,200 respectively). New York State earnings subject to income tax withholding were the same as that subject to federal income tax withholding. State income tax withholding totaled $87,300, with no local taxes withheld. The employer's New York State ID number is the same as the federal identification number. The form is signed by the President of the company, Harold Cameron (telephone #: 585-555-6281), and is submitted on the due date for paper filings.

DO NOT STAPLE

a Control number: 33333	For Official Use Only ▶ OMB No. 1545-0008		

b Kind of Payer (Check one): 941 [X] Military [ ] 943 [ ] 944 [ ] CT-1 [ ] Hshld. emp. [ ] Medicare govt. emp. [ ]

Kind of Employer (Check one): None apply [X] 501c non-govt. [ ] State/local non-501c [ ] State/local 501c [ ] Federal govt. [ ]   Third-party sick pay (Check if applicable) [ ]

c Total number of Forms W-2: 8	**d** Establishment number	**1** Wages, tips, other compensation: 1028945.00
		2 Federal income tax withheld: 116400.00
e Employer identification number (EIN): 11-1111111		**3** Social security wages: 839800.00
		4 Social security tax withheld: 52068.00
f Employer's name: Lucky Ties Apparel		**5** Medicare wages and tips: 1036770.00
		6 Medicare tax withheld: 15033.00
77 Main Street		**7** Social security tips
Rochester NY 14602		**8** Allocated tips
		9	**10** Dependent care benefits: 4200.00
		11 Nonqualified plans	**12a** Deferred compensation: 7825.00
g Employer's address and ZIP code		
h Other EIN used this year		**13** For third-party sick pay use only	**12b**
15 State: NY Employer's state ID number: 11-1111111		**14** Income tax withheld by payer of third-party sick pay
16 State wages, tips, etc.: 1028945.00	**17** State income tax: 87300.00	**18** Local wages, tips, etc.	**19** Local income tax
Contact person: Harold Cameron	Telephone number: (585) 555-6281	For Official Use Only
Email address	Fax number	

Under penalties of perjury, I declare that I have examined this return and accompanying documents and, to the best of my knowledge and belief, they are true, correct, and complete.

Signature ▶ *Harold Cameron*   Title ▶ President   Date ▶ 3/1/14

Form **W-3** Transmittal of Wage and Tax Statements   **2013**   Department of the Treasury Internal Revenue Service

Send this entire page with the entire Copy A page of Form(s) W-2 to the Social Security Administration (SSA). Photocopies are not acceptable. Do not send Form W-3 if you filed electronically with the SSA. Do not send any payment (cash, checks, money orders, etc.) with Forms W-2 and W-3.

The earnings subject to federal income tax in Box 1 were calculated as total compensation of $1,045,070, minus retirement plan contributions of $7,825, minus flexible spending account contributions of $8,300 (these two amounts are not subject to federal income tax withholding.

The Social Security wages in Box 3 are those on which Social Security tax is levied. Six of the eight employees had earnings subject to Social Security tax that exceeded the Social Security wage base of $113,700; therefore, this threshold represents their Social Security wages. Two other employees earned less than this amount; therefore, their entire compensation of $82,400 and $75,200 are subject to Social Security tax. Social Security wages of $839,800 are calculated as $113,700 x 6 employees + $82,400 + $75,200. Social Security tax in Box 4 is then calculated as Social Security wages of $839,800 x 6.2%.

Medicare wages in Box 5 are calculated as total compensation of $1,045,070 minus flexible spending account contributions of $8,300. The resulting $1,036,770 is multiplied by 1.45% to arrive at $15,033 of Medicare taxes in Box 6.

All other figures are taken from the information provided. The form is dated 3/1/14, as this is the due date for paper filing.

Concepts Review

All of the Concepts Review quizzes for this book are also available in the Student Resource Center. Check with your instructor on how to complete the quizzes (in the book or online).

True/False Questions

1. The lookback period runs from July 1 through June 30. *True   False*

2. FUTA tax must be remitted if the total FUTA tax owed exceeds $300 as of the end of the 2nd quarter. *True   False*

3. Form 941 is due by the last day of the first month after each quarter has ended. *True   False*

4. The Internal Revenue Service levies a small service fee for employers who utilize the Electronic Federal Tax Payment System. *True   False*

5. When an employer remits a federal tax payment via a check sent through the United States Postal Service, the check must arrive by the form's due date. *True   False*

6. Because Form 940 may not be remitted with a payment, no payment voucher can accompany the form. *True   False*

7. The total for Schedule A (Form 940) also appears on the first page of Form 940. *True   False*

8. Employers must furnish all employees with copies of the W-2 Form by January 31. *True   False*

9. The W-3 Form is submitted to the Social Security Administration independent of all other federal forms. *True   False*

10. Multiple due dates can apply to the W-3 Form, depending on whether a paper version is filed or the form is e-filed. *True   False*

Multiple Choice Questions

1. Which of the following taxes, when required to be paid, is due by the last day of the first month after a quarter ends?
   a. Social Security tax
   b. Federal Income Tax
   c. FUTA Tax
   d. Medicare tax

2. What is the annual federal tax threshold, above which an employer is deemed to be a semiweekly depositor?
   a. $500
   b. $7,000
   c. $50,000
   d. $113,700

3. The next-day deposit rule is triggered when taxes owed at the end of a day are greater than what amount?
   a. $500
   b. $2,500
   c. $50,000
   d. $100,000

4. Total taxes owed, against which total deposits are compared, are reported on which line of Form 941?
   a. Line 2
   b. Line 10
   c. Line 11
   d. Line 14

5. Which of the following is the due date for Form 940 when it is submitted without a payment?
   a. January 1
   b. January 15
   c. January 31
   d. February 10

6. Schedule A (Form 940) is used in each of the following circumstances except when:
   a. All of the employer's FUTA earnings are exempt from SUTA tax.
   b. The employer does not pay FUTA tax until the fourth quarter of the year.
   c. A portion of the employer's FUTA earnings are exempt from SUTA tax.
   d. The employer operates in a credit-reduction state.

7. Which copy of the W-2 Form is submitted by the employer to the Social Security Administration?
   a. Copy A
   b. Copy B
   c. Copy C
   d. Copy 2

8. Which of the following items is not reported on the W-2 Form?
   a. Dependent-care benefits
   b. Union dues
   c. Hours worked
   d. State income tax withheld

9. Which of the following is a true statement regarding the W-2 Form?
   a. Employers must submit the W-2 Form regardless of the amount of compensation paid to employees.
   b. Sending a copy of the W-2 Form to the employee is optional.
   c. The control number on the W-2 Form must be completed by the employer.
   d. The W-2 Form includes both federal and state tax information.

10. Which of the following items appear on the W-3 Form, but do not appear on the W-2 Form?
   a. Federal income tax withheld
   b. Kind of payer
   c. Social Security wages
   d. Dependent-care benefits

Knowledge Check A

For all assignments in this section, necessary IRS forms and/or Excel templates are located in the Student Resource Center.

KCa 6-1 Examine the Lookback Period

For each of the following independent circumstances, examine the lookback period to determine whether the company is a monthly or semiweekly depositor for 2014.

1. A company's total taxes owed (federal income tax withholding, Social Security tax, and Medicare tax) for six consecutive quarters were as follows:

2012; 1st Quarter	$21,000	2012; 4th Quarter	$11,100
2012; 2nd Quarter	$13,200	2013; 1st Quarter	$14,800
2012; 3rd Quarter	$9,750	2013; 2nd Quarter	$13,000

2. A company's total taxes owed (federal income tax withholding, Social Security tax, and Medicare tax) for six consecutive quarters were as follows:

2012; 1st Quarter	$14,500	2012; 4th Quarter	$10,900
2012; 2nd Quarter	$10,000	2013; 1st Quarter	$14,000
2012; 3rd Quarter	$13,850	2013; 2nd Quarter	$11,700

3. A company's total taxes owed (federal income tax withholding, Social Security tax, and Medicare tax) for six consecutive quarters were as follows:

2012; 1st Quarter	$18,000	2012; 4th Quarter	$13,000
2012; 2nd Quarter	$15,500	2013; 1st Quarter	$11,800
2012; 3rd Quarter	$17,400	2013; 2nd Quarter	$9,000

KCa 6-2 Record a Quarterly Federal Tax Payment Journal Entry

Walking Boots Company is a monthly depositor whose December federal taxes are displayed below. Record one journal entry to account for the month-end payment of the federal taxes. All tax payments are made in a timely manner on the payment due date (which, for this quarter, is not impacted by a weekend or holiday).

December Tax Totals			
Federal Income Tax	$604	Employer's Social Security Tax	$575
Employee's Social Security Tax	$575	Employer's Medicare Tax	$178
Employee's Medicare Tax	$178		

KCa 6-3 Record Quarterly FUTA & Voluntary Deduction Journal Entries

Cooking Cousins is a monthly depositor whose 4th quarter FUTA taxes and 4th quarter voluntary deductions are displayed below. Record one journal entry to account for the payment of federal unemployment taxes, and one journal entry to account for the payment of the voluntary deductions. Assume that each voluntary deduction is remitted to the respective organization on a quarterly basis on the last day of the first month after the end of the quarter. All tax payments are made in a timely manner on the payment due date (which, for this quarter, is not impacted by a weekend or holiday).

4th Quarter Totals

FUTA Tax	$26	Charitable Contribution	$80
Retirement Plan	$224	Cafeteria Plan	$400
Health Insurance	$350		

KCa 6-4 Complete Form 941

Complete Form 941 for the 2nd quarter of 2013 for Longneck Corp. (employer identification #22-2222222). Assume that Longneck Corp. (located at 518 State Street, Seattle, WA 98101) chooses to complete and mail Form 941 on the due date. Based on the lookback period, Longneck Corp. is a monthly depositor, and has deposited all tax amounts in a timely manner. All six employees worked during the first two months (only five employees worked during the third month), and the company does not choose to allow a third-party to discuss the form with the IRS. Second quarter earnings, and associated taxes withheld from employee earnings, are as follows:

	Month #1	Month #2	Month #3	2nd Quarter Payments	Associated Earnings
FWT	$850.00	$910.00	$880.00	$2,640.00	$11,291
Social Security	$225.06	$244.90	$230.08	$700.00	$11,291
Medicare	$52.64	$57.28	$53.81	$163.75	$11,291

KCa 6-5 Complete Form 940

Complete the 2013 Form 940 for Blacklist Associates (employer identification #44-4444444). Assume that Blacklist Associates (located at 504 Cyprus Avenue, Providence, RI 02801) chooses to complete and mail Form 940 on the due date. Round all figures entered on the form to whole dollar amounts and note that Blacklist Associates only pays SUTA tax in Rhode Island. The form is signed by the CEO of the company, James Scott (telephone #: 401-555-0492). The company elects to delay remitting FUTA tax until it is required to do so. Total employee compensation for the year was $452,870, and total dependent care contributions totaled $18,500. All earnings subject to FUTA tax are also subject to SUTA tax. Blacklist Associates allow its accountant (Wally Gorman, 401-555-9366, Pin #80515) to discuss the form with the IRS. Four employees of Blacklist Associates earned more than $7,000 in 2013 that was subject to FUTA tax (each exceeded this threshold in the first quarter), while a fifth employee hired during the fourth quarter earned only $3,200 in 2013 that was subject to FUTA tax.

KCa 6-6 Complete Form W-2

Complete the W-2 Form for the two employees of Flywheel Outfitters Inc. (employer identification #99-9999999). Flywheel Outfitters, Inc. (located at 909 Crispy Lane, Charleston, SC 29401) utilizes control numbers, and its South Carolina State ID number is the same as the federal identification number.

Julio Estevez (766 Mixing Road, Charleston, SC 29401), whose Social Security number is 777-77-7777, is an employee of Flywheel Outfitter's Inc. (Julio's control number is #1045). Gross earnings for federal income tax withholding, Social Security tax, and Medicare tax were $82,476.05 for the year, while these taxes were $8,645, $5,113.52, and $1,195.90 respectively. Dependent care benefits totaled $5,200 for the year, while the annual union dues were $625. South Carolina income tax withholding was $5,773.32 (based on the same gross earnings amount as above), with no local taxes withheld.

Albert Ochie (73 Scaring Place, Charleston, SC 29401), whose Social Security number is 888-88-8888, is an employee of Flywheel Outfitter's Inc. (Albert's control number is #1055). Gross earnings for federal income tax withholding, Social Security tax, and Medicare tax were $120,784.02 for the year, while these taxes were $13,270, $7,049.40, and $1,751.37 respectively. Annual union dues were $625, while Albert elects to have charitable contributions of $300 withheld. South Carolina income tax withholding was $7,944.03 (based on the same gross earnings amount as above), with no local taxes withheld.

KCa 6-7 Complete Form W-3

Complete the W-3 Form for Flywheel Outfitters, Inc., based on the W-2 Forms you completed in KCa 6-6 for the two employees of the company. The form is signed by the President of the company, Albert Ochie (telephone #: 843-555-8164), and is submitted on the due date for e-filing. The company files Form 941 during the year, and selects "none apply" in the *Kind of Employer* section.

KCa 6-8 Complete Form W-3

Complete the W-3 Form for Belt Buckle Industries (employer identification #88-8888888). The company (located at 435 Georgia Lane, Clifton, NJ 07011) does not use control numbers. Total employee compensation (gross pay) for the year was $527,000, and annual retirement plan contributions totaled $15,200. Federal income tax withholding totaled $73,100 for the year. Of the company's 4 employees, only one had earnings subject to Social Security tax that did not exceed $113,700 (this employee earned $48,200). New Jersey State earnings subject to income tax withholding were the same as that subject to federal income tax withholding. State income tax withholding totaled $53,000, with no local taxes withheld. The employer's New Jersey State ID number is the same as the federal identification number. The form is signed by the CEO of the company, Paul Goldstein (telephone #: 862-555-0052), and is submitted on the due date for e-filing. The company files Form 941 during the year, and selects "none apply" in the *Kind of Employer* section.

Knowledge Check B

For all assignments in this section, necessary IRS forms and/or Excel templates are located in the Student Resource Center.

KCb 6-1 Examine the Lookback Period

For each of the following independent circumstances, examine the lookback period to determine whether the company is a monthly or semiweekly depositor for 2014.

1. A company's total taxes owed (federal income tax withholding, Social Security tax, and Medicare tax) for six consecutive quarters were as follows:

2012; 1st Quarter	$8,200	2012; 4th Quarter	$9,000
2012; 2nd Quarter	$11,500	2013; 1st Quarter	$12,100
2012; 3rd Quarter	$10,400	2013; 2nd Quarter	$18,200

2. A company's total taxes owed (federal income tax withholding, Social Security tax, and Medicare tax) for six consecutive quarters were as follows:

2012; 1st Quarter	$18,300	2012; 4th Quarter	$14,200
2012; 2nd Quarter	$15,700	2013; 1st Quarter	$11,400
2012; 3rd Quarter	$13,400	2013; 2nd Quarter	$7,200

3. A company's total taxes owed (federal income tax withholding, Social Security tax, and Medicare tax) for six consecutive quarters were as follows:

2012; 1st Quarter	$14,900	2012; 4th Quarter	$10,000
2012; 2nd Quarter	$8,700	2013; 1st Quarter	$16,200
2012; 3rd Quarter	$11,100	2013; 2nd Quarter	$15,100

KCb 6-2 Record a Quarterly Federal Tax Payment Journal Entry

Decimal Corporation is a monthly depositor whose December federal taxes are displayed below. Record one journal entry to account for the month-end payment of the federal taxes. All tax payments are made in a timely manner on the payment due date (which, for this quarter, is not impacted by a weekend or holiday).

December Tax Totals			
Federal Income Tax	$3,250	Employer's Social Security Tax	$2,420
Employee's Social Security Tax	$2,420	Employer's Medicare Tax	$902
Employee's Medicare Tax	$902		

KCb 6-3 Record Quarterly FUTA & Voluntary Deduction Journal Entries

Alton's Arboreal Association is a monthly depositor whose 4th quarter FUTA taxes and 4th quarter voluntary deductions are displayed below. Record one journal entry to account for the payment of federal unemployment taxes, and one journal entry to account for the payment of the voluntary deductions. Assume that each voluntary deduction is remitted to the respective organization on a quarterly basis, on the last day of the first month after the end of the quarter. All tax payments are made in a timely manner, on the payment due date (which, for this quarter, is not impacted by a weekend or holiday).

4th Quarter Totals			
FUTA Tax	$370	Charitable Contribution	$700
Retirement Plan	$4,240	Cafeteria Plan	$5,560
Health Insurance	$3,020		

KCb 6-4 Complete Form 941

Complete Form 941 for the 1st quarter of 2013 for Bouncing Babies Co. (employer identification #33-3333333). Assume that Bouncing Babies Co. (located at 91 Bayberry Avenue, Baton Rouge, LA 70714) chooses to complete and mail Form 941 on the due date. Based on the lookback period, Bouncing Babies Co. is a monthly depositor and has deposited all tax amounts in a timely manner. All 32 employees worked during each of the three months, and the company elects to allow its accountant (William Gordon; 225-555-7846,; Pin # 83463) to discuss the form with the IRS. 1st quarter earnings, and associated taxes withheld from employee earnings, are as follows:

	Month #1	Month #2	Month #3	1st Quarter Payments	Associated Earnings
FWT	$12,400.00	$12,720.00	$12,120.00	$37,240.00	$331,200
Social Security	$7,579.50	$7,240.36	$7,990.13	$22,810.00	$367,903
Medicare	$1,772.63	$1,693.31	$1,868.66	$5,334.60	$367,903

KCb 6-5 Complete Form 940

Complete the 2013 Form 940 for KYG Corp. (employer identification #55-5555555). Assume that KYG Corp. (located at 81519 Duke Lane, Dayton, OH 45377) chooses to complete and mail Form 940 on the due date. Round all figures entered on the form to whole dollar amounts, and note that KYG Corp. only pays SUTA tax in Ohio. The form is signed by the President of the company, Marcelo Coleman (telephone #: 937-555-8825). The company elects to delay remitting FUTA tax until it is required to do so. Total employee compensation for the year was $751,000, total group-term life insurance contributions totaled $24,200, and total dependent-care contributions totaled $13,400. All earnings subject to FUTA tax are also subject to SUTA tax. KYG Corp. allows its accountant (Steve Kimmel, 937-555-0040, Pin #76134) to discuss the form with the IRS. Note that 9 employees of KYG Corp. earned more than $7,000 in 2013 that was subject to FUTA tax (each exceeded this threshold in the first quarter), while a tenth employee hired during the fourth quarter earned only $5,700 in 2013 that was subject to FUTA tax.

KCb 6-6 Complete Form W-2

Complete the W-2 Form for the two employees of Gameroom Associates Corp. (employer identification #55-5555555). Gameroom Associates Corp. (located at 87 Rose Way, Lexington, KY 40361) utilizes control numbers, and its Kentucky State ID number is the same as the federal identification number.

Rachel Flowers (4 Fiber Way, Lexington, KY 40361), whose Social Security number is 888-88-8888, is an employee of Gameroom Associates Corp. (Rachel's control number is #4407). Gross earnings for federal income tax withholding, Social Security tax, and Medicare tax were $101,470 for the year, while these taxes were $9,250, $6,291.14, and $1,471.32 respectively. The annual charitable contribution was $260. Kentucky income tax withholding was $6,088.20 (based on the same gross earnings amount as above), with no local taxes withheld. The employer's Kentucky State ID number is the same as the federal identification number.

Adrian Pitts (8765 Tripping Way, Lexington, KY 40361), whose Social Security number is 444-44-4444, is an employee of Gameroom Associates Corp. (Adrian's control number is #4408). Gross earnings for federal income tax withholding were $132,460 for the year, while gross earnings for Social Security tax and Medicare tax were $141,460 for the year. The federal income tax, Social Security tax, and Medicare tax were $16,350, $7049.40, and $2.051.17 respectively. The annual charitable contribution was $675, and the 401(k) retirement-plan contribution was $9,000. Kentucky income tax withholding was $10,382.73 (based on the same gross earnings amount as above), with no local taxes withheld. The employer's Kentucky State ID number is the same as the federal identification number.

KCb 6-7 Complete Form W-3

Complete the W-3 Form for Gameroom Associates Corp., based on the W-2 Forms you completed in KCb 6-6 for the two employees of the company. The form is signed by the CFO of the company, Rachel Flowers (telephone #: 859-555-2766), and is submitted on the due date for e-filing. The company files Form 941 during the year, and selects "none apply" in the *Kind of Employer* section.

KCb 6-8 Complete Form W-3

Complete the W-3 Form for Shipbuilders of New England (employer identification #33-3333333). The company (located at 2 Hickory Trail, Pawtucket, RI 02860) does not use control numbers. Total employee compensation (gross pay) for the year was $1,052,400, annual retirement-plan contributions totaled $27,500, and flexible spending account contributions ($8,500 of which were for dependent care) totaled $16,000. Federal income tax withholding totaled $122,300 for the year. Only 3 of the 9 employees have earnings subject to Social Security tax less than $113,700 (these employees earnings were $74,300, $42,500 and $106,200, respectively). Rhode Island State earnings subject to income tax withholding were the same as those subject to federal income tax withholding. State income tax withholding totaled $88,350, with no local taxes withheld. The employer's Rhode Island State ID number is the same as the federal identification number. The form is signed by the CFO of the company, Molly Richmond (telephone #: 401-555-9929), and is submitted on the due date for paper filings. The company files Form 941 during the year, and selects "none apply" in the *Kind of Employer* section.

Continuing Payroll Problem

For all assignments in this section, necessary IRS forms and/or Excel templates are located in the Student Resource Center.

CPP 6-1 Complete 4th Quarter & Year-End Payroll Reporting

Journalize the necessary entry to record payment of the 2nd quarter taxes in Form 941 for TCLH Industries, a manufacturer of cleaning products, as of July 15, 2013. Then complete Forms 941 & 940 as of year-end. Conclude by completing the W-2 Form for each of the four employees, as well as the associated W-3 Form.

1. Record the journal entry to account for the payment of federal income tax, Social Security tax, and Medicare tax with the 2nd Quarter Form 941. Assume that, aside from the signing bonus (see below), the employees earned the same amount during each of the 11 pay periods during the second quarter (the company was formed after the first two weeks of the 2nd quarter had passed), and had the same deductions for each pay period. Zachary Fox joined the company a few weeks after its inception, and therefore only worked 8 weeks during the 2nd quarter.

   Additionally, as was previously noted, Calvin Bell, Michaela Walton, and Suzanne Steinberg's taxable earnings for Social Security tax were $109,400, $141,000, and $113,100 respectively during their first two weeks of employment. These amounts include both their standard earnings and a discretionary signing bonus. Had they not received these bonuses, their pay during each of the first two weeks would have been the same as that of any other week. For these bonuses, assume a federal income tax withholding rate of 25%. Treat these bonuses the same as any other earnings for the purposes of FICA taxes.

2. Complete Form 941 for the 2nd quarter for TCLH Industries (employer identification #44-4444444). Assume that all necessary deposits were made on a timely basis (new businesses in their first year of operations are automatically monthly depositors), and that total deposits for the quarter equaled total taxes owed. Furthermore, note that the company had 3 pay periods during April, and 4 pay periods during both May and June. The company does not have a third-party designee, nor does it use a paid preparer. All forms are signed by the CEO of the company, Michael Sierra, and the form is submitted on the due date.

3. Complete Form 940 for 2013 for TCLH Industries. Assume that no additional employees joined the company for the remainder of 2013, and that all compensation data remained the same, and the form is submitted on the due date. for all four employees for every subsequent pay period through year-end. Both the 3rd and 4th quarters contained 13 pay periods, and the company does not remit FUTA tax until the latest date on which it is permitted to do so. Note that the life insurance for which employee withholdings were made is not group-term life insurance. Flexible Spending Accounts are reported on Form 940 as a Fringe Benefit, and all earnings subject to FUTA tax are also subject to SUTA tax.

4. Complete Form W-2 for each of the four employees of TCLH Industries. The company does not use control numbers, and its state identification number is the same as its federal identification number.

5. Complete Form W-3 for TCLH Industries. The company does not use establishment numbers, and both signs and submits the form on its paper-filing due date. The company selects "none apply" in the *Kind of Employer* section.

Critical Thinking

CT 6-1 Examine Quarterly State Payroll Forms

As you learned earlier in the chapter, Form 941 is completed by employers on a quarterly basis and submitted to the federal government. Most employers will similarly submit quarterly payroll forms to their respective states. Although Form NYS-45 (the New York quarterly payroll form) was shown earlier, it is important to examine the quarterly forms for your state, as the formats (and information required) are different from one state to another. In this exercise, you will use the internet to locate and review the quarterly payroll forms for your state.

Start by searching for the state payroll forms that apply to your state. Keep in mind that although a number of states do not levy an income tax on employees, they still require that quarterly forms be submitted. One reason for this is that State Unemployment tax must still be remitted in these states. Once you have located the form(s), write a paragraph of at least five sentences in which you discuss both the figures required on the form, and the differences between the state forms and Form 941.

Submit your final file(s) based on the guidelines provided by your instructor.

CT 6-2 Review the Electronic Federal Tax Payment System

The federal government strongly encourages the use of the Electronic Federal Tax Payment System (EFTPS). In comparison to the paper-based system that has traditionally been used, the EFTPS is far more efficient for the government, which is why its use is encouraged. However, the system also offers a variety of benefits to the employer. In this exercise, you will use the internet to examine the different uses of the EFTPS and the variety of ways that it can benefit the user.

Begin by navigating to the EFTPS website (the URL was provided earlier in the chapter), and learn more about the system. Then, search the internet to discover ways in which the EFTPS proves to be beneficial to employers. Write a paragraph of at least six sentences in which you first describe the various uses of the EFTPS, and then discuss how it provides benefits to the user. Be certain to focus on benefits yielded to the employer, and not to the government itself.

Submit your final file(s) based on the guidelines provided by your instructor.

Comprehensive Projects

These comprehensive projects are designed to be completed either manually, through the use of templates available in the Student Resource Center, or electronically through the use of Intuit QuickBooks. Consult with your instructor to determine which method should be used.

After examining the annual payroll process, it is important to practice using the skills you've learned. In this exercise chapter, two payroll-related projects are provided. The first project focuses on Ellipses Corp. For this company you will complete all payroll-related tasks for the month of December, and will then finalize all year-end reporting. The second project focuses on Ampersand, Inc. For this company you will complete all payroll-related tasks for the fourth quarter of the year, after which you will finalize all year-end payroll reporting.

One-Month Project

Ellipses Corp. is a small business that operates in Herndon, VA. The company is located at 10 Period Lane, Herndon, VA 20170. Its federal identification number is 77-7777777, and its president is John Parker (telephone #571-555-0073).

During 2013, four individuals were employed by Ellipses Corp. These employees are as follows:

Name	Address	Social Security #	Federal W/H Allowances	State W/H Allowances	Marital Status
Parker Cranston	85 Southern Road Herndon, VA 20170	111-11-1111	2	2	Married
Allison Harrison	203A Pine Court Herndon, VA 20170	777-77-7777	4	3	Married
John Parker	212 Tradition Lane Herndon, VA 20170	444-44-4444	1	1	Single
Pierre Sternberg	41 Seward Blvd. Herndon, VA 20170	333-33-3333	2	2	Married

Note that Pierre Sternberg was hired in November, and his first day of work was Monday, November 25th. Additionally, due to an economic downturn, Allison Harrison was laid off in mid-December, with her last day of work on Friday, December 13th.

All employees of Ellipses Corp. work a regular 40-hour workweek, receive overtime pay at a rate of 1.5 times the regular wage rate, and are paid weekly on Friday for the current week (which runs from Saturday – Friday, although employees never work on weekends). The SUTA tax rate applicable to Ellipses Corp. is 3.1%, while the SUTA wage base in Virginia is $8,000.

Earnings and voluntary deduction information for each of the four employees are as follows:

Name	Regular Wage Rate	Annual Salary	Weekly 401(k) Deduction	Weekly Charitable Contribution
Parker Cranston	$15/hour	N/A	6% of Gross Pay	$5
Allison Harrison	$23/hour	N/A	5% of Gross Pay	$5
John Parker	N/A	$203,000	N/A	$20
Pierre Sternberg	N/A	$112,000	1% of Gross Pay	N/A

The first eleven months of the year have passed, and all payroll-related activity has been properly accounted for as of 12/1/13. Payroll data for each of the four employees for the first three quarters of the year, as well as for the months of October & November, is as follows:

Parker Cranston

Period	Gross Earnings	Federal Income Tax	State Income Tax	Social Security Tax	Medicare Tax	401(k) Deduction	Charitable Cont.
1st Quarter	$7,800.00	$338.00	$286.00	$483.60	$113.10	$468.00	$65.00
2nd Quarter	$7,800.00	$338.00	$286.00	$483.60	$113.10	$468.00	$65.00
3rd Quarter	$7,800.00	$338.00	$286.00	$483.60	$113.10	$468.00	$65.00
October	$2,400.00	$104.00	$88.00	$148.80	$34.80	$144.00	$20.00
November	$3,000.00	$130.00	$110.00	$186.00	$43.50	$180.00	$25.00

Allison Harrison

Period	Gross Earnings	Federal Income Tax	State Income Tax	Social Security Tax	Medicare Tax	401(k) Deduction	Charitable Cont.
1st Quarter	$11,960.00	$585.00	$507.00	$741.52	$173.42	$598.00	$65.00
2nd Quarter	$11,960.00	$585.00	$507.00	$741.52	$173.42	$598.00	$65.00
3rd Quarter	$11,960.00	$585.00	$507.00	$741.52	$173.42	$598.00	$65.00
October	$3,680.00	$180.00	$156.00	$228.16	$53.36	$184.00	$20.00
November	$4,600.00	$225.00	$195.00	$285.20	$66.70	$230.00	$25.00

John Parker

Period	Gross Earnings	Federal Income Tax	State Income Tax	Social Security Tax	Medicare Tax	401(k) Deduction	Charitable Cont.
1st Quarter	$50,750.00	$12,277.98	$2,797.21	$3,146.50	$735.88	$0	$260.00
2nd Quarter	$50,750.00	$12,277.98	$2,797.21	$3,146.50	$735.88	$0	$260.00
3rd Quarter	$50,750.00	$12,277.98	$2,797.21	$756.40	$735.88	$0	$260.00
October	$15,615.38	$3,777.84	$860.68	$0	$226.42	$0	$80.00
November	$19,519.23	$4,722.30	$1,075.85	$0	$283.03	$0	$100.00

Pierre Sternberg

Period	Gross Earnings	Federal Income Tax	State Income Tax	Social Security Tax	Medicare Tax	401(k) Deduction	Charitable Cont.
1st Quarter	$0	$0	$0	$0	$0	$0	$0
2nd Quarter	$0	$0	$0	$0	$0	$0	$0
3rd Quarter	$0	$0	$0	$0	$0	$0	$0
October	$0	$0	$0	$0	$0	$0	$0
November	$2,153.85	$304.41	$113.52	$133.54	$31.23	$21.54	$0

Note that all tax payments and filings are made on the due date. Based on the data provided here, you will complete the following:

1. Establish an Employee Earnings Record for each of the company's four employees. Complete the top portion of each record.

2. Complete the Employee Earnings Record for December for each of the four employees. When calculating federal income tax withholding, use the withholding tables where possible, and only refer to the percentage method when necessary. Note that, as of December 9th, Parker Cranston requests (and Ellipses Corp. changes) his federal withholding allowances from 2 to 3. Additionally, for simplicity, calculate the State Income Tax Withholding as 5% of each employee's Gross Pay (recall that State Income Tax Withholding would ordinarily be calculated using the applicable state's withholding tables; this method was used to calculate the state withholding tax figures that have been provided for earlier periods). Payroll checks are remitted to the employees in the same order (Cranston, Harrison, Parker, Sternberg) each pay period, and are written from a bank account that is used solely for these payments. The first payroll check written in December is check #762.

Note that all charitable contributions are deemed to be made on the final day of each pay period. The following information will be required for the completion of these records for the two employees who are compensated with an hourly wage.

Weekly Hours Worked

Weekly Start Date	Parker Cranston	Allison Harrison
December 2nd	40	37
December 9th	38	41
December 16th	43.5	0
December 23rd	40	0
December 30th	16 (During 2013)	0

3. Establish and complete the Payroll Register for each weekly pay period during December. Additionally, establish and populate the Payroll Register for the week of December 30th with only 2013-related payroll data. If directed to do so by your instructor, record the necessary journal entries for each pay period.

4. Complete Form 941 for the fourth quarter. Note that the federal tax payments (which equaled the monthly calculations on line 16) differed slightly from the 4th quarter total tax owed (on line 6), resulting in an adjustment for fractions of cents on line 7. Furthermore, based on the lookback period, the company is a monthly depositor, which made timely payments throughout the entire year. Although Virginia quarterly state payroll forms are also filed by Ellipses Corp., you will not complete these. If directed to do so by your instructor, record the necessary journal entries associated with each Form 941 (including those required for any tax payments made).

5. Complete Form 940 for Ellipses Corp. Note that FUTA payments are only made when required (i.e., if the employer is permitted to postpone the payment of these taxes, it will do so until a point in time when payment must be remitted). Calculate total SUTA tax owed by the employer. Although Ellipses Corp. will file state forms in which this figure is reported, you are only required to calculate the total amount owed for the year. If directed to do so by your instructor, record the necessary journal entry associated with Form 940.

6. Complete Form W-2 for each of the four employees. State wages were the same as federal wages for each of the four employees, and the state identification number for Ellipses Corp. is the same as its federal identification number.

7. Complete Form W-3 for Ellipses Corp. Note that the company files the paper version of the form, and selects "none apply" in the *Kind of Employer* section.

Three-Month Project

Ampersand, Inc. is a small business that operates in Somerset, VT. The company is located at 732 Appalachian Way, Somerset, VT 05363. Its federal identification number is 44-4444444, and its president is Stacey Jones (telephone #802-555-3917).

During 2013, four individuals were employed by Ampersand, Inc. These employees are as follows:

Name	Address	Social Security #	Federal W/H Allowances	State W/H Allowances	Marital Status
Maggie Hough	13 Spruce Street Somerset, VT 05363	222-22-2222	1	1	Single
William Finnegan	7 Smith Blvd. Somerset, VT 05363	999-99-9999	2	2	Married
Stacey Jones	8110 Browning Pl. Somerset, VT 05363	555-55-5555	2	1	Single
Francine Stewart	101 Park Court Somerset, VT 05363	888-88-8888	3	3	Married

Note that Francine Stewart was hired in September, and her first day of work was Monday, September 23rd. Additionally, due to an economic downturn, Maggie Hough was laid off in late November, with her last day of work on Friday, November 22nd.

All employees of Ampersand, Inc. work a regular 40-hour workweek, receive overtime pay at a rate of 1.5 times the regular wage rate, and are paid weekly on Monday for the prior week (which runs from Saturday – Friday, although employees never work on weekends). The SUTA tax rate applicable to Ampersand, Inc. is 2.5%, while the SUTA wage base in Vermont is $16,000.

Earnings and voluntary deduction information for each of the four employees are as follows:

Name	Regular Wage Rate	Annual Salary	Weekly 401(k) Deduction	Weekly Charitable Contribution
Maggie Hough	$14/hour	N/A	5% of Gross Pay	$10
William Finnegan	$18/hour	N/A	4% of Gross Pay	$5
Stacey Jones	N/A	$262,000	N/A	$15
Francine Stewart	N/A	$94,000	2% of Gross Pay	N/A

The first three quarters of the year have passed, and all payroll-related activity has been properly accounted for as of 10/1/13. Quarterly payroll data for each of the four employees is as follows:

Maggie Hough

Quarter	Gross Earnings	Federal Income Tax	State Income Tax	Social Security Tax	Medicare Tax	401(k) Deduction	Charitable Cont.
1st Quarter	$7,280.00	$702.00	$187.33	$451.36	$105.56	$364.00	$130.00
2nd Quarter	$7,280.00	$702.00	$187.33	$451.36	$105.56	$364.00	$130.00
3rd Quarter	$7,280.00	$702.00	$187.33	$451.36	$105.56	$364.00	$130.00

William Finnegan

Quarter	Gross Earnings	Federal Income Tax	State Income Tax	Social Security Tax	Medicare Tax	401(k) Deduction	Charitable Cont.
1st Quarter	$9,360.00	$533.00	$178.75	$580.32	$135.72	$374.40	$65.00
2nd Quarter	$9,360.00	$533.00	$178.75	$580.32	$135.72	$374.40	$65.00
3rd Quarter	$9,360.00	$533.00	$178.75	$580.32	$135.72	$374.40	$65.00

Stacey Jones

Quarter	Gross Earnings	Federal Income Tax	State Income Tax	Social Security Tax	Medicare Tax	401(k) Deduction	Charitable Cont.
1st Quarter	$65,500.00	$16,562.00	$4,653.74	$4,061.00	$949.75	$0	$195.00
2nd Quarter	$65,500.00	$16,562.00	$4,653.74	$2,988.40	$949.75	$0	$195.00
3rd Quarter	$65,500.00	$16,562.00	$4,653.74	$0	$949.75	$0	$195.00

Francine Stewart

Quarter	Gross Earnings	Federal Income Tax	State Income Tax	Social Security Tax	Medicare Tax	401(k) Deduction	Charitable Cont.
1st Quarter	$0	$0	$0	$0	$0	$0	$0
2nd Quarter	$0	$0	$0	$0	$0	$0	$0
3rd Quarter	$1,807.69	$190.83	$57.58	$112.08	$26.21	$36.15	$0

Note that all tax payments and filings are made on the due date. Based on the data provided here, you will complete the following:

1. Establish an Employee Earnings Record for each of the company's four employees. Complete the top portion of each record.

2. Complete the Employee Earnings Record for the fourth quarter for each of the four employees. When calculating federal income tax withholding, use the withholding tables where possible, and only refer to the percentage method when necessary. Note that, as of December 2nd, Stacey Jones requests (and Ampersand, Inc. changes) her federal withholding allowances from 2 to 1. Additionally, for simplicity, calculate the State Income Tax Withholding as 5% of each employee's Gross Pay (recall that State Income Tax Withholding would ordinarily be calculated using the applicable state's withholding tables; this method was used to calculate the state withholding tax figures that have been provided for earlier periods). Payroll checks are remitted to the employees in the same order (Hough, Finnegan, Jones, Stewart) each pay period, and are written from a bank account that is used solely for these payments. The first payroll check written in October is check #4711.

Note that all charitable contributions are deemed to be made on the final day of each pay period. The following information will be required for the completion of these records for the two employees who are compensated with an hourly wage.

Weekly Hours Worked

Weekly Start Date	Maggie Hough	William Finnegan
September 30th	40	44
October 7th	42	37
October 14th	38	40
October 21st	40	46.5
October 28th	43.5	42
November 4th	40	45
November 11th	39	40

Weekly Start Date	Maggie Hough	William Finnegan
November 18th	41	34.5
November 25th	0	40
December 2nd	0	41
December 9th	0	43.5
December 16th	0	42.5
December 23rd	0	40
December 30th	0	17 (During 2013)

3. Establish and complete the Payroll Register for each weekly pay period during the fourth quarter. Additionally, establish and populate the Payroll Register for the week of December 30th with only 2013-related payroll data. If directed to do so by your instructor, record the necessary journal entries for each pay period.

4. Complete Form 941 for both the third and fourth quarters. Assume that the employees earned the same amount during each pay period of the third quarter, and that there were 5, 4, and 4 pay periods during the months of July, August, and September respectively. Note that the federal tax payments during both quarters (which equaled the monthly calculations on line 16) differed slightly from the quarterly total tax owed (on line 6), resulting in an adjustment for fractions of cents on line 7. Furthermore, based on the lookback period, the company is a monthly depositor, which made timely payments throughout the entire year. Although Vermont quarterly state payroll forms are also filed by Ampersand, Inc., you will not complete these. If directed to do so by your instructor, record the necessary journal entries associated with each Form 941 (including those required for any tax payments made).

5. Complete Form 940 for Ampersand, Inc. Note that FUTA payments are only made when required (i.e., if the employer is permitted to postpone the payment of these taxes, it will do so until a point in time when payment must be remitted). Calculate total SUTA tax owed by the employer. Although Ampersand, Inc. will file state forms in which this figure it reported, you are only required to calculate the total amount owed for the year. If directed to do so by your instructor, record the necessary journal entry associated with Form 940.

6. Complete Form W-2 for each of the four employees. State wages were the same as federal wages for each of the four employees, and the state identification number for Ampersand, Inc. is the same as its federal identification number.

7. Complete Form W-3 for Ampersand, Inc. Note that the company files the paper version of the form, and selects "none apply" in the *Kind of Employer* section.

2013 Federal Tax Tables

The following tables are updated annually by the IRS, and provided within the Circular E. Refer to these 2013 tables when determining federal income tax withholding throughout the textbook.

Percentage Method Tables for Income Tax Withholding

(For Wages Paid in 2013)

TABLE 1—WEEKLY Payroll Period

(a) SINGLE person (including head of household)—

If the amount of wages (after subtracting withholding allowances) is:

Not over $42 . . . . $0

Over—	But not over—	The amount of income tax to withhold is:	of excess over—
$42	—$214 . .	$0.00 plus 10%	—$42
$214	—$739 . .	$17.20 plus 15%	—$214
$739	—$1,732 . .	$95.95 plus 25%	—$739
$1,732	—$3,566 . .	$344.20 plus 28%	—$1,732
$3,566	—$7,703 . .	$857.72 plus 33%	—$3,566
$7,703	—$7,735 . .	$2,222.93 plus 35%	—$7,703
$7,735		$2,234.13 plus 39.6%	—$7,735

(b) MARRIED person—

If the amount of wages (after subtracting withholding allowances) is:

Not over $160 . . . . $0

Over—	But not over—	The amount of income tax to withhold is:	of excess over—
$160	—$503 . .	$0.00 plus 10%	—$160
$503	—$1,554 . .	$34.30 plus 15%	—$503
$1,554	—$2,975 . .	$191.95 plus 25%	—$1,554
$2,975	—$4,449 . .	$547.20 plus 28%	—$2,975
$4,449	—$7,820 . .	$959.92 plus 33%	—$4,449
$7,820	—$8,813 . .	$2,072.35 plus 35%	—$7,820
$8,813		$2,419.90 plus 39.6%	—$8,813

TABLE 2—BIWEEKLY Payroll Period

(a) SINGLE person (including head of household)—

If the amount of wages (after subtracting withholding allowances) is:

Not over $85 . . . . $0

Over—	But not over—	The amount of income tax to withhold is:	of excess over—
$85	—$428 . .	$0.00 plus 10%	—$85
$428	—$1,479 . .	$34.30 plus 15%	—$428
$1,479	—$3,463 . .	$191.95 plus 25%	—$1,479
$3,463	—$7,133 . .	$687.95 plus 28%	—$3,463
$7,133	—$15,406 . .	$1,715.55 plus 33%	—$7,133
$15,406	—$15,469 . .	$4,445.64 plus 35%	—$15,406
$15,469		$4,467.69 plus 39.6%	—$15,469

(b) MARRIED person—

If the amount of wages (after subtracting withholding allowances) is:

Not over $319 . . . . $0

Over—	But not over—	The amount of income tax to withhold is:	of excess over—
$319	—$1,006 . .	$0.00 plus 10%	—$319
$1,006	—$3,108 . .	$68.70 plus 15%	—$1,006
$3,108	—$5,950 . .	$384.00 plus 25%	—$3,108
$5,950	—$8,898 . .	$1,094.50 plus 28%	—$5,950
$8,898	—$15,640 . .	$1,919.94 plus 33%	—$8,898
$15,640	—$17,627 . .	$4,144.80 plus 35%	—$15,640
$17,627		$4,840.25 plus 39.6%	—$17,627

TABLE 3—SEMIMONTHLY Payroll Period

(a) SINGLE person (including head of household)—

If the amount of wages (after subtracting withholding allowances) is:

Not over $92 . . . . $0

Over—	But not over—	The amount of income tax to withhold is:	of excess over—
$92	—$464 . .	$0.00 plus 10%	—$92
$464	—$1,602 . .	$37.20 plus 15%	—$464
$1,602	—$3,752 . .	$207.90 plus 25%	—$1,602
$3,752	—$7,727 . .	$745.40 plus 28%	—$3,752
$7,727	—$16,690 . .	$1,858.40 plus 33%	—$7,727
$16,690	—$16,758 . .	$4,816.19 plus 35%	—$16,690
$16,758		$4,839.99 plus 39.6%	—$16,758

(b) MARRIED person—

If the amount of wages (after subtracting withholding allowances) is:

Not over $346 . . . . $0

Over—	But not over—	The amount of income tax to withhold is:	of excess over—
$346	—$1,090 . .	$0.00 plus 10%	—$346
$1,090	—$3,367 . .	$74.40 plus 15%	—$1,090
$3,367	—$6,446 . .	$415.95 plus 25%	—$3,367
$6,446	—$9,640 . .	$1,185.70 plus 28%	—$6,446
$9,640	—$16,944 . .	$2,080.02 plus 33%	—$9,640
$16,944	—$19,096 . .	$4,490.34 plus 35%	—$16,944
$19,096		$5,243.54 plus 39.6%	—$19,096

TABLE 4—MONTHLY Payroll Period

(a) SINGLE person (including head of household)—

If the amount of wages (after subtracting withholding allowances) is:

Not over $183 . . . . $0

Over—	But not over—	The amount of income tax to withhold is:	of excess over—
$183	—$927 . .	$0.00 plus 10%	—$183
$927	—$3,204 . .	$74.40 plus 15%	—$927
$3,204	—$7,504 . .	$415.95 plus 25%	—$3,204
$7,504	—$15,454 . .	$1,490.95 plus 28%	—$7,504
$15,454	—$33,379 . .	$3,716.95 plus 33%	—$15,454
$33,379	—$33,517 . .	$9,632.20 plus 35%	—$33,379
$33,517		$9,680.50 plus 39.6%	—$33,517

(b) MARRIED person—

If the amount of wages (after subtracting withholding allowances) is:

Not over $692 . . . . $0

Over—	But not over—	The amount of income tax to withhold is:	of excess over—
$692	—$2,179 . .	$0.00 plus 10%	—$692
$2,179	—$6,733 . .	$148.70 plus 15%	—$2,179
$6,733	—$12,892 . .	$831.80 plus 25%	—$6,733
$12,892	—$19,279 . .	$2,371.55 plus 28%	—$12,892
$19,279	—$33,888 . .	$4,159.91 plus 33%	—$19,279
$33,888	—$38,192 . .	$8,980.88 plus 35%	—$33,888
$38,192		$10,487.28 plus 39.6%	—$38,192

Publication 15 (2013)

Percentage Method Tables for Income Tax Withholding (continued)

(For Wages Paid in 2013)

TABLE 5—QUARTERLY Payroll Period

(a) SINGLE person (including head of household)—

If the amount of wages (after subtracting withholding allowances) is:		The amount of income tax to withhold is:	
Not over $550		$0	
Over—	**But not over—**		**of excess over—**
$550	—$2,781 . .	$0.00 plus 10%	—$550
$2,781	—$9,613 . .	$223.10 plus 15%	—$2,781
$9,613	—$22,513 . .	$1,247.90 plus 25%	—$9,613
$22,513	—$46,363 . .	$4,472.90 plus 28%	—$22,513
$46,363	—$100,138 . .	$11,150.90 plus 33%	—$46,363
$100,138	—$100,550 . .	$28,896.65 plus 35%	—$100,138
$100,550		$29,040.85 plus 39.6%	—$100,550

(b) MARRIED person—

If the amount of wages (after subtracting withholding allowances) is:		The amount of income tax to withhold is:	
Not over $2,075		$0	
Over—	**But not over—**		**of excess over—**
$2,075	—$6,538 . .	$0.00 plus 10%	—$2,075
$6,538	—$20,200 . .	$446.30 plus 15%	—$6,538
$20,200	—$38,675 . .	$2,495.60 plus 25%	—$20,200
$38,675	—$57,838 . .	$7,114.35 plus 28%	—$38,675
$57,838	—$101,663 . .	$12,479.99 plus 33%	—$57,838
$101,663	—$114,575 . .	$26,942.24 plus 35%	—$101,663
$114,575		$31,461.44 plus 39.6%	—$114,575

TABLE 6—SEMIANNUAL Payroll Period

(a) SINGLE person (including head of household)—

If the amount of wages (after subtracting withholding allowances) is:		The amount of income tax to withhold is:	
Not over $1,100		$0	
Over—	**But not over—**		**of excess over—**
$1,100	—$5,563 . .	$0.00 plus 10%	—$1,100
$5,563	—$19,225 . .	$446.30 plus 15%	—$5,563
$19,225	—$45,025 . .	$2,495.60 plus 25%	—$19,225
$45,025	—$92,725 . .	$8,945.60 plus 28%	—$45,025
$92,725	—$200,275 . .	$22,301.60 plus 33%	—$92,725
$200,275	—$201,100 . .	$57,793.10 plus 35%	—$200,275
$201,100		$58,081.85 plus 39.6%	—$201,100

(b) MARRIED person—

If the amount of wages (after subtracting withholding allowances) is:		The amount of income tax to withhold is:	
Not over $4,150		$0	
Over—	**But not over—**		**of excess over—**
$4,150	—$13,075 . .	$0.00 plus 10%	—$4,150
$13,075	—$40,400 . .	$892.50 plus 15%	—$13,075
$40,400	—$77,350 . .	$4,991.25 plus 25%	—$40,400
$77,350	—$115,675 . .	$14,228.75 plus 28%	—$77,350
$115,675	—$203,325 . .	$24,959.75 plus 33%	—$115,675
$203,325	—$229,150 . .	$53,884.25 plus 35%	—$203,325
$229,150		$62,923.00 plus 39.6%	—$229,150

TABLE 7—ANNUAL Payroll Period

(a) SINGLE person (including head of household)—

If the amount of wages (after subtracting withholding allowances) is:		The amount of income tax to withhold is:	
Not over $2,200		$0	
Over—	**But not over—**		**of excess over—**
$2,200	—$11,125 . .	$0.00 plus 10%	—$2,200
$11,125	—$38,450 . .	$892.50 plus 15%	—$11,125
$38,450	—$90,050 . .	$4,991.25 plus 25%	—$38,450
$90,050	—$185,450 . .	$17,891.25 plus 28%	—$90,050
$185,450	—$400,550 . .	$44,603.25 plus 33%	—$185,450
$400,550	—$402,200 . .	$115,586.25 plus 35%	—$400,550
$402,200		$116,163.75 plus 39.6%	—$402,200

(b) MARRIED person—

If the amount of wages (after subtracting withholding allowances) is:		The amount of income tax to withhold is:	
Not over $8,300		$0	
Over—	**But not over—**		**of excess over—**
$8,300	—$26,150 . .	$0.00 plus 10%	—$8,300
$26,150	—$80,800 . .	$1,785.00 plus 15%	—$26,150
$80,800	—$154,700 . .	$9,982.50 plus 25%	—$80,800
$154,700	—$231,350 . .	$28,457.50 plus 28%	—$154,700
$231,350	—$406,650 . .	$49,919.50 plus 33%	—$231,350
$406,650	—$458,300 . .	$107,768.50 plus 35%	—$406,650
$458,300		$125,846.00 plus 39.6%	—$458,300

TABLE 8—DAILY or MISCELLANEOUS Payroll Period

(a) SINGLE person (including head of household)—

If the amount of wages (after subtracting withholding allowances) divided by the number of days in the payroll period is:		The amount of income tax to withhold per day is:	
Not over $8.50		$0	
Over—	**But not over—**		**of excess over—**
$8.50	—$42.80 . .	$0.00 plus 10%	—$8.50
$42.80	—$147.90 . .	$3.43 plus 15%	—$42.80
$147.90	—$346.30 . .	$19.20 plus 25%	—$147.90
$346.30	—$713.30 . .	$68.80 plus 28%	—$346.30
$713.30	—$1,540.60 . .	$171.56 plus 33%	—$713.30
$1,540.60	—$1,546.90 . .	$444.57 plus 35%	—$1,540.60
$1,546.90		$446.78 plus 39.6%	—$1,546.90

(b) MARRIED person—

If the amount of wages (after subtracting withholding allowances) divided by the number of days in the payroll period is:		The amount of income tax to withhold per day is:	
Not over $31.90		$0	
Over—	**But not over—**		**of excess over—**
$31.90	—$100.60 . .	$0.00 plus 10%	—$31.90
$100.60	—$310.80 . .	$6.87 plus 15%	—$100.60
$310.80	—$595.00 . .	$38.40 plus 25%	—$310.80
$595.00	—$889.80 . .	$109.45 plus 28%	—$595.00
$889.80	—$1,564.00 . .	$191.99 plus 33%	—$889.80
$1,564.00	—$1,762.70 . .	$414.48 plus 35%	—$1,564.00
$1,762.70		$484.03 plus 39.6%	—$1,762.70

SINGLE Persons—WEEKLY Payroll Period
(For Wages Paid through December 2013)

At least	But less than	0	1	2	3	4	5	6	7	8	9	10
And the wages are—		And the number of withholding allowances claimed is—										
		The amount of income tax to be withheld is—										
$ 0	$55	$0	$0	$0	$0	$0	$0	$0	$0	$0	$0	$0
55	60	2	0	0	0	0	0	0	0	0	0	0
60	65	2	0	0	0	0	0	0	0	0	0	0
65	70	3	0	0	0	0	0	0	0	0	0	0
70	75	3	0	0	0	0	0	0	0	0	0	0
75	80	4	0	0	0	0	0	0	0	0	0	0
80	85	4	0	0	0	0	0	0	0	0	0	0
85	90	5	0	0	0	0	0	0	0	0	0	0
90	95	5	0	0	0	0	0	0	0	0	0	0
95	100	6	0	0	0	0	0	0	0	0	0	0
100	105	6	0	0	0	0	0	0	0	0	0	0
105	110	7	0	0	0	0	0	0	0	0	0	0
110	115	7	0	0	0	0	0	0	0	0	0	0
115	120	8	0	0	0	0	0	0	0	0	0	0
120	125	8	1	0	0	0	0	0	0	0	0	0
125	130	9	1	0	0	0	0	0	0	0	0	0
130	135	9	2	0	0	0	0	0	0	0	0	0
135	140	10	2	0	0	0	0	0	0	0	0	0
140	145	10	3	0	0	0	0	0	0	0	0	0
145	150	11	3	0	0	0	0	0	0	0	0	0
150	155	11	4	0	0	0	0	0	0	0	0	0
155	160	12	4	0	0	0	0	0	0	0	0	0
160	165	12	5	0	0	0	0	0	0	0	0	0
165	170	13	5	0	0	0	0	0	0	0	0	0
170	175	13	6	0	0	0	0	0	0	0	0	0
175	180	14	6	0	0	0	0	0	0	0	0	0
180	185	14	7	0	0	0	0	0	0	0	0	0
185	190	15	7	0	0	0	0	0	0	0	0	0
190	195	15	8	0	0	0	0	0	0	0	0	0
195	200	16	8	1	0	0	0	0	0	0	0	0
200	210	16	9	1	0	0	0	0	0	0	0	0
210	220	17	10	2	0	0	0	0	0	0	0	0
220	230	19	11	3	0	0	0	0	0	0	0	0
230	240	20	12	4	0	0	0	0	0	0	0	0
240	250	22	13	5	0	0	0	0	0	0	0	0
250	260	23	14	6	0	0	0	0	0	0	0	0
260	270	25	15	7	0	0	0	0	0	0	0	0
270	280	26	16	8	1	0	0	0	0	0	0	0
280	290	28	17	9	2	0	0	0	0	0	0	0
290	300	29	18	10	3	0	0	0	0	0	0	0
300	310	31	20	11	4	0	0	0	0	0	0	0
310	320	32	21	12	5	0	0	0	0	0	0	0
320	330	34	23	13	6	0	0	0	0	0	0	0
330	340	35	24	14	7	0	0	0	0	0	0	0
340	350	37	26	15	8	0	0	0	0	0	0	0
350	360	38	27	16	9	1	0	0	0	0	0	0
360	370	40	29	17	10	2	0	0	0	0	0	0
370	380	41	30	19	11	3	0	0	0	0	0	0
380	390	43	32	20	12	4	0	0	0	0	0	0
390	400	44	33	22	13	5	0	0	0	0	0	0
400	410	46	35	23	14	6	0	0	0	0	0	0
410	420	47	36	25	15	7	0	0	0	0	0	0
420	430	49	38	26	16	8	1	0	0	0	0	0
430	440	50	39	28	17	9	2	0	0	0	0	0
440	450	52	41	29	18	10	3	0	0	0	0	0
450	460	53	42	31	20	11	4	0	0	0	0	0
460	470	55	44	32	21	12	5	0	0	0	0	0
470	480	56	45	34	23	13	6	0	0	0	0	0
480	490	58	47	35	24	14	7	0	0	0	0	0
490	500	59	48	37	26	15	8	0	0	0	0	0
500	510	61	50	38	27	16	9	1	0	0	0	0
510	520	62	51	40	29	17	10	2	0	0	0	0
520	530	64	53	41	30	19	11	3	0	0	0	0
530	540	65	54	43	32	20	12	4	0	0	0	0
540	550	67	56	44	33	22	13	5	0	0	0	0
550	560	68	57	46	35	23	14	6	0	0	0	0
560	570	70	59	47	36	25	15	7	0	0	0	0
570	580	71	60	49	38	26	16	8	1	0	0	0
580	590	73	62	50	39	28	17	9	2	0	0	0
590	600	74	63	52	41	29	18	10	3	0	0	0

Publication 15 (2013)

SINGLE Persons—WEEKLY Payroll Period

(For Wages Paid through December 2013)

And the wages are—		And the number of withholding allowances claimed is—										
At least	But less than	0	1	2	3	4	5	6	7	8	9	10
		The amount of income tax to be withheld is—										
$600	$610	$76	$65	$53	$42	$31	$20	$11	$4	$0	$0	$0
610	620	77	66	55	44	32	21	12	5	0	0	0
620	630	79	68	56	45	34	23	13	6	0	0	0
630	640	80	69	58	47	35	24	14	7	0	0	0
640	650	82	71	59	48	37	26	15	8	0	0	0
650	660	83	72	61	50	38	27	16	9	1	0	0
660	670	85	74	62	51	40	29	17	10	2	0	0
670	680	86	75	64	53	41	30	19	11	3	0	0
680	690	88	77	65	54	43	32	20	12	4	0	0
690	700	89	78	67	56	44	33	22	13	5	0	0
700	710	91	80	68	57	46	35	23	14	6	0	0
710	720	92	81	70	59	47	36	25	15	7	0	0
720	730	94	83	71	60	49	38	26	16	8	1	0
730	740	95	84	73	62	50	39	28	17	9	2	0
740	750	97	86	74	63	52	41	29	18	10	3	0
750	760	100	87	76	65	53	42	31	20	11	4	0
760	770	102	89	77	66	55	44	32	21	12	5	0
770	780	105	90	79	68	56	45	34	23	13	6	0
780	790	107	92	80	69	58	47	35	24	14	7	0
790	800	110	93	82	71	59	48	37	26	15	8	0
800	810	112	95	83	72	61	50	38	27	16	9	1
810	820	115	96	85	74	62	51	40	29	17	10	2
820	830	117	99	86	75	64	53	41	30	19	11	3
830	840	120	101	88	77	65	54	43	32	20	12	4
840	850	122	104	89	78	67	56	44	33	22	13	5
850	860	125	106	91	80	68	57	46	35	23	14	6
860	870	127	109	92	81	70	59	47	36	25	15	7
870	880	130	111	94	83	71	60	49	38	26	16	8
880	890	132	114	95	84	73	62	50	39	28	17	9
890	900	135	116	97	86	74	63	52	41	29	18	10
900	910	137	119	100	87	76	65	53	42	31	20	11
910	920	140	121	102	89	77	66	55	44	32	21	12
920	930	142	124	105	90	79	68	56	45	34	23	13
930	940	145	126	107	92	80	69	58	47	35	24	14
940	950	147	129	110	93	82	71	59	48	37	26	15
950	960	150	131	112	95	83	72	61	50	38	27	16
960	970	152	134	115	96	85	74	62	51	40	29	17
970	980	155	136	117	99	86	75	64	53	41	30	19
980	990	157	139	120	101	88	77	65	54	43	32	20
990	1,000	160	141	122	104	89	78	67	56	44	33	22
1,000	1,010	162	144	125	106	91	80	68	57	46	35	23
1,010	1,020	165	146	127	109	92	81	70	59	47	36	25
1,020	1,030	167	149	130	111	94	83	71	60	49	38	26
1,030	1,040	170	151	132	114	95	84	73	62	50	39	28
1,040	1,050	172	154	135	116	97	86	74	63	52	41	29
1,050	1,060	175	156	137	119	100	87	76	65	53	42	31
1,060	1,070	177	159	140	121	102	89	77	66	55	44	32
1,070	1,080	180	161	142	124	105	90	79	68	56	45	34
1,080	1,090	182	164	145	126	107	92	80	69	58	47	35
1,090	1,100	185	166	147	129	110	93	82	71	59	48	37
1,100	1,110	187	169	150	131	112	95	83	72	61	50	38
1,110	1,120	190	171	152	134	115	96	85	74	62	51	40
1,120	1,130	192	174	155	136	117	99	86	75	64	53	41
1,130	1,140	195	176	157	139	120	101	88	77	65	54	43
1,140	1,150	197	179	160	141	122	104	89	78	67	56	44
1,150	1,160	200	181	162	144	125	106	91	80	68	57	46
1,160	1,170	202	184	165	146	127	109	92	81	70	59	47
1,170	1,180	205	186	167	149	130	111	94	83	71	60	49
1,180	1,190	207	189	170	151	132	114	95	84	73	62	50
1,190	1,200	210	191	172	154	135	116	97	86	74	63	52
1,200	1,210	212	194	175	156	137	119	100	87	76	65	53
1,210	1,220	215	196	177	159	140	121	102	89	77	66	55
1,220	1,230	217	199	180	161	142	124	105	90	79	68	56
1,230	1,240	220	201	182	164	145	126	107	92	80	69	58
1,240	1,250	222	204	185	166	147	129	110	93	82	71	59

$1,250 and over	Use Table 1(a) for a **SINGLE person** on page 44. Also see the instructions on page 42.

MARRIED Persons—WEEKLY Payroll Period

(For Wages Paid through December 2013)

And the wages are—		And the number of withholding allowances claimed is—										
At least	But less than	0	1	2	3	4	5	6	7	8	9	10
		The amount of income tax to be withheld is—										
$ 0	$160	$0	$0	$0	$0	$0	$0	$0	$0	$0	$0	$0
160	165	0	0	0	0	0	0	0	0	0	0	0
165	170	1	0	0	0	0	0	0	0	0	0	0
170	175	1	0	0	0	0	0	0	0	0	0	0
175	180	2	0	0	0	0	0	0	0	0	0	0
180	185	2	0	0	0	0	0	0	0	0	0	0
185	190	3	0	0	0	0	0	0	0	0	0	0
190	195	3	0	0	0	0	0	0	0	0	0	0
195	200	4	0	0	0	0	0	0	0	0	0	0
200	210	5	0	0	0	0	0	0	0	0	0	0
210	220	6	0	0	0	0	0	0	0	0	0	0
220	230	7	0	0	0	0	0	0	0	0	0	0
230	240	8	0	0	0	0	0	0	0	0	0	0
240	250	9	1	0	0	0	0	0	0	0	0	0
250	260	10	2	0	0	0	0	0	0	0	0	0
260	270	11	3	0	0	0	0	0	0	0	0	0
270	280	12	4	0	0	0	0	0	0	0	0	0
280	290	13	5	0	0	0	0	0	0	0	0	0
290	300	14	6	0	0	0	0	0	0	0	0	0
300	310	15	7	0	0	0	0	0	0	0	0	0
310	320	16	8	1	0	0	0	0	0	0	0	0
320	330	17	9	2	0	0	0	0	0	0	0	0
330	340	18	10	3	0	0	0	0	0	0	0	0
340	350	19	11	4	0	0	0	0	0	0	0	0
350	360	20	12	5	0	0	0	0	0	0	0	0
360	370	21	13	6	0	0	0	0	0	0	0	0
370	380	22	14	7	0	0	0	0	0	0	0	0
380	390	23	15	8	0	0	0	0	0	0	0	0
390	400	24	16	9	1	0	0	0	0	0	0	0
400	410	25	17	10	2	0	0	0	0	0	0	0
410	420	26	18	11	3	0	0	0	0	0	0	0
420	430	27	19	12	4	0	0	0	0	0	0	0
430	440	28	20	13	5	0	0	0	0	0	0	0
440	450	29	21	14	6	0	0	0	0	0	0	0
450	460	30	22	15	7	0	0	0	0	0	0	0
460	470	31	23	16	8	1	0	0	0	0	0	0
470	480	32	24	17	9	2	0	0	0	0	0	0
480	490	33	25	18	10	3	0	0	0	0	0	0
490	500	34	26	19	11	4	0	0	0	0	0	0
500	510	35	27	20	12	5	0	0	0	0	0	0
510	520	36	28	21	13	6	0	0	0	0	0	0
520	530	38	29	22	14	7	0	0	0	0	0	0
530	540	39	30	23	15	8	0	0	0	0	0	0
540	550	41	31	24	16	9	1	0	0	0	0	0
550	560	42	32	25	17	10	2	0	0	0	0	0
560	570	44	33	26	18	11	3	0	0	0	0	0
570	580	45	34	27	19	12	4	0	0	0	0	0
580	590	47	35	28	20	13	5	0	0	0	0	0
590	600	48	37	29	21	14	6	0	0	0	0	0
600	610	50	38	30	22	15	7	0	0	0	0	0
610	620	51	40	31	23	16	8	1	0	0	0	0
620	630	53	41	32	24	17	9	2	0	0	0	0
630	640	54	43	33	25	18	10	3	0	0	0	0
640	650	56	44	34	26	19	11	4	0	0	0	0
650	660	57	46	35	27	20	12	5	0	0	0	0
660	670	59	47	36	28	21	13	6	0	0	0	0
670	680	60	49	38	29	22	14	7	0	0	0	0
680	690	62	50	39	30	23	15	8	0	0	0	0
690	700	63	52	41	31	24	16	9	1	0	0	0
700	710	65	53	42	32	25	17	10	2	0	0	0
710	720	66	55	44	33	26	18	11	3	0	0	0
720	730	68	56	45	34	27	19	12	4	0	0	0
730	740	69	58	47	35	28	20	13	5	0	0	0
740	750	71	59	48	37	29	21	14	6	0	0	0
750	760	72	61	50	38	30	22	15	7	0	0	0
760	770	74	62	51	40	31	23	16	8	1	0	0
770	780	75	64	53	41	32	24	17	9	2	0	0
780	790	77	65	54	43	33	25	18	10	3	0	0
790	800	78	67	56	44	34	26	19	11	4	0	0

Publication 15 (2013)

MARRIED Persons—WEEKLY Payroll Period

(For Wages Paid through December 2013)

And the wages are—		And the number of withholding allowances claimed is—										
At least	But less than	0	1	2	3	4	5	6	7	8	9	10
		The amount of income tax to be withheld is—										
$800	$810	$80	$68	$57	$46	$35	$27	$20	$12	$5	$0	$0
810	820	81	70	59	47	36	28	21	13	6	0	0
820	830	83	71	60	49	38	29	22	14	7	0	0
830	840	84	73	62	50	39	30	23	15	8	0	0
840	850	86	74	63	52	41	31	24	16	9	1	0
850	860	87	76	65	53	42	32	25	17	10	2	0
860	870	89	77	66	55	44	33	26	18	11	3	0
870	880	90	79	68	56	45	34	27	19	12	4	0
880	890	92	80	69	58	47	35	28	20	13	5	0
890	900	93	82	71	59	48	37	29	21	14	6	0
900	910	95	83	72	61	50	38	30	22	15	7	0
910	920	96	85	74	62	51	40	31	23	16	8	1
920	930	98	86	75	64	53	41	32	24	17	9	2
930	940	99	88	77	65	54	43	33	25	18	10	3
940	950	101	89	78	67	56	44	34	26	19	11	4
950	960	102	91	80	68	57	46	35	27	20	12	5
960	970	104	92	81	70	59	47	36	28	21	13	6
970	980	105	94	83	71	60	49	38	29	22	14	7
980	990	107	95	84	73	62	50	39	30	23	15	8
990	1,000	108	97	86	74	63	52	41	31	24	16	9
1,000	1,010	110	98	87	76	65	53	42	32	25	17	10
1,010	1,020	111	100	89	77	66	55	44	33	26	18	11
1,020	1,030	113	101	90	79	68	56	45	34	27	19	12
1,030	1,040	114	103	92	80	69	58	47	35	28	20	13
1,040	1,050	116	104	93	82	71	59	48	37	29	21	14
1,050	1,060	117	106	95	83	72	61	50	38	30	22	15
1,060	1,070	119	107	96	85	74	62	51	40	31	23	16
1,070	1,080	120	109	98	86	75	64	53	41	32	24	17
1,080	1,090	122	110	99	88	77	65	54	43	33	25	18
1,090	1,100	123	112	101	89	78	67	56	44	34	26	19
1,100	1,110	125	113	102	91	80	68	57	46	35	27	20
1,110	1,120	126	115	104	92	81	70	59	47	36	28	21
1,120	1,130	128	116	105	94	83	71	60	49	38	29	22
1,130	1,140	129	118	107	95	84	73	62	50	39	30	23
1,140	1,150	131	119	108	97	86	74	63	52	41	31	24
1,150	1,160	132	121	110	98	87	76	65	53	42	32	25
1,160	1,170	134	122	111	100	89	77	66	55	44	33	26
1,170	1,180	135	124	113	101	90	79	68	56	45	34	27
1,180	1,190	137	125	114	103	92	80	69	58	47	35	28
1,190	1,200	138	127	116	104	93	82	71	59	48	37	29
1,200	1,210	140	128	117	106	95	83	72	61	50	38	30
1,210	1,220	141	130	119	107	96	85	74	62	51	40	31
1,220	1,230	143	131	120	109	98	86	75	64	53	41	32
1,230	1,240	144	133	122	110	99	88	77	65	54	43	33
1,240	1,250	146	134	123	112	101	89	78	67	56	44	34
1,250	1,260	147	136	125	113	102	91	80	68	57	46	35
1,260	1,270	149	137	126	115	104	92	81	70	59	47	36
1,270	1,280	150	139	128	116	105	94	83	71	60	49	38
1,280	1,290	152	140	129	118	107	95	84	73	62	50	39
1,290	1,300	153	142	131	119	108	97	86	74	63	52	41
1,300	1,310	155	143	132	121	110	98	87	76	65	53	42
1,310	1,320	156	145	134	122	111	100	89	77	66	55	44
1,320	1,330	158	146	135	124	113	101	90	79	68	56	45
1,330	1,340	159	148	137	125	114	103	92	80	69	58	47
1,340	1,350	161	149	138	127	116	104	93	82	71	59	48
1,350	1,360	162	151	140	128	117	106	95	83	72	61	50
1,360	1,370	164	152	141	130	119	107	96	85	74	62	51
1,370	1,380	165	154	143	131	120	109	98	86	75	64	53
1,380	1,390	167	155	144	133	122	110	99	88	77	65	54
1,390	1,400	168	157	146	134	123	112	101	89	78	67	56

$1,400 and over	Use Table 1(b) for a **MARRIED person** on page 44. Also see the instructions on page 42.

SINGLE Persons—BIWEEKLY Payroll Period
(For Wages Paid through December 2013)

And the wages are–		And the number of withholding allowances claimed is—										
At least	But less than	0	1	2	3	4	5	6	7	8	9	10
		The amount of income tax to be withheld is—										
$ 0	$105	$0	$0	$0	$0	$0	$0	$0	$0	$0	$0	$0
105	110	2	0	0	0	0	0	0	0	0	0	0
110	115	3	0	0	0	0	0	0	0	0	0	0
115	120	3	0	0	0	0	0	0	0	0	0	0
120	125	4	0	0	0	0	0	0	0	0	0	0
125	130	4	0	0	0	0	0	0	0	0	0	0
130	135	5	0	0	0	0	0	0	0	0	0	0
135	140	5	0	0	0	0	0	0	0	0	0	0
140	145	6	0	0	0	0	0	0	0	0	0	0
145	150	6	0	0	0	0	0	0	0	0	0	0
150	155	7	0	0	0	0	0	0	0	0	0	0
155	160	7	0	0	0	0	0	0	0	0	0	0
160	165	8	0	0	0	0	0	0	0	0	0	0
165	170	8	0	0	0	0	0	0	0	0	0	0
170	175	9	0	0	0	0	0	0	0	0	0	0
175	180	9	0	0	0	0	0	0	0	0	0	0
180	185	10	0	0	0	0	0	0	0	0	0	0
185	190	10	0	0	0	0	0	0	0	0	0	0
190	195	11	0	0	0	0	0	0	0	0	0	0
195	200	11	0	0	0	0	0	0	0	0	0	0
200	205	12	0	0	0	0	0	0	0	0	0	0
205	210	12	0	0	0	0	0	0	0	0	0	0
210	215	13	0	0	0	0	0	0	0	0	0	0
215	220	13	0	0	0	0	0	0	0	0	0	0
220	225	14	0	0	0	0	0	0	0	0	0	0
225	230	14	0	0	0	0	0	0	0	0	0	0
230	235	15	0	0	0	0	0	0	0	0	0	0
235	240	15	0	0	0	0	0	0	0	0	0	0
240	245	16	1	0	0	0	0	0	0	0	0	0
245	250	16	1	0	0	0	0	0	0	0	0	0
250	260	17	2	0	0	0	0	0	0	0	0	0
260	270	18	3	0	0	0	0	0	0	0	0	0
270	280	19	4	0	0	0	0	0	0	0	0	0
280	290	20	5	0	0	0	0	0	0	0	0	0
290	300	21	6	0	0	0	0	0	0	0	0	0
300	310	22	7	0	0	0	0	0	0	0	0	0
310	320	23	8	0	0	0	0	0	0	0	0	0
320	330	24	9	0	0	0	0	0	0	0	0	0
330	340	25	10	0	0	0	0	0	0	0	0	0
340	350	26	11	0	0	0	0	0	0	0	0	0
350	360	27	12	0	0	0	0	0	0	0	0	0
360	370	28	13	0	0	0	0	0	0	0	0	0
370	380	29	14	0	0	0	0	0	0	0	0	0
380	390	30	15	0	0	0	0	0	0	0	0	0
390	400	31	16	1	0	0	0	0	0	0	0	0
400	410	32	17	2	0	0	0	0	0	0	0	0
410	420	33	18	3	0	0	0	0	0	0	0	0
420	430	34	19	4	0	0	0	0	0	0	0	0
430	440	35	20	5	0	0	0	0	0	0	0	0
440	450	37	21	6	0	0	0	0	0	0	0	0
450	460	38	22	7	0	0	0	0	0	0	0	0
460	470	40	23	8	0	0	0	0	0	0	0	0
470	480	41	24	9	0	0	0	0	0	0	0	0
480	490	43	25	10	0	0	0	0	0	0	0	0
490	500	44	26	11	0	0	0	0	0	0	0	0
500	520	47	28	13	0	0	0	0	0	0	0	0
520	540	50	30	15	0	0	0	0	0	0	0	0
540	560	53	32	17	2	0	0	0	0	0	0	0
560	580	56	34	19	4	0	0	0	0	0	0	0
580	600	59	36	21	6	0	0	0	0	0	0	0
600	620	62	39	23	8	0	0	0	0	0	0	0
620	640	65	42	25	10	0	0	0	0	0	0	0
640	660	68	45	27	12	0	0	0	0	0	0	0
660	680	71	48	29	14	0	0	0	0	0	0	0
680	700	74	51	31	16	1	0	0	0	0	0	0
700	720	77	54	33	18	3	0	0	0	0	0	0
720	740	80	57	35	20	5	0	0	0	0	0	0
740	760	83	60	38	22	7	0	0	0	0	0	0
760	780	86	63	41	24	9	0	0	0	0	0	0
780	800	89	66	44	26	11	0	0	0	0	0	0

Publication 15 (2013)

SINGLE Persons—BIWEEKLY Payroll Period
(For Wages Paid through December 2013)

| And the wages are— | | And the number of withholding allowances claimed is— | | | | | | | | | | |
At least	But less than	0	1	2	3	4	5	6	7	8	9	10
		The amount of income tax to be withheld is—										
$800	$820	$92	$69	$47	$28	$13	$0	$0	$0	$0	$0	$0
820	840	95	72	50	30	15	0	0	0	0	0	0
840	860	98	75	53	32	17	2	0	0	0	0	0
860	880	101	78	56	34	19	4	0	0	0	0	0
880	900	104	81	59	36	21	6	0	0	0	0	0
900	920	107	84	62	39	23	8	0	0	0	0	0
920	940	110	87	65	42	25	10	0	0	0	0	0
940	960	113	90	68	45	27	12	0	0	0	0	0
960	980	116	93	71	48	29	14	0	0	0	0	0
980	1,000	119	96	74	51	31	16	1	0	0	0	0
1,000	1,020	122	99	77	54	33	18	3	0	0	0	0
1,020	1,040	125	102	80	57	35	20	5	0	0	0	0
1,040	1,060	128	105	83	60	38	22	7	0	0	0	0
1,060	1,080	131	108	86	63	41	24	9	0	0	0	0
1,080	1,100	134	111	89	66	44	26	11	0	0	0	0
1,100	1,120	137	114	92	69	47	28	13	0	0	0	0
1,120	1,140	140	117	95	72	50	30	15	0	0	0	0
1,140	1,160	143	120	98	75	53	32	17	2	0	0	0
1,160	1,180	146	123	101	78	56	34	19	4	0	0	0
1,180	1,200	149	126	104	81	59	36	21	6	0	0	0
1,200	1,220	152	129	107	84	62	39	23	8	0	0	0
1,220	1,240	155	132	110	87	65	42	25	10	0	0	0
1,240	1,260	158	135	113	90	68	45	27	12	0	0	0
1,260	1,280	161	138	116	93	71	48	29	14	0	0	0
1,280	1,300	164	141	119	96	74	51	31	16	1	0	0
1,300	1,320	167	144	122	99	77	54	33	18	3	0	0
1,320	1,340	170	147	125	102	80	57	35	20	5	0	0
1,340	1,360	173	150	128	105	83	60	38	22	7	0	0
1,360	1,380	176	153	131	108	86	63	41	24	9	0	0
1,380	1,400	179	156	134	111	89	66	44	26	11	0	0
1,400	1,420	182	159	137	114	92	69	47	28	13	0	0
1,420	1,440	185	162	140	117	95	72	50	30	15	0	0
1,440	1,460	188	165	143	120	98	75	53	32	17	2	0
1,460	1,480	191	168	146	123	101	78	56	34	19	4	0
1,480	1,500	195	171	149	126	104	81	59	36	21	6	0
1,500	1,520	200	174	152	129	107	84	62	39	23	8	0
1,520	1,540	205	177	155	132	110	87	65	42	25	10	0
1,540	1,560	210	180	158	135	113	90	68	45	27	12	0
1,560	1,580	215	183	161	138	116	93	71	48	29	14	0
1,580	1,600	220	186	164	141	119	96	74	51	31	16	1
1,600	1,620	225	189	167	144	122	99	77	54	33	18	3
1,620	1,640	230	192	170	147	125	102	80	57	35	20	5
1,640	1,660	235	197	173	150	128	105	83	60	38	22	7
1,660	1,680	240	202	176	153	131	108	86	63	41	24	9
1,680	1,700	245	207	179	156	134	111	89	66	44	26	11
1,700	1,720	250	212	182	159	137	114	92	69	47	28	13
1,720	1,740	255	217	185	162	140	117	95	72	50	30	15
1,740	1,760	260	222	188	165	143	120	98	75	53	32	17
1,760	1,780	265	227	191	168	146	123	101	78	56	34	19
1,780	1,800	270	232	195	171	149	126	104	81	59	36	21
1,800	1,820	275	237	200	174	152	129	107	84	62	39	23
1,820	1,840	280	242	205	177	155	132	110	87	65	42	25
1,840	1,860	285	247	210	180	158	135	113	90	68	45	27
1,860	1,880	290	252	215	183	161	138	116	93	71	48	29
1,880	1,900	295	257	220	186	164	141	119	96	74	51	31
1,900	1,920	300	262	225	189	167	144	122	99	77	54	33
1,920	1,940	305	267	230	192	170	147	125	102	80	57	35
1,940	1,960	310	272	235	197	173	150	128	105	83	60	38
1,960	1,980	315	277	240	202	176	153	131	108	86	63	41
1,980	2,000	320	282	245	207	179	156	134	111	89	66	44
2,000	2,020	325	287	250	212	182	159	137	114	92	69	47
2,020	2,040	330	292	255	217	185	162	140	117	95	72	50
2,040	2,060	335	297	260	222	188	165	143	120	98	75	53
2,060	2,080	340	302	265	227	191	168	146	123	101	78	56
2,080	2,100	345	307	270	232	195	171	149	126	104	81	59

$2,100 and over Use Table 2(a) for a **SINGLE person** on page 44. Also see the instructions on page 42.

MARRIED Persons—BIWEEKLY Payroll Period

(For Wages Paid through December 2013)

And the wages are—		And the number of withholding allowances claimed is—										
At least	But less than	0	1	2	3	4	5	6	7	8	9	10
		The amount of income tax to be withheld is—										
$ 0	$320	$0	$0	$0	$0	$0	$0	$0	$0	$0	$0	$0
320	330	1	0	0	0	0	0	0	0	0	0	0
330	340	2	0	0	0	0	0	0	0	0	0	0
340	350	3	0	0	0	0	0	0	0	0	0	0
350	360	4	0	0	0	0	0	0	0	0	0	0
360	370	5	0	0	0	0	0	0	0	0	0	0
370	380	6	0	0	0	0	0	0	0	0	0	0
380	390	7	0	0	0	0	0	0	0	0	0	0
390	400	8	0	0	0	0	0	0	0	0	0	0
400	410	9	0	0	0	0	0	0	0	0	0	0
410	420	10	0	0	0	0	0	0	0	0	0	0
420	430	11	0	0	0	0	0	0	0	0	0	0
430	440	12	0	0	0	0	0	0	0	0	0	0
440	450	13	0	0	0	0	0	0	0	0	0	0
450	460	14	0	0	0	0	0	0	0	0	0	0
460	470	15	0	0	0	0	0	0	0	0	0	0
470	480	16	1	0	0	0	0	0	0	0	0	0
480	490	17	2	0	0	0	0	0	0	0	0	0
490	500	18	3	0	0	0	0	0	0	0	0	0
500	520	19	4	0	0	0	0	0	0	0	0	0
520	540	21	6	0	0	0	0	0	0	0	0	0
540	560	23	8	0	0	0	0	0	0	0	0	0
560	580	25	10	0	0	0	0	0	0	0	0	0
580	600	27	12	0	0	0	0	0	0	0	0	0
600	620	29	14	0	0	0	0	0	0	0	0	0
620	640	31	16	1	0	0	0	0	0	0	0	0
640	660	33	18	3	0	0	0	0	0	0	0	0
660	680	35	20	5	0	0	0	0	0	0	0	0
680	700	37	22	7	0	0	0	0	0	0	0	0
700	720	39	24	9	0	0	0	0	0	0	0	0
720	740	41	26	11	0	0	0	0	0	0	0	0
740	760	43	28	13	0	0	0	0	0	0	0	0
760	780	45	30	15	0	0	0	0	0	0	0	0
780	800	47	32	17	2	0	0	0	0	0	0	0
800	820	49	34	19	4	0	0	0	0	0	0	0
820	840	51	36	21	6	0	0	0	0	0	0	0
840	860	53	38	23	8	0	0	0	0	0	0	0
860	880	55	40	25	10	0	0	0	0	0	0	0
880	900	57	42	27	12	0	0	0	0	0	0	0
900	920	59	44	29	14	0	0	0	0	0	0	0
920	940	61	46	31	16	1	0	0	0	0	0	0
940	960	63	48	33	18	3	0	0	0	0	0	0
960	980	65	50	35	20	5	0	0	0	0	0	0
980	1,000	67	52	37	22	7	0	0	0	0	0	0
1,000	1,020	69	54	39	24	9	0	0	0	0	0	0
1,020	1,040	72	56	41	26	11	0	0	0	0	0	0
1,040	1,060	75	58	43	28	13	0	0	0	0	0	0
1,060	1,080	78	60	45	30	15	0	0	0	0	0	0
1,080	1,100	81	62	47	32	17	2	0	0	0	0	0
1,100	1,120	84	64	49	34	19	4	0	0	0	0	0
1,120	1,140	87	66	51	36	21	6	0	0	0	0	0
1,140	1,160	90	68	53	38	23	8	0	0	0	0	0
1,160	1,180	93	71	55	40	25	10	0	0	0	0	0
1,180	1,200	96	74	57	42	27	12	0	0	0	0	0
1,200	1,220	99	77	59	44	29	14	0	0	0	0	0
1,220	1,240	102	80	61	46	31	16	1	0	0	0	0
1,240	1,260	105	83	63	48	33	18	3	0	0	0	0
1,260	1,280	108	86	65	50	35	20	5	0	0	0	0
1,280	1,300	111	89	67	52	37	22	7	0	0	0	0
1,300	1,320	114	92	69	54	39	24	9	0	0	0	0
1,320	1,340	117	95	72	56	41	26	11	0	0	0	0
1,340	1,360	120	98	75	58	43	28	13	0	0	0	0
1,360	1,380	123	101	78	60	45	30	15	0	0	0	0
1,380	1,400	126	104	81	62	47	32	17	2	0	0	0
1,400	1,420	129	107	84	64	49	34	19	4	0	0	0
1,420	1,440	132	110	87	66	51	36	21	6	0	0	0
1,440	1,460	135	113	90	68	53	38	23	8	0	0	0
1,460	1,480	138	116	93	71	55	40	25	10	0	0	0
1,480	1,500	141	119	96	74	57	42	27	12	0	0	0

Publication 15 (2013)

MARRIED Persons—BIWEEKLY Payroll Period
(For Wages Paid through December 2013)

And the wages are–		And the number of withholding allowances claimed is—										
At least	But less than	0	1	2	3	4	5	6	7	8	9	10
		The amount of income tax to be withheld is—										
$1,500	$1,520	$144	$122	$99	$77	$59	$44	$29	$14	$0	$0	$0
1,520	1,540	147	125	102	80	61	46	31	16	1	0	0
1,540	1,560	150	128	105	83	63	48	33	18	3	0	0
1,560	1,580	153	131	108	86	65	50	35	20	5	0	0
1,580	1,600	156	134	111	89	67	52	37	22	7	0	0
1,600	1,620	159	137	114	92	69	54	39	24	9	0	0
1,620	1,640	162	140	117	95	72	56	41	26	11	0	0
1,640	1,660	165	143	120	98	75	58	43	28	13	0	0
1,660	1,680	168	146	123	101	78	60	45	30	15	0	0
1,680	1,700	171	149	126	104	81	62	47	32	17	2	0
1,700	1,720	174	152	129	107	84	64	49	34	19	4	0
1,720	1,740	177	155	132	110	87	66	51	36	21	6	0
1,740	1,760	180	158	135	113	90	68	53	38	23	8	0
1,760	1,780	183	161	138	116	93	71	55	40	25	10	0
1,780	1,800	186	164	141	119	96	74	57	42	27	12	0
1,800	1,820	189	167	144	122	99	77	59	44	29	14	0
1,820	1,840	192	170	147	125	102	80	61	46	31	16	1
1,840	1,860	195	173	150	128	105	83	63	48	33	18	3
1,860	1,880	198	176	153	131	108	86	65	50	35	20	5
1,880	1,900	201	179	156	134	111	89	67	52	37	22	7
1,900	1,920	204	182	159	137	114	92	69	54	39	24	9
1,920	1,940	207	185	162	140	117	95	72	56	41	26	11
1,940	1,960	210	188	165	143	120	98	75	58	43	28	13
1,960	1,980	213	191	168	146	123	101	78	60	45	30	15
1,980	2,000	216	194	171	149	126	104	81	62	47	32	17
2,000	2,020	219	197	174	152	129	107	84	64	49	34	19
2,020	2,040	222	200	177	155	132	110	87	66	51	36	21
2,040	2,060	225	203	180	158	135	113	90	68	53	38	23
2,060	2,080	228	206	183	161	138	116	93	71	55	40	25
2,080	2,100	231	209	186	164	141	119	96	74	57	42	27
2,100	2,120	234	212	189	167	144	122	99	77	59	44	29
2,120	2,140	237	215	192	170	147	125	102	80	61	46	31
2,140	2,160	240	218	195	173	150	128	105	83	63	48	33
2,160	2,180	243	221	198	176	153	131	108	86	65	50	35
2,180	2,200	246	224	201	179	156	134	111	89	67	52	37
2,200	2,220	249	227	204	182	159	137	114	92	69	54	39
2,220	2,240	252	230	207	185	162	140	117	95	72	56	41
2,240	2,260	255	233	210	188	165	143	120	98	75	58	43
2,260	2,280	258	236	213	191	168	146	123	101	78	60	45
2,280	2,300	261	239	216	194	171	149	126	104	81	62	47
2,300	2,320	264	242	219	197	174	152	129	107	84	64	49
2,320	2,340	267	245	222	200	177	155	132	110	87	66	51
2,340	2,360	270	248	225	203	180	158	135	113	90	68	53
2,360	2,380	273	251	228	206	183	161	138	116	93	71	55
2,380	2,400	276	254	231	209	186	164	141	119	96	74	57
2,400	2,420	279	257	234	212	189	167	144	122	99	77	59
2,420	2,440	282	260	237	215	192	170	147	125	102	80	61
2,440	2,460	285	263	240	218	195	173	150	128	105	83	63
2,460	2,480	288	266	243	221	198	176	153	131	108	86	65
2,480	2,500	291	269	246	224	201	179	156	134	111	89	67
2,500	2,520	294	272	249	227	204	182	159	137	114	92	69
2,520	2,540	297	275	252	230	207	185	162	140	117	95	72
2,540	2,560	300	278	255	233	210	188	165	143	120	98	75
2,560	2,580	303	281	258	236	213	191	168	146	123	101	78
2,580	2,600	306	284	261	239	216	194	171	149	126	104	81
2,600	2,620	309	287	264	242	219	197	174	152	129	107	84
2,620	2,640	312	290	267	245	222	200	177	155	132	110	87
2,640	2,660	315	293	270	248	225	203	180	158	135	113	90
2,660	2,680	318	296	273	251	228	206	183	161	138	116	93
2,680	2,700	321	299	276	254	231	209	186	164	141	119	96

$2,700 and over	Use Table 2(b) for a **MARRIED person** on page 44. Also see the instructions on page 42.

SINGLE Persons—SEMIMONTHLY Payroll Period

(For Wages Paid through December 2013)

And the wages are–		And the number of withholding allowances claimed is—										
At least	But less than	0	1	2	3	4	5	6	7	8	9	10
		The amount of income tax to be withheld is—										
$ 0	$115	$0	$0	$0	$0	$0	$0	$0	$0	$0	$0	$0
115	120	3	0	0	0	0	0	0	0	0	0	0
120	125	3	0	0	0	0	0	0	0	0	0	0
125	130	4	0	0	0	0	0	0	0	0	0	0
130	135	4	0	0	0	0	0	0	0	0	0	0
135	140	5	0	0	0	0	0	0	0	0	0	0
140	145	5	0	0	0	0	0	0	0	0	0	0
145	150	6	0	0	0	0	0	0	0	0	0	0
150	155	6	0	0	0	0	0	0	0	0	0	0
155	160	7	0	0	0	0	0	0	0	0	0	0
160	165	7	0	0	0	0	0	0	0	0	0	0
165	170	8	0	0	0	0	0	0	0	0	0	0
170	175	8	0	0	0	0	0	0	0	0	0	0
175	180	9	0	0	0	0	0	0	0	0	0	0
180	185	9	0	0	0	0	0	0	0	0	0	0
185	190	10	0	0	0	0	0	0	0	0	0	0
190	195	10	0	0	0	0	0	0	0	0	0	0
195	200	11	0	0	0	0	0	0	0	0	0	0
200	205	11	0	0	0	0	0	0	0	0	0	0
205	210	12	0	0	0	0	0	0	0	0	0	0
210	215	12	0	0	0	0	0	0	0	0	0	0
215	220	13	0	0	0	0	0	0	0	0	0	0
220	225	13	0	0	0	0	0	0	0	0	0	0
225	230	14	0	0	0	0	0	0	0	0	0	0
230	235	14	0	0	0	0	0	0	0	0	0	0
235	240	15	0	0	0	0	0	0	0	0	0	0
240	245	15	0	0	0	0	0	0	0	0	0	0
245	250	16	0	0	0	0	0	0	0	0	0	0
250	260	16	0	0	0	0	0	0	0	0	0	0
260	270	17	1	0	0	0	0	0	0	0	0	0
270	280	18	2	0	0	0	0	0	0	0	0	0
280	290	19	3	0	0	0	0	0	0	0	0	0
290	300	20	4	0	0	0	0	0	0	0	0	0
300	310	21	5	0	0	0	0	0	0	0	0	0
310	320	22	6	0	0	0	0	0	0	0	0	0
320	330	23	7	0	0	0	0	0	0	0	0	0
330	340	24	8	0	0	0	0	0	0	0	0	0
340	350	25	9	0	0	0	0	0	0	0	0	0
350	360	26	10	0	0	0	0	0	0	0	0	0
360	370	27	11	0	0	0	0	0	0	0	0	0
370	380	28	12	0	0	0	0	0	0	0	0	0
380	390	29	13	0	0	0	0	0	0	0	0	0
390	400	30	14	0	0	0	0	0	0	0	0	0
400	410	31	15	0	0	0	0	0	0	0	0	0
410	420	32	16	0	0	0	0	0	0	0	0	0
420	430	33	17	1	0	0	0	0	0	0	0	0
430	440	34	18	2	0	0	0	0	0	0	0	0
440	450	35	19	3	0	0	0	0	0	0	0	0
450	460	36	20	4	0	0	0	0	0	0	0	0
460	470	37	21	5	0	0	0	0	0	0	0	0
470	480	39	22	6	0	0	0	0	0	0	0	0
480	490	40	23	7	0	0	0	0	0	0	0	0
490	500	42	24	8	0	0	0	0	0	0	0	0
500	520	44	26	9	0	0	0	0	0	0	0	0
520	540	47	28	11	0	0	0	0	0	0	0	0
540	560	50	30	13	0	0	0	0	0	0	0	0
560	580	53	32	15	0	0	0	0	0	0	0	0
580	600	56	34	17	1	0	0	0	0	0	0	0
600	620	59	36	19	3	0	0	0	0	0	0	0
620	640	62	38	21	5	0	0	0	0	0	0	0
640	660	65	41	23	7	0	0	0	0	0	0	0
660	680	68	44	25	9	0	0	0	0	0	0	0
680	700	71	47	27	11	0	0	0	0	0	0	0
700	720	74	50	29	13	0	0	0	0	0	0	0
720	740	77	53	31	15	0	0	0	0	0	0	0
740	760	80	56	33	17	1	0	0	0	0	0	0
760	780	83	59	35	19	3	0	0	0	0	0	0
780	800	86	62	37	21	5	0	0	0	0	0	0

Publication 15 (2013)

SINGLE Persons—SEMIMONTHLY Payroll Period

(For Wages Paid through December 2013)

At least	But less than	0	1	2	3	4	5	6	7	8	9	10
And the wages are–		And the number of withholding allowances claimed is—										
		The amount of income tax to be withheld is—										
$800	$820	$89	$65	$40	$23	$7	$0	$0	$0	$0	$0	$0
820	840	92	68	43	25	9	0	0	0	0	0	0
840	860	95	71	46	27	11	0	0	0	0	0	0
860	880	98	74	49	29	13	0	0	0	0	0	0
880	900	101	77	52	31	15	0	0	0	0	0	0
900	920	104	80	55	33	17	1	0	0	0	0	0
920	940	107	83	58	35	19	3	0	0	0	0	0
940	960	110	86	61	37	21	5	0	0	0	0	0
960	980	113	89	64	40	23	7	0	0	0	0	0
980	1,000	116	92	67	43	25	9	0	0	0	0	0
1,000	1,020	119	95	70	46	27	11	0	0	0	0	0
1,020	1,040	122	98	73	49	29	13	0	0	0	0	0
1,040	1,060	125	101	76	52	31	15	0	0	0	0	0
1,060	1,080	128	104	79	55	33	17	0	0	0	0	0
1,080	1,100	131	107	82	58	35	19	2	0	0	0	0
1,100	1,120	134	110	85	61	37	21	4	0	0	0	0
1,120	1,140	137	113	88	64	40	23	6	0	0	0	0
1,140	1,160	140	116	91	67	43	25	8	0	0	0	0
1,160	1,180	143	119	94	70	46	27	10	0	0	0	0
1,180	1,200	146	122	97	73	49	29	12	0	0	0	0
1,200	1,220	149	125	100	76	52	31	14	0	0	0	0
1,220	1,240	152	128	103	79	55	33	16	0	0	0	0
1,240	1,260	155	131	106	82	58	35	18	2	0	0	0
1,260	1,280	158	134	109	85	61	37	20	4	0	0	0
1,280	1,300	161	137	112	88	64	39	22	6	0	0	0
1,300	1,320	164	140	115	91	67	42	24	8	0	0	0
1,320	1,340	167	143	118	94	70	45	26	10	0	0	0
1,340	1,360	170	146	121	97	73	48	28	12	0	0	0
1,360	1,380	173	149	124	100	76	51	30	14	0	0	0
1,380	1,400	176	152	127	103	79	54	32	16	0	0	0
1,400	1,420	179	155	130	106	82	57	34	18	2	0	0
1,420	1,440	182	158	133	109	85	60	36	20	4	0	0
1,440	1,460	185	161	136	112	88	63	39	22	6	0	0
1,460	1,480	188	164	139	115	91	66	42	24	8	0	0
1,480	1,500	191	167	142	118	94	69	45	26	10	0	0
1,500	1,520	194	170	145	121	97	72	48	28	12	0	0
1,520	1,540	197	173	148	124	100	75	51	30	14	0	0
1,540	1,560	200	176	151	127	103	78	54	32	16	0	0
1,560	1,580	203	179	154	130	106	81	57	34	18	2	0
1,580	1,600	206	182	157	133	109	84	60	36	20	4	0
1,600	1,620	210	185	160	136	112	87	63	39	22	6	0
1,620	1,640	215	188	163	139	115	90	66	42	24	8	0
1,640	1,660	220	191	166	142	118	93	69	45	26	10	0
1,660	1,680	225	194	169	145	121	96	72	48	28	12	0
1,680	1,700	230	197	172	148	124	99	75	51	30	14	0
1,700	1,720	235	200	175	151	127	102	78	54	32	16	0
1,720	1,740	240	203	178	154	130	105	81	57	34	18	1
1,740	1,760	245	206	181	157	133	108	84	60	36	20	3
1,760	1,780	250	209	184	160	136	111	87	63	38	22	5
1,780	1,800	255	214	187	163	139	114	90	66	41	24	7
1,800	1,820	260	219	190	166	142	117	93	69	44	26	9
1,820	1,840	265	224	193	169	145	120	96	72	47	28	11
1,840	1,860	270	229	196	172	148	123	99	75	50	30	13
1,860	1,880	275	234	199	175	151	126	102	78	53	32	15
1,880	1,900	280	239	202	178	154	129	105	81	56	34	17
1,900	1,920	285	244	205	181	157	132	108	84	59	36	19
1,920	1,940	290	249	209	184	160	135	111	87	62	38	21
1,940	1,960	295	254	214	187	163	138	114	90	65	41	23
1,960	1,980	300	259	219	190	166	141	117	93	68	44	25
1,980	2,000	305	264	224	193	169	144	120	96	71	47	27
2,000	2,020	310	269	229	196	172	147	123	99	74	50	29
2,020	2,040	315	274	234	199	175	150	126	102	77	53	31
2,040	2,060	320	279	239	202	178	153	129	105	80	56	33
2,060	2,080	325	284	244	205	181	156	132	108	83	59	35
2,080	2,100	330	289	249	208	184	159	135	111	86	62	37
2,100	2,120	335	294	254	213	187	162	138	114	89	65	40
2,120	2,140	340	299	259	218	190	165	141	117	92	68	43

$2,140 and over — Use Table 3(a) for a **SINGLE person** on page 44. Also see the instructions on page 42.

MARRIED Persons—SEMIMONTHLY Payroll Period

(For Wages Paid through December 2013)

And the wages are–		And the number of withholding allowances claimed is—										
At least	But less than	0	1	2	3	4	5	6	7	8	9	10
		The amount of income tax to be withheld is—										
$ 0	$350	$0	$0	$0	$0	$0	$0	$0	$0	$0	$0	$0
350	360	1	0	0	0	0	0	0	0	0	0	0
360	370	2	0	0	0	0	0	0	0	0	0	0
370	380	3	0	0	0	0	0	0	0	0	0	0
380	390	4	0	0	0	0	0	0	0	0	0	0
390	400	5	0	0	0	0	0	0	0	0	0	0
400	410	6	0	0	0	0	0	0	0	0	0	0
410	420	7	0	0	0	0	0	0	0	0	0	0
420	430	8	0	0	0	0	0	0	0	0	0	0
430	440	9	0	0	0	0	0	0	0	0	0	0
440	450	10	0	0	0	0	0	0	0	0	0	0
450	460	11	0	0	0	0	0	0	0	0	0	0
460	470	12	0	0	0	0	0	0	0	0	0	0
470	480	13	0	0	0	0	0	0	0	0	0	0
480	490	14	0	0	0	0	0	0	0	0	0	0
490	500	15	0	0	0	0	0	0	0	0	0	0
500	520	16	0	0	0	0	0	0	0	0	0	0
520	540	18	2	0	0	0	0	0	0	0	0	0
540	560	20	4	0	0	0	0	0	0	0	0	0
560	580	22	6	0	0	0	0	0	0	0	0	0
580	600	24	8	0	0	0	0	0	0	0	0	0
600	620	26	10	0	0	0	0	0	0	0	0	0
620	640	28	12	0	0	0	0	0	0	0	0	0
640	660	30	14	0	0	0	0	0	0	0	0	0
660	680	32	16	0	0	0	0	0	0	0	0	0
680	700	34	18	2	0	0	0	0	0	0	0	0
700	720	36	20	4	0	0	0	0	0	0	0	0
720	740	38	22	6	0	0	0	0	0	0	0	0
740	760	40	24	8	0	0	0	0	0	0	0	0
760	780	42	26	10	0	0	0	0	0	0	0	0
780	800	44	28	12	0	0	0	0	0	0	0	0
800	820	46	30	14	0	0	0	0	0	0	0	0
820	840	48	32	16	0	0	0	0	0	0	0	0
840	860	50	34	18	2	0	0	0	0	0	0	0
860	880	52	36	20	4	0	0	0	0	0	0	0
880	900	54	38	22	6	0	0	0	0	0	0	0
900	920	56	40	24	8	0	0	0	0	0	0	0
920	940	58	42	26	10	0	0	0	0	0	0	0
940	960	60	44	28	12	0	0	0	0	0	0	0
960	980	62	46	30	14	0	0	0	0	0	0	0
980	1,000	64	48	32	16	0	0	0	0	0	0	0
1,000	1,020	66	50	34	18	1	0	0	0	0	0	0
1,020	1,040	68	52	36	20	3	0	0	0	0	0	0
1,040	1,060	70	54	38	22	5	0	0	0	0	0	0
1,060	1,080	72	56	40	24	7	0	0	0	0	0	0
1,080	1,100	74	58	42	26	9	0	0	0	0	0	0
1,100	1,120	77	60	44	28	11	0	0	0	0	0	0
1,120	1,140	80	62	46	30	13	0	0	0	0	0	0
1,140	1,160	83	64	48	32	15	0	0	0	0	0	0
1,160	1,180	86	66	50	34	17	1	0	0	0	0	0
1,180	1,200	89	68	52	36	19	3	0	0	0	0	0
1,200	1,220	92	70	54	38	21	5	0	0	0	0	0
1,220	1,240	95	72	56	40	23	7	0	0	0	0	0
1,240	1,260	98	74	58	42	25	9	0	0	0	0	0
1,260	1,280	101	77	60	44	27	11	0	0	0	0	0
1,280	1,300	104	80	62	46	29	13	0	0	0	0	0
1,300	1,320	107	83	64	48	31	15	0	0	0	0	0
1,320	1,340	110	86	66	50	33	17	1	0	0	0	0
1,340	1,360	113	89	68	52	35	19	3	0	0	0	0
1,360	1,380	116	92	70	54	37	21	5	0	0	0	0
1,380	1,400	119	95	72	56	39	23	7	0	0	0	0
1,400	1,420	122	98	74	58	41	25	9	0	0	0	0
1,420	1,440	125	101	77	60	43	27	11	0	0	0	0
1,440	1,460	128	104	80	62	45	29	13	0	0	0	0
1,460	1,480	131	107	83	64	47	31	15	0	0	0	0
1,480	1,500	134	110	86	66	49	33	17	1	0	0	0
1,500	1,520	137	113	89	68	51	35	19	3	0	0	0
1,520	1,540	140	116	92	70	53	37	21	5	0	0	0
1,540	1,560	143	119	95	72	55	39	23	7	0	0	0
1,560	1,580	146	122	98	74	57	41	25	9	0	0	0
1,580	1,600	149	125	101	76	59	43	27	11	0	0	0

Publication 15 (2013)

MARRIED Persons—SEMIMONTHLY Payroll Period

(For Wages Paid through December 2013)

And the wages are—		And the number of withholding allowances claimed is—										
At least	But less than	0	1	2	3	4	5	6	7	8	9	10
		The amount of income tax to be withheld is—										
$1,600	$1,620	$152	$128	$104	$79	$61	$45	$29	$13	$0	$0	$0
1,620	1,640	155	131	107	82	63	47	31	15	0	0	0
1,640	1,660	158	134	110	85	65	49	33	17	0	0	0
1,660	1,680	161	137	113	88	67	51	35	19	2	0	0
1,680	1,700	164	140	116	91	69	53	37	21	4	0	0
1,700	1,720	167	143	119	94	71	55	39	23	6	0	0
1,720	1,740	170	146	122	97	73	57	41	25	8	0	0
1,740	1,760	173	149	125	100	76	59	43	27	10	0	0
1,760	1,780	176	152	128	103	79	61	45	29	12	0	0
1,780	1,800	179	155	131	106	82	63	47	31	14	0	0
1,800	1,820	182	158	134	109	85	65	49	33	16	0	0
1,820	1,840	185	161	137	112	88	67	51	35	18	2	0
1,840	1,860	188	164	140	115	91	69	53	37	20	4	0
1,860	1,880	191	167	143	118	94	71	55	39	22	6	0
1,880	1,900	194	170	146	121	97	73	57	41	24	8	0
1,900	1,920	197	173	149	124	100	76	59	43	26	10	0
1,920	1,940	200	176	152	127	103	79	61	45	28	12	0
1,940	1,960	203	179	155	130	106	82	63	47	30	14	0
1,960	1,980	206	182	158	133	109	85	65	49	32	16	0
1,980	2,000	209	185	161	136	112	88	67	51	34	18	2
2,000	2,020	212	188	164	139	115	91	69	53	36	20	4
2,020	2,040	215	191	167	142	118	94	71	55	38	22	6
2,040	2,060	218	194	170	145	121	97	73	57	40	24	8
2,060	2,080	221	197	173	148	124	100	75	59	42	26	10
2,080	2,100	224	200	176	151	127	103	78	61	44	28	12
2,100	2,120	227	203	179	154	130	106	81	63	46	30	14
2,120	2,140	230	206	182	157	133	109	84	65	48	32	16
2,140	2,160	233	209	185	160	136	112	87	67	50	34	18
2,160	2,180	236	212	188	163	139	115	90	69	52	36	20
2,180	2,200	239	215	191	166	142	118	93	71	54	38	22
2,200	2,220	242	218	194	169	145	121	96	73	56	40	24
2,220	2,240	245	221	197	172	148	124	99	75	58	42	26
2,240	2,260	248	224	200	175	151	127	102	78	60	44	28
2,260	2,280	251	227	203	178	154	130	105	81	62	46	30
2,280	2,300	254	230	206	181	157	133	108	84	64	48	32
2,300	2,320	257	233	209	184	160	136	111	87	66	50	34
2,320	2,340	260	236	212	187	163	139	114	90	68	52	36
2,340	2,360	263	239	215	190	166	142	117	93	70	54	38
2,360	2,380	266	242	218	193	169	145	120	96	72	56	40
2,380	2,400	269	245	221	196	172	148	123	99	74	58	42
2,400	2,420	272	248	224	199	175	151	126	102	77	60	44
2,420	2,440	275	251	227	202	178	154	129	105	80	62	46
2,440	2,460	278	254	230	205	181	157	132	108	83	64	48
2,460	2,480	281	257	233	208	184	160	135	111	86	66	50
2,480	2,500	284	260	236	211	187	163	138	114	89	68	52
2,500	2,520	287	263	239	214	190	166	141	117	92	70	54
2,520	2,540	290	266	242	217	193	169	144	120	95	72	56
2,540	2,560	293	269	245	220	196	172	147	123	98	74	58
2,560	2,580	296	272	248	223	199	175	150	126	101	77	60
2,580	2,600	299	275	251	226	202	178	153	129	104	80	62
2,600	2,620	302	278	254	229	205	181	156	132	107	83	64
2,620	2,640	305	281	257	232	208	184	159	135	110	86	66
2,640	2,660	308	284	260	235	211	187	162	138	113	89	68
2,660	2,680	311	287	263	238	214	190	165	141	116	92	70
2,680	2,700	314	290	266	241	217	193	168	144	119	95	72
2,700	2,720	317	293	269	244	220	196	171	147	122	98	74
2,720	2,740	320	296	272	247	223	199	174	150	125	101	77

$2,740 and over   Use Table 3(b) for a **MARRIED person** on page 44. Also see the instructions on page 42.

SINGLE Persons—MONTHLY Payroll Period

(For Wages Paid through December 2013)

And the wages are—		And the number of withholding allowances claimed is—										
At least	But less than	0	1	2	3	4	5	6	7	8	9	10
		The amount of income tax to be withheld is—										
$ 0	$220	$0	$0	$0	$0	$0	$0	$0	$0	$0	$0	$0
220	230	4	0	0	0	0	0	0	0	0	0	0
230	240	5	0	0	0	0	0	0	0	0	0	0
240	250	6	0	0	0	0	0	0	0	0	0	0
250	260	7	0	0	0	0	0	0	0	0	0	0
260	270	8	0	0	0	0	0	0	0	0	0	0
270	280	9	0	0	0	0	0	0	0	0	0	0
280	290	10	0	0	0	0	0	0	0	0	0	0
290	300	11	0	0	0	0	0	0	0	0	0	0
300	320	13	0	0	0	0	0	0	0	0	0	0
320	340	15	0	0	0	0	0	0	0	0	0	0
340	360	17	0	0	0	0	0	0	0	0	0	0
360	380	19	0	0	0	0	0	0	0	0	0	0
380	400	21	0	0	0	0	0	0	0	0	0	0
400	420	23	0	0	0	0	0	0	0	0	0	0
420	440	25	0	0	0	0	0	0	0	0	0	0
440	460	27	0	0	0	0	0	0	0	0	0	0
460	480	29	0	0	0	0	0	0	0	0	0	0
480	500	31	0	0	0	0	0	0	0	0	0	0
500	520	33	0	0	0	0	0	0	0	0	0	0
520	540	35	2	0	0	0	0	0	0	0	0	0
540	560	37	4	0	0	0	0	0	0	0	0	0
560	580	39	6	0	0	0	0	0	0	0	0	0
580	600	41	8	0	0	0	0	0	0	0	0	0
600	640	44	11	0	0	0	0	0	0	0	0	0
640	680	48	15	0	0	0	0	0	0	0	0	0
680	720	52	19	0	0	0	0	0	0	0	0	0
720	760	56	23	0	0	0	0	0	0	0	0	0
760	800	60	27	0	0	0	0	0	0	0	0	0
800	840	64	31	0	0	0	0	0	0	0	0	0
840	880	68	35	3	0	0	0	0	0	0	0	0
880	920	72	39	7	0	0	0	0	0	0	0	0
920	960	76	43	11	0	0	0	0	0	0	0	0
960	1,000	82	47	15	0	0	0	0	0	0	0	0
1,000	1,040	88	51	19	0	0	0	0	0	0	0	0
1,040	1,080	94	55	23	0	0	0	0	0	0	0	0
1,080	1,120	100	59	27	0	0	0	0	0	0	0	0
1,120	1,160	106	63	31	0	0	0	0	0	0	0	0
1,160	1,200	112	67	35	2	0	0	0	0	0	0	0
1,200	1,240	118	71	39	6	0	0	0	0	0	0	0
1,240	1,280	124	76	43	10	0	0	0	0	0	0	0
1,280	1,320	130	82	47	14	0	0	0	0	0	0	0
1,320	1,360	136	88	51	18	0	0	0	0	0	0	0
1,360	1,400	142	94	55	22	0	0	0	0	0	0	0
1,400	1,440	148	100	59	26	0	0	0	0	0	0	0
1,440	1,480	154	106	63	30	0	0	0	0	0	0	0
1,480	1,520	160	112	67	34	2	0	0	0	0	0	0
1,520	1,560	166	118	71	38	6	0	0	0	0	0	0
1,560	1,600	172	124	75	42	10	0	0	0	0	0	0
1,600	1,640	178	130	81	46	14	0	0	0	0	0	0
1,640	1,680	184	136	87	50	18	0	0	0	0	0	0
1,680	1,720	190	142	93	54	22	0	0	0	0	0	0
1,720	1,760	196	148	99	58	26	0	0	0	0	0	0
1,760	1,800	202	154	105	62	30	0	0	0	0	0	0
1,800	1,840	208	160	111	66	34	1	0	0	0	0	0
1,840	1,880	214	166	117	70	38	5	0	0	0	0	0
1,880	1,920	220	172	123	74	42	9	0	0	0	0	0
1,920	1,960	226	178	129	80	46	13	0	0	0	0	0
1,960	2,000	232	184	135	86	50	17	0	0	0	0	0
2,000	2,040	238	190	141	92	54	21	0	0	0	0	0
2,040	2,080	244	196	147	98	58	25	0	0	0	0	0
2,080	2,120	250	202	153	104	62	29	0	0	0	0	0
2,120	2,160	256	208	159	110	66	33	1	0	0	0	0
2,160	2,200	262	214	165	116	70	37	5	0	0	0	0
2,200	2,240	268	220	171	122	74	41	9	0	0	0	0
2,240	2,280	274	226	177	128	79	45	13	0	0	0	0
2,280	2,320	280	232	183	134	85	49	17	0	0	0	0
2,320	2,360	286	238	189	140	91	53	21	0	0	0	0
2,360	2,400	292	244	195	146	97	57	25	0	0	0	0

Publication 15 (2013)

SINGLE Persons—MONTHLY Payroll Period

(For Wages Paid through December 2013)

And the wages are—		And the number of withholding allowances claimed is—										
At least	But less than	0	1	2	3	4	5	6	7	8	9	10
		The amount of income tax to be withheld is—										
$2,400	$2,440	$298	$250	$201	$152	$103	$61	$29	$0	$0	$0	$0
2,440	2,480	304	256	207	158	109	65	33	0	0	0	0
2,480	2,520	310	262	213	164	115	69	37	4	0	0	0
2,520	2,560	316	268	219	170	121	73	41	8	0	0	0
2,560	2,600	322	274	225	176	127	79	45	12	0	0	0
2,600	2,640	328	280	231	182	133	85	49	16	0	0	0
2,640	2,680	334	286	237	188	139	91	53	20	0	0	0
2,680	2,720	340	292	243	194	145	97	57	24	0	0	0
2,720	2,760	346	298	249	200	151	103	61	28	0	0	0
2,760	2,800	352	304	255	206	157	109	65	32	0	0	0
2,800	2,840	358	310	261	212	163	115	69	36	4	0	0
2,840	2,880	364	316	267	218	169	121	73	40	8	0	0
2,880	2,920	370	322	273	224	175	127	78	44	12	0	0
2,920	2,960	376	328	279	230	181	133	84	48	16	0	0
2,960	3,000	382	334	285	236	187	139	90	52	20	0	0
3,000	3,040	388	340	291	242	193	145	96	56	24	0	0
3,040	3,080	394	346	297	248	199	151	102	60	28	0	0
3,080	3,120	400	352	303	254	205	157	108	64	32	0	0
3,120	3,160	406	358	309	260	211	163	114	68	36	3	0
3,160	3,200	412	364	315	266	217	169	120	72	40	7	0
3,200	3,240	420	370	321	272	223	175	126	77	44	11	0
3,240	3,280	430	376	327	278	229	181	132	83	48	15	0
3,280	3,320	440	382	333	284	235	187	138	89	52	19	0
3,320	3,360	450	388	339	290	241	193	144	95	56	23	0
3,360	3,400	460	394	345	296	247	199	150	101	60	27	0
3,400	3,440	470	400	351	302	253	205	156	107	64	31	0
3,440	3,480	480	406	357	308	259	211	162	113	68	35	3
3,480	3,520	490	412	363	314	265	217	168	119	72	39	7
3,520	3,560	500	419	369	320	271	223	174	125	76	43	11
3,560	3,600	510	429	375	326	277	229	180	131	82	47	15
3,600	3,640	520	439	381	332	283	235	186	137	88	51	19
3,640	3,680	530	449	387	338	289	241	192	143	94	55	23
3,680	3,720	540	459	393	344	295	247	198	149	100	59	27
3,720	3,760	550	469	399	350	301	253	204	155	106	63	31
3,760	3,800	560	479	405	356	307	259	210	161	112	67	35
3,800	3,840	570	489	411	362	313	265	216	167	118	71	39
3,840	3,880	580	499	417	368	319	271	222	173	124	76	43
3,880	3,920	590	509	427	374	325	277	228	179	130	82	47
3,920	3,960	600	519	437	380	331	283	234	185	136	88	51
3,960	4,000	610	529	447	386	337	289	240	191	142	94	55
4,000	4,040	620	539	457	392	343	295	246	197	148	100	59
4,040	4,080	630	549	467	398	349	301	252	203	154	106	63
4,080	4,120	640	559	477	404	355	307	258	209	160	112	67
4,120	4,160	650	569	487	410	361	313	264	215	166	118	71
4,160	4,200	660	579	497	416	367	319	270	221	172	124	75
4,200	4,240	670	589	507	426	373	325	276	227	178	130	81
4,240	4,280	680	599	517	436	379	331	282	233	184	136	87
4,280	4,320	690	609	527	446	385	337	288	239	190	142	93
4,320	4,360	700	619	537	456	391	343	294	245	196	148	99
4,360	4,400	710	629	547	466	397	349	300	251	202	154	105
4,400	4,440	720	639	557	476	403	355	306	257	208	160	111
4,440	4,480	730	649	567	486	409	361	312	263	214	166	117
4,480	4,520	740	659	577	496	415	367	318	269	220	172	123
4,520	4,560	750	669	587	506	425	373	324	275	226	178	129
4,560	4,600	760	679	597	516	435	379	330	281	232	184	135
4,600	4,640	770	689	607	526	445	385	336	287	238	190	141
4,640	4,680	780	699	617	536	455	391	342	293	244	196	147
4,680	4,720	790	709	627	546	465	397	348	299	250	202	153
4,720	4,760	800	719	637	556	475	403	354	305	256	208	159
4,760	4,800	810	729	647	566	485	409	360	311	262	214	165
4,800	4,840	820	739	657	576	495	415	366	317	268	220	171
4,840	4,880	830	749	667	586	505	424	372	323	274	226	177
4,880	4,920	840	759	677	596	515	434	378	329	280	232	183
4,920	4,960	850	769	687	606	525	444	384	335	286	238	189
4,960	5,000	860	779	697	616	535	454	390	341	292	244	195
5,000	5,040	870	789	707	626	545	464	396	347	298	250	201
5,040	5,080	880	799	717	636	555	474	402	353	304	256	207

$5,080 and over   Use Table 4(a) for a **SINGLE person** on page 44. Also see the instructions on page 42.

MARRIED Persons—MONTHLY Payroll Period

(For Wages Paid through December 2013)

And the wages are–		And the number of withholding allowances claimed is—										
At least	But less than	0	1	2	3	4	5	6	7	8	9	10
		The amount of income tax to be withheld is—										
$ 0	$680	$0	$0	$0	$0	$0	$0	$0	$0	$0	$0	$0
680	720	1	0	0	0	0	0	0	0	0	0	0
720	760	5	0	0	0	0	0	0	0	0	0	0
760	800	9	0	0	0	0	0	0	0	0	0	0
800	840	13	0	0	0	0	0	0	0	0	0	0
840	880	17	0	0	0	0	0	0	0	0	0	0
880	920	21	0	0	0	0	0	0	0	0	0	0
920	960	25	0	0	0	0	0	0	0	0	0	0
960	1,000	29	0	0	0	0	0	0	0	0	0	0
1,000	1,040	33	0	0	0	0	0	0	0	0	0	0
1,040	1,080	37	4	0	0	0	0	0	0	0	0	0
1,080	1,120	41	8	0	0	0	0	0	0	0	0	0
1,120	1,160	45	12	0	0	0	0	0	0	0	0	0
1,160	1,200	49	16	0	0	0	0	0	0	0	0	0
1,200	1,240	53	20	0	0	0	0	0	0	0	0	0
1,240	1,280	57	24	0	0	0	0	0	0	0	0	0
1,280	1,320	61	28	0	0	0	0	0	0	0	0	0
1,320	1,360	65	32	0	0	0	0	0	0	0	0	0
1,360	1,400	69	36	4	0	0	0	0	0	0	0	0
1,400	1,440	73	40	8	0	0	0	0	0	0	0	0
1,440	1,480	77	44	12	0	0	0	0	0	0	0	0
1,480	1,520	81	48	16	0	0	0	0	0	0	0	0
1,520	1,560	85	52	20	0	0	0	0	0	0	0	0
1,560	1,600	89	56	24	0	0	0	0	0	0	0	0
1,600	1,640	93	60	28	0	0	0	0	0	0	0	0
1,640	1,680	97	64	32	0	0	0	0	0	0	0	0
1,680	1,720	101	68	36	3	0	0	0	0	0	0	0
1,720	1,760	105	72	40	7	0	0	0	0	0	0	0
1,760	1,800	109	76	44	11	0	0	0	0	0	0	0
1,800	1,840	113	80	48	15	0	0	0	0	0	0	0
1,840	1,880	117	84	52	19	0	0	0	0	0	0	0
1,880	1,920	121	88	56	23	0	0	0	0	0	0	0
1,920	1,960	125	92	60	27	0	0	0	0	0	0	0
1,960	2,000	129	96	64	31	0	0	0	0	0	0	0
2,000	2,040	133	100	68	35	3	0	0	0	0	0	0
2,040	2,080	137	104	72	39	7	0	0	0	0	0	0
2,080	2,120	141	108	76	43	11	0	0	0	0	0	0
2,120	2,160	145	112	80	47	15	0	0	0	0	0	0
2,160	2,200	149	116	84	51	19	0	0	0	0	0	0
2,200	2,240	155	120	88	55	23	0	0	0	0	0	0
2,240	2,280	161	124	92	59	27	0	0	0	0	0	0
2,280	2,320	167	128	96	63	31	0	0	0	0	0	0
2,320	2,360	173	132	100	67	35	2	0	0	0	0	0
2,360	2,400	179	136	104	71	39	6	0	0	0	0	0
2,400	2,440	185	140	108	75	43	10	0	0	0	0	0
2,440	2,480	191	144	112	79	47	14	0	0	0	0	0
2,480	2,520	197	148	116	83	51	18	0	0	0	0	0
2,520	2,560	203	154	120	87	55	22	0	0	0	0	0
2,560	2,600	209	160	124	91	59	26	0	0	0	0	0
2,600	2,640	215	166	128	95	63	30	0	0	0	0	0
2,640	2,680	221	172	132	99	67	34	2	0	0	0	0
2,680	2,720	227	178	136	103	71	38	6	0	0	0	0
2,720	2,760	233	184	140	107	75	42	10	0	0	0	0
2,760	2,800	239	190	144	111	79	46	14	0	0	0	0
2,800	2,840	245	196	148	115	83	50	18	0	0	0	0
2,840	2,880	251	202	153	119	87	54	22	0	0	0	0
2,880	2,920	257	208	159	123	91	58	26	0	0	0	0
2,920	2,960	263	214	165	127	95	62	30	0	0	0	0
2,960	3,000	269	220	171	131	99	66	34	1	0	0	0
3,000	3,040	275	226	177	135	103	70	38	5	0	0	0
3,040	3,080	281	232	183	139	107	74	42	9	0	0	0
3,080	3,120	287	238	189	143	111	78	46	13	0	0	0
3,120	3,160	293	244	195	147	115	82	50	17	0	0	0
3,160	3,200	299	250	201	153	119	86	54	21	0	0	0
3,200	3,240	305	256	207	159	123	90	58	25	0	0	0
3,240	3,280	311	262	213	165	127	94	62	29	0	0	0
3,280	3,320	317	268	219	171	131	98	66	33	1	0	0
3,320	3,360	323	274	225	177	135	102	70	37	5	0	0
3,360	3,400	329	280	231	183	139	106	74	41	9	0	0

Publication 15 (2013)

MARRIED Persons—MONTHLY Payroll Period

(For Wages Paid through December 2013)

And the wages are—		And the number of withholding allowances claimed is—										
At least	But less than	0	1	2	3	4	5	6	7	8	9	10
		The amount of income tax to be withheld is—										
$3,400	$3,440	$335	$286	$237	$189	$143	$110	$78	$45	$13	$0	$0
3,440	3,480	341	292	243	195	147	114	82	49	17	0	0
3,480	3,520	347	298	249	201	152	118	86	53	21	0	0
3,520	3,560	353	304	255	207	158	122	90	57	25	0	0
3,560	3,600	359	310	261	213	164	126	94	61	29	0	0
3,600	3,640	365	316	267	219	170	130	98	65	33	0	0
3,640	3,680	371	322	273	225	176	134	102	69	37	4	0
3,680	3,720	377	328	279	231	182	138	106	73	41	8	0
3,720	3,760	383	334	285	237	188	142	110	77	45	12	0
3,760	3,800	389	340	291	243	194	146	114	81	49	16	0
3,800	3,840	395	346	297	249	200	151	118	85	53	20	0
3,840	3,880	401	352	303	255	206	157	122	89	57	24	0
3,880	3,920	407	358	309	261	212	163	126	93	61	28	0
3,920	3,960	413	364	315	267	218	169	130	97	65	32	0
3,960	4,000	419	370	321	273	224	175	134	101	69	36	4
4,000	4,040	425	376	327	279	230	181	138	105	73	40	8
4,040	4,080	431	382	333	285	236	187	142	109	77	44	12
4,080	4,120	437	388	339	291	242	193	146	113	81	48	16
4,120	4,160	443	394	345	297	248	199	150	117	85	52	20
4,160	4,200	449	400	351	303	254	205	156	121	89	56	24
4,200	4,240	455	406	357	309	260	211	162	125	93	60	28
4,240	4,280	461	412	363	315	266	217	168	129	97	64	32
4,280	4,320	467	418	369	321	272	223	174	133	101	68	36
4,320	4,360	473	424	375	327	278	229	180	137	105	72	40
4,360	4,400	479	430	381	333	284	235	186	141	109	76	44
4,400	4,440	485	436	387	339	290	241	192	145	113	80	48
4,440	4,480	491	442	393	345	296	247	198	150	117	84	52
4,480	4,520	497	448	399	351	302	253	204	156	121	88	56
4,520	4,560	503	454	405	357	308	259	210	162	125	92	60
4,560	4,600	509	460	411	363	314	265	216	168	129	96	64
4,600	4,640	515	466	417	369	320	271	222	174	133	100	68
4,640	4,680	521	472	423	375	326	277	228	180	137	104	72
4,680	4,720	527	478	429	381	332	283	234	186	141	108	76
4,720	4,760	533	484	435	387	338	289	240	192	145	112	80
4,760	4,800	539	490	441	393	344	295	246	198	149	116	84
4,800	4,840	545	496	447	399	350	301	252	204	155	120	88
4,840	4,880	551	502	453	405	356	307	258	210	161	124	92
4,880	4,920	557	508	459	411	362	313	264	216	167	128	96
4,920	4,960	563	514	465	417	368	319	270	222	173	132	100
4,960	5,000	569	520	471	423	374	325	276	228	179	136	104
5,000	5,040	575	526	477	429	380	331	282	234	185	140	108
5,040	5,080	581	532	483	435	386	337	288	240	191	144	112
5,080	5,120	587	538	489	441	392	343	294	246	197	148	116
5,120	5,160	593	544	495	447	398	349	300	252	203	154	120
5,160	5,200	599	550	501	453	404	355	306	258	209	160	124
5,200	5,240	605	556	507	459	410	361	312	264	215	166	128
5,240	5,280	611	562	513	465	416	367	318	270	221	172	132
5,280	5,320	617	568	519	471	422	373	324	276	227	178	136
5,320	5,360	623	574	525	477	428	379	330	282	233	184	140
5,360	5,400	629	580	531	483	434	385	336	288	239	190	144
5,400	5,440	635	586	537	489	440	391	342	294	245	196	148
5,440	5,480	641	592	543	495	446	397	348	300	251	202	153
5,480	5,520	647	598	549	501	452	403	354	306	257	208	159
5,520	5,560	653	604	555	507	458	409	360	312	263	214	165
5,560	5,600	659	610	561	513	464	415	366	318	269	220	171
5,600	5,640	665	616	567	519	470	421	372	324	275	226	177
5,640	5,680	671	622	573	525	476	427	378	330	281	232	183
5,680	5,720	677	628	579	531	482	433	384	336	287	238	189
5,720	5,760	683	634	585	537	488	439	390	342	293	244	195
5,760	5,800	689	640	591	543	494	445	396	348	299	250	201
5,800	5,840	695	646	597	549	500	451	402	354	305	256	207
5,840	5,880	701	652	603	555	506	457	408	360	311	262	213

$5,880 and over   Use Table 4(b) for a **MARRIED person** on page 44. Also see the instructions on page 42.

SINGLE Persons—DAILY Payroll Period

(For Wages Paid through December 2013)

And the wages are—		And the number of withholding allowances claimed is—										
At least	But less than	0	1	2	3	4	5	6	7	8	9	10
		The amount of income tax to be withheld is—										
$0	$12	$0	$0	$0	$0	$0	$0	$0	$0	$0	$0	$0
12	15	1	0	0	0	0	0	0	0	0	0	0
15	18	1	0	0	0	0	0	0	0	0	0	0
18	21	1	0	0	0	0	0	0	0	0	0	0
21	24	1	0	0	0	0	0	0	0	0	0	0
24	27	2	0	0	0	0	0	0	0	0	0	0
27	30	2	1	0	0	0	0	0	0	0	0	0
30	33	2	1	0	0	0	0	0	0	0	0	0
33	36	3	1	0	0	0	0	0	0	0	0	0
36	39	3	1	0	0	0	0	0	0	0	0	0
39	42	3	2	0	0	0	0	0	0	0	0	0
42	45	4	2	1	0	0	0	0	0	0	0	0
45	48	4	2	1	0	0	0	0	0	0	0	0
48	51	4	3	1	0	0	0	0	0	0	0	0
51	54	5	3	1	0	0	0	0	0	0	0	0
54	57	5	3	2	0	0	0	0	0	0	0	0
57	60	6	4	2	1	0	0	0	0	0	0	0
60	63	6	4	2	1	0	0	0	0	0	0	0
63	66	7	4	3	1	0	0	0	0	0	0	0
66	69	7	5	3	1	0	0	0	0	0	0	0
69	72	8	5	3	2	0	0	0	0	0	0	0
72	75	8	6	4	2	1	0	0	0	0	0	0
75	78	8	6	4	2	1	0	0	0	0	0	0
78	81	9	7	4	3	1	0	0	0	0	0	0
81	84	9	7	5	3	1	0	0	0	0	0	0
84	87	10	8	5	3	2	0	0	0	0	0	0
87	90	10	8	6	4	2	1	0	0	0	0	0
90	93	11	8	6	4	2	1	0	0	0	0	0
93	96	11	9	7	4	3	1	0	0	0	0	0
96	99	12	9	7	5	3	1	0	0	0	0	0
99	102	12	10	8	5	3	2	0	0	0	0	0
102	105	13	10	8	6	4	2	1	0	0	0	0
105	108	13	11	8	6	4	2	1	0	0	0	0
108	111	13	11	9	7	4	3	1	0	0	0	0
111	114	14	12	9	7	5	3	1	0	0	0	0
114	117	14	12	10	8	5	3	2	0	0	0	0
117	120	15	13	10	8	6	4	2	1	0	0	0
120	123	15	13	11	8	6	4	2	1	0	0	0
123	126	16	13	11	9	7	4	3	1	0	0	0
126	129	16	14	12	9	7	5	3	1	0	0	0
129	132	17	14	12	10	8	5	3	2	0	0	0
132	135	17	15	13	10	8	6	4	2	1	0	0
135	138	17	15	13	11	8	6	4	2	1	0	0
138	141	18	16	13	11	9	7	4	3	1	0	0
141	144	18	16	14	12	9	7	5	3	1	0	0
144	147	19	17	14	12	10	8	5	3	2	0	0
147	150	19	17	15	13	10	8	6	4	2	1	0
150	153	20	17	15	13	11	8	6	4	2	1	0
153	156	21	18	16	13	11	9	7	4	3	1	0
156	159	22	18	16	14	12	9	7	5	3	1	0
159	162	22	19	17	14	12	10	8	5	3	2	0
162	165	23	19	17	15	13	10	8	6	4	2	1
165	168	24	20	17	15	13	11	8	6	4	2	1
168	171	25	21	18	16	13	11	9	7	4	3	1
171	174	25	22	18	16	14	12	9	7	5	3	1
174	177	26	22	19	17	14	12	10	8	5	3	2
177	180	27	23	19	17	15	13	10	8	6	4	2
180	183	28	24	20	17	15	13	11	8	6	4	2
183	186	28	25	21	18	16	13	11	9	7	4	3
186	189	29	25	22	18	16	14	12	9	7	5	3
189	192	30	26	22	19	17	14	12	10	8	5	3
192	195	31	27	23	19	17	15	13	10	8	6	4
195	198	31	28	24	20	17	15	13	11	8	6	4
198	201	32	28	25	21	18	16	13	11	9	7	4
201	204	33	29	25	22	18	16	14	12	9	7	5
204	207	34	30	26	22	19	17	14	12	10	8	5
207	210	34	31	27	23	19	17	15	13	10	8	6
210	213	35	31	28	24	20	17	15	13	11	8	6
213	216	36	32	28	25	21	18	16	13	11	9	7
216	219	37	33	29	25	22	18	16	14	12	9	7

Publication 15 (2013)

SINGLE Persons—DAILY Payroll Period

(For Wages Paid through December 2013)

And the wages are—		And the number of withholding allowances claimed is—										
At least	But less than	0	1	2	3	4	5	6	7	8	9	10
		The amount of income tax to be withheld is—										
$219	$222	$37	$34	$30	$26	$22	$19	$17	$14	$12	$10	$8
222	225	38	34	31	27	23	19	17	15	13	10	8
225	228	39	35	31	28	24	20	17	15	13	11	8
228	231	40	36	32	28	25	21	18	16	13	11	9
231	234	40	37	33	29	25	22	18	16	14	12	9
234	237	41	37	34	30	26	22	19	17	14	12	10
237	240	42	38	34	31	27	23	19	17	15	13	10
240	243	43	39	35	31	28	24	20	17	15	13	11
243	246	43	40	36	32	28	25	21	18	16	13	11
246	249	44	40	37	33	29	25	22	18	16	14	12
249	252	45	41	37	34	30	26	22	19	17	14	12
252	255	46	42	38	34	31	27	23	19	17	15	13
255	258	46	43	39	35	31	28	24	20	17	15	13
258	261	47	43	40	36	32	28	25	21	18	16	13
261	264	48	44	40	37	33	29	25	22	18	16	14
264	267	49	45	41	37	34	30	26	22	19	17	14
267	270	49	46	42	38	34	31	27	23	19	17	15
270	273	50	46	43	39	35	31	28	24	20	17	15
273	276	51	47	43	40	36	32	28	25	21	18	16
276	279	52	48	44	40	37	33	29	25	22	18	16
279	282	52	49	45	41	37	34	30	26	22	19	17
282	285	53	49	46	42	38	34	31	27	23	19	17
285	288	54	50	46	43	39	35	31	28	24	20	17
288	291	55	51	47	43	40	36	32	28	25	21	18
291	294	55	52	48	44	40	37	33	29	25	22	18
294	297	56	52	49	45	41	37	34	30	26	22	19
297	300	57	53	49	46	42	38	34	31	27	23	19
300	303	58	54	50	46	43	39	35	31	28	24	20
303	306	58	55	51	47	43	40	36	32	28	25	21
306	309	59	55	52	48	44	40	37	33	29	25	22
309	312	60	56	52	49	45	41	37	34	30	26	22
312	315	61	57	53	49	46	42	38	34	31	27	23
315	318	61	58	54	50	46	43	39	35	31	28	24
318	321	62	58	55	51	47	43	40	36	32	28	25
321	324	63	59	55	52	48	44	40	37	33	29	25
324	327	64	60	56	52	49	45	41	37	34	30	26
327	330	64	61	57	53	49	46	42	38	34	31	27
330	333	65	61	58	54	50	46	43	39	35	31	28
333	336	66	62	58	55	51	47	43	40	36	32	28
336	339	67	63	59	55	52	48	44	40	37	33	29
339	341	67	63	60	56	52	48	45	41	37	33	30
341	343	68	64	60	56	53	49	45	41	38	34	30
343	345	68	64	61	57	53	49	46	42	38	34	31
345	347	69	65	61	57	54	50	46	42	39	35	31
347	349	69	65	62	58	54	50	47	43	39	35	32
349	351	70	66	62	58	55	51	47	43	40	36	32
351	353	70	66	63	59	55	51	48	44	40	36	33
353	355	71	67	63	59	56	52	48	44	41	37	33
355	357	72	67	64	60	56	52	49	45	41	37	34
357	359	72	68	64	60	57	53	49	45	42	38	34
359	361	73	68	65	61	57	53	50	46	42	38	35
361	363	73	69	65	61	58	54	50	46	43	39	35
363	365	74	70	66	62	58	54	51	47	43	39	36
365	367	74	70	66	62	59	55	51	47	44	40	36
367	369	75	71	67	63	59	55	52	48	44	40	37
369	371	75	71	67	63	60	56	52	48	45	41	37
371	373	76	72	68	64	60	56	53	49	45	41	38
373	375	77	72	68	64	61	57	53	49	46	42	38
375	377	77	73	69	65	61	57	54	50	46	42	39
377	379	78	73	69	65	62	58	54	50	47	43	39
379	381	78	74	70	66	62	58	55	51	47	43	40
381	383	79	75	70	66	63	59	55	51	48	44	40
383	385	79	75	71	67	63	59	56	52	48	44	41
385	387	80	76	72	67	64	60	56	52	49	45	41
387	389	80	76	72	68	64	60	57	53	49	45	42
389	391	81	77	73	68	65	61	57	53	50	46	42

$391 and over — Use Table 8(a) for a **SINGLE person** on page 45. Also see the instructions on page 42.

MARRIED Persons—DAILY Payroll Period
(For Wages Paid through December 2013)

At least	But less than	0	1	2	3	4	5	6	7	8	9	10
		\$0	\$0	\$0	\$0	\$0	\$0	\$0	\$0	\$0	\$0	\$0
$ 0	$36	0	0	0	0	0	0	0	0	0	0	0
36	39	1	0	0	0	0	0	0	0	0	0	0
39	42	1	0	0	0	0	0	0	0	0	0	0
42	45	1	0	0	0	0	0	0	0	0	0	0
45	48	1	0	0	0	0	0	0	0	0	0	0
48	51	2	0	0	0	0	0	0	0	0	0	0
51	54	2	1	0	0	0	0	0	0	0	0	0
54	57	2	1	0	0	0	0	0	0	0	0	0
57	60	3	1	0	0	0	0	0	0	0	0	0
60	63	3	1	0	0	0	0	0	0	0	0	0
63	66	3	2	0	0	0	0	0	0	0	0	0
66	69	4	2	1	0	0	0	0	0	0	0	0
69	72	4	2	1	0	0	0	0	0	0	0	0
72	75	4	3	1	0	0	0	0	0	0	0	0
75	78	4	3	1	0	0	0	0	0	0	0	0
78	81	5	3	2	0	0	0	0	0	0	0	0
81	84	5	4	2	1	0	0	0	0	0	0	0
84	87	5	4	2	1	0	0	0	0	0	0	0
87	90	6	4	3	1	0	0	0	0	0	0	0
90	93	6	4	3	1	0	0	0	0	0	0	0
93	96	6	5	3	2	0	0	0	0	0	0	0
96	99	7	5	4	2	1	0	0	0	0	0	0
99	102	7	5	4	2	1	0	0	0	0	0	0
102	105	7	6	4	3	1	0	0	0	0	0	0
105	108	8	6	4	3	1	0	0	0	0	0	0
108	111	8	6	5	3	2	0	0	0	0	0	0
111	114	9	7	5	4	2	1	0	0	0	0	0
114	117	9	7	5	4	2	1	0	0	0	0	0
117	120	10	7	6	4	3	1	0	0	0	0	0
120	123	10	8	6	4	3	1	0	0	0	0	0
123	126	10	8	6	5	3	2	0	0	0	0	0
126	129	11	9	7	5	4	2	1	0	0	0	0
129	132	11	9	7	5	4	2	1	0	0	0	0
132	135	12	10	7	6	4	3	1	0	0	0	0
135	138	12	10	8	6	4	3	1	0	0	0	0
138	141	13	10	8	6	5	3	2	0	0	0	0
141	144	13	11	9	7	5	4	2	1	0	0	0
144	147	14	11	9	7	5	4	2	1	0	0	0
147	150	14	12	10	7	6	4	3	1	0	0	0
150	153	15	12	10	8	6	4	3	1	0	0	0
153	156	15	13	10	8	6	5	3	2	0	0	0
156	159	15	13	11	9	7	5	4	2	1	0	0
159	162	16	14	11	9	7	5	4	2	1	0	0
162	165	16	14	12	10	7	6	4	3	1	0	0
165	168	17	15	12	10	8	6	4	3	1	0	0
168	171	17	15	13	10	8	6	5	3	2	0	0
171	174	18	15	13	11	9	7	5	4	2	1	0
174	177	18	16	14	11	9	7	5	4	2	1	0
177	180	19	16	14	12	10	7	6	4	3	1	0
180	183	19	17	15	12	10	8	6	4	3	1	0
183	186	19	17	15	13	10	8	6	5	3	2	0
186	189	20	18	15	13	11	9	7	5	4	2	1
189	192	20	18	16	14	11	9	7	5	4	2	1
192	195	21	19	16	14	12	10	7	6	4	3	1
195	198	21	19	17	15	12	10	8	6	4	3	1
198	201	22	19	17	15	13	10	8	6	5	3	2
201	204	22	20	18	15	13	11	9	7	5	4	2
204	207	23	20	18	16	14	11	9	7	5	4	2
207	210	23	21	19	16	14	12	10	7	6	4	3
210	213	24	21	19	17	15	12	10	8	6	4	3
213	216	24	22	19	17	15	13	10	8	6	5	3
216	219	24	22	20	18	15	13	11	9	7	5	4
219	222	25	23	20	18	16	14	11	9	7	5	4
222	225	25	23	21	19	16	14	12	10	7	6	4
225	228	26	24	21	19	17	15	12	10	8	6	4
228	231	26	24	22	19	17	15	13	10	8	6	5
231	234	27	24	22	20	18	15	13	11	9	7	5
234	237	27	25	23	20	18	16	14	11	9	7	5
237	240	28	25	23	21	19	16	14	12	10	7	6
240	243	28	26	24	21	19	17	15	12	10	8	6

Publication 15 (2013)

MARRIED Persons—DAILY Payroll Period

(For Wages Paid through December 2013)

And the wages are—		And the number of withholding allowances claimed is—										
At least	But less than	0	1	2	3	4	5	6	7	8	9	10
		The amount of income tax to be withheld is—										
$243	$246	$28	$26	$24	$22	$19	$17	$15	$13	$10	$8	$6
246	249	29	27	24	22	20	18	15	13	11	9	7
249	252	29	27	25	23	20	18	16	14	11	9	7
252	255	30	28	25	23	21	19	16	14	12	10	7
255	258	30	28	26	24	21	19	17	15	12	10	8
258	261	31	28	26	24	22	19	17	15	13	10	8
261	264	31	29	27	24	22	20	18	15	13	11	9
264	267	32	29	27	25	23	20	18	16	14	11	9
267	270	32	30	28	25	23	21	19	16	14	12	10
270	273	33	30	28	26	24	21	19	17	15	12	10
273	276	33	31	28	26	24	22	19	17	15	13	10
276	279	33	31	29	27	24	22	20	18	15	13	11
279	282	34	32	29	27	25	23	20	18	16	14	11
282	285	34	32	30	28	25	23	21	19	16	14	12
285	288	35	33	30	28	26	24	21	19	17	15	12
288	291	35	33	31	28	26	24	22	19	17	15	13
291	294	36	33	31	29	27	24	22	20	18	15	13
294	297	36	34	32	29	27	25	23	20	18	16	14
297	300	37	34	32	30	28	25	23	21	19	16	14
300	303	37	35	33	30	28	26	24	21	19	17	15
303	306	37	35	33	31	28	26	24	22	19	17	15
306	309	38	36	33	31	29	27	24	22	20	18	15
309	312	38	36	34	32	29	27	25	23	20	18	16
312	315	39	37	34	32	30	28	25	23	21	19	16
315	318	40	37	35	33	30	28	26	24	21	19	17
318	321	41	37	35	33	31	28	26	24	22	19	17
321	324	41	38	36	33	31	29	27	24	22	20	18
324	327	42	38	36	34	32	29	27	25	23	20	18
327	330	43	39	37	34	32	30	28	25	23	21	19
330	333	44	40	37	35	33	30	28	26	24	21	19
333	336	44	41	37	35	33	31	28	26	24	22	19
336	339	45	41	38	36	33	31	29	27	24	22	20
339	341	46	42	38	36	34	32	29	27	25	23	20
341	343	46	42	39	36	34	32	30	27	25	23	21
343	345	47	43	39	37	34	32	30	28	25	23	21
345	347	47	43	40	37	35	32	30	28	26	23	21
347	349	48	44	40	37	35	33	30	28	26	24	21
349	351	48	44	41	38	35	33	31	29	26	24	22
351	353	49	45	41	38	36	33	31	29	27	24	22
353	355	49	45	42	38	36	34	31	29	27	25	22
355	357	50	46	42	38	36	34	32	29	27	25	23
357	359	50	46	43	39	36	34	32	30	27	25	23
359	361	51	47	43	39	37	35	32	30	28	26	23
361	363	51	47	44	40	37	35	33	30	28	26	24
363	365	52	48	44	40	37	35	33	31	28	26	24
365	367	52	48	45	41	38	35	33	31	29	26	24
367	369	53	49	45	41	38	36	33	31	29	27	24
369	371	53	49	46	42	38	36	34	32	29	27	25
371	373	54	50	46	42	39	36	34	32	30	27	25
373	375	54	50	47	43	39	37	34	32	30	28	25
375	377	55	51	47	43	40	37	35	32	30	28	26
377	379	55	51	48	44	40	37	35	33	30	28	26
379	381	56	52	48	44	41	38	35	33	31	29	26
381	383	56	52	49	45	41	38	36	33	31	29	27
383	385	57	53	49	45	42	38	36	34	31	29	27
385	387	57	53	50	46	42	38	36	34	32	29	27
387	389	58	54	50	46	43	39	36	34	32	30	27
389	391	58	54	51	47	43	39	37	35	32	30	28
391	393	59	55	51	47	44	40	37	35	33	30	28
393	395	59	55	52	48	44	40	37	35	33	31	28
395	397	60	56	52	48	45	41	38	35	33	31	29
397	399	60	56	53	49	45	41	38	36	33	31	29
399	401	61	57	53	49	46	42	38	36	34	32	29

| $401 and over | | Use Table 8(b) for a **MARRIED person** on page 45. Also see the instructions on page 42. |

Annual Federal Payroll Tax Calendar

The following calendar displays those payroll-related due dates that affect the majority of employers.

January

15-Jan	Monthly Depositor payment of December Federal Income Tax, Social Security Tax, and Medicare Tax
31-Jan	Form 941 – 4th Quarter of prior year (additional 10 days to file if timely deposits in full payment of quarterly taxes were made)
31-Jan	Form 940 – (additional 10 days to file if all FUTA tax was deposited when due)
31-Jan	Deposit FUTA Tax – May be included with Form 940 (that is filed on 1/31) if undeposited FUTA tax does not exceed $500
31-Jan	W-2 Forms must be provided to all employees
31-Jan	1099-MISC Forms must be provided to all independent contractors

February

15-Feb	Monthly Depositor payment of January Federal Income Tax, Social Security Tax, and Medicare Tax

March

1-Mar	If paper copies are being remitted, W-2 & W-3 forms are due to be sent to the Social Security Administration
1-Mar	Form 1096 & 1099-MISC forms are due to be sent to the IRS
15-Mar	Form 1120 & 1120S Corporate Tax Returns
15-Mar	Monthly Depositor payment of February Federal Income Tax, Social Security Tax, and Medicare Tax
31-Mar	If e-filing, W-2 & W-3 forms are due to be sent to the Social Security Administration

April

15-Apr	Form 1040 Individual Tax Return
15-Apr	Monthly Depositor payment of March Federal Income Tax, Social Security Tax, and Medicare Tax
30-Apr	Form 941 – 1st Quarter (additional 10 days to file if timely deposits in full payment of quarterly taxes were made)
30-Apr	Deposit FUTA Tax – Only if undeposited FUTA tax exceeds $500

May

15-May	Monthly Depositor payment of April Federal Income Tax, Social Security Tax, and Medicare Tax

June

15-Jun	Monthly Depositor payment of May Federal Income Tax, Social Security Tax, and Medicare Tax

July	
15-Jul	Monthly Depositor payment of June Federal Income Tax, Social Security Tax, and Medicare Tax
31-Jul	Form 941 – 2nd Quarter (additional 10 days to file if timely deposits in full payment of quarterly taxes were made)
31-Jul	Deposit FUTA Tax – Only if undeposited FUTA tax exceeds $500

August	
15-Aug	Monthly Depositor payment of July Federal Income Tax, Social Security Tax, and Medicare Tax

September	
15-Sep	Monthly Depositor payment of August Federal Income Tax, Social Security Tax, and Medicare Tax

October	
15-Oct	Monthly Depositor payment of September Federal Income Tax, Social Security Tax, and Medicare Tax
31-Oct	Form 941 – 3rd Quarter (additional 10 days to file if timely deposits in full payment of quarterly taxes were made)
31-Oct	Deposit FUTA Tax – Only if undeposited FUTA tax exceeds $500

November	
15-Nov	Monthly Depositor payment of October Federal Income Tax, Social Security Tax, and Medicare Tax

December	
15-Dec	Monthly Depositor payment of November Federal Income Tax, Social Security Tax, and Medicare Tax

Note: Any due dates falling on a weekend or legal holiday are extended to the next business day.

Note: Semiweekly Depositors must make payments either by the subsequent Wednesday (for Wednesday – Friday paydays) or the subsequent Friday (for Saturday – Tuesday paydays).

Note: Federal tax payment must be made on the following business day if the liability exceeds $100,000 (Next-Day Deposit Rule).

State Tax Department Websites

It's important to understand not only the federal payroll tax considerations discussed throughout this book, but also the state payroll tax requirements that apply to you. The following websites will enable you to further research these requirements.

Alabama
http://www.alabama.gov/portal/
secondary.jsp?id=taxes

Alaska
http://tax.alaska.gov/

Arizona
http://www.azdor.gov/

Arkansas
http://www.dfa.arkansas.gov/

California
http://www.taxes.ca.gov/

Colorado
http://www.colorado.gov/revenue

Connecticut
http://www.ct.gov/drs/

Delaware
http://revenue.delaware.gov/

Florida
http://dor.myflorida.com/dor/

Georgia
https://etax.dor.ga.gov/

Hawaii
http://tax.hawaii.gov/

Idaho
http://tax.idaho.gov/

Illinois
http://www.revenue.state.il.us

Indiana
http://www.in.gov/dor/

Iowa
http://www.iowa.gov/tax/

Kansas
http://www.ksrevenue.org/

Kentucky
http://revenue.ky.gov/

Louisiana
http://www.rev.state.la.us/

Maine
http://www.maine.gov/revenue/

Maryland
http://www.dat.state.md.us/

Massachusetts
http://www.mass.gov/dor/

Michigan
http://www.michigan.gov/treasury

Minnesota
http://www.revenue.state.mn.us

Mississippi
https://www.dor.ms.gov/

Missouri
http://dor.mo.gov/

Montana
http://revenue.mt.gov/

Nebraska
http://www.revenue.nebraska.gov/

Nevada
http://tax.nv.gov/

New Hampshire
http://www.revenue.nh.gov/

New Jersey
http://www.state.nj.us/treasury/
taxation/

New Mexico
http://www.tax.newmexico.gov/

New York
http://www.tax.ny.gov/

North Carolina
http://www.dornc.com/

North Dakota
https://www.nd.gov/tax/

Ohio
http://www.tax.ohio.gov/

Oklahoma
http://www.tax.ok.gov/

Oregon
http://www.oregon.gov/DOR/

Pennsylvania
http://www.revenue.state.pa.us/

Rhode Island
http://www.tax.ri.gov/

South Carolina
http://www.sctax.org/

South Dakota
http://dor.sd.gov/

Tennessee
http://www.tennessee.gov/revenue/

Texas
http://www.window.state.tx.us/

Utah
http://tax.utah.gov/

Vermont
http://www.state.vt.us/tax/

Virginia
http://www.tax.virginia.gov/

Washington
http://dor.wa.gov/

West Virginia
http://www.wva.state.wv.us/wvtax/

Wisconsin
http://www.revenue.wi.gov/

Wyoming
http://revenue.wyo.gov/

American Samoa
http://americansamoa.gov/index.php/
taxforms

Guam
https://www.guamtax.com/

Northern Mariana Islands
http://www.cnmidof.net/rev/

Puerto Rico
http://www.hacienda.gobierno.pr/

U.S. Virgin Islands
http://www.vibir.gov/

Washington D.C.
http://otr.cfo.dc.gov/

Glossary

bonuses   Additional employee earnings that may be either planned or unplanned.

Cafeteria Plans   Plans in which tax-free funds may be contributed (through voluntary withholdings from earnings) in order to provide a range of benefits to the employee.

Circular E   An employer's tax guide (also referred to as *Publication 15*), distributed by the IRS, that provides guidance on variety of payroll-related topics.

commissions   Employee earnings calculated as a percentage of sales.

Current Tax Payment Act of 1943   An Act that modified the federal income tax system, directing that payments could no longer be made in the subsequent year, but instead must be paid during the year in which the associated income is earned. This act resulted in employers withholding taxes from employees' pay.

deductions   Amounts withheld from employee pay, and which are therefore not included in employee's paychecks.

discretionary bonus   An unplanned bonus that is not contingent on an employee reaching specific goals.

Electronic Federal Tax Payment System (EFTPS)   A telephone- and internet-based system that provides employers with the most convenient method for remitting federal tax payments.

employee earnings record   A record maintained by the employer for each employee displaying key employee information and payroll figures for a given year.

Employee Retirement Income Security Act   An act, passed in 1974, setting forth regulations that must be followed by employers who offer retirement plans to their employees. Often referred to as *ERISA*.

employer identification number (EIN)   A unique number that an employer must obtain from the IRS prior to submitting payroll-related forms.

Equal Pay Act (EPA)   An amendment, passed in 1963, to the Fair Labor Standards Act dictating that no employer may discriminate against any employee by paying a lower wage than what is paid to someone of the opposite sex for a similar job.

Fair Labor Standards Act (FLSA)   An act, passed into law in 1938, dictating labor conditions and regulations that must be followed by the majority of employers.

Federal Income Tax Withholding   Tax withheld from employee earnings, used to fund a range of governmental agencies and services. Also called *Federal Income Tax*.

federal minimum wage   The lowest wage that may be paid to employees for whom an exception (or a higher State Minimum Wage) does not apply.

Federal Unemployment Tax (FUTA)   A tax levied on employers, based on the taxable earnings of their employees. These taxes are used by the federal government to provide unemployment compensation to individuals who are out of work.

Flexible Spending Account   A type of cafeteria plan in which employees may be reimbursed for qualified benefits, such as dependent care expenses and medical expenses.

gross pay   The total amount earned by an employee.

gross wages   Total employee earnings prior to subtracting taxes and other withholding amounts.

Immigration Reform and Control Act (IRCA)   An act, passed in 1986, that strengthened U.S. immigration law, and which led to the requirement that employers maintain I-9 Forms for all employees.

incentive plans   Plans that tie increased employee earnings to increases in productivity.

independent contractors   Individuals who perform services for an employer without qualifying as employees.

Local Income Tax Withholding   Tax withheld from employee earnings (by certain local municipalities), used to fund local operations. Also called *Local Income Tax*.

lookback period   A time period used by employers to determine the applicable payment increment for Federal Income tax, Social Security Tax, and Medicare Tax; it encompasses the previous July 1 through June 30 for a given year.

mandatory deductions   Amounts that are required, by either federal or state government, to be withheld from employee earnings.

Medical Plans   Plans in which funds are set aside (through voluntary withholdings from employee earnings) to cover medical costs.

Medicare Tax (HI)   Tax withheld from employee earnings, used to operate the Medicare federal health insurance program covering individuals 65 years of age or older, as well as certain disabled individuals.

monthly depositor   An employer who must remit payment of Federal Income Tax, Social Security Tax, and Medicare Tax on a monthly basis.

net pay   The amount paid to an employee within the paycheck.

Net Self-Employment Income   The income of a self-employed individual after certain business expenses have been subtracted.

next-day deposit rule   A rule dictating that an employer must remit all owed taxes on the next business day if the total accumulated amount owed exceeds $100,000 at the end of any day.

non-discretionary bonus   A planned bonus paid by an employer as a result of a specific metric being met.

pay-as-you-go   A type of system in which income tax must be paid as the associated income is earned.

paycheck   A typical form of payment provided to employees.

Payroll Deduction IRA   A simple retirement plan option often used by self-employed individuals.

Payroll Register   A record maintained by an employer in which all employee earnings for a single period are displayed.

payroll service   An outside company that handles a variety of payroll-related tasks for an employer.

paystub   A paycheck attachment displaying the breakdown of an employee's earnings.

pay period   A specific period during which employees earn their pay; common types include weekly, bi-weekly, semi-monthly, and monthly.

Percentage Method   A method for determining an employee's federal income tax withholding in which a three-step process, that includes referencing the Percentage Method tables, is used.

Personal Responsibility and Work Opportunity Reconciliation Act of 1996 (PRWORA)   An act that significantly strengthened the child support program throughout the United States, and which led to the mandatory reporting of new employees.

piecework   An employee compensation system in which earnings are determined based on the number of units produced.

Retirement Plans   Plans providing funds to employees after retirement, which may be funded through voluntary withholdings from employee earnings.

salary   An annual pay amount, typically agreed upon by the employer and employee.

Self-Employment Contributions Act of 1954   An act establishing that self-employed individuals must pay Self-Employment Taxes.

self-employment income   The earnings of an individual who works for him/herself, on which taxes must be paid.

semiweekly depositor   An employer who must remit payment of Federal Income Tax, Social Security Tax, and Medicare Tax twice each week.

SIMPLE IRA   A retirement savings plan designed for employees of small businesses.

Social Security Tax (OASDI)   Tax withheld from employee earnings, used to fund the social security system, which pays benefits to retired or disabled workers and their dependents or survivors. Also known as *Old Age, Survivors, and Disability Insurance Tax*.

State Disability Insurance Tax   Tax withheld from employee earnings (by a small number of states/territories), used to provide benefits to temporarily disabled employees who are unable to work for a period of time.

State Income Tax Withholding   Tax withheld from employee earnings (by the majority of states), used to fund state operations. Also called *State Income Tax*.

State Unemployment Tax (SUTA)   A tax levied on employers, based on the taxable earnings of their employees. Along with Federal Unemployment Taxes, these taxes are used to operate unemployment programs.

time card   A document that tracks the hours worked by an employee.

tip pool   An acceptable method under the Fair Labor Standards Act for dividing tips, in which all tips are added together and then divided amongst employees.

Union Dues   Dues paid by unionized employees which may be voluntarily withheld from employee earnings.

voluntary deductions   Amounts that an employee may elect to have withheld from his/her earnings.

wage   A compensation amount paid to employees, typically on an hourly basis.

Wage-Bracket Method   A method for determining an employee's federal income tax withholding in which Federal Income Tax Withholding Tables are used.

wage garnishment   The withholding of a portion of an employee's earnings, in compliance with a court order or other legal proceeding.

Workers' Compensation   A form of insurance that provides financial assistance to employees injured during the course of their employment.

workweek   Any 7-day period, designated by the employer, that begins and ends consistently each week.

401(k) Plan   A defined-contribution retirement plan in which a set amount of tax-deferred funds may be withheld from gross earnings each pay period.

403(b) Plan   A retirement savings plan, similar to a 401(k), which is available only to certain employees of specific types of institutions; also referred to as a Tax-Sheltered Annuity (TSA) Plan.

Index